Praise for *Trend Following*

"Michael Covel's Trend Following*: essential."*

—Ed Seykota, trend follower and original market wizard

"Trend Following by Michael Covel? I'm 'long' this book."

—Bob Spear, developer of Trading Recipes Software

"Michael Covel's Trend Following *is a breakthrough book that captures the essence of what really makes markets tick. Diligently researched and comprehensive in scope, it will replace* The Market Wizards *as the must-read bible for a new generation of traders."*

—Jonathan Hoenig, portfolio manager, Capitalistpig Hedge Fund LLC and Fox News contributor

"Investment books that have a lasting appeal offer insight that resonates with a large number of investors. We believe Michael Covel's Trend Following *will be such a book."*

—Richard E. Cripps, Legg Mason chief market strategist

*"Please read [*Trend Following*] whether you think you have an interest in trend following or are not sure...Covel has hit a home run with it."*

—Gail Osten, editor-in-chief, *Stocks, Futures, & Options* magazine

"Michael Covel has written the definitive book on trend following. With careful research and clear insight, he has captured the essence of the most successful of all trading strategies. Michael knows his subject matter and he writes about it with passion, conviction, and enthusiasm. This enjoyable and well written book is destined to become a classic."

—Charles LeBeau, author of *Technical Traders Guide to Computer Analysis of the Futures Markets*

*"*Trend Following *is an engrossing and educational journey through the principles, pitfalls, players, and psychology of aggressive technical trading of the investment markets. [It is] rich in its wisdom and historical study."*

—Gerald Appel, president of Signalert Corporation and publisher of *Systems and Forecasts* newsletter

"*Conventional wisdom says buy low and sell high, but what do you do now that your favorite market—be it a stock, bond, or commodity—is at an all-time high or low? For a completely different perspective, from people who actually make money at this business, take a look inside. Michael Covel has written a timely and entertaining account of trend following—how it works, how to do it, and who can do it. While it's not for everybody, it might be for you.*"

—Charles Faulkner, NLP modeler and trading coach, featured in numerous books including *The New Market Wizards*

"*I think the book did a superb job of covering the philosophy and thinking behind trend following (basically, why it works). You might call it the Market Wizards of Trend Following.*"

—Van K. Tharp, Ph.D., president, International Institute of Trading Mastery, Inc. Van was originally profiled in *The Market Wizards* by Jack Schwager.

"*I think that this book documents a great deal of what has made trend following managers a successful part of the money management landscape (how they manage risk and investment psychology). It serves as a strong educational justification on why investors should consider using trend following managers as a part of an overall portfolio strategy.*"

—Tom Basso, retired CEO, Trendstat Capital Management, Inc. Tom was originally profiled in *The New Market Wizards* by Jack Schwager.

"*Michael Covel mixes a unique blend of trend following matters with the thoughts and quotes of successful traders, investors and society's leaders. This is a valuable contribution and some of the best writing on trend following I've seen.*"

—Robert (Bucky) Isaacson, managed money and trend following pioneer for more than 30 years

"Trend Following: *Definitely required reading for the aspiring trader.*"

—David S. Druz, tactical investment management and trend follower for 25 years

"*Michael Covel reveals the real secret about trading—that there is no secret. His points are peppered with wisdom from experts across the industry.*"

—John Ehlers, president, MESA Software

Trend Following
(Updated Edition)

Trend Following
(Updated Edition)

Learn to Make Millions
in Up or Down Markets

Michael W. Covel

Vice President, Publisher: Tim Moore
Associate Publisher and Director of Marketing: Amy Neidlinger
Executive Editor: Jim Boyd
Editorial Assistants: Myesha Graham and Pamela Boland
Operations Manager: Gina Kanouse
Digital Marketing Manager: Julie Phifer
Publicity Manager: Laura Czaja
Assistant Marketing Manager: Megan Colvin
Cover Designer: Chuti Prasertsith
Managing Editor: Kristy Hart
Project Editor: Betsy Harris
Copy Editor: Deadline Driven Publishing
Proofreader: Kathy Ruiz
Senior Indexer: Cheryl Lenser
Compositor: Nonie Ratcliff
Manufacturing Buyer: Dan Uhrig

This book is sold with the understanding that neither the author nor the publisher is engaged in rendering legal, accounting or other professional services or advice by publishing this book. Each individual situation is unique. Thus, if legal or financial advice or other expert assistance is required in a specific situation, the services of a competent professional should be sought to ensure that the situation has been evaluated carefully and appropriately. The author and the publisher disclaim any liability, loss, or risk resulting directly or indirectly, from the use or application of any of the contents of this book.

FT Press offers excellent discounts on this book when ordered in quantity for bulk purchases or special sales. For more information, please contact U.S. Corporate and Government Sales, 1-800-382-3419, corpsales@pearsontechgroup.com. For sales outside the U.S., please contact International Sales at international@pearson.com.

Company and product names mentioned herein are the trademarks or registered trademarks of their respective owners.

Printed in the United States of America

Fifth Printing: June 2010

ISBN-10: 0-13-702018-X
ISBN-13: 978-0-13-702018-8

Pearson Education Ltd.
Pearson Education Australia PTY, Limited.
Pearson Education Singapore, Pte. Ltd.
Pearson Education North Asia, Ltd.
Pearson Education Canada, Ltd.
Pearson Educación de Mexico, S.A. de C.V.
Pearson Education—Japan
Pearson Education Malaysia, Pte. Ltd.

The Library of Congress Cataloging-in-Publication data is on file.

For Uyen.

Contents

Foreword . . . . **xiii**

Preface . . . . **xvii**

Acknowledgments . . . . **xxi**

Part I 1

1 Trend Following 3
    The Market 3
    Winning Versus Losing 4
    Investor Versus Trader 6
    Fundamental Versus Technical 7
    Discretionary Versus Mechanical 11
    In Plain Sight 12
    Change 15
    Modus Operandi: Price 17
    Follow the Trend 18
    Loss 22
    Conclusion 23

2 Great Trend Followers **27**
    David Harding 29
    Bill Dunn 32
    John W. Henry 45
    Ed Seykota 58
    Keith Campbell 67
    Jerry Parker 71

Salem Abraham 74
Richard Dennis 78
Richard Donchian 85
Jesse Livermore and Dickson Watts 90

Part II   95

3 Performance Data 97
Absolute Returns 98
Fear of Volatility and Confusion with Risk 99
Drawdowns 106
Correlation 111
Zero Sum Nature of the Markets 114
George Soros and Zero Sum 116

4 Big Events, Crashes, and Panics 123
Event #1: 2008 Stock Market Bubble and Crash 126
Day-by-Day Analysis 136
Event #2: 2000–2002 Stock Market Bubble 138
Event #3: Long-Term Capital Management Collapse 151
Event #4: Asian Contagion 164
Event #5: Barings Bank 168
Event #6: Metallgesellschaft 172
Final Thoughts 175
The Always "New" Coming Storm 178

5 Baseball: Thinking Outside the Batter's Box 181
The Home Run 182
Moneyball and Billy Beane 185
John W. Henry Enters the Game 186
Red Sox 2003–2007 188

Part III   191

6 Human Behavior 193
Prospect Theory 194
Emotional Intelligence: Daniel Goleman 200
Charles Faulkner 201
Ed Seykota's Trading Tribe 202
Curiosity Is the Answer, Not Degrees 204
Commitment to Habitual Success 206

7 Decision Making 211
Occam's Razor 212
Fast and Frugal Decision Making 213
The Innovator's Dilemma 216
Process Versus Outcome 218

8 Science of Trading **221**
   Critical Thinking 222
   Chaos Theory: Linear Versus Nonlinear 224
   Compounding 229

9 Holy Grails **231**
   Buy and Hold 232
   Warren Buffett 234
   Losers Average Losers 235
   Crash and Panic 238
   Analysis Paralysis 241
   Final Thoughts 243

Part IV **245**

10 Trading Systems **247**
   Risk, Reward, and Uncertainty 248
   Five Questions for a Trading System 253
   Your Trading System 265
   Frequently Asked Questions 266

11 The Game **277**
   Slow Acceptance 278
   Blame Game 279
   Understand the Game 280
   Decrease Leverage; Decrease Return 281
   Fortune Favors the Bold 282

   Afterword **285**
   Acceptance 285
   Inefficient Markets 288
   Trend Following Critics 290
   Critic Geetesh Bhardwaj 294
   Final Thoughts 296

   Foreword to the First Edition by Charles Faulkner **299**

Appendices **303**

   Introduction to Appendices **305**

A Trend Following for Stocks **307**
   Does Trend Following Work on Stocks? 307
   Short Selling 318
   Tax Efficiency 318
   The Capitalism Distribution: Observations of Individual
   Common Stock Returns, 1983–2006 331
   Charts 338

B   Performance Guide **347**
    Trend Following Historical Performance Data 347
    Abraham Trading Company 347
    Campbell & Company, Inc.—Financial Metals & Energy—
    Large Program 349
    Chesapeake Capital Corporation—Diversified Program 352
    Clarke Capital Management, Inc.—Millennium Program 354
    Drury Capital, Inc.—Diversified Trend Following Program 355
    DUNN Capital Management, Inc.—World Monetary Assets 356
    Eckhardt Trading Company—Standard Program 359
    John W. Henry & Company, Inc.—Financials and Metals Program 361
    Millburn Ridgefield Corporation—Diversified Program 363
    Rabar Market Research, Inc.—Diversified 366
    Sunrise Capital Partners LLC—Expanded Diversified 368
    Superfund 370
    Transtrend B.V.—Diversified Trend Program—Enhanced Risk (USD) 371
    Winton Capital Management Ltd—Diversified Winton Futures Fund 372
    Risk Disclaimer 374

C   Short-Term Trading **375**

D   Personality Traits of Successful Traders **377**

E   Trend Following Models **381**

F   Trading System Example from Mechanica **385**
    System Background Information 385
    System Details 386
    A Canadian Dollar Trade 388
    System Performance 389
    Summary 392

G   Critical Questions for Trading Systems **395**

Resources **397**

Endnotes **399**

Bibliography **423**

Index **431**

Foreword

"No good decision was ever made in a swivel chair."
—General George S. Patton, Jr.

Larry Hite

When I started trading in the commodity futures markets over 35 years ago, the industry didn't even have a name. Today, the business has grown to the point where there are a myriad of ways to describe the funds that operate and their many styles of investing. The particular discipline of trading that I practiced, even before the nomenclature existed, is now plainly and aptly termed "trend following." In fact, while I have seen many strategies come and go, most of the other managers that I have known to survive and thrive over the past few decades in global futures markets are also trend followers. For having made my living as a trend follower, I've yet to come across a more compelling study, so clearly distilled, than has been offered by Michael Covel in *Trend Following*.

I first met Michael Covel when he was working on this book. I was a little hesitant at first about sharing some of the rather simple secrets of my trade. And, I didn't make it easy on Covel. I started interviewing *him* on his investments and how he managed his risk. He quickly made me realize that he not only understood trend following, but that he embraced it much like me. We delved into the roots of trend following and my investment strategies to explore why they work rather than just accepting the results. In reading *Trend Following*, I now see how well he was able to translate his knowledge, and the perspectives of many of my colleagues, to paper.

A large fraction of traffic accidents are of the type "driver looked but failed to see." Here, drivers collide with pedestrians in plain view, with cars directly in front of them, and even run into trains. That's right—run into trains, not the other way around. In such cases, information from the world is entering the driver's eyes. But at some point along the way, this information is lost, causing the driver to lose connection with reality. They are looking, but they are not seeing.

Ronald A. Rensink

It's important to have a plan, remain disciplined in executing that plan, and pay attention to what is actually happening rather than what you expect to happen. We try to be as objective as possible in our analyses...It's not always easy for people who are involved every day to stay with a plan when misfortune occurs for a time. You always encounter the unexpected and this can push discipline right out of the way in the name of prudence. But prudence almost always dictates staying with the approach that has made you successful. I see that as one of my primary roles. I often encourage everyone during difficult days to remain patient. I don't blame people for the unexpected.

John W. Henry

CME Magazine, Premier Issue

Back in the 1970s, most of the guys I knew traded individual markets. The ones who traded wheat did not talk to the guys who traded sugar. And, the guys who invested stocks did not care to talk to either one, because commodities were for "speculators" and not "investors." Further, the bond crowd thought the stock guys were cowboys. Each group had developed its own superiority complexes and fundamentally believed that only industry experts like them could understand the subtle dynamics of their markets. I guess that's part of the reason that no one cared much for trend followers like me—I viewed every market the same way and each represented nothing more than a trade to me. Today, for all the different facets, I believe everyone has come to speak the same language. It's the language of risk.

In my early days, there was only one guy I knew who seemed to have a winning track record year after year. This fellow's name was Jack Boyd. Jack was also the only guy I knew who traded lots of different markets. If you followed any *one* of Jack's trades, you never really knew how you were going to do. But, if you were like me and actually counted *all* of his trades, you would have made about 20 percent a year. So, that got me more than a little curious about the idea of trading futures markets "across the board." Although each individual market seemed risky, when you put them together, they tended to balance each other out and you were left with a nice return with less volatility.

I could always see, after I got to Wall Street, how, for all the confusion, markets were driven by people and their emotions. That was what all of these markets had in common—people—and people just don't change. So, I set out to understand similarities in the way that markets moved. When I added up Jack's trades, only a few big trades made him all the money. For each of these big winners, I was there when "experts" told Jack that these markets couldn't go any higher, but they did. Then, when I looked at Jack's losses, they tended to be relatively small. Although it took me many years to put it all together—remember, there were no books like this back then—these seemingly small observations became the foundation for me of two important, intertwined investment themes: trend following and risk management. Jack was not so much a trend follower, but he did practice the first rule of trend following: Cut your losers and let your winners run.

Most of the guys that I knew who lost a lot of money actually tended to be more right than wrong. They just lost a lot on a few big losers. I believe that people put too much of a premium on being right. In some ways, it's one of the drawbacks for people who went to the best schools and always got straight As—they are too used to always being right. It gets back to people and emotions. Everyone is happy to take lots of little winners—it makes them feel good. When their trades go against them, on the other hand, they hold on because they don't want to accept being wrong. Many times, these trades come back and they are able to capture their small profit. To me, that kind of trading is a little bit like picking up nickels in front of a steamroller.

Thankfully, the markets don't care about me or you or where we went to school. They don't care if you're short or tall. I was never very good in school and I wasn't a good athlete either. With my background, the way I saw it, I never had any problem with the idea that I could be wrong. So, I have always built in an assumption of wrongness to anything that I do. We now kindly refer to this practice as risk management, but I just wanted to answer the question: "What's the worst thing that could happen to me?" I never wanted to do anything that could kill me. Knowing that I was not likely to be right that often, I had to trade in a way that would make me a lot of money when I was right and not lose me a lot of money when I was wrong. If that wasn't enough, it also had to be simple enough for me to understand.

After many years of searching and learning things the hard way, I evolved my own version of trend following. The idea made sense and I had some good examples to follow. Still, I wanted to prove to myself that it worked without betting real money. I had to test what would have happened had I traded that way in the past. These were the early days of computers and we even had to "borrow" time on university computers to test and prove our theories. It was a painstaking task, but it gave me the comfort that I needed. Now, in reading *Trend Following*, the do-it-yourselfers might argue that having a book that illustrates these same basic principles takes some of the fun out of it.

Actually, Covel, like any good trend follower, has not focused solely on the endpoint. He gives you a deep understanding of the most important part: the path. Unlike so many other books that

A prudent investor's best safeguard against risk is not retreat, but diversification. [And] true diversification is difficult to achieve by [simply] spreading an investment among different stocks (or different equity managers), or even by mixing stocks and bonds, because the two are not complementary.

David Harding
Winton Capital

[Trend following firm] Aspect Capital is aptly named. Its group of physics-trained leaders took it from the aspect ratio of plane design, that is, the wider the wing span, the more stable the plane. As such, Aspect trades not only futures of its early roots but European equities, bonds and currencies in various forms, covering a so-called wider wing span. The London-based hedge fund was the brainchild of Martin Lueck, Eugene Lambert and Anthony Todd. Founded in 1997, the principals were involved in the development of AHL (now owned by Man) with a track record stretching back to 1983. Aspect's disciplined approach has successfully generated returns from both longs and shorts in difficult markets environments.

Futures Magazine and
Aspect Capital

have been written about investing, *Trend Following* goes beyond the results to explore the journey of this outstanding group of traders.

For my staff at Hite Capital, Covel's *Trend Following* is required reading. For my daughters at home, it has finally settled the question I seemed never to have been able to clearly answer myself, "Daddy, what do you do for a living?" This book captures and conveys what so many traders have taken careers and large losses to learn. And lucky for all of us, you don't have to be Phi Beta Kappa to understand it.

We no longer live in that world of wheat guys, sugar guys, and stock guys. Trend following trading is an important force in every market and should be a part of any diverse investment portfolio. For me, the discipline of trend following goes beyond trading and money management. Trend following is a way of thinking that can be employed in many parts of life as we all tend to continue to do the things that work for us and stop doing those activities that don't.

The way I see it, you have two choices—you can do what I did and work for 30-plus years, cobbling together scraps of information, seeking to create a money-making strategy, or you can spend a few days reading Covel's book and skip that three-decade learning curve.

About Larry Hite

Larry Hite founded Mint Investments in 1983. By 1990, Mint Investments had become the largest commodity trading advisor in the world in terms of assets under management. Mint's achievements won Hite and his team industry-wide acclaim, and in 1990, Jack Schwager dedicated an entire chapter of his bestselling book, Market Wizards, to Hite's trading and risk management philosophy.

Preface

"Men wanted for hazardous journey. Small wages.
Bitter cold. Long months of complete darkness.
Constant danger. Safe return doubtful. Honor and
recognition in case of success."[1]

This book is the result of a 14-year "hazardous journey" for the truth about trend following trading. It fills a void in a marketplace inundated with books about buying low and selling high, index investing, and all other types of fundamental analysis, but lacking any resource or, for that matter, practically any reference to what I believe is the single best strategy to consistently make money in the markets. That strategy is known as **trend following.** Author Van Tharp has described it succinctly:

> "Let's break down the term 'trend following' into its components. The first part is 'trend.' Every trader needs a trend to make money. If you think about it, no matter what the technique, if there is not a trend after you buy, then you will not be able to sell at higher prices ... 'following' is the next part of the term. We use this word because trend followers always wait for the trend to shift first, then 'follow' it."[2]

Trend following trading seeks to capture the majority of a market trend, up or down, for profit. It aims for profits in all major asset classes—stocks, bonds, currencies, and commodities. Unfortunately, however simple the basic concepts about trend following are, they have been widely misunderstood by the public. My desire to correct this state of affairs is what, in part, launched my research.

When it is a question of money, everyone is of the same religion.

Voltaire

I wanted to be as objective as possible, so I based my writing on all available data:

- Trend followers' month-by-month performance histories
- Trend followers' published words and comments over the last 30 years
- News accounts of financial disasters
- News accounts of the losers in those financial disasters
- Charts of markets traded by trend followers
- Charts of markets traded by losers in the financial disasters

Education rears disciples, imitators, and routinists, not pioneers of new ideas and creative geniuses. The schools are not nurseries of progress and improvement, but conservatories of tradition and unvarying modes of thought.
Ludwig von Mises

If I could have written a book comprising only numbers, charts, and graphs of trend following performance data, I would have. However, without any explanation, few readers would have appreciated the ramifications of what the data alone showed. Therefore, my approach to writing *Trend Following* became similar to the one Jim Collins describes in his book *Good to Great*, in which a team of researchers generated questions, accumulated data in their open-ended search for answers, and then energetically debated it.

However, unlike Collins who was writing about generally well known public companies, trend followers form a sort of underground network of relatively unknown traders who, except for an occasional article, the mainstream press has virtually ignored. What I have attempted to do is lift the veil, for the first time, on who these enormously successful traders are, how they trade, and what is to be learned from their approach to trading that we might all apply to our own portfolios.

Trend Following challenges much of the conventional wisdom about successful trading and traders. To avoid the influences of conventional wisdom, I was determined to avoid being influenced by institutionalized knowledge defined by Wall Street and was adamant about fighting "flat earth" thinking. During my research, starting with an assumption and then finding data to support it was avoided. Instead, questions were asked and then, objectively, doggedly, and slowly, answers were revealed.

If there was one factor that motivated me to work in this manner, it was simple curiosity. The more I uncovered about trend followers, the more I wanted to know. For example, one of the earliest questions (without an answer already) was learning who profited when Barings Bank collapsed. My research unearthed a connection between Barings Bank and trend follower John W. Henry (now the majority owner of the Boston Red Sox). Henry's track record generated new questions, such as, "How did he discover trend following in the first place?" and "Has his approach changed in any significant way in the past 30 years?"

I was also curious about who won the $1.9 billion hedge fund Long Term Capital Management lost during the summer of 1998. Why did the biggest banks on Wall Street invest $100 billion in an options pricing model with so much inherent risk? Further, considering what mutual fund and hedge fund managers lost during October 2008 and what successful trend followers earned during the same time, I could not understand why so few investors were oblivious to even the existence of trend following trading. Other questions quickly appeared:

The important thing in science is not so much to obtain new facts as to discover new ways of thinking about them.

Sir William Bragg

- How do trend followers win in the zero-sum game of trading?
- Why has trend following been the most profitable style of trading?
- What is the philosophical framework of trend followers' success?
- What are the timeless principles of trend following trading?
- What are trend followers' worldview of market behavior?
- What are the reasons why trend following is enduring?

Many of the trend followers studied are reclusive and extremely low key. Some discovered trend following on their own and used it to make their fortunes out of home offices. Bill Dunn, a successful trend follower who has beaten the markets for over 30 years, works out of a quiet, Spartan office in a Florida coastal town. For Wall Street, this approach to trading is tantamount to sacrilege. It goes against all the customs, rituals, trappings, and myths we have grown accustomed to with Wall Street success. In fact, it is my hope that my profiles of trend followers will correct the public's misconception of a successful trader as a harried, intense workaholic who spends 24/7 in the labyrinth of a Wall Street trading firm, surrounded by monitors and screaming into a phone.

When the first edition of *Trend Following* hit the streets in April 2004 I hoped to assemble the first comprehensive look at trend following trading. Almost five years since initial publication, that goal was realized. How do I know? Since the first edition of *Trend Following*, I have met literally dozens of trend following traders managing collectively billions upon billions of dollars. Their feedback has been the validation. I never would have expected that an obscure book put together five years ago would lead me to having conversations with the likes of Nobel Prize winner Harry Markowitz and hedge fund managers Boone Pickens and David Harding, but it did.

Validation aside, October and November 2008 made me want another bite at the apple, another chance to "work" on this book. And lucky for me, the 2008 market chaos gave me that window. There is no doubt that October and November 2008 were the most historic market months since the Great Depression. Most people, most mutual funds, and most hedge funds lost unimaginable sums of money. It has long been said that "genius is leverage in a rising market," and when the bubble popped in 2008 clearly people who had long been positioned as genius weren't that smart after all. Already guessed where I am headed with this rant? Yes, while the rest of the world got creamed in 2008, trend followers made fortunes. Performance numbers for top trend following traders for October 2008 alone ranged from +5 percent to +40 percent. Making that much in one month when much of the rest of the world was losing big time is noteworthy to say the least. My publisher Jim Boyd agreed with me.

Fish see the bait, but not the hook; men see the profit, but not the peril.

Chinese proverb

This new edition of *Trend Following* includes many new sections and insights, surrounding the same core timeless lessons from the first edition. I updated the book throughout and worked to make material accessible and interesting enough so it might give an occasional "aha" experience. However, if you're looking for trading "secrets," you need to look elsewhere. There is no such thing. If you're in the mood for stories about what it's like inside a typical Wall Street firm (at least in those firms before they all went under in 2008!) or how greedy traders sow the seeds of their own destruction, your needs will not be met with my writing. But if you are looking for something different, looking for something to fill a void in your understanding of how big returns are actually made year after year, but didn't know where to turn for honest information, I hope my insights give you the confidence that ultimately helps you to make some big money.

To be aware how fruitful the playful mood can be is to be immune to the propaganda of the alienated, which extols resentment as a fuel of achievement.

Eric Hoffer

Acknowledgments

It is a pleasure to recognize the traders, colleagues, mentors, writers, and friends who contributed directly and indirectly to *Trend Following*.

Justin Vandergrift and William W. Noel, III must be singled out for special mention. This book would not have come together without their hard work.

I am particularly grateful to those traders—Ed Seykota, Bill Dunn, Daniel Dunn, Mark Rzepczynski, Jason Russell, Easan Katir, Jonathan Hoenig, Cole Wilcox, Eric Crittenden, Michael Martin, Salem Abraham, Ajay Jani, and Paul Mulvaney—who were generous with their feedback under tight writing deadlines. Thanks also to Martin Bergin for the initial introduction to Bill Dunn.

The support of Charles Faulkner must be acknowledged as well. He shared his intellect, enthusiasm, and most of all, his time, reading and critiquing various drafts. Additionally, John O'Donnell of Online Trading Academy was gracious with his time and energy.

I also want to thank Peter Borish, Bill Miller of Legg Mason, Michael Mauboussin of Legg Mason, Richard Cripps of Legg Mason, David Harding of Winton Capital, William Fung, Toby Crabel of Crabel Capital, Grant Smith of Millburn Corporation, Mark Abraham, Bernard Drury of Drury Capital, Larry Hite of Hite Capital Management, Michael Clarke of Clarke Capital Management, Mark Rosenberg of SSARIS Advisors, LLC, Jon Sundt of Altegris, Christian Baja of Superfund, David Beach of Beach Capital, and Alejandro Knoepffler of Cipher Investment Management for their generous personal time and consideration. I want to especially thank Jerry Parker of Chesapeake Capital for answering questions early on.

Additionally, Celia Straus, Jeff Kopiwoda, Chris Koomey, Jerry Mullins, Molly Alton Mullins, Beneva Schulte, Withers Hurley, Elizabeth Ellen, Justice Litle, Barry Ritholtz, Mark Rostenko, Arthur Maddock, Brett Steenbarger, Austin Guu, and Bob Spear all made valuable contributions.

Throughout years of research, I've benefited repeatedly from the trading wisdom and experience of John W. Henry, Jonathan Craven, Mark Hawley, John Hoade, Shaun Jordan, Carol Kaufman, Jane Martin, Leo Melamed, Larry Mollner, Kim Hunter, Gibbons Burke, Chuck LeBeau, and Leon Rose. A sincere thank you also goes out to Oliver Alliker, James Altucher, Gerald Appel, Aspect Capital, Hunter Baldwin, Tom Basso, John Boik, Bob Brooks, Wade Brorsen, Ursula Burger, Jake Carriker, Celeste Cave, Art Collins, Cory Colvin, Allan Como, Larry Connors, Chip Dempsey, Tim Dempsey, Rolf Dobelli, Edward Dobson, David Dolak, Woody Dorsey, David Druz, Patrick Dyess, Stephen Eckett, William Eckhardt, Marc Faber, Mark Fitzsimmons, Ed Foster, Nelson Freeburg, Mitsuru Furukawa, Dave Goodboy, Jayanthi Gopalakrishnan, Stephanie Haase, Scott Hicks, James Holter, Scott A. Houdek, Robert (Bucky) Isaacson, Christian Jund, MaryAnn Kiely, Eddie Kwong, Pete Kyle, Eric Laing, Elina Manevich, Bill Mann, Jon Markman, Michael Martin, John Mauldin, Timothy M. McCann, Lizzie McLoughlin, James Montier, Georgia Nakou, Peter Navarro, Gail Osten, Michael Panzner, Bob Pardo, Baron Robertson, Jim Rogers, Murray Ruggiero, Michael Seneadza, Takaaki Sera, Tom Shanks, Howard Simons, Barry Sims, Aaron Smith, Michael Stephani, Richard Straus, Nassim Nicholas Taleb, Stephen Taub, Ken Tower, Ken Tropin, Tomoko Uchiyama, Thomas Vician, Jr., Robert Webb, Kate Welling, Gabriel Wisdom, Brent Wood, and Patrick L. Young for all of their efforts and support.

And thank you to the following publications and writers who generously allowed me to quote from their work: Sol Waksman and Barclay Managed Futures Report, *Futures Magazine*, Managed Account Reports, Michael Rulle of Graham Capital Management, and *Technical Analysis of Stocks and Commodities Magazine*.

I am also indebted to the following authors whose works continue to be treasure troves of information and insight: Morton Baratz, Peter Bernstein, Clayton Christensen, Jim Collins, Jay Forrester, Tom Friedman, Gerd Gigerenzer, Daniel Goleman, Stephen Jay Gould, Alan Greenberg, Larry Harris, Robert Koppel, Edwin Lefevere, Michael Lewis, Jesse Livermore, Roger Lowenstein,

Ludwig von Mises, Lois Peltz, Ayn Rand, Jack Schwager, Denise Shekerjian, Robert Shiller, Van Tharp, Edward Thorp, Peter Todd, Brenda Ueland, and Dickson Watts.

This book could only have come to fruition with the editorial guidance of Jim Boyd at FT Press, as well as the able assistance and attention to detail of Dennis Higbee. I also want to thank Donna Cullen-Dolce, Lisa Iarkowski, Stephen Crane, John Pierce, and Lucy Petermark. To Paul Donnelly at Oxford University Press, I owe a special debt of gratitude for seeing potential in my initial proposal—even though he passed!

—Michael W. Covel
January 2009

About the Author

Michael Covel is a highly respected author, director, and entrepreneur who founded the internationally known website TurtleTrader.com in 1996. Covel's first book was the best selling *Trend Following: How Great Traders Make Millions in Up or Down Markets* (FT Press April 2004 and November 2005 Expanded Edition). The book profiles great trend following traders who have won millions, if not billions, in the market. The original edition, expanded edition, and paperback edition have sold 100,000 plus copies. It is also available in German, Japanese, Chinese (complex and simplified), Korean, French, Arabic, Turkish, and Russian.

Covel's second book *The Complete TurtleTrader: The Legend, the Lessons, the Results* (Collins, October 2007) is the definitive inside look at the legendary trader Richard Dennis and his student traders, 'The Turtles.' The book has received wide acclaim and is headed toward bestseller status. It is also available in German, Korean, and Chinese (complex and simplified).

Building off his book success, Covel wrote, directed, and produced a theatrical release documentary titled *Broke: The New American Dream*, built around the subject of behavioral finance, specifically investigating the 2007–2008 market crisis and crash. Face-to-face interviews with Nobel Prize winners Dr. Harry Markowitz and Dr. Vernon Smith, famed mutual fund investor Bill Miller of Legg Mason, David Harding of hedge fund Winton Capital, plus dozens of other Wall Street pros, along with average investors were conducted over 2007 and 2008. The film was shot in New York, DC, Miami, Dallas, San Diego, Baltimore, Las Vegas, Richmond, London, Tokyo, Singapore, Macau, and on a sheep farm outside of Harrisonburg, Virginia.

Fear touches everyone—even the successful people, the golden boys, the people who give the appearance of passing through life with their hands deep in their pockets, a whistle on their lips. To take on risk, you need to conquer fear, at least temporarily, at least occasionally. It can be done, especially if you look outside yourself for a strong ledge to stand on.
Denise Shekerjian[1]

Michael Covel has had unparalleled face-to-face access with the great traders of our time. Interviewing dozens of fund managers managing collectively well over $10 billion USD has given Covel a unique understanding.

Not afraid of a crowd or controversy, Covel is known for engaging and provocative speeches presented to audiences from Tokyo to Paris to Macau (China) to Vienna (Austria) to Hong Kong to Dallas (US). His writings have appeared in *Trader Monthly Magazine, Stocks, Futures and Options Magazine, Futures Magazine, Technical Analysis of Stocks and Commodities Magazine,* TradingMarkets.com, Yahoo Finance, *Market Technicians Association Newsletter*, and *Futures Japan Magazine*. Covel has been quoted and interviewed by likes of Bloomberg Radio, *Technical Analysis Magazine*, Barrons, and dozens of radio programs.

Covel can be reached directly at www.michaelcovel.com.

Part I

Trend Following

1

"Speculation is dealing with the uncertain conditions of the unknown future. Every human action is a speculation in that it is embedded in the flux of time."—Ludwig von Mises[1]

The Market

A market is simply a place where buyers and sellers gather to trade and exchange goods, buying and selling for any number of reasons across all types of instruments (for instance, stocks, currencies, commodities, and so on). Markets perform the essential role of exchange. The New York Stock Exchange and the National Association of Securities Dealers Automated Quotation System (NASDAQ) are two exchanges. There are also futures exchanges, such as the Chicago Mercantile Exchange. All of these exchanges have many markets where traders can buy and sell whatever they want. They are the place where organized speculation takes place.

Although this might sound simple and might sound as if I am focusing on a minor point, I am not. The markets' capability to provide a "price" for buyers and sellers to rely on as fact in the course of speculation is crucial. Ludwig von Mises, the noted Austrian economist, puts it into perspective:

The people that I know who are the most successful at trading are passionate about it. They fulfill what I think is the first requirement: developing intuitions about something they care about deeply, in this case, trading. They are the people who study years of charts, or commodity annuals... They develop a deep knowledge of whatever form of analysis they use. Out of that passion and knowledge, their trading ideas, insights, and intuitions emerge.

Charles Faulkner[2]

3

"It is the very essence of prices that they are the offshoot of the actions of individuals and groups of individuals acting on their own behalf. The catallactic concept of exchange ratios and prices precludes anything that is the effect of actions of a central authority, of people resorting to violence and threats in the name of society or the state or of an armed pressure group. In declaring that it is not the business of the government to determine prices, we do not step beyond the borders of logical thinking. A government can no more determine prices than a goose can lay hen's eggs."[3]

Although government can't determine prices in the long run, in the short term as we have all seen with the popping of the credit bubble, the government can greatly affect the market system. However, at the end of the day, all we have are prices and speculation. Because that is the case, finding out how to best "speculate" using market prices is a worthy endeavor.

Winning Versus Losing

The joy of winning and the pain of losing are right up there with the pain of winning and the joy of losing. Also to consider are the joy and pain of not participating. The relative strengths of these feelings tend to increase with the distance of the trader from his commitment to being a trader.

Ed Seykota[4]

Because of the corporate and market scandals of the last decade, it is understandable that the general public equates "winning" with simply abusing the financial market system. October and November 2008 are the latest to leave the public feeling abused and on the outside looking in. However, there are disciplined men and women trading in the markets with the utmost integrity who achieve spectacular returns year after year. Examine their beliefs and self-perceptions so you understand what keeps their earnings honest. However, before you examine others' perspectives, take a moment to consider your own. How do you approach investing?

For example, does this describe you? At the end of the 1990s, just when you were feeling good about yourself because you were more secure financially, the dot-com bubble burst, and by the time it was over, you had lost a significant amount of money. The same thing happened again in October and November 2008. You found yourself angry with the analysts, experts, brokers, or money managers whose advice you had taken. You didn't do anything wrong except follow their advice. Now you doubt that you will meet your investment goals or retire. You've held on to your remaining investments believing that they will eventually turn around, but deciding how to invest your 401k monies is paralyzing. You still believe that buying and holding is the way to go. You've now begun to think that winning in the markets is just plain dumb luck.

Or, maybe you view your money world like this: Sure, you lost some cash in the bear market and sure you lost more in October and November 2008, but, win or lose, you enjoy the thrill of investing in stock in the hopes of making a profit. Investing is entertainment for you. Plus, you like to boast about your investments for the admiration of others. You know you can be depressed and angry when you lose, but you also know that when you win you feel terrific. It's a great high. Because your main goal is to invest for quick profits, you're going to keep on doing what you've always done. After all, there was one time a few years ago when trading off a "hot tip" made you a nice profit.

If you think education is expensive, try ignorance.
Derek Bok

There is a much better way to think about making money. How would you feel about embracing this perspective? Your approach is objective and rational. You have enough confidence in your own decision making that you don't seek out investment recommendations from others. You're content to wait patiently until the right opportunity comes along. Yet, you're never too proud to buy a stock that is making new highs. For you, buying opportunities are usually market breakouts. Conversely, when you recognize that you are wrong, you exit immediately. You view a loss as an opportunity to learn, move on, and save your money for another day. What good is obsessing on the past going to do for you? You approach your trading as a business, making note of what you buy or sell and why in the same matter-of-fact way that you balance your checkbook. By not personalizing your trading decisions, you can make them without emotional indecision.

That is a stark contrast in perspectives. The first is that of a generally a market loser; the latter is that of a potential market winner. Don't be in such a hurry to choose the winning approach until you've found out just what making such a choice entails. On the other hand, I hope you'll find in *trend following trading* the inspiration to step up to the plate and go for it without fear or reservation. And don't be shy about it. You have to want to make money. You have to want to get ahead and be successful, the critics' condemnation be damned. Speculation, as von Mises has noted, is

The perfect speculator must know when to get in; more important, he must know when to stay out; and most important, he must know when to get out once he's in.

not only honorable, but a lifeblood. Profit-seeking speculation is *the* driving force of the market.[5]

Investor Versus Trader

Do you consider yourself an investor or a trader? Most people think of themselves as investors. However, if you knew that the biggest winners in the markets call themselves traders, wouldn't you want to know why? Simply put, they don't invest; they trade.

Investors put their money, or capital, into a market, such as stocks or real estate, under the assumption that the value will always increase over time. As the value increases, so does the person's "investment." Investors typically do not have a plan for when their investment value decreases. They usually hold on to their investment, hoping that the value will reverse itself and go back up. Investors typically succeed in bull markets and lose in bear markets.

This is because investors anticipate bear (down) markets with fear and trepidation, and therefore, they are unable to plan how to respond when they start to lose. They choose to "hang tight," and they continue to lose. They have an idea that a different approach to their losing involves more complicated trading techniques such as "selling short," of which they know little and don't care to learn. If the mainstream press continually positions investing as "good" or "safe" and trading as "bad" or "risky," people are reluctant to align themselves with traders or even seek to understand what trading is about.

A trader has a defined plan or strategy to put capital into a market to achieve a single goal: profit. Traders don't care what they own or what they sell as long as they end up with more money than they started with. They are not investing in anything. They are trading. It is a critical distinction.

Tom Basso, a longtime trader, has said that a person is a trader whether or not he is actually trading. Some people think they must be in and out of the markets every day to call themselves traders. What makes someone a trader has more to do with his perspective on life more so than making a given trade. For example, a great trader's perspective includes extreme patience. Like the African lion waiting for days for the right moment to strike its unsuspecting

Nothing has changed during the 21 years we've been managing money. Government regulation and intervention have been, are, and will continue to be present for as long as society needs rules by which to live. Today's governmental intervention or decree is tomorrow's opportunity. For example, governments often act in the same way that cartels act. Easily the most dominant and effective cartel has been OPEC, and even OPEC has been unable to create an ideal world from the standpoint of pricing its product. Free markets will always find their own means of price discovery.

Keith Campbell[6]

prey, a trend follower can wait weeks or months for the right trade that puts the odds on his side.

Additionally, and ideally, traders go short as often as they go long, enabling them to make money in both up and down markets. However, a majority of traders won't or can't go short. They struggle with the concept of making money when a market declines. I hope that after reading *Trend Following*, the confusion and hesitation associated with making money in down markets, markets that are dropping or crashing, will dissipate.

Trend followers are traders, so I generally use the word "trader" instead of "investor" throughout.

Fundamental Versus Technical

There are two basic theories that are used to trade in the markets. The first theory is fundamental analysis. It is the study of external factors that affect the supply and demand of a particular market. Fundamental analysis uses factors such as weather, government policy, domestic and foreign political and economic events, price-earnings ratios, and balance sheets to make buy and sell decisions. By monitoring "fundamentals" for a particular market, one can supposedly predict a change in market direction before that change has been reflected in the price of the market with the belief that you can then make money from that knowledge.

Whenever we get a period of poor performance, most investors conclude something must be fixed. They ask if the markets have changed. But trend following presupposes change.

John W. Henry[7]

The vast majority of Wall Street uses fundamental analysis alone. They are the academics, brokers, and analysts who spoke highly of the new economy during the dot-com craze. These same Wall Street players brought millions of players into the real estate and credit bubbles of 2008. Millions bought into their rosy fundamental projections and rode bubbles straight up with no clue how to exit when those bubbles finally burst. Consider an exchange between a questioner and President Bush at a December 17, 2007 press conference:

> Q: "I wanted to ask you [Mr. President]—I'm a financial advisor here in Fredericksburg [Virginia], and I wanted to ask you what your thoughts are on the market going forward for '08, and if any of your policies would make any difference?"
>
> The President: "No (laughter), I'm not going to answer your question. If I were an investor, I would be looking at the basic fundamentals of the economy. Early on in my

presidency, somebody asked me about the stock market, and I thought I was a financial genius, and it was a mistake (laughter). The fundamentals of this nation are strong. One of the interesting developments has been the role of exports in overall GDP growth. When you open up markets for goods and services, and we're treated fairly, we can compete just about with anybody, anywhere. And exports have been an integral part, at least of the 3rd quarter growth. But far be it for me—I apologize—for not being in the position to answer your question. But I don't think you want your President opining on whether the Dow Jones is going to—(laughter)—be going up or down."

One of our basic philosophical tendencies is that change is constant, change is random, and trends will reappear if we go through a period of non-trending markets. It's only a precursor to future trends and we feel if there is an extended period of non-trending markets, this really does set up a base for very dynamic trends in the future.

Former Head of Research at John W. Henry[8]

The President's view is a typical fundamental view shared by the vast majority of market participants. Consider further an excerpt found in Yahoo! Finance's commentary; it outlines a single market day:

"It started off decent, but ended up the fourth straight down day for stocks...early on, the indices were in the green, mostly as a continuation from the bounce Monday afternoon...but as the day wore on and the markets failed to show any upward momentum, the breakdown finally occurred...The impetus this time was attributed to the weakness in the dollar, even though the dollar was down early in the day while stocks were up...also, oil prices popped higher on wishful thinking statements from a Venezuelan official about OPEC cutting production... whether or not these factors were simply excuses for selling, or truly perceived as fundamental factors hardly matters...."

Millions of readers read this type of drivel every day. Worse, thousands watch Jim Cramer of *Mad Money* fame promote similar nonsensical beliefs every day. Predictions based off of fundamental analysis don't work for the vast majority of market participants. Great example? Not many predicted the October/November 2008 market crash! On top of not being able to predict, fundamental analysis leaves many with trying to pick bottoms or trust that conditions will always improve. One of the great traders of the twentieth century, Ed Seykota, nailed the problem with fundamental analysis:

"One evening, while having dinner with a fundamentalist, I accidentally knocked a sharp knife off the edge of the table. He watched the knife twirl through the air, as it came to rest with the pointed end sticking into his shoe. 'Why didn't you move your foot?' I exclaimed. 'I was waiting for it to come back up,' he replied."[9]

Don't we all know an investor who is waiting for "his" market to come back? The financial website marketer Motley Fool has a back-story, a narrative behind how it started, that reflects the folly of literally banking on fundamental analysis as a solution for making money:

"It all started with chocolate pudding. When they were young, brothers David and Tom Gardner learned about stocks and the business world from their father at the supermarket. Dad, a lawyer and economist, would tell them, 'See that pudding? We own the company that makes it! Every time someone buys that pudding, it's good for our company. So go get some more!' The lesson stuck."[10]

The Motley Fools' David and Tom Gardner's pudding story might be cute, but it is *Forrest Gump*-like simplistic (and wrong). Their plan gets you in, but it doesn't tell you when to get out or how much of the pudding stock you must buy. Unfortunately, many people believe that simple story is a good strategy for making money. That is a sad state of affairs.

A second market theory, technical analysis, operates in stark contrast to fundamental analysis. This approach is based on the belief that at any given point in time market prices reflect all known factors affecting supply and demand for that particular market. Instead of evaluating fundamental factors, technical analysis looks at the market prices themselves. Technical traders believe that a careful analysis of daily price action is an effective means of trading for profit.

Now here is where an understanding of technical analysis becomes complicated. There are essentially two forms of technical analysis. One form is based on an ability to "read" charts and use "indicators" to predict market direction. Here is an example of the mentality behind a predictive view of technical analysis:

But I think our ace in the hole is that the governments usually screw things up and don't maintain their sound money and policy coordination. And about the time we're ready to give up on what usually has worked, and proclaim that the world has now changed, the governments help us out by creating unwise policy that helps produce dislocations and trends.

Jerry Parker[11]

While a fundamental analyst may be able to properly evaluate the economics underlying a stock, I do not believe they can predict how the masses will process this same information. Ultimately, it is the dollar-weighted collective opinion of all market participants that determines whether a stock goes up or down. This consensus is revealed by analyzing price.

Mark Abraham
Quantitative Capital Management, L.P.

"I often hear people swear they make money with technical analysis. Do they really? The answer, of course, is that they do. People make money using all sorts of strategies, including some involving tea leaves and sunspots. The real question is: Do they make more money than they would investing in a blind index fund that mimics the performance of the market as a whole? Most academic financial experts believe in some form of the random-walk theory and consider technical analysis almost indistinguishable from a pseudoscience whose predictions are either worthless or, at best, so barely discernibly better than chance as to be unexploitable because of transaction costs."[12]

Markets aren't chaotic, just as the seasons follow a series of predictable trends, so does price action.
Stocks are like everything else in the world: They move in trends, and trends tend to persist.

Jonathan Hoenig
Portfolio Manager,
Capitalistpig Hedge Fund LLC

This is the view of technical analysis held by most people who know of technical analysis—that it is some form of mysterious chart reading technique, such as astrology. Equity research from a major bank furthers my prediction distinction point:

"The question of whether technical analysis works has been a topic of contention for over three decades. Can past prices forecast future performance?"[13]

However, there is another type of technical analysis that neither tries to predict nor forecast. This type is based on reacting to price action. Trend followers are the group of technical traders who use reactive technical analysis. Instead of trying to predict a market direction, their strategy is to react to the market's movements whenever they occur. This enables them to focus on the market's actual moves and not get emotionally involved with trying to predict direction or duration.

It is not the strongest of the species that survive, nor the most intelligent, but the ones most responsive to change.

Charles Darwin

However, this type of price analysis never allows trend followers to enter at the exact bottom of a trend or exit at the exact top of the trend. Second, with price analysis, they don't necessarily trade every day. Instead, trend followers wait patiently for the right market conditions instead of forcing the market. Third, there should be no performance goals with price analysis. Some traders might embrace a strategy that dictates, for example, "I must make $400 dollars a day." Trend followers would counter with, "Sure, but what if the markets don't move on a given day?"

One trend follower summarized the conundrum:

"I could not analyze 20 markets fundamentally and make money. One of the reasons [trend following] works is because you don't try to outthink it. You are a trend follower, not a trend predictor."[14]

Discretionary Versus Mechanical

I have established the concept that you can be an investor or trader. I have established that trading can be fundamentally or technically based. Further, technical trading can be predictive or reactive. And I've explained how trend followers are traders who use a reactive technical approach based on price. However, there is even more distinction. Traders can also be discretionary or mechanical.

It is when the unimaginable occurs that the systematic trader remains calm, presciently knowing when to buy, sell, or adjust their exposure.

Mark Abraham
Quantitative Capital Management, L.P.

John W. Henry, one of the best trend followers over the last 25 years, makes a clear distinction between the two strategies: "[I] believe that an investment strategy can only be as successful as the discipline of the manager to adhere to the requirements in the face of market adversity. Unlike discretionary traders, whose decisions may be subject to behavioral biases, [I] practice a disciplined investment process."[15]

When Henry speaks of decisions that may be subject to behavioral biases, he is referring to the legions of traders who make their buy and sell decisions based on the sum of their market knowledge, their view of the current market environment, or any number of other factors. In other words, they use their discretion—hence, the use of discretionary to describe their approach to trading.

Decisions made at the "discretion" of the trader are subjective and can be changed or second-guessed. There are no ironclad assurances that these discretionary trading decisions are not colored by personal bias. Of course, a trader's initial choice to launch a trading system is discretionary. You must make discretionary decisions such as choosing a system, selecting your portfolio, and determining a risk percentage. However, after you've decided on the basics, you can choose to systematize these discretionary decisions and from that point forward, make them systematic.

The trend is your friend except at the end when it bends.

Ed Seykota[18]

Mechanical trading systems, generally used by trend followers, are based on an objective and automated set of rules. Traders rigidly follow these trading rules (often putting them into computer programs) to get themselves in (buy) and out (sell) of a market. A mechanical trading system can make life easier by eliminating emotion from trading decisions. It forces discipline. If you break your mechanical trading system rules, you will go broke.

Henry puts into perspective the downsides of discretionary trading:

I feel sorry for the traders who watch CNBC all day, every day. They hope to eek out some competitive advantage from the comments of some guy who has never traded an S&P contract in his life. Even if the media happened to have something relevant to say, the news is already reflected in the open, high, low, close, open interest and daily volume.

Christian Baha
CEO Superfund

"Unlike discretionary traders, whose decisions may be subject to behavioral biases, JWH practices a disciplined investment process. By quantifying the circumstances under which key investment decisions are made, the JWH methodology offers investors a consistent approach to markets, unswayed by judgmental bias."[16]

It seems a bit rigid to say you can't even use just a little discretion when faced with a trading decision, doesn't it? After all, where's the fun if all you ever do is follow a mechanical model? But then trend following isn't supposed to be about fun. It's supposed to be about winning profits. A researcher at Campbell and Company, one of the oldest and most successful trend following firms, is adamant about avoiding discretion:

"One of our strengths is to follow our models and not use discretion. This rule is written in stone at Campbell."[17]

You can see throughout this book that trend followers choose their words carefully and deliberately. It was encouraging to me to find that there are few, if any, instances when their words are not reflected in their philosophies and ultimately their performance data.

In Plain Sight

Trend following is not something new. It goes back decades. The strategy is simply discovered by new generations of traders at different times:

"Salem Abraham, a trend following trader, began research-ing the markets by asking a simple question: Who is making money? The answer was trend followers and his journey began."[19]

But few people have made the journey with Abraham. During the dot-com era of the late 1990s, during the 2008 real estate and credit bubbles, so many investors and traders with so little strategy were making so much money that trend followers disappeared from the radar screen, even though they kept right on making money.

Since trend following has nothing to do with short-term trading, cutting edge technologies, or Wall Street Holy Grails, its appeal is always negligible during market bubbles. It's not sexy. If investors can jump on the bandwagon of practically any "long only" mutual or hedge fund manager or turn a profit trading themselves by simply buying Internet, energy, or real estate stocks and holding on to them, what need would there ever be to adopt a strategy such as trend following?

However, if we look at how much money trend followers have made since assorted stock market bubbles have popped, trend following becomes far more relevant to the bottom line. The following chart (Chart 1.1) shows a hypothetical index of three longtime trend following firms compared against the S&P stock index. The chart combines Dunn Capital Management, Campbell and Co., and John W. Henry and Co. into an equally weighted index:

Defining a trend is like defining love. We know it when we see it, but we are rarely sure exactly what it is. Fung and Hsieh's paper goes a long way to doing for trends what poets have been trying to do for love since time immemorial. They give us a working model that quantitatively defines their value for us. Traders will not be surprised to learn that trend following advisors performed best during extreme market moves, especially during bad months for equities.[20]

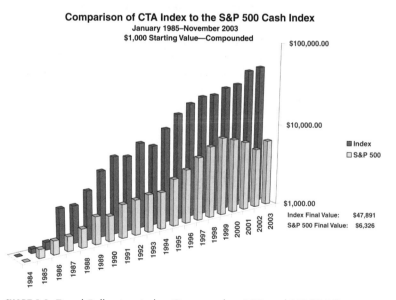

Comparison of CTA Index to the S&P 500 Cash Index
January 1985–November 2003
$1,000 Starting Value—Compounded

$100,000.00

$10,000.00

■ Index
☐ S&P 500

$1,000.00

| Index Final Value: | $47,891 |
| S&P 500 Final Value: | $6,326 |

CHART 1.1: Trend Following Index Compared to S&P and NASDAQ

Change is not merely necessary to life—it is life.

         Alvin Toffler

Yet, even when trend following success is brought to their attention, investors are often skeptical. They say the markets have changed and that trend following no longer works. Their concerns usually stem from a random press story of a trend follower who supposedly "blew up" and lost all of his clients' money. But the truth is that trend following hasn't changed, even though a single trend follower may make a mistake.

Let's put change in perspective. Markets behave the same as they did 300 years ago. In other words, markets are the same today because they always change. This is the philosophical underpinning of trend following trading. A few years ago, for example, German mark trading had significant trading volume. Now the Euro has replaced the German mark. This was a huge, yet typical, change. If you are flexible, market changes, like changes in life, don't have to impact you negatively. Trend traders traded the mark; now they trade the Euro.

Accepting the inevitability of change is the first step to understanding trend following philosophy. One trend follower describes the benefits of understanding change:

> "But what won't change? Change. When a period of difficult performance continues, however, most investors' natural conclusion is that something must be done to fix the problem. Having been through these draw downs before, we know that they are unpleasant, but they do not signal that something is necessarily wrong with the future. During these periods, almost everyone asks the same question in these exact words: 'Have the markets changed?' I always tell them the truth: 'Yes.' Not only have they changed, but they will continue to change as they have throughout history and certainly throughout our 19 years. Trend following presupposes change. It is based on change."[21]

Markets go up, down, and sideways. They trend. They flow. They surprise. No one can forecast a trend's beginning or end until it becomes a matter of record, just like the weather. However, if your trading strategy is designed to adapt to change, you can take advantage of the changes to make money as John W. Henry noted:

> "If you have a valid basic philosophy, the fact that things change turns out to be a benefit. At least you can survive. At the very least, you will survive over the long term. But if

you don't have a valid basic philosophy, you won't be successful because change will eventually kill you. I knew I could not predict anything, and that is why we decided to follow trends, and that is why we've been so successful. We simply follow trends. No matter how ridiculous those trends appear to be at the beginning, and no matter how extended or how irrational they seem at the end, we follow trends."[22]

What does Henry mean by "a valid basic philosophy?" He is talking about a trading strategy that can be defined, quantified, written down, and measured in terms of numbers—as a way to track trends. Do you have one of those? Does your broker have one? Does your mutual fund manager have one? Does your high-flying hedge fund have one? Trend followers do not guess if they must buy or sell. They know what to do because they have their "valid basic philosophy" codified in a specific plan. What is behind the source of those trends, those profits? The Man Group, one of the largest trend following traders, sees "trends as a persistent price phenomenon that stem[s] from changes in risk premiums—the amount of return investors demand to compensate the risks they are taking. Risk premiums vary massively over time in response to new market information, changes in economic environment, or even intangible factors such as shifts in investor sentiment. When risk premiums decrease or increase, underlying assets have to be priced again. Because investors typically have different expectations, large shifts in markets result over several months or even years as expectations are gradually adjusted. As long as there is uncertainty about the future, there will be trends for [trend followers] to capture."

Change

There are plenty of people who ignore trend following's tremendous track record and argue that it is outdated, inferior, or it plain doesn't work.

"Has Trend Following Changed?" was the topic of a panel at a Managed Fund Association's conference. Patrick Welton saw that there is no evidence that trend following has changed. To prove this fact, he constructed 120 trend following models. Some were reversal-based, and others were not. Some were breakout style trading systems based on price action with others relying on

The people who excel in any field are people who realize that the moment is there to be seized—that there are opportunities at every turn. They are more alive to the moment.

Charles Faulkner[23]

The four most expensive words in the English language are "this time it's different."

Sir John Templeton

While conceding tacitly or explicitly that over the long run daily price movements are serially independent (move randomly) technical analysts focus on recurring short term patterns and trends. They are like surfboard riders, who study the movements of the waves, not in order to understand why they behave as they do, but simply in order to be on hand whenever they surge, to catch them at their crest, or as soon thereafter as possible to ride them as far as they possible can, and to dissemble before they change direction.

Morton S. Baratz[25]

By honest I don't mean that you only tell what's true. But you make clear the entire situation. You make clear all the information that is required for somebody else who is intelligent to make up their mind.

Richard Feynman

volatility and band-style breakouts. The average holding periods ranged from two weeks to one year. The results gave almost identical performance characteristics in periods covering the late 1980s, early 1990s, and late 1990s.

Welton also addressed the misconception that the sources of return for trend following had changed. He pointed out that starting from first principles, it was a fact that the source of return for trend following resulted from sustained market price movements. Human reaction to such events, and the stream of information describing them, takes time and runs its course unpredictably. The resulting magnitude and rate of price change could not be reliably forecast. This is the precise reason why trend following works.[24]

Burt Kozloff, a consultant in the fund industry, also confronted trend-trading skeptics head on two decades before trend followers' fantastic October 2008 returns:

"In February, 1985, on a tour of Germany sponsored by the Deutsche Terminborse, several advisors and pool operators were making a presentation to a group of German institutional investors. Among them were two trend-based traders, Campbell & Co. and John W. Henry & Co. During the question-and-answer period, one man stood and proclaimed: 'But isn't it true that Trend Following is dead?' At this point, the moderator asked that slides displaying the performance histories for Campbell and Henry be displayed again. The moderator marched through the declines, saying: 'Here's the first obituary for trend-based trading. Here's the next one...and the next but these traders today are at new highs, and they consistently decline to honor the tombstones that skeptics keep erecting every time there's a losing period.' Campbell and JWH have made their investors hundreds of millions of dollars since that time. It might, therefore, be a mistake to write yet another series of obituaries."[26]

A new trend following obituary, often oblivious to real facts, and often rooted in ignorance, will be written every few years by mutual fund defenders, player haters, and cranks despite the incredible amounts of money made by trend following practitioners. Perplexed at Wall Street's lack of acceptance, one trend follower responded:

"How can someone buy high and short low and be successful for two decades unless the underlying nature of markets is to trend? On the other hand, I've seen year-after-year, brilliant men buying low and selling high for a while successfully and then going broke because they thought they understood why a certain investment instrument had to perform in accordance with their personal logic."[27]

I have found though that trend followers generally seem to be oblivious to those who question their strategies. Why spend massive energy constantly defending yourself when you are producing monster returns year after year? That said, I do enjoy spending time to make the defense for them. The subject is too important and too valuable for the average investor to let it go under the radar.

Modus Operandi: Price

In an increasingly uncertain and, these days, downright unfriendly world, it is extremely efficient and effective if our decision making is based on this single, simple, reliable truth. The constant barrage of fundamental data, such as price-earnings ratios, crop reports, and economic studies, plays into traders' tendencies to make trading more complicated than it needs to be. Yet, factoring in every possible fundamental still does not tell a trader how much and when to buy, or how much and when to sell. The truth of "price" always seems to win out over all of these other analytical methods.

But even if you digest price as the key trading variable, it is not unusual for many traders to become familiar with and focus on only one market (usually stocks in their home countries) to the exclusion of all other global opportunities. Seeking to maintain a maximum degree of comfort, they follow this one familiar market's movements faithfully. If they specialize in stocks, they wouldn't dream of branching out into currencies or futures. How can a stock trader know anything about currencies? That's the fear. The idea that you could know enough about Cisco and soybeans to trade them both seems unfathomable to many. But think about what cotton, crude oil, Cisco, GE, the U.S. dollar, the Australian dollar, wheat, Apple, Google, and Berkshire Hathaway all have in common. The answer? Price.

[Trend following] is motivated by a very broad interpretation of the universe. The underlying belief is that economic systems adjust to changes in fundamentals gradually and over long periods of time, and that the consequent trends are evident everywhere in human history and commerce. Political, economic, and social regime changes trigger price adjustments in markets that don't happen instantaneously. For example, the growth and decline of the Roman Empire took place, not in a day, but over hundreds of years. A major problem, of course, is that markets don't move from one state to another in a straight line: There are periods of countertrend shock and volatility. We spend most of our time trying to find ways to deal with those unsettling but inevitable events. That being said, it is really not difficult to put together a simple trend following system that can generate positive returns over a realistic holding period and there are many, many commercial systems that have been generating strong, albeit volatile, returns for a long time. So there are definitely firm grounds for believing in Santa Claus.

Paul Mulvaney
CIO of
Mulvaney Capital Management Ltd.

Market prices are the objective data. Accepting that truth allows you to compare and study prices and measure their movements, even if you know nothing about those markets themselves. You can look at individual price histories and charts without knowing which market is which and trade them successfully. Think about that. That is not what they teach at Wharton, but it is the foundation of making millions.

Follow the Trend

Don't try to guess how far a trend will go. You can't. Peter Borish, former second-in-command with Paul Tudor Jones, lays bare the only concern a trader must have:

> "Price makes news, not the other way around. A market is going to go where a market is going to go."[28]

The concept of price as the trading cue is just too darn simple for people to accept. This is seen in the mainstream press that always emphasizes the *wrong* numbers. Bill Griffith, an anchor at CNBC, once pondered:

> "At some point, investing is an act of faith. If you can't believe the numbers, annual reports, etc., what numbers can you believe?"

Griffith misses the point when he asks what numbers you can believe if you can't believe a company's annual report. It doesn't matter whether you can or cannot believe the earnings statement. All of these numbers can be doctored, fixed, or cooked. The traded market price can't be fixed. It's the only number to believe. You can see it every day in the paper or online. However, this simple fact does not diminish the confusion. Alan Sloan, by all accounts a fine finance reporter, searches for numbers to trust without ever understanding how futile his search will be:

> "If some of the smartest people on Wall Street can't trust the numbers, you wonder who can trust the numbers."

What numbers is Sloan talking about? Balance sheets? Price-earnings ratios? You can't ever trust those numbers. Someone can always alter them. Beyond that, even if you knew accurate balance sheet numbers, how can they can help you determine when or how much to buy or sell? A critical lesson from John W. Henry:

"...Political uncertainty is one reason why investment decisions are not driven by discretionary judgments. How, for example, do you measure the impact of statements from Messrs. Greenspan, Rubin, Summers, Miyazawa, or Sakakibara? Even if [we] knew all the linkages between fundamentals and prices, unclear policy comments would limit our ability to generate returns...trying to interpret the tea leaves in Humphreys-Hawkins testimony or the minds of Japanese policy authorities does not lend itself to disciplined systematic investing. Instead of trying to play a loser's game of handicapping policy statements, our models let market prices do the talking. Prices may be volatile, but they do not cloud the truth in market reactions. Our job is to systematically sift price data to find trends and act on them and not let the latest news flashes sway our market opinions."[29]

You can't read tea leaves. Nobody can. William Eckhardt, a longtime trend follower and former partner of trend follower Richard Dennis (the father of the 'Turtles'), builds off Henry's wisdom by describing how price is what traders live and die by:

"An important feature of our approach is that we work almost exclusively with price, past and current...Price is definitely the variable traders live and die by, so it is the obvious candidate for investigation...Pure price systems are close enough to the North Pole that any departure tends to bring you farther south."[30]

How does a trend follower implement Dennis' philosophy? Trend trader Ed Seykota told me a story about trading sugar. He had been buying sugar—thousands of sugar contracts [futures]. Every day, the market was closing limit up. Every day, the market was going higher and higher. He just kept buying more and more sugar each day limit up. A broker was watching all this. One day, the broker called Seykota after the market was closed, because he had extra contracts of sugar that were not balanced out, and he said to Seykota, "I bet you want to buy these other 5,000 contracts of sugar." Seykota replied, "Sold."

Think about that: After the market has closed limit up for days in a row, Seykota says, "Sure, I'll buy more sugar contracts at the absolute top of the market." Why is this an important lesson?

Ed Seykota is a genius and a great trader who has been phenomenally successful. When I first met Ed he had recently graduated from MIT and had developed some of the first computer programs for testing and trading technical systems...Ed provided an excellent role model. For example, one time, he was short silver and the market just kept eking down, a half penny a day. Everyone else seemed to be bullish, talking about why silver had to go up because it was so cheap, but Ed just stayed short. Ed said, "The trend is down, and I'm going to stay short until the trend changes." I learned patience from him in the way he followed the trend.

Michael Marcus[31]

Be less curious about people and more curious about ideas.

Marie Curie

The wisest trend follower I know has said that every 5 years some famous trader blows up and everyone declares trend following to be dead. Then, 5 years later, some famous trader blows up and everyone declares trend following to be dead. Then, 5 years later...well, was the problem trend following or the trader?

[Trend following] is similar to being long options because the stop loss creates a limited downside, and the continuation of the trend creates the large upside. This is why the phrase for this approach to trading is to "cut losses" and to "let profits run." Of course, if trends continually fail to materialize, these limited losses can accumulate to large losses. This is also true for any option purchase strategy. For trend followers, the "option premium" is "paid" for after an unsuccessful trade is closed when a stop loss has been reached. The premium can also be "paid" after markets have moved a great deal, profits have been made, and a reversal causes a trailing stop to be hit, and some of the profits reversed.

Michael S. Rulle, President, Graham Capital Management[34]

Everybody instinctively wants to buy sugar on the dip. Let it come down low. Get a bargain. Trend following works by doing the opposite: by buying higher prices.

Even Good Traders Confuse Price

The trading histories of Julian Robertson and Louis Bacon, two famous hedge fund managers, underscore the importance of price for decision making.

A few years back, Julian Robertson shut his long running hedge fund down. He was a global macro trader who relied on fundamentals for decision making. He had a close relationship with another global macro trader, Louis Bacon. Bacon is extremely secretive to the extent that it's nearly impossible to find out his performance numbers unless you are a client. I do know from the little bit of writing available on Bacon that he's pulled hundreds of millions, if not billions, of profit from the marketplace. Although Bacon does not advertise himself as a trend follower, the following excerpt leaves no doubt that he is focused on price action just as much as a trend followers:

"If a stock goes from 100 to 90, an investor who looks at fundamentals will think maybe it's a better buy," explains one source. "But with Louis [Bacon], he will figure he must have been wrong about something and get out." Contrast that, say, with [Julian] Robertson, who, even after shutting down his firm, was doggedly holding on to massive positions in such stocks as U.S. Airways Group and United Asset Management Corp... [Bacon made the comment] in an investor letter that 'those traders with a futures background [trend trading] are more sensitive to market action, whereas value-based equity traders are trained to react less to the market and focus much more on their assessment of a company's or situation's viability.'"[32]

Today, Louis Bacon is still trading and following price.

Trend followers know that attempting to pinpoint the beginning of a trending market is futile. When trends begin, they often arise from a flat market that doesn't appear to be trending in any direction. The idea is to take small bets early on in a market to see if the trend does, indeed, mature and get big enough to make big money. How do trend following strategies succeed? Michael Rulle of Graham Capital Management offers:

> "The ability of trend following strategies to succeed depends on two obvious but important assumptions about markets. First, it assumes that price trends occur regularly in markets. Secondly, it assumes that trading systems can be created to profit from these trends. The basic trading strategy that all trend followers try to systematize is to 'cut losses' and 'let profits run.'"[33]

I asked Charles Faulkner, a modeler of top traders, to expand upon what at first glance appears to be a simple idea:

> "...the first rule of trading is to, 'Cut your losses, and let your profits run.' And then, that it's the hardest thing to do. Seldom do any of them wonder why, and yet this is exactly where the efficient market hypothesis breaks down, and the psychological nature of the markets shows through. When we lose or misplace something, we expect to find it later. The cat comes back. We find our car keys. But we know a dollar on the street will not be there with the next person who passes by. So experience teaches us that losses are unlikely and gains are hard. 'A bird in the hand is worth two in the bush.' This is when I tell them that they earn their trading profits by doing the hard thing—by going against human nature. This is where the discipline comes in, the psychological preparation, the months of system testing that give the trader the confidence to actually trade against his natural tendencies."

If cutting losses and letting profits run is the trend follower's mantra, it is because harsh reality dictates that you can't play the game if you run out of money. Nor can you predict the trend direction, as trend trader Christopher Cruden points out:

> "I would prefer to finish with a certain currency forecast, based upon my own fundamental reading of the market and one that underpins my personal investment philosophy... The only problem is I can't tell you when this will happen or which event will be first. On that basis alone, it seems best to stay with our systematic approach."[35]

In Patton, *my favorite scene is when U.S. General George S. Patton has just spent weeks studying the writing of his German adversary Field Marshall Erwin Rommel and is crushing him in an epic tank battle in Tunisia. Patton, sensing victory as he peers onto the battlefield from his command post, growls, "Rommel, you magnificent bastard. I read your book!"*

Paul Tudor Jones as quoted in the Foreword to *The Alchemy of Finance*

Are you a bull market baby? Can you survive in any situation?

A good example of not letting profits run can be seen in trading strategies that take profits off the table before a trend is over. For example, one broker told me that one of his strategies was to ride a stock up for a 30 percent gain and then exit. That was his strategy. Let it go up 30 percent and get out. Sounds reasonable. However, a strategy that uses profit targets is problematic. The biggest problem is that it goes against the math of getting rich, which is to let your profits run. If you can't predict the end or top of a trend, why get out early and risk leaving profits on the table?

For example, you start with $50,000. The market takes off and your account swells to $80,000. You could, at that point, quickly pull your $30,000 profit off the table. Your misconception is that if you don't take those profits immediately, they will be gone.

Trend followers know that a $50,000 account may go to $80,000, back to $55,000, back up to $90,000, and from there, perhaps, all the way up to $200,000. The person who took profits at $80,000 is not around to take the ride up to $200,000. Letting your profits run is tough psychologically. But understand that in trying to protect every penny of your profit, you actually prevent yourself from making the big profits.

Loss

I began to realize that the big money must necessarily be in the big swing.

Jesse Livermore

You are going to have ups and downs in your trading account. Losses are a part of the trading game. You say you want no losses? You want positive returns every month? Well, you could have had your money with the Ponzi-scheme of Bernard Madoff, but we all know how that turned out! Life equals having losses and you're going to have losses with trend following. "You can't make money if you are not willing to lose. It's like breathing in, but not being willing to breathe out."[36]

If you don't have losses, you are not taking risks. If you don't risk, you won't ever win big. Losses aren't the problem. It's how you deal with them. Ignore losses with no plan and they will come back to haunt you and your account size. Consider:

"Theoretically, really big losses rarely befall a trend follower because he eliminates or reverses his position as soon as the market goes against him. A lot of little losses are inevitable…The rationale for hanging in is that any price move could be the beginning of a trend, and the occasional big breakout justifies a string of small losses."[37]

Conclusion

Ed Seykota once told me a story about being in Bermuda with a new trader who wanted to learn the "secrets." "Just give me the quick-and-dirty version of your magical trading secrets," the neophyte said. Seykota took the new trader out to the beach. They stood there watching the waves break against the shoreline. The neophyte asked, "What's your point?" Seykota said, "Go down to the shoreline where the waves break. Now begin to time them. Run out with the waves as they recede and run in as the waves come in. Can you see how you could get into rhythm with the waves? You follow the waves out and you follow them in. You just follow their lead."

In my search for the facts about trend following, it became clear that its basic tenets, its philosophical underpinnings, are relevant not only to trading, but to our lives in general, from business to personal relationships. I also found in my conversations with the old pro trend followers that trend following works best when pursued with unbridled passion.

How important is passion? Author Brett Steenbarger puts passion into perspective:

Many people would sooner die than think; in fact, they do so.

Bertrand Russell

"Find your passion: the work that stimulates, fascinates, and endlessly challenges you. Identify what you find meaningful and rewarding, and pour yourself into it. If your passion happens to be the markets, you will find the fortitude to outlast your learning curve and to develop the mastery needed to become a professional. If your passion is not the markets, then invest your funds with someone who possesses an objective track record and whose investment aims match your own. Then go forth and pour yourself into those facets of life that will keep you springing out of bed each morning, eager to face each day."[38]

While assembling *Trend Following*, it became clear that when used within the context of passion, the term "trend following" could

Among people who take the trouble to understand what the business is about instead of assuming it involves speculating on live cattle, it is readily understood.

Bruce Cleland,
Campbell and Co.[40]

also be substituted throughout for other activities in life. This insight crystallized with me while rereading a passage from a 1938 book on creative writing by Brenda Ueland:

> "Whenever I say writing in this book, I also mean anything that you love and want to do or to make. It may be a six-act tragedy in blank verse, it may be dressmaking or acrobatics, or inventing a new system of double entry accounting…but you must be sure that your imagination and love are behind it, that you are not working just from grim resolution, i.e., to impress people."[39]

Trend followers I met don't seem to trade with grim resolve or with an intention to impress others. They are playing the game to win and enjoying every moment of it. Like other high-level performers, such as professional athletes and world-class musicians, they understand how critical it is to maintain a winning attitude for success. And as Larry Hite reminded, good trend traders ask themselves straightforward questions:

> "The first question you have to ask yourself: 'who are you?' I'm not kidding. And don't look at your driver's license! But what you got to say to yourself: 'what am I comfortable doing?' Am I an arbitrager? Am I a short-term trader? …it is really important that you understand who you are and what you want to do. The next thing you have to ask yourself, one of the real details, 'what are you going to do?' What are you going to do exactly? What has to be done? Is it hard to you? Is it easy? Do you have the materials to do it? One of the great things about the market is the markets don't care about you. The market doesn't care what color you are. The markets don't care if you are short or tall. They don't care about anything. They don't care whether you leave or stay. The last question you have to ask yourself: 'what follows?' You have to ask yourself, 'if I do this and it works, where am I? What have I got?' Now what I've said may really sound like it's pretty simple and common sense, [but think about the failed hedge fund Long Term Capital Management]…those were some very, very smart people [Nobel Prize winners] who did some pretty stupid things. And they did it because they didn't ask themselves the basic questions."

Key Points

- Seykota: "All profitable systems trade trends; the difference in price necessary to create the profit implies a trend."

- Trend following is based on simple universal laws we can all learn.

- No one knows how high or how low a market will go. No one knows when a market will move. You can't undo the past, and you can't predict the future. Prices, not traders, predict the future.

- Trend followers buy high and sell short low. This is counterintuitive for most.

- Using "common sense" is not a good way to judge or trade markets.

- Losses are a cost of doing business. No one can be right all the time. No one can make money all the time. Trend followers expect and handle losses with objectivity and detachment. If you don't have losses, you are not taking risks. If you don't risk, you won't win.

- Price goes either up, down, or sideways. No advances in technology, leaps of modern science, or radical shifts in perception will alter this fact.

- What if they told you that the best way to get to point B, without bumping into walls, would be to bump into the walls and not worry about it? Don't worry about getting to point B, but just enjoy bumping into the walls.[43]

- "If you take emotion—would be, could be, should be—out of it, and look at what is, and quantify it," says John W. Henry, reflecting from the owner's box at Fenway Park, "I think you have a big advantage over most human beings."

If you take emotion—would be, could be, should be—out of it, and look at what is, and quantify it, I think you have a big advantage over most human beings.

John W. Henry[41]

A trend is a trend is a trend, Gertrude Stein would have said if she were a trader...Once you have a game plan, the differences are pretty idiosyncratic.

Richard Dennis[42]

Great Trend Followers

2

"Most of us don't have the discipline to stay focused on a single goal
for five, ten, or twenty years, giving up everything to bring it off, but
that's what's necessary to become an Olympic champion, a world class
surgeon, or a Kirov ballerina. Even then, of course, it may be all in vain.
You may make a single mistake that wipes out all the work. It may ruin
the sweet, lovable self you were at seventeen. That old adage is true: You
can do anything in life; you just can't do everything. That's what Bacon
meant when he said a wife and children were hostages to fortune. If you
put them first, you probably won't run the three-and-a-half-minute-mile,
make your first $10 million, write the great American novel,
or go around the world on a motorcycle.
Such goals take complete dedication."
—Jim Rogers[1]

The best way to understand trend following is not by only
reading rules that might make up a particular trend trading strategy,
but also by meeting the men and women who practice it. Unfortunately, investors today are reluctant to concede that they might do
better when it comes to their finances with mentoring or guidance.
Although they will sign up for a cooking course, they won't take
advantage of wisdom from those who have made fortunes. They
prefer "reinventing the wheel" to modeling their behavior after
proven excellence. However, because I consider role modeling to be
critical to learning correct trading, this chapter profiles excellent
trend followers.

Technical trading is not glamorous. It will rarely tell that you bought at the lows and sold at the highs. But trading should be a business, and a systematic program is a plan to profit over time, rather than from a single trade. High expectations are essential to success, but unrealistic ones just waste time. Computers do not tell the user how to make profits in the market; they can only verify our own ideas. We consider using a computer to develop trading programs to be a sensible, conservative approach.

Cognitrend GMBH

As an observer of trend following, I've come to realize that if you take historical and current trend following performance data seriously, you must make a choice. You can accept the data as fact, make an honest assessment of yourself and your approach to making money, and make a commitment to change. Or, you can pretend the performance data of great trend traders doesn't exist and keep on buying and holding. If you think you're likely to make the latter choice, reconsider whether trend following is for you.

Trend followers are generalists when it comes to their trading strategy. Tom Friedman, a great author in the field of international relations, explained this important distinction:

"The great strategists of the past kept forests as well as trees in views. They were generalists, and they operated from an ecological perspective. They understood the world is a web, in which adjustments made here are bound to have effects over there—that everything is interconnected. Where might one find generalists today? The dominant trend within universities and the think tanks is toward ever-narrower specialization: a higher premium is placed on functioning deeply within a single field than broadly across several. And yet, without some awareness of the whole—without some sense of how means converge to accomplish or to frustrate ends—there can be no strategy. And without strategy, there is only drift."[2]

The men profiled here see the whole. They see the connections. They also know how to separate their emotions from their financial decision making. One "market wizard," Charles Faulkner, explained how crucial it is to know who you are:

"Being able to trade your system instead of your psychology means separating yourself from your trading. This can begin with your language. 'I'm in the trading business' and 'I work as a trader' are very different from 'I'm a trader' or 'I own a few stocks and bonds' (from a major East Coast speculator). The market wizards I've met seem to live by William Blake's phrase, 'I must make my own system or be enslaved by another's.' They have made their own systems—in their trading and in their lives and in their language. They don't allow others to define them or their terms. And they are sometimes considered abrupt, difficult, iconoclastic, or full of themselves as a result. And they know the greater truth—they are themselves and they know what works for them.”

This chapter starts with a trend following trader not originally profiled in my first edition of this book from 2004. David Harding, Bernard Drury, Christian Baha, Michael Clarke and the trend-trading firm TransTrend have all established themselves as new trend followers of great success. And the leader of a new breed of trend followers is currently Harding. After introducing Harding, the old pros of trend following are all still profiled; they provide great insights and lessons to all aspiring trend following traders.

When I first got into commodities, no one was interested in a diversified approach. There were cocoa men, cotton men, grain men—they were worlds apart. I was almost the first one who decided to look at all commodities together. Nobody before had looked at the whole picture and had taken a diversified position with the idea of cutting losses short and going with a trend.

Richard Donchian

David Harding

David Harding has had tremendous success as a trend following trader. Today, his trend following fund for clients exceeds $10 billion in assets, give or take a billion or two to the upside. He typically makes 20 percent a year. How did he reach that pinnacle?

Born in London and reared in Oxfordshire, Harding had always been interested in investing—a result of his father’s influence, a horticulturalist who enjoyed betting on the markets. His mother by comparison was a French teacher. As a young man, he had a natural inclination for science and quickly found a way to put the talent to use. Early in his career, he took a job at Sabre Fund Management where he designed trading systems. Soon thereafter, he met Michael Adam and Martin Lueck. The trio went on to launch Adam, Harding, and Lueck (AHL), a trend following firm managing money for clients. In two years, the Man Group bought AHL out and built its trend following firm and systems into a monster with $21 billion under management.[3] Harding, while wealthy from the sale, knew much of Man Group’s success was built around his trading systems. But he wanted more than to rest on his buyout winnings and over time built his new firm Winton Capital into a trend-trading juggernaut. All of that success comes with a basic philosophical underpinning. But, before jumping into his philosophies, consider his performance, the main reason I am writing about him (see Chart 2.1).

CHART 2.1: Monthly Performance Data for Winton Futures Fund

Recent Returns	Latest Month	Last 3 Months	Last 6 Months	Last 12 Months	Last 2 Years	Last 3 Years	Last 4 Years	Last 5 Years	Last 7 Years	Last 10 Years
Manager	(3.10)	(2.91)	(2.61)	22.95	36.32	41.85	93.41	130.59	223.81	358.79
Benchmark	1.22	(8.39)	(3.06)	(12.48)	(1.05)	5.74	16.88	28.05	13.86	34.83

	JAN	FEB	MAR	APR	MAY	JUN	JUL	AUG	SEP	OCT	NOV	DEC	Year
2008	3.85	7.95	(0.66)	(0.99)	1.99	5.06	(4.63)	(3.00)	(0.41)	3.73	4.97	2.17	21.08
2007	3.86	(5.93)	(3.95)	6.46	5.05	1.91	(1.18)	(0.88)	6.99	2.52	2.42	0.24	17.97
2006	4.20	(2.58)	4.01	5.66	(2.94)	(1.17)	(0.47)	4.54	(1.10)	1.48	3.24	2.14	17.84
2005	(5.38)	6.58	4.64	(4.21)	6.62	3.13	(1.85)	7.63	(6.17)	(2.95)	7.32	(4.37)	9.73
2004	2.72	11.56	(0.80)	(8.62)	0.28	(2.96)	1.33	3.09	5.14	4.03	6.37	(0.19)	22.62
2003	5.95	11.95	(10.80)	2.45	10.19	(5.20)	(0.68)	0.62	0.26	4.72	(2.48)	10.27	27.76
2002	(10.13)	(6.04)	12.62	(3.76)	(3.96)	7.95	4.71	6.04	7.63	(7.96)	(0.69)	14.16	18.33
2001	4.38	0.56	7.09	(5.31)	(2.61)	(2.66)	0.66	0.56	4.64	13.75	(7.10)	(5.15)	7.12
2000	(3.96)	1.72	(3.28)	2.06	(0.26)	(1.27)	(4.58)	3.23	(7.76)	2.09	7.33	16.81	10.43
1999	(1.38)	3.61	(3.98)	10.51	(8.39)	5.29	(2.01)	(3.47)	(0.17)	(6.20)	13.93	9.04	15.08
1998	1.50	3.27	7.38	(1.63)	8.53	2.97	1.51	10.99	4.51	(5.70)	1.15	9.50	52.17
1997										(12.97)	9.96	8.14	3.49

I have had the opportunity to interview Harding on two occasions. Both times he came across as a down-to-earth, hard worker, but also highly competitive. He wants to win. Did Harding start out with that great trading performance? No silver spoon for him. He worked. He practiced:

"I worked for a company [early on], and the people who ran that took a very old-fashioned approach to trading. About 10 people and I spent the first half of every day drawing about 400 charts by hand. It was very tedious. I did this for about two years. The act of laboriously updating these charts forces you to focus in much more minute detail on data than you normally would, and over a period of time, I became completely convinced the market was not efficient, contrary to the theory at the time.[4] I became convinced that markets weren't efficient and absolutely trended...We trade everything using trend-following systems, and it works. By simulation, you come up with ideas and hypotheses, and you test those. Over the years, what we've done, essentially, is conduct experiments. But instead of using a microscope or a telescope, the computer is our laboratory instrument. And instead of looking at the stars, we're looking at data and simulation languages...it's counterintuitive to think in terms of statistics and probability. It takes discipline and training; it tortures the machinery. People are much better, for instance, at judging whether another person is cheating in a human relationship. We're hugely social creatures. We're keen on our intuition. But when our intuition is wrong, we'll still be very resistant to being corrected. What are traders' biggest failures about understanding risk? There's a human desire to seek spurious certainty. We try to come to a yes-no answer, one that's absolute, when the right answer might be neither yes nor no. People see things in black and white when often they need to be comfortable with shades of gray."[5]

Shades of gray are tough medicine to follow, a tough philosophy to believe down to your core. No one wants to think that way when it comes to their money, we want to imagine uniform precision is possible, but if the guys who make the most money think like Harding, isn't it worth it for everyone else to try to think that way, too? At the end of the day, perhaps the best lessons I took from Harding came from his original marketing materials titled "The Winton Papers." His explanation about human decision making should be absorbed by everyone before they ever put a dollar to work in the markets:

"The aggregate effect of shared mental biases and imitation results in patterns of behavior, which while they are nonconsistent with Mr. Spock-like, rational decision making or with informational efficiency, are demonstrably systematic. The market equivalent of these behavioral patterns is trending, whereby prices tend to move persistently in one direction or another in response to information. The widespread adoption of investing fashions, like indexation, introduces market mechanisms, which magnify herding behavior on a large scale."[6]

Although Harding's words were written before the events of 2008, his insights explain how the crash unfolded. To those who want to learn how to trade better, to those who don't just want to affix blame for down performance, Harding offers a way out. But, he knows his "agnostic" approach to investing has critics. "Most people believe it doesn't work, or if it did it soon won't work. We almost never do anything based on our opinions. If we do, it's based on opinions about mathematical phenomenon and statistical distribution, not opinions about Fed policy."

Bill Dunn

Whenever you can, count.
Sir Francis Galton[8]

Bill Dunn, like Harding, is a trend follower. He made 50 percent in 2002 when the majority of investors were losing big. He made 21 percent in the one month of October 2008 when most of Wall Street was melting down. He never hesitates to swing for the home run because for Dunn, it can be all or nothing. I originally started this chapter with a profile of Dunn because his performance data is a clear, consistent, and *dramatic* demonstration of trend following.

Dunn is founder and chairman of Dunn Capital Management, Inc. He is one of the purest trend followers alive because he trades his trading system full throttle, aiming for huge returns. Dunn Capital has no defined "target" for an annual return (other than positive). There is nothing in Dunn Capital's risk management that precludes annual returns approaching 100 percent. There is no policy that if, for example, a Dunn program were to be up 50 percent by mid-year that the company would "rest on its laurels," so to speak, and dial back trading for the rest of the calendar year. Further, it is not surprising to see Dunn down 20 percent or more every three or four years, and in some cases down 50 percent, but whatever the level of volatility, this independent, self-disciplined, long-term trend follower never deviates from his core strategy. His son Daniel Dunn offers:

"We have a risk budgeting scheme that certainly was ahead of its time in 1974 and is still—in our opinion—state of the art in 2008."[7]

It is not difficult to believe that Dunn adheres to principles set forth 30 years ago if you have read Jim Collins' work *Good to Great*:

"Essentially, whatever you find will be as true 10 years from now, 20 years from now, 30 or 50 years from now as it is today and as it was 50 years ago. And if you can put your finger on those truths, then you've made a contribution."[9]

Dunn has always believed that in order to make money, you must be able to live with a certain amount of volatility. Clients who invest their money with Dunn must have absolute, "no-questions-asked" trust in Dunn's decision making. This trend follower has no patience for anyone who questions his ability to take and accept losses. He is not a role model for the faint-hearted. His "full throttle" approach has proven itself for 30 years, making Dunn himself and his clients rich.

His "risk-budgeting scheme" or money management is based on objective decision making. "Caution is costly" could be his motto. At a certain point, he enters a market, and, if the market goes down, at a certain point he exits that market. To Dunn, trading without a predefined exit strategy is a recipe for disaster.

Dunn's risk management system enables him to balance the overall volatility of his portfolio—something the average or even professional investor generally ignores. The more volatile a market, the less he trades. The less volatile a market, the more he trades. For Dunn, if risk-taking is a necessary means to potential profit, then position size should always be titrated to maintain the targeted risk constraint, which in turn should be set at the maximum level acceptable to the investor. Their system of risk management ensures that they exit a market when the trade goes against them:

"One of our areas of expertise in the risk-budgeting process is how risk is going to be allocated to say a yen trade and how much risk is going to be allocated to an S&P trade and what is the optimal balance of that for a full 22 market portfolio. The risk parameters are really defined by their buy and sell signals so it is just a matter of how much you are going to commit to that trade so that if it goes against you, you are going to lose only x percent."[12]

The novice trader is at a disadvantage because the intuitions that he is going to have about the market are going to be the ones that are typical of beginners. The expert is someone who sees beyond those typical responses and has an understanding of the deeper workings of the market.

Charles Faulkner[10]

Like so many others who share his libertarian views, Bill's journey to Free Minds and Free Markets began in 1963 when he read Ayn Rand's short collection of essays on ethics.

Reason Magazine[11]

Extreme Performance Numbers

Like Dunn, this chart (Chart 2.2) assumes an "in-your-face" attitude. The performance data compares the returns if you had hypothetically invested $1,000 with Dunn and $1,000 with the S&P. The data demands a choice—either put your money with Dunn Capital Management, learn to trend follow yourself, or pretend trend following does not exist.

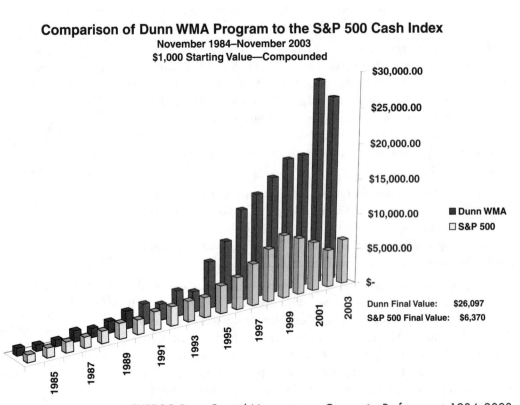

Comparison of Dunn WMA Program to the S&P 500 Cash Index
November 1984–November 2003
$1,000 Starting Value—Compounded

Dunn Final Value: $26,097
S&P 500 Final Value: $6,370

CHART 2.2: Dunn Capital Management: Composite Performance 1984–2003

How does Dunn do it? Here are two charts that reflect different periods of his trading history but tell the same story about his approach to trading. The first one (Chart 2.3) is the Japanese Yen trade from December 1994 to June 1996, where Dunn made a killing.

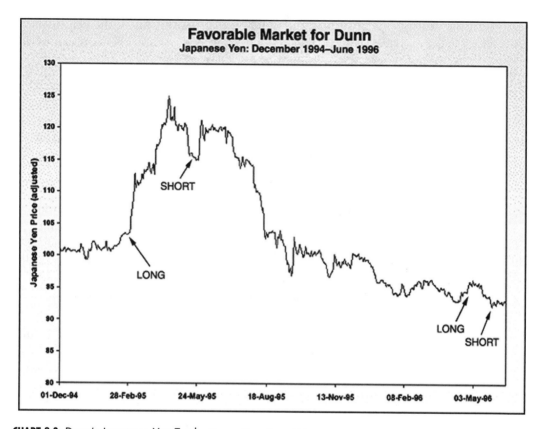

CHART 2.3: Dunn's Japanese Yen Trade   Source: Dunn Capital Management

1995 was a great year for Dunn. In 2003, for the first time, he publicly walked through his thought processes—his trend following process—with an audience of investors, who came away with an invaluable lesson:

> "This is 18 months of the Japanese yen and as you can see, it went up and down and there was some significant trends so we should have had an opportunity to make some money and it turns out we did. Because the WMA is a reversal system, it's always in the market, it's either long or short, trying to follow and identify the major trends. So while this is the first signal ... that's shown on the chart and is long, we obviously must have been short coming in [to this] big rise. [The rise] was enough to tell us we should quit being short and start being long and it seemed like a pretty smart thing do ... after we saw that [big rise up]."[13]

He is riding the trend up that first big hill of the yen in March 1995. He is making his decisions within the context of his mechanical system. He continues:

"Then we have significant retracement, which caused a short signal for the WMA program; our model has always incorporated near-term volatility and this volatility [as we went long] was far less than the volatility that was going on [when we went short]."[14]

Dunn summarizes the trade:

"Now also because the volatility was very high here ... this rise was—not enough to give us a long signal and as a result, we rode this short position for nearly a year all the way down—where we got a long signal that was wrong and we reversed and went down to short. Now that was a very, very good market for our program, but some markets are not so good ... "[15]

Unfortunately, the confidence of his tone and delivery cannot be replicated in print.

Be Nimble

Dunn once opined with a straight face after riding a trend to great profit: "The recent volatility in the energy complex has been quite exciting and potentially rewarding for the nimble."[16]

What exactly does Dunn mean by the word nimble? He means he is ready to make decisions based on market movement. When an opportunity to get on a potential trend appears, he is prepared. He takes the leap. He is nimble when, relying on his system, he reacts to the Japanese yen move with alacrity because he trusts his trading plan and his management of risk.

The second chart is the British pound (Chart 2.4) where, unlike the Japanese yen, the market proved unfavorable for Dunn. It was a typical whipsaw market, which is always difficult for trend followers because small losses add up. You can see how he entered and was stopped out; then entered and was stopped out again. Remember, trend followers don't predict markets, they react to them—so the small losses were part of the game. He managed the small losses because the British pound was only a portion of his portfolio. His yen trade more than made up for his losses on the British pound trade, because no matter how uncomfortable others are with his approach, for Dunn, big winners offset small losers in the long run.

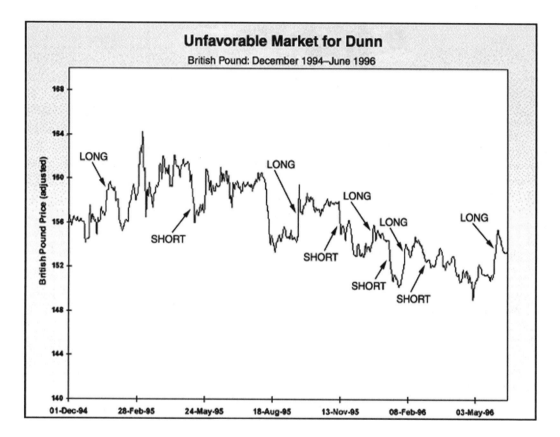

CHART 2.4: Dunn's British Pound Trade   Source: Dunn Capital Management

If you told Dunn that his approach made you uncomfortable, I know what he would say, because he has said it often:

"We don't make market predictions. We just ride the bucking bronco."[17]

Dunn's failed trades on the British pound—the up and down, go nowhere trend—is exactly what he means when he says, "We just ride the bucking bronco." In hindsight, you might ask yourself why he was trading the British pound if he was losing. The simple answer is that neither he nor anyone else could have predicted whether or not the British pound would be the next great home run. The real question is, "Do you stay out of the game because you can't predict how the game is going to unfold?"

Dunn Early Years

"I made the decision [to concentrate on managing money] four or five years ago when I realized that I would make far more money—with the skill set that I have—with a whole lot less work than with anything else," Robert Pardo says. That is when he entered into a fee-sharing agreement with CTA Dunn Capital Management. Pardo calls his relationship with Dunn a match made in heaven. Dunn funds his CTA with the company's proprietary capital and does the execution and the paperwork. For that, they share in the fees and participate equally in the technology. It also frees Pardo to continue building models that Dunn can eventually use for excess capacity.[21]

Dunn grew up in Kansas City and Southern California. After graduating from high school, he served three years with the U.S. Marine Corps. In the ensuing years, he received a bachelor degree in engineering physics from the University of Kansas in 1960 and a doctorate in theoretical physics from Northwestern University. For the next two years, he held research and faculty positions at the University of California and Pomona College. He then worked for research organizations near Washington, D.C., developing and testing logistical and operational systems for the Department of Defense. Bottom line: Dunn enjoyed the R&D side of things, but also understood the real world's need for applications beyond the theoretical. The markets are his real world.

Around the age of 35, Dunn "got it." At the time, he was working out of his home in suburban Fairfax, Virginia. He came across a newsletter touting a commodity trading system, "which almost sounded too good to be true." Upon testing it, that turned out to be the case [and he set about developing his new system]... Using daily data, Dunn's system looked for big trends, as defined by a percentage of a price move from a recent low or high. It traded each market three to five times a year, automatically reversing if the trend moved in the other direction. [Dunn determined] position size by risking 2 percent to 6 percent of equity under management on each trade."[18]

It's not uncommon for long-term trend followers to have trades in place for well over a year, hence the term "long." If you want day trading insanity or the feeling of exhilaration in Las Vegas, Dunn is not the person you should choose as a trading role model.

Following his computerized trading system, Dunn holds long-term positions in major trends typically trading only two to five times per year in each market. The original system was and still is a reversal system, whereby it is always in the market, either long or short. Dunn says he's held winning positions for as long as a year and half.[19]

Early on Dunn needed more capital to execute his particular plan of trading attack. He found it, in the person of Ralph Klopenstein. "Klopenstein ... helped launch Dunn by giving him a $200,000 house account to manage. Dunn, a Defense Department systems analyst...[had] realized his trading hobby would require a whole lot of other people's money to use a promising system he developed."[20]

Ed Seykota, another trend follower profiled later in this chapter, is fond of pointing out that when you stop trying to please others and concentrate on pleasing yourself, you gradually become aware of what you are passionate about in life. And when that happens, all sorts of people come out of the woodwork to help you achieve your goals. Dunn is proof positive.

Life at Dunn Capital

Back in the mid-nineties Marty Bergin arranged for me to visit Stuart, Florida, and spend a day at Dunn Capital. In one of those classic small world stories Bergin had been my baseball coach when I was sixteen in Northern Virginia. Today, he is a key member of Dunn's firm.

Dunn's office is on a quiet street, located off a waterway in the heart of Stuart, a quiet retirement community 30 miles from West Palm Beach. There is no receptionist at Dunn Capital, so after you enter the office, your only recourse is to saunter down a hallway to see if anyone is in. It feels more like an accountant's office than a high-powered trading firm. In fact, the atmosphere is so casual that there is no atmosphere. Dunn is a shining example of why location, pretentious offices, and intense activity have little to do with trading success.

There are only a handful of employees at Dunn because it doesn't take many employees to run his fund (which stands around $500 million total as of fall of 2008). Plus, employees are not all traders. The hardest thing to deal with when running a hedge fund is not the trading decisions, but the accounting and regulatory concerns. No one at Dunn is tied to screens watching the market because trades are entered only after an alarm at a PC goes off indicating a buy or sell signal and thus the need to place an order.

Another reason Dunn has so few employees is because he has a relatively few well-chosen clients. In fact, he's fond of saying, "If people want to invest with me, they know where to find me." Dunn's investors benefit from the fact that there is no disconnect between his bottom line as a fund manager and the investor's bottom line— to wit, trading profits.

Dunn's fund is different than many because he compounds absolute returns. He leaves his money on the table by reinvesting in the fund. As a result, Dunn's trading capital is not only made up of clients, but rather the result of systematically reinvesting profits of his own over a long period of time.

By focusing on profits and incentive fees, Dunn makes money only when the fund (read: clients) makes money. He doesn't charge a management fee. With no management fee, there is no incentive to constantly raise capital. The only incentive is to make money. If Dunn makes money, he gets a portion of the profits. Compounding, or reinvesting your profits, makes sense if you're serious about making money, and Dunn is serious.

He's also direct. In the time I spent with him, I was impressed with his matter-of-fact, "no B.S." attitude. He was polite without being effusive; interested without being encouraging. He was wearing a pair of khakis and a Hawaiian shirt, and he made it clear that it was his way or the highway.

No Profit Targets

Dunn doesn't say, "I want 15 percent a year." The market can't be ordered to give a trader a steady 15 percent rate of return, but even if it could, is a steady 15 percent the right way to approach trading in the first place? If you started with $1,000, what rate of return would you rather have over a period of three years? +15 percent, +15 percent, and +15 percent or the unpredictable –5 percent, +50 percent, and +20 percent? At the end of three years, the first hypothetical investment opportunity would be worth $1520 but the second investment would be worth $1710. The second one would be a stream of returns representative of a Dunn type of trading style.

You can't dial in a certain amount return for a given year. There are no profit targets that work well, as Dunn states:

Confidence comes from success, to be sure, but it can also come from recognizing that a lot of carefully examined failures are themselves one path to success.

Denise Shekerjian[22]

Profit targets imply a trader can predict the future. Profit targets are profit-limiting. Trend followers stay in the moment of now, avoid prognostication, and let markets run as far as they go.

**Thomas Vician, Jr.
Student of Ed Seykota's**

"We only have two systems. The first system is the one I
started with in 1974. The other system, we developed and
launched in 1989. The major strategic elements of these
two models—how and when to trade, how much to buy and
sell—have never changed in almost 30 years. We expect
change. None of the things that have happened in the
development of new markets over the past 30 years strike
us as making the marketplace different in any essential
way. The markets are just the markets. I know that is
unusual. I know in the past five years a lot of competitors
have purposefully lowered the risk on their models i.e. they
are deleveraging them or trying to mix them with other
things to reduce the volatility. Of course, they have also
reduced their returns."[23]

He is addressing a critical issue here: reducing risk to reduce
volatility to appeal to nervous clients. The result is always lower
absolute returns. If you remain fixated on volatility as your enemy,
instead of correctly realizing volatility is the actual source of profit,
you will never "get" trend following trading.

Dunn is very good at using risk management—more commonly
called money management (see Chapter 10, "Trading Systems") to
his advantage. His money management techniques enable him to
score big. In June 2002, Dunn returned +24.26 percent, then
followed with +14.84 percent for the month of July. By that time, he
was up +37 percent for the same year in which buy-and-holders of
the NASDAQ for this period were crushed. He finished 2002 up
more than 50 percent. His 2008 performance is right there again—
big up when others are down.

*Money management is the
true survival key.*

Bill Dunn[24]

How does Dunn do it?

- **He cuts his losses**.
- **He never changes his core strategy:** His performance is not a
  result of human judgment. Dunn's trend following is
  quantitative and systematic, with no discretionary overrides of
  his system-generated trade signals. This is a foreign concept to
  those investors who watch CNBC for stock tips. His trading
  style doesn't drift.
- **Long-term holding:** For holding periods of approximately 3.75
  years and beyond, all returns are positive for Dunn. Lesson?
  Stay with a system for the long haul and you do well.

- **Compounding:** Dunn compounds relentlessly. He plows profits back into his trading system and builds upon fresh gains.
- **Recovery:** Dunn had losing years of 27.1 percent in 1976 and 32.0 percent in 1981 followed by multiyear gains of 500 percent and 300 percent, respectively. You must be able to accept drawdowns and understand that recovery is, by the nature of trend trading, around the corner.
- **Going short:** Dunn goes short as often as he goes long. In general buy-and-holders never consider the "short side." If you are not biased to trend direction, you can win either way.

Drawdowns Are Part of the Game

Dunn Capital has had its share of drawdowns, but his approach to losses is clear and calm:

> "Some experience losses and then wait for gains, which they hope will come soon...But sometimes they don't come soon and sometimes they don't come at all. And [the traders] perish."[25]

But don't think for a second that you are not going to suffer pain, either by trading like Dunn or letting Dunn manage your money. Because drawdowns—a.k.a. your account going down—will make you feel like you need an extra dose of Prilosec.

Dunn Capital in Print

There are great lessons to be learned from the performance data of Dunn, but you can find insight from their writings as well. The Dunn Capital monthly newsletter adopts a brutally honest tone when communicating with clients, as evidenced by the following excerpts from monthly newsletters throughout the spring of 2003:[26]

1. "As global monetary, fiscal, and political conditions grow increasingly unsustainable, the trend following strategy that DUNN steadfastly employs may possibly be one of the few beneficiaries."

2. "The only thing that can be said with certainty about the current state of the world economy is that there are many large, unsustainable imbalances and structural problems that must be corrected. Perhaps the equity markets are correctly predicting a rapid return to more stable and prosperous times. Perhaps not. Regardless, there seems to be more than ample fodder for the creation of substantial trends in the coming months."

3. "It seems that Mr. Greenspan's twin bubbles, equities and housing, working along side the federal, municipal, and external deficits, will make the coming weeks and months more interesting than anyone may really care to witness. If this all seems a bit too grim, do not forget that California, on its own, would be the fifth largest economy in the world. Currently, the state has a 33 billion dollar budget gap, which seems almost certain to result in the peaceful overthrow of the state's chief executive in November. Also remember that the analysis presented here may be nothing more than an incorrect interpretation of the facts. On the truly bright side, it is comforting to know that the opinions expressed in this letter will have absolutely no bearing on the time-tested methods that DUNN uses to generate trading profits and manage risk."

Change is not merely necessary to life—it is life.
Alvin Toffler

I love the fact that even though Dunn has strong political opinions, he knows that his opinions mean zilch when it comes to properly trading the market. His political and or economic opinions do not form the basis of when he buys and sells.

Clients

What problems can prevent clients from seeing Dunn's way?

- Clients usually do not understand the nature of trend following. They often panic and pull out just before a big move makes them a lot of money.

- Clients may start asking for the trader to change his approach. Although they may not have articulated this directly to the fund manager, they really wanted the trend following strategy customized for them before investing their money in the first place. The manager is then faced with a difficult decision: Take the client's money and make money through management fees (which can be lucrative) or trade the capital as originally designed. Trading a trend following system as originally designed is the optimal path in the long run.

If clients try to change or adjust how Dunn trades, he either lets them go or doesn't take them on as a client in the first place:

> "A person must be an optimist to be in this business, but I also believe it's a cyclical phenomenon for several other reasons. In our 18 years of experience, we've had to endure a number of long and nasty periods during which we've asked ourselves this same question. In late 1981, our accounts had lost about 42 percent over the previous 12 months, and we and our clients were starting to wonder if we would ever see good markets again. We continued to trade our thoroughly researched system, but our largest client got cold feet and withdrew about 70 percent of our total equity under management. You guessed it. Our next month was up 18 percent, and in the 36 months following, their withdrawal of our accounts made 430 percent!"[27]

This observation always made me wonder why Dunn is not studied in MBA programs. Are Harvard MBAs aware of Dunn's trading when they graduate?

Check Your Ego at the Door

What is it like to work at Dunn? They once posted a job wanted ad on a job board. Part of it read:

> "Candidates...must NOT be constrained by any active noncompete agreement and will be required to enter into a confidentiality and noncompete agreement. Only long-term, team players need apply (no prima donnas). Salary: competitive base salary, commensurate with experience, with bonus potential and attractive benefits, beginning at $65,000."[28]

Notice how Dunn says, "[N]o prima donnas." In other words, readers of this ad can choose either to work for Dunn or attempt to be Dunn on their own, but they cannot have both. Trend following demands taking personal responsibility for one's actions, and Dunn makes it clear that he is responsible for Dunn Capital.

One of the interesting traits of the many trend followers I spoke with personally or observed from afar is their honesty. If you listen closely to their words and review their performance data, they are more than happy to tell you exactly what they are doing and why.

Key Points

- Dunn's attitude captures the essence of trend following. His performance data is one of the clearest, most consistent, most dramatic demonstrations of trend-following success available.

- Dunn goes short as often as long.

- Dunn's average rolling 60-month period has yielded a return of about 231 percent.

- Dunn's designed risk is a 1 percent chance of a 20 percent or greater loss in a month.

Men's expectations manifest in trends
John W. Henry[29]

John W. Henry

The performance data of Bill Dunn and John W. Henry shows them to be trend followers cut from similar cloth. They are both astonishingly successful self-made men who started without formal association to Wall Street. They developed trading systems in the 1970s that have made them millions of dollars again and again. Their correlated performance data shows that they both trade for absolute returns and often trade in the same trends at the same time.

Henry's performance is clear (Chart 2.5):

Henry has captured some of the great trends of our generation. By all available evidence, Henry was on the other side of the Barings Bank blowout in 1995. In the zero-sum game, he won what Barings Bank lost. More recently, in 2002, Henry was up 40 percent while the NASDAQ was spiraling downwards. He, like Dunn, doesn't have a strategy that could be remotely considered "active or day trading," but when his trading system tells him, "It's time," he can literally blow the doors off the barn with spectacular returns in short order. Can he have down years? Yes, and he does from time to time, but he was right there again making huge money in 2008 when everyone else was seemingly losing.

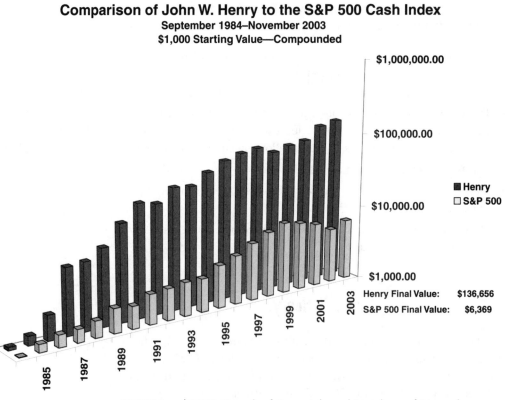

Comparison of John W. Henry to the S&P 500 Cash Index
September 1984–November 2003
$1,000 Starting Value—Compounded

Henry Final Value: $136,656
S&P 500 Final Value: $6,369

CHART 2.5: $1000 Growth of Financials and Metals as of November, 2003

Also, I can't help but notice that, as the owner of the Boston Red Sox, Henry applies the basic tenets of trend following—simple heuristics for decision making, mathematics, statistics, and application of a system—to the world of sports. Henry and baseball are connected clearly, as discussed in Chapter 5, "Baseball: Thinking Outside the Batter's Box."

Prediction Is Futile

Henry was blunt: "I don't believe that I am the only person who cannot predict future prices. No one consistently can predict anything, especially investors. Prices, not investors, predict the future. Despite this, investors hope or believe that they can predict the future, or someone else can. A lot of them look to you to predict what the next macroeconomic cycle will be. We rely on the fact that other investors are convinced that they can predict the future, and I believe that's where our profits come from. I believe it's that simple."

Because trend following is primarily based on a single piece of data—the price—it can be difficult to paint the true story of what that really means. Henry has always been able to articulate clearly and consistently how he trades, year after year, to those willing to listen carefully. To generate his profits, he relies on the fact that other traders think they can predict where the market will go and often end up as losers. Henry will tell you that he routinely wins the losses of the market losers in the zero-sum trading game.

About John W. Henry

John W. Henry was born in Quincy, Illinois to a successful farming family. For a Midwestern farm boy in the '50s, there was nothing in the world like baseball, and from the time nine-year-old Henry went to his first major league game, he was hooked. In the summer, he would listen in rapt attention to the great St. Louis Cardinals broadcaster Harry Caray night after night. Henry described himself as having average intelligence, but a knack for numbers, and like many young baseball fans, he crunched batting averages in his head.

Henry attended community colleges and took numerous night courses, but never received his college degree. It wasn't for lack of interest, however. When he was attending a class taught by Harvey Brody at UCLA, they collaborated on and published a strategy for beating the odds at blackjack. When his father died, Henry took over the family farms, teaching himself hedging techniques. He began speculating in corn, wheat, and soybeans. And it wasn't long before he was trading for clients. In 1981, he founded John W. Henry and Company, Inc., in Newport Beach, California.[31]

If Henry's first managed account was staked with $16,000 and he now owns the Boston Red Sox, don't you think the best question to ask is, "How?" A former president at his trading firm paints what appears to be at first glance a simplistic portrait depicting their firm's success:

There is no Holy Grail. There is no perfect way to capture that move from $100/ounce to $800/ounce in gold.

John W. Henry[30]

How are we able to make money by following trends year in and year out? I think it's because markets react to news, but ultimately major change takes place over time. Trends develop because there's an accumulating consensus on future prices, consequently there's an evolution to the "believed true price value" over time. Because investors are human and they make mistakes, they're never 100 percent sure of their vision and whether or not their view is correct. So price adjustments take time as they fluctuate and a new consensus is formed in the face of changing market conditions and new facts. For some changes, this consensus is easy to reach, but there are other events that take time to formulate a market view. It's those events that take time that form the basis of our profits.

John W. Henry

"There has been surprisingly little change. Models we developed 20 years ago are still in place today. Obviously, we trade a different mix of markets. We've also added new programs over the last 20 years, but relative to many of our peers, we have not made significant adjustments in our trading models. We believe that markets are always changing and adjusting, and the information that's important to investors will also change. In the 1980s, everyone was interested in the money supply figures... everyone would wait by their phones until that number came out. In the 1990s, the information du jour was unemployment numbers. But people's reactions to the markets are fairly stable. Uncertainty creates trends and that's what we're trying to exploit. Even if you have better and faster dissemination of information, the one thing we haven't really improved is people's ability to process information. We're trying to exploit people's reaction, which is embedded in prices and leads to trends. These reactions are fairly stable and may not require major adjustments of models."[32]

He reiterates an important philosophical tenet of trend following: In looking at the long term, change is constant. And because change is constant, uncertainty is constant. From uncertainty, trends emerge. It is the exploitation of these trends that forms the basis of trend following profit. All of the cutting edge technology and news-gathering capabilities in the world are not going to help you trade trends. That is white noise, static if you will.

We have made our business managing risk. We are comfortable with risk and we get our reward from risk.

John W. Henry[34]

When I spoke with Henry's president, he offered insight regarding all aspects of their trading business:

- "We stick to our knitting."
- "Most people don't have the discipline to do what they need to do.
- "We like to keep it sophisticatedly simple."
- "Our best trading days are when we don't trade."
- "We make more money the less we trade."
- "Some of our best trades are when we are sitting on our hands doing nothing."

- "We don't want to be the smartest person in the market. Trying to be the smart person in the market is a losing game."

He was not being flippant. He was direct and gracious. His tone was matter of fact. He wanted people to understand why John W. Henry and Co. does what it does. A few years ago, he gave a great analogy about the emotional ups and downs you must cope with to reach trend following success:

> *Life is a school of probability.*
> Walter Bagehot[35]

> "Looking at the year as a mountain ride...Anyone who has ridden the trains in mountainous Switzerland will remember the feeling of anxiety and expectations as you ascend and descend the rugged terrain. During the decline, there is anxiety because you often do not know how far you will fall. Expectations are heightened as you rise out of the valley because you cannot always see the top of the mountain."[33]

A World-View Philosophy

Trend followers like Henry and Dunn could not have developed their trading systems without first deciding how they were going to view the world. Each, through experience, education, and research, came to an understanding of how markets work before they determined how to trade them. What each of them found, separately, was that market trends are more pervasive than people think, and could have been traded in the same way 200 years ago as they are today.

To that end Henry spent years studying historical price data from the 18th and 19th centuries in order to prove to himself that there was only one successful way to approach trading. When he explains his investment philosophy, he is crystal clear about what it is and what it is not:

- **Long-term trend identification:** Trading systems ignore short-term volatility in the attempt to capture superior returns during major trending markets. Trends can last as long as a few months or years.
- **Highly disciplined investment process:** Methodology is designed to keep discretionary decision making to a minimum.

- **Risk management:** Traders adhere to a strict formulaic risk management system that includes market exposure weightings, stop-loss provisions, and capital commitment guidelines that attempt to preserve capital during trendless or volatile periods.

- **Global diversification:** By participating in more than 70 markets and not focusing on one country or region, they have access to opportunities that less diversified firms may miss.

As I have seen, some traders dismiss trend following as simply predictive technical analysis. Henry is not some "technical indicator guru" trying to make predictions:

> "...'Some people call what we do technical analysis, but JWH just identifies and follows trends. It's like, if you are in the fashion world, you have to follow trends, or you're yesterday's news.' But as with technical analysis, trend followers believe that markets are smarter than any of their individual participants. In fact, they make it their business not to try to figure out why markets are going up or down or where they're going to stop."[36]

Henry's use of fashion as a metaphor for trend following hits the nail on the head and goes beyond obvious comparison between trends in clothing and trends in markets. He explains that to be fashionable, you have no choice but to follow stylistic trends of the moment. Likewise, trend followers have no choice but to react to trends, and like those who dictate fashion, successful trend followers exploit trends long before the public is paying attention.

We don't predict the future, but we do know that the next five years will not look like the last five years. That just doesn't happen. Markets change. And our results over the next three years will not replicate the last three. They never do.

John W. Henry[39]

Trend followers would agree with H. L. Mencken when he said, "We are here and it is now. Further than that, all human knowledge is moonshine." They understand that attending to what is taking place in the market from moment to moment isn't a technique; it is what is and that is all. The moment, the here and now, is the only place that is truly measurable. Henry showed how he applies this philosophy in a past coffee trade:

> "All fundamentals were bearish: The International Coffee Organization was unable to agree on a package to support prices, there was an oversupply of coffee, and the freeze season was over in Brazil...his system signaled an unusually large long position in coffee. He bought, placing 2 percent of the portfolio on the trade. The system was

right. Coffee rallied to $2.75 per lb. from $1.32 in the last quarter of the year, and he made a 70 percent return. 'The best trades are the ones I dislike the most. The market knows more than I do.'"[37]

It's What You Think You Know That Gets You into Trouble

Henry knows that the complicated, difficult elements of trend following are not about what you must master, but what you must eliminate from your market view.

On why the long-term approaches work best over decades:

"There is an overwhelming desire to act in the face of adverse market moves. Usually it is termed 'avoiding volatility' with the assumption that volatility is bad. However, I found avoiding volatility really inhibits the ability to stay with the long-term trend. The desire to have close stops to preserve open trade equity has tremendous costs over decades. Long-term systems do not avoid volatility; they patiently sit through it. This reduces the occurrence of being forced out of a position that is in the middle of a long-term major move."[38]

On stocks:

"The current thinking is that stocks have outperformed everything else for 200 years. They may have a little relevance for the next 25 years. But there is no one in the year 2000 that you can convince to jettison the belief that 200 years of performance will not cause stocks to grow to the sky. Right now people believe in data that supports the inevitable growth in prices of stocks within a new landscape or new economy. What will be new to them is an inevitable bear market."[40]

For all his talk about avoiding predictions, Henry is making one here. He is predicting that stocks can't go up forever because eventually trends reverse themselves. He is also pointing out that as a trend follower, he will be prepared whenever they do to take action and potentially profit (which he did to great profit during the market crash of October 2008).

Let's take a look at the type of markets we face around the world. There is a constant barrage of information, but often this information can be conflicting and, in some cases, does not come out with the frequency that we would like. For example, monetary policy can serve as a simple case. There are only a limited number of Fed meetings a year; however, this is supposed to help us infer the direction of interest rates and help us manage risk on a daily basis. How do you manage risk in markets that move 24 hours a day, when the fundamental inputs do not come frequently? In the grain markets, crop reports are fairly limited, and demand information comes with significant lags, if at all. How can this information be best incorporated in the daily price action? Under these types of conditions, simple approaches, such as following prices, may be better.

Mark S. Rzepczynski, President & Chief Investment Officer, John W. Henry & Co.[41]

It Starts with Research

Henry has influenced many traders. One of his former employees presented observations in his new firm's marketing materials:

- The time frame of the trading system is long term in nature, with the majority of profitable trades lasting longer than six weeks and some lasting for several months.
- The system is neutral in markets until a signal to take a position is generated.
- It is not uncommon for markets to stay neutral for months at a time, waiting for prices to reach a level that warrants a long or short position.
- The system incorporates predefined levels of initial trade risk. If a new trade turns quickly unprofitable, the risk control parameters in place for every trade will force a liquidation when the preset stop-loss level is reached. In such situations, a trade can last for as little as one day.

This same former employee participated in a conference seminar while working at John W. Henry and Co. The conference was sparsely attended, and as happens when someone speaks to a small audience, the conversation became more informal and more revealing of the early years working with Henry:

"We are very well aware of the trends that have taken place in the last 20 years and we are just curious to see are we in a period in this century that trend following seems to work? Have we lucked out that we happen to be in this industry during trends for the last decade or two? We went back to the 1800s and looked at interest rates, currency fluctuations, and grain prices to see if there was as much volatility in an era that most people don't know much about as there has been this decade. Much to our relief and maybe also surprise, we found out that there were just as many trends, currencies, interest rates, and grain prices back in the 1800s as there has been exhibited this last decade. Once again, we saw the trends were relatively random, unpredictable, and just further supported our philosophy of

We can't always take advantage of a particular period. But in an uncertain world, perhaps the investment philosophy that makes the most sense, if you study the implications carefully, is trend following. Trend following consists of buying high and selling low. For 19 years we have consistently bought high and sold low. If trends were not the underlying nature of markets, our type of trading would have very quickly put us out of business. It wouldn't take 19 years or even 19 months of buying high and selling low ALL of the time to bankrupt you. But trends are an integral, underlying reality in life. How can someone buy high and sell low and be successful for two decades unless the underlying nature of markets is to trend? On the other hand, I've seen year-after-year, brilliant men buying low and selling high for a while successfully and then going broke because they thought they understood why a certain investment instrument had to perform in accordance with their personal logic.

John W. Henry[43]

being fully diversified, and don't alter your system to work in any specific time period."

"Hours and hours were spent in the depths of the university library archives. They gave us Xerox burns on our hands, I think, photo copying grain prices, and interest rate data—not only in the U.S., but also around the world. We looked at overseas interest rates back to that time period. A lot of it is a little bit sketchy, but it was enough to give us the fact that things really jumped around back then as they do now."[42]

It reminded me of the scene in the *Wizard of Oz* when Toto pulls back the curtain to reveal how the wizard really works his magic. It was clear that there were no secret formulas or hidden strategies with Henry. There were no short cuts. This was slow, painstaking trench warfare in the bowels of a research library, armed only with a photocopying machine to memorialize price histories for their analysis.

Years later, I was inspired to do my own price research. My objective was not to use price data at that time in a trading system but to see instead how little markets had changed. One of the best places to research historical market data in newspapers and magazines from over 100 years ago is the U.S. National Agricultural Library. Don't be misled by the word "Agricultural." You can review the stacks at this library and spend hours pouring over magazines from the 1800s. Like Henry's firm, I discovered that markets were indeed basically the same then as now.

John W. Henry on the Record

I had the chance to hear Henry speak in person at an FIA Research Division Dinner held in New York City years back. This was only months after the Barings Bank debacle. During the Q&A, Henry revealed some of the qualities shared by all successful trend followers. This excerpt from the post-dinner Q&A shows Henry at his best, full of grace and good humor. He refused to waste time discussing fundamentals and offered a genuine appreciation of the nature of change:

Moderator: The question that always comes up for technicians is, "Do you believe the markets have changed?"

Henry: It always comes up whenever there are losses, especially prolonged losses. I heard it, in fact, when I started my career 14 years ago. They were worrying, "Is there too much money going into trend following?" You laugh, but I can show you evidence in writing of this. My feeling is that markets are always changing. But if you have a basic philosophy that's sound, you're going to be able to take advantage of those changes to greater or lesser degrees. It is the same with using good, sound business principles—the changing world is not going to materially hurt you if your principles are designed to adapt. So the markets HAVE changed. But that's to be expected and it's good.

Everything flows.

Heraclitus

Female Voice: John, you're noted for your discipline. How did you create that, and how do you maintain that?

Henry: Well, you create discipline by having a strategy you really believe in. If you really believe in your strategy, that brings about discipline. If you don't believe in it, in other words, if you haven't done your homework properly, and haven't made assumptions that you can really live with when you're faced with difficult periods, then it won't work. It really doesn't take much discipline, if you have a tremendous confidence in what you're doing.

Male Voice: I'd like to know if your systems are completely black box.

Henry: We don't use any black boxes. I know people refer to technical trend following as "black box," but what you have is really a certain philosophy of trading. Our philosophy is that there is an inherent return in trend following. I know CTAs that have been around a lot longer than I have, who have been trading trends: Bill Dunn, Millburn, and others who have done rather well over the last 20 to 30 years. I don't think it's luck year after year after year.

Successful trend followers are often described as simply profiting from their "good luck" when in fact, it is not luck but discipline that enables them to win absolute returns.

What this transcript cannot recreate on the page is the audience's reaction. I remember looking around at all the Henry fans jammed into that Wall Street hotel suite and thinking, "Everyone in this room is far more interested in viewing Henry as a personality—a rock star—instead of figuring out what he does to make money." Henry is one of the best traders for the last 25 years. But shouldn't the goal be to try and find similar success in whatever walk of life you pursue rather than only applaud Henry's?

Change Is Overrated

Often more vocal than other trend followers over the years, Henry has been publicly forthright about trend following for years. For instance, his presentation in Geneva, Switzerland could have been a semester course in trend following for anyone open to the message:

> "We began trading our first program, in 1981 and this was after quite a bit of research into the practical aspects of a basic philosophy of what drives markets. The world was frighteningly different in those days than it is today when I was designing what turned out to be a trend following system. That approach—a mechanical and mathematical system—has not really changed at all. Yet the system continues to be successful today, even though there has been virtually no change to it over the last 18 years."[44]

I can't help but notice that the "we haven't changed our system" chorus is sung not only by Dunn, but by Henry and numerous other trend followers as well. And how does this timeless system work? Here is an example of a winning trend for Henry (see Chart 2.6):

> "We took a position around March or April 1998 in the South African rand, short (which would be this particular chart; this is the dollar going up against the rand). You can see it takes time for these things and if you're patient, you can have huge profits, especially if you don't set a profit objective."[45]

When people are in doubt, they tend to look to others to confirm their behavior. Some people would rather adopt others' opinions rather than form their own.

Jon C. Sundt
President
Altegris Investments
1st Quarter 2004 Commentary

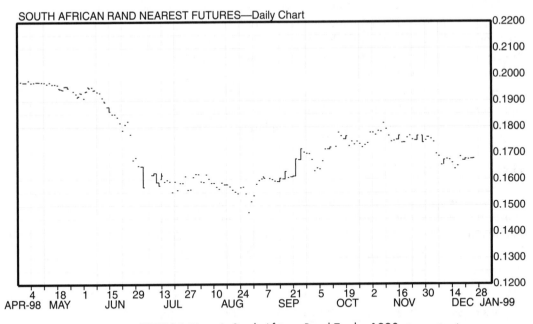

SOUTH AFRICAN RAND NEAREST FUTURES—Daily Chart

CHART 2.6: Henry's South African Rand Trade, 1998 Source: Barchart.com

Moreover, just like Dunn, Henry did well in a historical Japanese yen trade (see Chart 2.7).

Henry concluded: "You can see that in this enormous move, when the dollar/yen went from 100 to 80 in that particular month we were up 11% just in the Japanese yen that quarter."[46]

Fade the Fed

Regular overreaction to Federal Reserve announcements is part of Wall Street life. Some so-called pros take the Federal Reserve's words and act on them even if there is no real way to know what any of it even means at that moment. And does it make logical sense to worry about what the Fed is going to do if there is no clear way to decipher where they might go to begin with? The Fed, to the best of my knowledge, has never offered any statement you could rely on that would dictate, "Buy 1000 share of GOOG today."

JAPANESE YEN NEAREST FUTURES—Weekly Chart

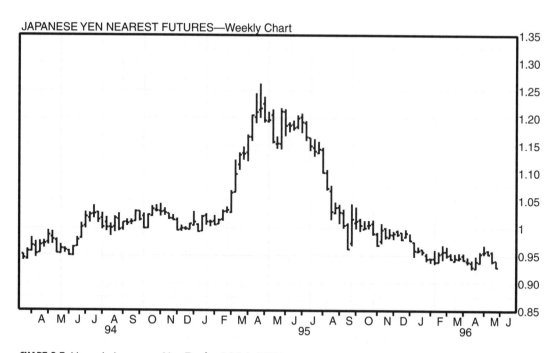

CHART 2.7: Henry's Japanese Yen Trade, 1994–1996 Source: Barchart.com

Henry's trend following system is predicated on price action, not Bernanke's words. Henry is ready for a change in price at all times. The moving lips of a Fed's head have no impact if a trading style has been developed from the ground up to respond to change:

> "I know that when the Fed first raises interest rates after months of lowering them, you do not see them the next day lowering interest rates. And they don't raise rates and then a few days later or a few weeks later lower them. They raise, raise, raise, raise...[PAUSE]...raise, raise, raise. And then once they lower, they don't raise, lower, raise, lower, raise, lower. Rather they lower, lower, lower, lower. There are trends that tend to exist, whether they are capital flows or interest rates...if you have enough discipline, or if you only trade a few markets, you don't need a computer to trade this way."[47]

Henry knows human minds can create anxiety by conjuring up terrifying future market scenarios, so he relies on his system to keep him focused in the present on what he can actually control—his system.

Key Points

- Henry's first managed fund was staked with $16,000 in 1981. He now owns the Boston Red Sox baseball team.

- Henry has a four-point investment philosophy: long-term trend identification, highly disciplined investment process, risk management, and global diversification.

- Henry understands change. This understanding gives him a distinct advantage.

Ed Seykota

Win or lose, everybody gets what they want out of the market. Some people seem to like to lose, so they win by losing money.

Ed Seykota[48]

After you enter the world of markets and investing, you will eventually run across the book *Market Wizards* by Jack Schwager. Of all the trader interviews in *Market Wizards*, the most memorable is the one with Ed Seykota. While some may perceive Seykota's manner as extremely direct, most will agree Seykota is unique in the way he thinks. One profound and now famous statement of his is, "Everybody gets what they want out of the market." This was a response to a question about trading, but I feel certain that Seykota would say it also applies to life.

Although almost completely unknown to both traders and laymen alike, Seykota's achievements rank him as one of the best trend followers (and traders) of our time. I first met Seykota at a small beachside cafe. I had received an invitation from Seykota to get together to discuss the outreach possibilities of the Internet. During our first meeting, he asked me what I thought Richard Dennis was looking for when he hired his student traders the Turtles (Seykota knew I had a website called TurtleTrader.com). My reply was to say I thought Dennis was looking for students who could think in terms of odds. Seykota's response was to ask me if my reply was my own thinking or something I was told by someone else. This was my first indoctrination to Seykota's "direct nature."

Fortune tellers live in the future. So do people who want to put things off. So do fundamentalists.

Ed Seykota[49]

The following story passed along from an associate is "pure Seykota":

"I attended a day-long seminar in February 1995 in Toronto, Canada where Seykota was one of the guest speakers. The WHOLE audience peppered Seykota with questions like: Do you like gold, where do you think the Canadian $ is headed, how do you know when there is a top, how do you know when the trend is up etc.? To each of these, he replied: 'I like gold—it's shiny, pretty—makes nice jewelry' or 'I have no idea where the Canadian dollar is headed or the trend is up when price is moving up, etc.' His replies were simple, straight-forward answers to the questions asked of him. Later, I learned through the event organizer that a large majority of the audience (who paid good money, presumably to learn the 'secrets' of trading from a market wizard) were not impressed. Many felt they had wasted their time and money listening to Seykota. Seykota's message couldn't be clearer to anyone who cared to listen. The answers were found in the very questions each person asked. Don't ask, 'How do you know the trend is moving up?' Instead, ask, 'What is going to tell me the trend is up?' Not, 'What do you think of gold?' Instead, ask, 'Am I correctly trading gold?' Seykota's answers effectively placed everyone in front of a huge mirror, reflecting their trading self back at them. If you don't even know the question to ask about trading, much less the answers, get out of the business and spend your life doing something you enjoy."[50]

> *Pyramiding instructions appear on dollar bills. Add smaller and smaller amounts on the way up. Keep your eye open at the top.*
>
> Ed Seykota[52]

How would you have reacted to Seykota's speech? Walk out or be curious? Think about it.

Performance Second to None

What are Seykota's performance numbers? "Seykota earned, after fees, nearly 60 percent on average each year from 1990 to 2000 managing proprietary money in his managed futures program."[51]

But Seykota is different than Harding, Henry, and Dunn. He literally has been a one-man shop his entire career. There is no fancy office or other employees. He does not hold himself out as a money manager and he is extremely selective of his clients. He doesn't really care whether people have money that they want him to trade or not. I've had the chance to review his monthly performance data for the decade of the 1990s. The month-by-month numbers are eye popping. Seykota takes big risks, and he gets big rewards.

About Ed Seykota

Seykota was born in 1946. He earned his Bachelor of Science from MIT in 1969 and by 1972 had embarked on the trading career he pursues to this day—investing for his own account and the accounts of a few select others. He was self-taught, but influenced in his career by Amos Hostetter and Richard Donchian.

Early in his career, Seykota was hired by a major broker. He conceived and developed the first commercial computerized trading system for client money in the futures markets. According to Jack Schwager's *Market Wizards*, he increased one client's account from $5,000 to $15,000,000 in just 12 years.

For the past few years, Seykota has worked from a home office in Incline Village, Nevada. His trading is largely confined to the few minutes it takes to run his internally written computer program, which generates trading signals for the next day. He also mentors traders through his Web site and his Trading Tribe, a widespread community of like-minded traders. He has served as a teacher and mentor to some great traders, including Michael Marcus and David Druz. Seykota's Trading Tribe is discussed further in Chapter 6, "Human Behavior."

The Seykota "Secret"

Seykota's style is direct. He enjoys debunking market ignorance with terse, Zen-like statements that force the listener to look inward:

> "The biggest secret about success is that there isn't any big secret about it, or if there is, then it's a secret from me, too. The idea of searching for some secret for trading success misses the point."[53]

That self-deprecating response emphasizes process over outcome, but don't be misled by his modesty, because he gets impatient with hypocrisy and mindlessness. He is a fearless trader and does not suffer fools gladly. Yet when he remembers his first trade, I saw how he uncovered the passion for what he does:

> "The first trade I remember, I was about five years old in Portland, OR. My father gave me a gold-colored medallion, a sales promotion trinket. I traded it to a neighbor kid for

five magnifying lenses. I felt as though I had participated in a rite of passage. Later, when I was 13, my father showed me how to buy stocks. He explained that I should buy when the price broke out of the top of a box and to sell when it broke out of the bottom. And that's how I got started."[54]

On how he first started trading:

"I saw a letter published by Richard Donchian, which implied that a purely mechanical trend following system could beat the markets. This too seemed impossible to me. So I wrote computer programs (on punch cards in those days) to test the theories. Amazingly, his [Donchian] theories tested true. To this day, I'm not sure I understand why or whether I really need to. Anyhow, studying the markets, and backing up my opinions with money, was so fascinating compared to my other career opportunities at the time, that I began trading full time for a living."[55]

Trading was in his blood at a young age and at age 23, he went out on his own with about a half-dozen accounts in the $10,000–25,000 range.[56]

Seykota had found an alternative to a Wall Street career built only on commissions. From the beginning, he worked for incentive fees alone. If he made money for his clients, he got paid. If he did not make money, he did not get paid. Does your broker, mutual fund manager, or hedge fund work like that?

Amos Hostetter: "Never Mind the Cheese"

As a new trader, Seykota passed through Commodities Corp, a trader training ground then based in Princeton, New Jersey. One of his mentors was Amos Hostetter. Hostetter made phenomenal amounts of money trading. (He died early in an auto accident, but his son is a billionaire today.) When a market's supply-and-demand prospects looked promising, Hostetter would put up one-third of his ultimate position. If he lost 25 percent of that stake, he'd get out. "Never mind the cheese," he'd crack, "let me out of the trap." But when the market swung his way, he'd add another third, taking a final position when prices climbed half as high as he thought they'd go. Hostetter's strategies were so successful that they were computerized so other traders could learn to duplicate his success.[57]

If a gambler places bets on the input symbol to a communication channel and bets his money in the same proportion each time a particular symbol is received, his capital will grow (or shrink) exponentially. If the odds are consistent with the probabilities of occurrence of the transmitted symbols (i.e., equal to their reciprocals), the maximum value of this exponential rate of growth will be equal to the rate of transmission of information. If the odds are not fair, i.e., not consistent with the transmitted symbol probabilities but consistent with some other set of probabilities, the maximum exponential rate of growth will be larger than it would have been with no channel by an amount equal to the rate of transmission of information.

J. L. Kelly, Jr[60]

His "get-out-of-the-trap" strategies influenced many top traders of the last 30 years. Who else passed through Commodities Corporation? Traders with names like Paul Tudor Jones, Bruce Kovner, Louis Bacon, and Michael Marcus paid their dues at Commodities Corporation. Interestingly, in the mid-1990s, long after the majority of the trend followers had moved on to their own firms, I visited Commodities Corporation's offices. Midway through our tour, we bumped into a stressed-out energy trader. After a few minutes of conversation, we began to chat about his trading style, which was based on fundamentals. Throughout our entire conversation, he was glued to the monitor. When I brought up trend following, he assured me that it did not work. I was surprised that a trader working for a famous firm, known for training brilliant trend followers, was completely blinded to even the possibility that trend following worked. I realized then that even the people closest to trend following did not necessarily have an appreciation for it.

Jay Forrester: System Dynamics

Along with Hostetter, Jay Forrester, a professor of Seykota's at MIT, was a strong influence on the then young Seykota:

"One of my mentors, Jay Forrester, was a stickler for clear writing, a sign of clear thinking."[58]

Forrester taught Seykota about System Dynamics. "It is a method for studying the world around us. Unlike other scientists, who study the world by breaking it up into smaller and smaller pieces, system dynamicists look at things as a whole. The central concept to system dynamics is understanding how all the objects in a system interact with one another. A system can be anything from a steam engine, to a bank account, to a basketball team. The objects and people in a system interact through "feedback" loops, where a change in one variable affects other variables over time, which in turn affects the original variable, and so on. An example of this is money in a bank account. Money in the bank earns interest, which increases the size of the account. Now that the account is larger, it earns even more interest, which adds more money to the account. This goes on and on. What system dynamics attempts to do is understand the basic structure of a system, and thus understand the behavior it can produce. Many of these systems and problems that are analyzed can be built as models on a computer. System dynamics takes advantage of the fact that a computer model can be of much greater complexity and carry out more simultaneous calculations than can the mental model of the human mind."[59]

This type of thought process and computer modeling is not only a foundation of Seykota's success, but it can be seen across the trend following success landscape.

Seykota.com

Seykota gives visitors ample amounts of wisdom and whimsy in answers to the emails he receives on his website. Here are some examples of Seykota's "clear" responses, selected by both him and us from his website:[61]

> *For a system trader, it's way more important to have your trading size down than it is to fine tune your entry and exit points.*
>
> **David Druz[62]**

"To avoid whipsaw losses, stop trading."

Lesson: You will have losses. Accept them.

"Here's the essence of risk management: Risk no more than you can afford to lose, and also risk enough so that a win is meaningful. If there is no such amount, don't play."

Lesson: Money management is crucial. This is further investigated in Chapter 10.

"Trend following is an exercise in observing and responding to the ever-present moment of now. Traders who predict the future dwell upon a nonexistent place, and to the extent they also park their ability to act out there, they can miss opportunities to act in the now."

Lesson: All we have is now. It is much better to react to the fact of market movements in present time than a future time that doesn't exist.

"Markets are fundamentally volatile. No way around it. Your problem is not in the math. There is no math to get you out of having to experience uncertainty."

Lesson: You can crunch all the numbers you like, but your "gut" still has to handle the ups and downs. You have to live with and feel the uncertainty.

"I recall, in the old days, people showing a lot of concern that markets are different and trend following methods no longer work."

I'd say the most important benefit I attained from my time in the Incline Tribe was how I learned to incorporate my feelings around uncertainty into my trading. Ed and I worked on it until I finally got the Aha: that my need for uncertainty is a natural part of my emotional constitution. And if my clients don't eventually get it, I may need new clients, or they may need T-Bills. Their money-drama is not part of my system.

Michael Martin
Student of Ed Seykota's

Lesson: Today or yesterday, skeptics abound. They sound like broken records in their desires to see trend following debunked.

"It can be very expensive to try to convince the markets you are right."

Lesson: Go with the flow. Leave your personal or fundamental opinions at the door. Do you want to be right or make money? The losers profiled in Chapter 4, "Big Events, Crashes, and Panics," tried to convince everyone that they were right and lost big time.

"When magazine covers get pretty emotional, get out of the position. There's nothing else in the magazine that works very well, but the covers are pretty good. This is not an indictment of the magazine people, it's just that at the end of a big move there is a communal psychological abreaction that shows up on the covers of magazines."[63]

Lesson: Crowd psychology is real, and the price reflects all.

Seykota Students

Easan Katir: Seykota Student #1

Seykota's track record is incredible, but one of his students, Easan Katir, offered a warning when it comes to making comparisons:

"Journalists, interviewers, and such like to hedge their praise and use phrases such as 'one of the best traders,' etc. If one looks at Ed Seykota's model account record and compares it with anyone else, historical or contemporary, he is the best trader in history, period. Isn't he? Who else comes close? I don't know of anyone. Livermore made fortunes, but had drawdowns to zero. There are numerous examples of managers with a few years of meteoric returns who subsequently blow up. The household names, Buffett and Soros, are less than half of Ed's return each year. One might apply filters such as Sharpe ratios, AUM, etc., and perhaps massage the results. But as far as the one central metric—raw percentage profit—Ed is above anyone else I know, and I've been around managing money for 20 years."

Jason Russell: Seykota Student #2

Russell is a student of Ed Seykota's. He provided me a glimpse into the process of training with Seykota:

> "Through working with Ed, I have learned many things in the past couple of years, one of the most important being: Apply trend following to your life as well as to your trading. Freeing yourself from the need to understand "why" is as useful when dealing with family, friends, and foes as it is when entering or exiting a trade. It also has the added benefit of making you a much better trader."

Most traders cannot recognize how simple life really is. This is similar to what Russell describes as Seykota's view of simplicity:

> "There is simplicity beyond sophistication. Ed spends a lot of time there. He listens, he feels, he speaks with clarity. He is a master of his craft. Before working with Ed, I spent years learning, reading, and earning various designations. All of this has been useful as it provides me with a high level of technical proficiency. However, somehow through this whole process, I have gained a strong appreciation for simplifying. Miles Davis was once asked what went through his mind when he listened to his own music. He said: 'I always listen to what I can leave out.' That sounds like Ed."

David Druz: Seykota Student #3

Druz once described what it was like to work with Seykota:

> "It was one of the most incredible experiences of my life. He is the smartest trader I have ever seen. I don't think anybody comes close. He has the greatest insights into how markets work and how people operate. It's almost scary being in his presence. It was tough surviving working with him because of the mental gymnastics involved. If you have a personality weakness, he finds it—fast. But it's a positive thing because successful traders must understand themselves and their psychological weaknesses. My time with Ed was one of the greatest times of my life and gave me tremendous confidence—but I don't trade any differently because of it. A guy like Ed Seykota is magic."[64]

The difference between a successful person and others is not a lack of strength, not a lack of knowledge, but rather a lack of will.

Vince Lombardi

Seykota would be the first to say that he is no magician. Although it may be human nature to attribute phenomenal trading success to magical powers, trend following is actually a form of trial and error. The errors are all the small losses incurred while trying to find those big trends.

Jim Hamer: Seykota Student #4

Jim Hamer, a trend follower based out of Williamburg, Virginia, felt it was important to tell me about Seykota's life beyond the markets:

"I lived with Ed and his family for a little over two months in early 1997. One of the more amazing things I observed about Ed is that he has gifts in so many areas, trading being just one of them. He showed me a music video that he produced many years ago. It was an excellent production. He also recorded an album several years before the video. He is a very talented musician. My favorite song was *Bull Market*, which he used to play for me on his acoustic guitar. During the time I was with him, he was very involved in experiments that attempted to redefine airflows as they relate to the Bernoulli Principle. He spent an enormous amount of time putting together academic papers and sending them to several experts in the field concerning this work. He is the consummate scientist. One day, we took a 'field trip' to visit Ed's state legislator to discuss Charter School legislation and the impact on Ed's children and the students of Nevada. Not long after I left, Ed ran for the local school board. He has a keen interest in and knowledge of education. Ed Seykota will never be defined solely by trading. He has a love of learning and is a modern-day Renaissance man."

Charles Faulkner, profiled in Chapter 6, once said that if Seykota had wanted to stay in academia, he would have won a Nobel Prize. That said, Seykota would have abhorred life in an ivory tower and the accompanying politics. This is a man who relishes the here and now, where he can confront real problems and provide real solutions. He chooses to live real trading, not admire it.

Key Points

- Seykota: "Win or lose, everybody gets what they want out of the market. Some people seem to like to lose, so they win by losing money."
- Seykota: "To avoid whipsaw losses, stop trading."
- Seykota: "Risk no more than you can afford to lose and also risk enough so that a win is meaningful."
- Seykota: "Trend following is an exercise in observing and responding to the ever-present moment of now."
- Seykota: "Fundamentalists and anticipators may have difficulties with risk control because a trade keeps looking 'better' the more it goes against them."
- Seykota: "Until you master the basic literature and spend some time with successful traders, you might consider confining your trading to the supermarket."
- Seykota: "I don't predict a nonexisting future."

Keith Campbell

Considering he's one of the largest (in terms of client assets) and oldest trend followers, Keith Campbell and his company, Campbell and Company, are nearly nonexistent in terms of visibility. Do the requisite Google search and you'll find almost no information about their trading. You would think that with billions in client capital, Campbell & Co. would be as well known as Fidelity—not true.

However, when you have a very reclusive trader, access to his monthly performance data makes up for a lack of information due to any self-imposed anonymity. The data (see Chart 2.8) speaks the truth about the success of a trend follower such as Campbell even if he's reluctant to do so.

You've got to have a longer perspective and confidence in the veracity of the approach that you're using.

Bruce Cleland, President and Chief Executive Officer at Campbell & Co. in Towson, Md.[65]

Comparison of Campbell Program to the S&P 500 Cash Index
April 1983–November 2003
$1,000 Starting Value—Compounded

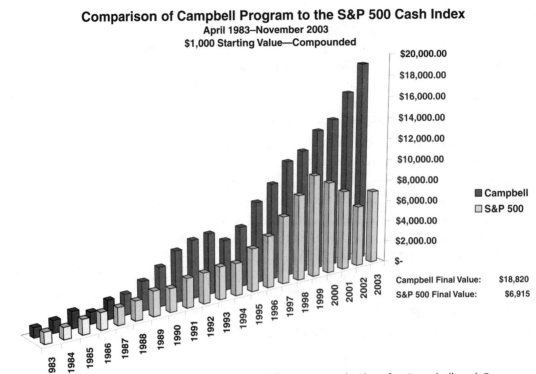

Campbell Final Value: $18,820
S&P 500 Final Value: $6,915

CHART 2.8:   Hypothetical $1000 Growth Chart for Campbell and Co.

About Keith Campbell

Measure what is measurable, and make measurable what is not so.

Galileo Galilei[66]

Perhaps one reason trend followers respect the unexpected is because many of them did not set out to become traders. When unexpectedly exposed to trading many realized how well suited they were for it and eventually came upon trend following as the ideal strategy. In the 1960s, Campbell took a job in California where he could both ski and surf. When his roommate moved out of their California apartment, he advertised for a replacement and ended up with Chet Conrad, a commodity broker. Campbell recalled that, "(Conrad) got me into trading as a customer. But he was always moaning he didn't have enough money to trade." Campbell then put together $60,000 from 12 investors to form his first futures fund with three advisors—a fundamentalist, a bar chartist, and a point-and-figure advocate. When that fund struggled, he started the Campbell Fund and then took it over on January 1, 1972. A few years later, Campbell and Conrad went their separate ways. Conrad relocated to Lake Tahoe, Nevada on a gutsy sugar trade that turned a borrowed $10,000 into $3 million. Campbell remained with his fund, which today is the oldest commodity fund still trading.[67]

However, it is unfair to refer to Campbell and Co. as a "commodity fund" because Campbell trades more than just commodities. Jim Little of Campbell and Co. makes this clear when he describes the widely diverse markets they trade, which include stocks:

"We always are looking for non-correlated absolute return strategies that can produce higher quality risk adjusted returns; whether that is more managed futures strategy models or long/short equities or whatever. We have 30 years of experience doing long/short stock indexes, bond futures, and currencies; to do it in individual equities (stocks) isn't that much different."

But, like John W. Henry, trading diverse markets doesn't translate into complicated trading strategies. Campbell also believes in keeping it simple:

"I'm very uncomfortable with black box trading where I'm dealing with algorithms I don't understand. Everything we do we could do on the back of an envelope with a pencil."[68]

Campbell's "back of an envelope" remark must be a revelation to those people who imagine trading to be wildly complex. The real lesson with Campbell like other great trend followers is the discipline to stick to his rules in the tough times.

Campbell Compared to Benchmarks

While I am no proponent of benchmarking, the following chart (Chart 2.9) shows drawdown comparisons across asset classes:

CHART 2.9: Worst Case Cumulative Percentage Decline, Jan. 1972–Dec. 1995

- S&P—43% (12/72–9/74)
- Fidelity Magellan—63% (6/72–9/74)
- Campbell's Oldest Fund—36% (9/74–3/76)
- Lehman Brothers Government Bond Index—12% (1/94–10/94)

There was a time when a lot of people thought that the models or algorithms that we used were king— that everything else was ancillary to the mathematics. I think today as an industry, we have a much more realistic and a better balanced approach. The mathematics are very important, but it's only one piece of the puzzle. The most important thing overall is the total investment process, of which the signal generator is an important part. Portfolio structuring, risk management, execution strategies, capital management, and leverage management may not be directly connected to the algorithm that generates the buy and sell signals, but they are all hugely important.

Bruce Cleland, President and CEO, Campbell and Co.[69]

Many skeptics like to think trend followers are the only ones with drawdowns. The chart, however, shows the truth of drawdowns across several indexes and fund types.

The key is to accept drawdowns and be able to manage them when they occur. Otherwise, you are left watching the NASDAQ drop 77 percent peak to trough over 2000—2002 with no plan on what to do next. Buy and hope?

Campbell and Company analyzes only technical market data, not any economic factors external to market prices.[71]

Still, Campbell's strategies were often doubted by Wall Street, especially the "old guard" who like to gripe how supposedly risky trend following is. Campbell refutes that:

"A common perception is that futures markets are extremely volatile, and that investing in futures is therefore very risky, much riskier than equity investments. The reality is that generally futures prices are less volatile than common stocks prices. It is the amount of leverage available in futures which creates the perception of high risk, not market volatility. The actual risk involved in futures trading depends, among other things, upon how much leverage is used."[70]

Managing the use of leverage is a crucial component of trend followers' risk management. It is the part of the trading strategy that allows them to keep coming back day after day and year after year to trade and win.

Correlation and Consistency

Most trend followers earn their returns at different times than common benchmark measures, such as the S&P stock index. Campbell (see Chart 2.10), like John W. Henry & Company and other longtime trend followers, is not correlated with major stock market indexes.

CHART 2.10: Correlation Analysis Between Campbell Composite and S&P 500 Index, January 1980–November 2003. Source: Campbell and Co.

Both Positive	96 of 287 Months
Opposite	150 of 287 Months
Both Negative	41 of 287 Months

Even more remarkable than his lack of correlation to the S&P benchmark, Campbell's performance (see Chart 2.11) is consistent over total months, total years, and 12-, 24-, 36-, 48-, and 60-month rolling time windows:

CHART 2.11:   Past Consistency of the Campbell Composite, January 1980–November 2003 (estimates). Source: Campbell and Co.

January 1980–November 2003 (estimates)	Number of Time Periods	Number of Profitable Periods	Number of Unprofitable Periods	Percentage Profitable
Total Months	287	161	126	56.10%
Total Years	31	26	5	83.87%
12-Month Rolling Windows	276	217	59	78.62%
24-Month Rolling Windows	264	228	36	86.36%
36-Month Rolling Windows	252	226	26	89.68%
48-Month Rolling Windows	240	240	0	100.00%
60-Month Rolling Windows	228	228	0	100.00%

Are you any more knowledgeable about Campbell and Co. now? Qualitatively perhaps not, but quantitatively their performance numbers demonstrate, yet again, a validity in trend following trading.

Our trend-following methods do not pretend to determine the value of what we are trading, nor do they determine what that value ought to be, but they do produce absolute returns fairly consistently.

Jim Little, Campbell and Co.[72]

Key Point

• Campbell and Co.: "Everything we do we could do on the back of an envelope with a pencil."

Jerry Parker

I first visited Jerry Parker's original office in Manakin-Sabot, Virginia in 1994. Manakin-Sabot is a rural Richmond suburb. It's in the "sticks." Why make that point? Because a few months before, I was in Salomon Brothers' office in lower Manhattan gazing across, for the first time, their huge trading floor, which seemed like the epicenter of Wall Street. The light bulb of geographic irrelevance went off when Parker's unpretentious offices in Manakin-Sabot hit my eyes for the first time. You never would have guessed that this was where the thoughtful, laid-back CEO of Chesapeake Capital Management managed over $1 billion. For Parker, like Bill Dunn, trappings appeared meaningless.

Parker grew up in Lynchburg, Virginia, graduating from the University of Virginia. He was working as an accountant in Richmond when he applied to Richard Dennis' training program and was the first student Dennis accepted. Pragmatic and consistent, he went on to start his own money management firm, Chesapeake Capital, in 1988. He made the decision to risk less and make less for clients, so he took his Turtle trading approach, a trend following strategy, and ratcheted it down a degree. In other words, he took an aggressive system for making money and customized it to investors who were comfortable with lower leverage.

Even though he was shooting for lower risk he returned 61.82 percent on his money in one incredible year of 1993. That put his firm on the map (see Chart 2.12). However, he is generally in the 12–14 percent return range today. His more conservative approach to trend following is different from Dunn or Seykota who have always pushed their systems for absolute returns. Parker does it a little differently, but no less successfully. I always walked away from Parker impressed each time at how straightforward and unassuming he was.

A Virginian

Technical traders do not need to have a particular expertise in each market that they trade. They do not need to be an authority on meteorological phenomena, geopolitical occurrences or the economic impact of specific worldwide events on a particular market.

Jerry Parker[73]

Parker spoke at the annual Futures and Options Expo in Chicago at the height of the dot-com bubble. At the time trend following seemed stodgy, especially when the speaker was as self-deprecating as Parker. His address covered a full range of trend following philosophies. He left half his allotted time for Q&A, however, and this is where attendees were able to gain more specific insight into his firm's trading techniques. However skeptical Parker's audience, it did not prevent him from offering simple, direct, and solid advice about trading to those willing to accept it.

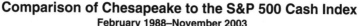

Comparison of Chesapeake to the S&P 500 Cash Index
February 1988–November 2003
$1,000 Starting Value—Compounded

Chesapeake Final Value: $12,633
S&P 500 Final Value: $4,114

CHART 2.12: Hypothetical $1000 Growth Chart for Chesapeake Capital

On the dangers of a buy-and-hold mentality:

"The strategy of buy and hold is bad. Hold for what? A key to successful traders is their ability to leverage investments ...many [traders] are too conservative in their willingness to leverage."[74]

On the folly of predicting where markets may be headed:

"I don't know nor do I care. The system that we use at Chesapeake is about the market knowing where it's going."[75]

On his trend following trading system:

"This flies in the face of what clients want: fancy schools, huge research, an intuitive approach that knows what's going to happen before it happens, e.g., be overweight in the

I participated in the Richard Dennis "Turtle Program." The methods we were taught and the trading experience received were all a technical approach to trading the commodity markets. The most important experience that led me to utilize a technical approach was the amount of success that I experienced trading Rich's system.

Jerry Parker[80]

stock market before the rate cut. But obviously you can't know what's going to happen before it happens, and maybe the rate cut is the start of a major trend, and maybe it's okay to get in after. That's our approach. No bias short or long."[76]

On counter-trend or day trading:

"The reason for it is a lot of traders as well as clients don't like trend following. It's not intuitive, not natural, too long term, not exciting enough."[77]

On the wishful thinking of victims of recent market disasters:

"They said 'the market's wrong, it'll come back'. The market is never wrong."[78]

Ask yourself if you want to be right or do you want to win. They are different questions.

Parker Downplays Intelligence

Trend following success is much more predicated on discipline than pure academic achievement. Parker is candid about the intelligence required at his firm:

"We have a system in which we do not have to rely on our intellectual capabilities. One of the main reasons why what we do works in the markets is that no one can figure out what is happening."[79]

The best trend followers are willing to admit that pure I.Q. is not the key. They also know that the latest news flash of the day is not information that figures into their decisions about when to buy, when to sell, or how much to buy or sell at any time. Parker adds, "Our pride and opinions should not interfere with sound trading approaches."[81]

Parker has also trained and influenced other traders. Look no further than an associate of Parker's, Salem Abraham.

Salem Abraham

Salem Abraham does it differently than most trend followers. He truly proves physical location is meaningless for success.

It would be hard to find a financial firm in the United States as removed from Wall Street, geographically and culturally, as the Abraham Trading Company. Housed in the same building where his grandfather Malouf Abraham once chewed the fat with local politicians and ranchers while building a sizable land-speculation business, the company has evolved into one of the nation's most unusual trading operations.[82]

It was while he was a student at Notre Dame University that Abraham found he had a natural ability for and interest in trading. Like Greg Smith, one of Seykota's students, he researched which traders were the most successful and discovered trend following. Abraham returned home to the family ranch in Canadian, Texas after graduating and discussed the idea of trading for a living with his "granddad," who cautiously agreed to help him get started. According to Abraham, he was to "try it out for six months," and then discard the idea ("throw the quote machine out the window") if he failed.[83]

There was no failure for Abraham. He quickly developed a Wall Street business in the most anti-Wall Street way. Abraham's firm's culture is astonishingly different from what people might expect from a top trader:

> "No one at the company has an Ivy League degree. Most of the employees at Abraham Trading have backgrounds working at the area's feedlots or natural-gas drilling and pipeline companies. Their training in the complexities of trading and arbitrage is provided on the job. 'This beats shoveling manure at 6 in the morning,' said Geoff Dockray, who was hired as a clerk for Mr. Abraham after working at a feedlot near Canadian. The financial markets are complicated but they're not as relentless as dealing with livestock all the time."[84]

Abraham's "meat-and-potatoes" approach to trading is no nonsense:

> "The underlying premise of ATC's [Abraham Trading Company] trading approach is that commodity interests will, from time to time, enter into periods of major price change to either a higher or lower level. These price changes are known as trends, which have been observed and recorded since the beginning of market history. There

I think the only cardinal evil on earth is that of placing your prime concern within other men. I've always demanded a certain quality in the people I liked. I've always recognized it at once— and it's the only quality I respect in men. I chose my friends by that. Now I know what it is. A self-sufficient ego. Nothing else matters.

Ayn Rand[86]

Abraham Trading was up +74.65 percent for 2003.

is every reason to believe that in free markets prices will continue to trend. The trading approach used by ATC is designed to exploit these price moves."[85]

When asked about his relationship with Parker, Abraham gave an example of six degrees of separation and the randomness of life:

"We do in fact know Jerry Parker with Chesapeake Capital. The shortest version I can give you is he is my dad's sister's husband's brother's daughter's husband. I'm not sure you can call that related but something like that. I first learned about the futures industry by talking to him while he visited in-laws in Texas."

A lesson learned? Keep your eyes open to possibilities, as you never know where opportunity will appear. Parker knows Abraham's age (and success) can cause problems:

"Sometimes people have a tendency to resent a young guy who's making so much money," said Jerry Parker, himself a hedge fund manager from Richmond, Virginia, who has been an investor in Mr. Abraham's fund for the last five years. "I just think he has a lot of guts."[87]

Consider Abraham's trading performance (see Chart 2.13).

If there is a lesson to be learned from Abraham, it is simply that if you want to become a trend follower, it doesn't hurt to get out there and meet the players.

Parker and Abraham are ultimately realists. They play the zero-sum game hard in similar ways and excel at it, but they have also found a way to balance key components of their lives. Without compromising integrity, they have found a way to apply their trading philosophy and at the same time please clients.

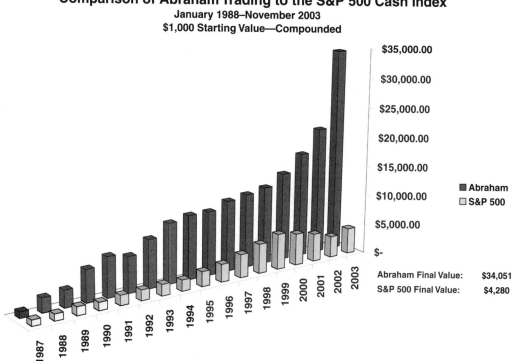

CHART 2.13: Hypothetical $1000 Growth Chart for Abraham Trading Company

---

Key Points

- Parker: "A key to successful traders is their ability to leverage investments...many [traders] are too conservative in their willingness to leverage."

- Parker: "A lot of traders as well as clients don't like trend following. It's not intuitive, not natural, too long term, not exciting enough."

- Parker: "The market is never wrong."

- Trend following success is not predicated on academic achievement.

- More on Parker and Abraham can be found in my second book *The Complete TurtleTrader* (Collins, 2007).

Richard Dennis

Richard Dennis is retired from trading. Unfortunately, his exit has been misinterpreted by some in the press as sounding the death-knell of trend following. It is true that Dennis' career had big ups and downs, but trend following itself is doing just fine.

Dennis was born and raised in Chicago in close proximity to the exchanges. He began trading as a teenager with $400 saved from his pizza delivery job. Because he was too young to qualify for membership on the exchange, he would send signals to his father, who would do the actual trading. At 17, he finally landed a job in the pit as a runner on the exchange floor and started trading.[88]

Dennis' Students: The Turtles

Eventually, Dennis would achieve fantastic wealth with profits in the hundreds of millions of dollars. However, his real fame would come from his experiment in teaching trading to new traders.

In 1983, he made a bet with his partner William Eckhardt. Dennis believed that trading could be taught. Eckhardt belonged to the "you're born with it or you're not" camp. They decided to experiment by seeing whether they could teach novices successful trading. Twenty-plus students were accepted into two separate training programs. Dennis called his students "Turtles," after visiting a turtle-breeding farm in Singapore.

How did it start? Dennis ran classified ads saying "Trader Wanted" and was immediately overwhelmed by some 1,000 queries from would-be traders. He picked 20+ novices, trained them for two weeks, and then gave them money to trade for his firm. His turtle traders included two professional gamblers, a fantasy-game designer, an accountant, and a juggler. Jerry Parker, the former accountant who now manages more than $1 billion, was one of several who went on to become top money managers.[90]

Although Dennis appears to own the mantle of trend following teaching professor, there are many other trend followers, including Seykota, Dunn, and Henry, who have served as teachers to a number of successful traders. Also keep in mind that not all the Turtles turned out to be winners. After they left Dennis' tutelage and traded on their own, there were several Turtles who failed (e.g. Curtis Faith). Their root problems might be traced to poor personal discipline coupled with an incomplete understanding of the psychology needed to win. Perhaps, after some Turtles went out on their own, they could not cope without the safety net of being under Dennis' wing. Of course, Jerry Parker is a monster exception to this theory—he is absolutely the most successful of the turtle traders.

This is not a criticism of the system Dennis taught his students. It is rather an acknowledgement that some people could not stick with the trading system as it was taught them or perhaps were never comfortable with it to begin with. In stark contrast, Bill Dunn was completely unknown to the general public when the Turtles burst onto the scene in the 1980s. Since that time, Dunn has slowly overtaken most, if not all, trend followers in terms of absolute performance. You have to wonder if something about the initial small one-man shop of Dunn set in motion the habits that enabled him to roar past the Turtles that seemingly had the superior head start. For years, many of the Turtles also refused to acknowledge they were even trend followers while Dunn was always candid. Did the hype and mystery of the Turtles set forward in the *Market Wizards* books help most of them in the long run?

All this said, the story of the Turtles is so widespread that the criteria Dennis used to select his students is still insightful (see more in *The Complete TurtleTrader*, my second book).

Turtle Selection Process

Dale Dellutri, a former executive at Dennis' firm, managed the Turtle group. He said they were looking for "smarts and for people who had odd ideas." Ultimately, they selected several blackjack players, an actor, a security guard, and a designer of the fantasy game Dungeons and Dragons. One of the ways they screened candidates was by having them answer true or false questions. What questions were asked?

There's nothing quite as good or bad as trading. They give you a number every day. That's what's good about it, and that's what's bad about it. That's what makes it hard. That's what makes it worth doing.

Richard Dennis[92]

The following true/false questions were sent out to the second group of Turtles. These questions were used to help decide who was picked and who was not:

1. One should favor being long or being short, whichever one is comfortable with.

2. On initiation, one should know precisely at what price to liquidate if a profit occurs.

3. One should trade the same number of contracts in all markets.

4. If one has $100,000 to risk, one ought to risk $25,000 on every trade.

5. On initiation, one should know precisely where to liquidate if a loss occurs.

6. You can never go broke taking profits.

7. It helps to have the fundamentals in your favor before you initiate.

8. A gap up is a good place to initiate if an uptrend has started.

9. If you anticipate buy stops in the market, wait until they are finished and buy a little higher than that.

10. Of three types of orders (market, stop, and resting), market orders cost the least skid.

11. The more bullish news you hear and the more people are going long, the less likely the uptrend is to continue after a substantial uptrend.

12. The majority of traders are always wrong.

13. Trading bigger is an overall handicap to one's trading performance.

14. Larger traders can "muscle" markets to their advantage.

15. Vacations are important for traders to keep the proper perspective.

16. Under trading is almost never a problem.

17. Ideally, average profits should be about three or four times average losses.

18. A trader should be willing to let profits turn into losses.

19. A very high percentage of trades should be profits.

20. A trader should like to take losses.

21. It is especially relevant when the market is higher than it's been in 4 and 13 weeks.

22. Needing and wanting money are good motivators to good trading.

23. One's natural inclinations are good guides to decision making in trading.

24. Luck is an ingredient in successful trading over the long run.

25. When you're long, "limit up" is a good place to take a profit.

26. It takes money to make money.

27. It's good to follow hunches in trading.

28. There are players in each market one should not trade against.

29. All speculators die broke.

30. The market can be understood better through social psychology than through economics.

31. Taking a loss should be a difficult decision for traders.

32. After a big profit, the next trend-following trade is more likely to be a loss.

33. Trends are not likely to persist.

34. Almost all information about a commodity is at least a little useful in helping make decisions.

35. It's better to be an expert in one to two markets rather than try to trade ten or more markets.

36. In a winning streak, total risk should rise dramatically.

37. Trading stocks is similar to trading commodities.

38. It's a good idea to know how much you are ahead or behind during a trading session.

39. A losing month is an indication of doing something wrong.

40. A losing week is an indication of doing something wrong.

41. The big money in trading is made when one can get long at lows after a big downtrend.

42. It's good to average down when buying.

43. After a long trend, the market requires more consolidation before another trend starts.

44. It's important to know what to do if trading in commodities doesn't succeed.

45. It is not helpful to watch every quote in the markets one trades.

46. It is a good idea to put on or take off a position all at once.

47. Diversification in commodities is better than always being in one or two markets.

48. If a day's profit or loss makes a significant difference to your net worth, you're overtrading.

49. A trader learns more from his losses than his profits.

50. Except for commission and brokerage fees, execution "costs" for entering orders are minimal over the course of a year.

51. It's easier to trade well than to trade poorly.

52. It's important to know what success in trading will do for you later in life.

53. Uptrends end when everyone gets bearish.

54. The more bullish news you hear, the less likely a market is to break out on the upside.

55. For an off-floor trader, a long-term trade ought to last three or four weeks or less.

56. Others' opinions of the market are good to follow.

57. Volume and open interest are as important as price action.

58. Daily strength and weakness is a good guide for liquidating long-term positions with big profits.

59. Off-floor traders should spread different markets of different market groups.

60. The more people are going long, the less likely an uptrend is to continue in the beginning of a trend.

61. Off-floor traders should not spread different delivery months of the same commodity.

62. Buying dips and selling rallies is a good strategy.

63. It's important to take a profit most of the time.

Not all the questions were true or false. Dennis also asked candidates essay questions:

1. What were your standard test results on college entrance exams?

2. Name a book or movie you like and why.

3. Name a historical figure you like and why.

4. Why would you like to succeed at this job?

5. Name a risky thing you have done and why.

6. Explain a decision you have made under pressure and why that was your decision.

7. Hope, fear, and greed are said to be enemies of good traders. Explain a decision you may have made under one of these influences and how you view that decision now.

8. What are some good qualities you have that might help in trading?

9. What are some bad qualities you have that might hurt in trading?

10. In trading would you rather be good or lucky? Why?

11. Is there anything else you'd like to add?

At first glance, these questions might seem simplistic, but Dennis did not care what anyone might think:

> "I suppose I didn't like the idea that everyone thought I was crazy or going to fail, but it didn't make any substantial difference because I had an idea what I wanted to do and how I wanted to do it."[93]

Dennis placed the passion to achieve at the top of his list. You have to wake up with that inner drive and desire to make it happen. You have to go for it. Dennis also outlined the problem with profit targets (a key lesson taught to the Turtles):

> "When you have a position, you put it on for a reason, and you've got to keep it until the reason no longer exists. Don't take profits just for the sake of taking profits."[94]

Dennis makes it clear that if you don't know when a trend will end, but you do know it can go significantly higher, then why get off?

Whatever you use should be applied in some quantitative, rigorous fashion. You should use science to determine what works and quantify it. I'm still surprised today at how I can expect so strongly that a trading methodology will be profitable but, after running it though a simulation, I discover it's a loser.

Paul Rabar[95]

Aftermath

Although some of his Turtle students have had successful money management careers (some not), Dennis seems to especially not do well when trading for clients. If Dennis just traded for himself, he might be fine (and much richer). His problems seem to

No trader can control volatility completely, but you can improve your odds.

Observation made by a student of Richard Dennis

arise when he trades for clients who do not truly understand the nature of trend following trading. His most recent stab at managing money for others, which ended in the fall of 2000, resulted in a compounded annual return of 26.9 percent (after fees), including two years when performance exceeded 100 percent. But, he stopped trading for clients after a drawdown in 2000. His clients pulled their money right before his trading would have gone straight up. Doubt me that he would have gone up? Use Dunn Capital Management and just about any other trend follower as a proxy and you will see what happened in the fall of 2000. If those impatient clients had stayed with Dennis from the fall of 2000 to the present, they would have been richly rewarded, far surpassing stock market buy and hold gains by comparison.

One of the biggest lessons a trader can learn is that trading for your own account and trading for clients are two different things. John W. Henry told me that it never gets easy losing money for clients. Traders who concentrate on expanding just their own capital often have a great advantage over money managers. Money managers must deal with the pressure and expectations of clients at all times.

I don't think trading strategies are as vulnerable to not working if people know about them, as most traders believe. If what you are doing is right, it will work even if people have a general idea about it. I always say that you could publish trading rules in the newspaper and no one would follow them. A key is consistency and discipline.

Richard Dennis[96]

There may have been other reasons for Dennis' problems beyond pressure and expectations from clients. For example, Dennis said he could not program a computer if it walked in and bit him. He outsourced his programming, as many traders do. But there is something to be said about knowing how everything under the hood works. Ed Seykota is generally acknowledged to have programmed the first computerized trading system. Bill Dunn and his staff wrote their original programming for their trading systems. In other words, there may be value in learning all you can about every aspect of trading if you are going to trade a trend following trading system.

Key Points

- Dennis: "Trading was even more teachable than I imagined. In a strange sort of way, it was almost humbling."

- Dennis: "When you have a position, you put it on for a reason, and you've got to keep it until the reason no longer exists.

Don't take profits just for the sake of taking profits. You have to have a strategy to trade, know how it works, and follow through on it."

- Dennis: "You don't get any profits from fundamental analysis; you get profit from buying and selling."

More on Dennis can be found in my second book, *The Complete TurtleTrader*.

Richard Donchian

The Father of Trend Following

Although Richard Donchian passed away many years ago, his influence resonates. He is known as the father of trend following. His original technical trading system became the foundation on which later trend followers would build their systems. Where do you think the Turtle system evolved from? He is noteworthy among traders in general, as he was the originator of the managed money industry. From the time he started the industry's first managed fund in 1949 until his death, he shared his research and served as a teacher and mentor to numerous present-day trend followers.

About Richard Donchian

Donchian was born in 1905 in Hartford, Connecticut. He graduated from Yale in 1928 with a BA in economics. He was so fascinated by trading that even after losing his investments in the 1929 stock market crash, he returned to work on Wall Street.

In 1930, he managed to borrow some capital to trade shares in Auburn Auto, what William Baldwin in his article on Donchian called, "the Apple Computer of its day." The moment after he made several thousand dollars on the trade, he became a market "technician," charting prices and formulating buy and sell strategies without concern for an investment's basic value.[98]

From 1933 to 1935, Donchian wrote a technical market letter for Hemphill, Noyes & Co. He stopped his financial career to serve as an Air Force statistical control officer in World War II, but returned to Wall Street after the war and he became a market letter writer for Shearson Hamill & Company. He began to keep detailed,

I became a computer applicant of Dick's [Donchian] ideas. He was one of the only people at the time who was doing simulation of any kind. He was generous with his ideas, making a point to share what he knew; it delighted him to get others to try systems. He inspired a great many people and spawned a whole generation of traders, providing courage and a road map.

Ed Seykota[97]

We started our database using punch cards in 1968, and we collected commodity price data back to July 1959. We back-tested the 5 and 20 and the weekly rules for Dick. I think the weekly method was the best thing that anyone had ever done. Of all Dick's contributions, the weekly rules helped identify the trend and helped you act on it. Dick is one of those people who today likes to beat the computer—only he did it by hand. He enjoyed the academics of the process, the excitement of exploring new ideas and running the numbers.

Dennis D. Dunn, Dunn & Hargitt[99]

technical records on futures prices, recording daily price data in a ledger book. Barbara Dixon, one of his students, observed how he computed his moving averages, posted his own charts by hand, and developed his market signals—without the benefit of an accurate database, software, or any computing capability. His jacket pockets were always loaded down with pencils and a pencil sharpener.[100]

Much of Donchian's work went unnoticed by the numerous stars of finance that followed him. Dixon makes it clear that her mentor's work preceded and prefigured that of the academic theorists who developed the foundations of the modern theory of finance. Long before Harvard's John Litner published his quantitative analysis of the benefits of including managed futures in a portfolio with stocks and bonds, Donchian used concepts like diversification and risk control, key elements of modern portfolio theory that won William Sharpe and Harry Markowitz Nobel prizes in economics in 1990.[101]

Donchian: The Personification of Persistence

Was Donchian an overnight sensation? After 42 years, Donchian was still managing only $200,000, despite his detailed graphs of price charts for stocks and commodities. Then, in his mid-60s, everything came together, and a decade later, he was managing $27 million at Shearson American Express making $1 million a year in fees and commissions and another million in trading profits on his own money.[102]

Mid-60s? What patience and persistence! Like all of the other great trend followers, the importance of price was critical for Donchian:

"He didn't predict price movements, he just followed them. His explanation for his success was simple and as old as the 'Dow Theory' itself: 'Trends persist.' 'A lot of people say things like: Gold has got to come down. It went up too fast. That's why 85 percent of commodities investors lose money,' he says. He was never distracted from his system. 'The fundamentals are supposed to be bullish in copper,' he says. 'But I'm on the short side now because the trend is down.'"[104]

I remember in 1979 or 1980, at one of the early MAR conferences, being impressed by the fact that I counted 19 CTAs who were managing public funds, and I could directly identify 16 of the 19 with Dick Donchian. They had either worked for him or had had monies invested with him. To me, that's the best evidence of his impact in the early days. Dick has always been very proud of the fact that his people have prospered. He also was proud that after too many years in which his was the lone voice in the wilderness, his thinking eventually came to be the dominant thinking of the industry.

Brett Elam,
Elam Management Corp.[103]

What were his rules? The following Donchian trading guidelines were first published in 1934:

General Guides

1. Beware of acting immediately on a widespread public opinion. Even if correct, it will usually delay the move.

2. From a period of dullness and inactivity, watch for and prepare to follow a move in the direction in which volume increases.

3. Limit losses and ride profits, irrespective of all other rules.

4. Light commitments are advisable when market position is not certain. Clearly defined moves are signaled frequently enough to make life interesting and concentration on these moves will prevent unprofitable whip-sawing.

5. Seldom take a position in the direction of an immediately preceding three-day move. Wait for a one-day reversal.

6. Judicious use of stop orders is a valuable aid to profitable trading. Stops may be used to protect profits, to limit losses, and from certain formations such as triangular foci to take positions. Stop orders are apt to be more valuable and less treacherous if used in proper relation to the chart formation.

7. In a market in which upswings are likely to equal or exceed downswings, heavier position should be taken for the upswings for percentage reasons— a decline from 50 to 25 will net only 50 percent profit, whereas an advance from 25 to 50 will net 100 percent profit.

8. In taking a position, price orders are allowable. In closing a position, use market orders.

9. Buy strong-acting, strong-background commodities and sell weak ones, subject to all other rules.

10. Moves in which rails lead or participate strongly are usually more worth following than moves in which rails lag.

11. A study of the capitalization of a company, the degree of activity of an issue, and whether an issue is a lethargic truck horse or a spirited race horse is fully as important as a study of statistical reports.

Donchian Technical Guidelines

1. A move followed by a sideways range often precedes another move of almost equal extent in the same direction as the original move. Generally, when the second move from the sideways range has run its course, a counter move approaching the sideways range may be expected.

2. Reversal or resistance to a move is likely to be encountered:

   a. On reaching levels at which in the past, the commodity has fluctuated for a considerable length of time within a narrow range

   b. On approaching highs or lows

3. Watch for good buying or selling opportunities when trend lines are approached, especially on medium or dull volume. Be sure such a line has not been hugged or hit too frequently.

4. Watch for "crawling along" or repeated bumping of minor or major trend lines and prepare to see such trend lines broken.

5. Breaking of minor trend lines counter to the major trend gives most other important position taking signals. Positions can be taken or reversed on stop at such places.

6. Triangles of ether slope may mean either accumulation or distribution depending on other considerations, although triangles are usually broken on the flat side.

7. Watch for volume climax, especially after a long move.

8. Don't count on gaps being closed unless you can distinguish between breakaway gaps, normal gaps, and exhaustion gaps.

9. During a move, take or increase positions in the direction of the move at the market the morning following any one-day reversal, however slight the reversal may be, especially if volume declines on the reversal.

Donchian's Student

Barbara Dixon was one of the more successful female trend traders in the business. She graduated from Vassar College in 1969, but because she was a woman and a history major, no one would hire her as a stockbroker. Undaunted, she finally took a job at

Shearson as a secretary for Donchian. Dixon received three years of invaluable tutelage in trend following under Donchian. When Donchian moved to Connecticut, she stayed behind to strike out on her own in 1973. Before long, she had some 40 accounts, ranging from $20,000 to well over $1 million.

Losing an illusion makes you wiser than finding a truth.

Ludwig Borne

Dixon saw an uncomplicated genius in Donchian's trading:

"I'm not a mathematician. I believe that the simple solution is the most elegant and the best. Nobody has ever been able to demonstrate to me that a complex mathematical equation can answer the question, 'Is the market moving in an uptrend, downtrend, or sideways.' Any better than looking at a price chart and having simple rules to define those three sets of circumstances. These are the same rules I used back in the late 70s."[105]

Donchian was, once again, ahead of his time when he taught the critical importance of fast and simple decision making, a subject covered in Chapter 7, "Decision Making."

Dixon was fond of pointing out that a good system is one that keeps you alive and keeps your equity intact when there are no trends. She explained that the reason for any system is to get you into the market when a trend establishes itself. Her message is clear: "[D]on't give up the system, even after a string of losses…that is important because that's just when the profits are due."[106]

Dixon doesn't attempt to predict price moves, nor expect to be right every time. She knows she can't forecast the top or bottom of a price move. The hope is that it continues indefinitely because you expect to make money over the long run, but on individual trades, you admit when you're wrong and move on.[107]

Today, most people fixate on the new and fresh fast money idea of the day, yet I still find almost every word Donchian (or Dixon) wrote newer, fresher, and more honest than anything currently broadcast on CNBC. My favorite Donchian wisdom tackles an issue that people are still struggling with in 2009:

"It doesn't matter if you're trading stocks or soybeans. Trading is trading, and the name of the game is increasing your wealth. A trader's job description is stunningly simple: Don't lose money. This is of utmost importance to new traders, who are often told do your research. This is good advice, but should be considered carefully. Research alone won't ensure a profit, and at the end of the day, your main goal should be to make money, not to get an A in How to Read a Balance Sheet."

Donchian's blunt talk may explain why Harvard's finance curriculum does not include mention of Dunn, Henry, Seykota, Campbell, Parker, Abraham, or Donchian himself.

Key Points

Can one know absolutely when price will trend? No. Does one have to know absolutely in order to have a profitable business? No. In fact, a great number of businesses are based on the probability that a time-based series will trend. In fact, if you look at insurance, gambling, and other related businesses, you will come to the conclusion that even a small positive edge can mean great profits.

Chat Forum Post

- Donchian's account dropped below zero following the 1929 stock market crash.
- He was one of the Pentagon whiz kids in World War II. He served as a cryptanalyst and worked closely with Robert McNamara during his Air Force tenure.
- Donchian did not start his trend following fund until age 65. He traded into his 90s. He personally trained legions in the art of trend following. He trained women at a time when women had little respect on Wall Street.
- Donchian: "Nobody has ever been able to demonstrate to me that a complex mathematical equation can answer the question, 'Is the market moving in an up trend, downtrend, or sideways.'"

Jesse Livermore and Dickson Watts

Ed Seykota found wisdom and inspiration through the work of Richard Donchian. But who else influenced trend followers? How long ago did this style of trading start? Trend followers would point to Jesse Livermore, an early twentieth-century stock and commodity trader, who traded as a trend follower long before the term existed.

Livermore was born in South Acton, Massachusetts in 1877. At the age of 15, he went to Boston and began working in Paine Webber's Boston brokerage office. He studied price movements and began to trade their price fluctuations. When Livermore was in his 20s, he moved to New York City to speculate in the stock and commodities markets. After 40 years of trading, he developed a knack for speculating on price movements. One of his foremost rules was, "Never act on tips."

The unofficial biography of Livermore was *Reminiscences of a Stock Operator* first published in 1923 and written by journalist Edwin Lefevre. Readers likely guessed Lefevre as a pseudonym for Livermore himself. *Reminiscences of a Stock Operator* went on to become a Wall Street classic. Numerous quotations and euphemisms from the book are so embedded in trading lore that traders today don't have the slightest idea of their origination. I've selected a few of his best:[108]

1. "It takes a man a long time to learn all the lessons of his mistakes. They say there are two sides to everything. But there is only one side to the stock market; and it is not the bull side or the bear side, but the right side."

2. "I think it was a long step forward in my trading education when I realized at last that when old Mr. Partridge kept on telling the other customers, 'Well, you know this is a bull market!' he really meant to tell them that the big money was not in the individual fluctuations but in the main movements—that is, not in reading the tape, but in sizing up the entire market and its trend."

3. "The reason is that a man may see straight and clearly and yet become impatient or doubtful when the market takes its time about doing as he figured it must do. That is why so many men in Wall Street, who are not at all in the sucker class, not even in the third grade, nevertheless lose money. The market does not beat them. They beat themselves, because though they have brains they cannot sit tight. Old Turkey was dead right in doing and saying what he did. He had not only the courage of his convictions but the intelligent patience to sit tight."

4. " ...The average man doesn't wish to be told that it is a bull or bear market. What he desires is to be told specifically which particular stock to buy or sell. He wants to get something for nothing. He does not wish to work. He doesn't even wish to have to think. It is too much bother to have to count the money that he picks up from the ground."

We love volatility and days like the one in which the stock market took a big plunge, for being on the right side of moving markets is what makes us money. A stagnant market in any commodity, such as grain has experienced recently, means there's no opportunity for us to make money.

Dinesh Desai[109]

5. "A man will risk half his fortune in the stock market with less reflection than he devotes to the selection of a medium-priced automobile."

Think about the wild speculation that took place during the dot-com bubble of the late 1990s, the wild speculation that ended with the October 2008 market crash, and then remember Livermore was referring to the market environment of 75 years ago, not today.

Livermore did write one book: *How to Trade in Stocks: The Livermore Formula for Combining Time, Element, and Price.* It was published in 1940. The book is rare and difficult to find, but a little persistence paid off for me. Livermore was by no means a perfect trader (and he says so). He was no role model. His trading style was bold and extremely volatile. He went broke several times making and losing millions. That said, his personal trading performance does not detract from the wisdom of his words.

Was Livermore the first trend follower? I doubt it. One trader who had an influence on Livermore was Dickson Watts. Watts was president of the New York Cotton Exchange between 1878 and 1880, yet his words are as relevant as ever:

"What is speculation? All business is more or less speculation. The term speculation, however, is commonly restricted to business of exceptional uncertainty. The uninitiated believe that chance is so large a part of speculation that it is subject to no rules, is governed by no laws. This is a serious error. Let us first consider the qualities essential to the equipment of a speculator:

1. Self-reliance: A man must think for himself, must follow his own convictions. Self-trust is the foundation of successful effort.

2. Judgment: That equipoise, that nice adjustment of the facilities one to the other, which is called good judgment, is an essential to the speculator.

3. Courage: That is, confidence to act on the decisions of the mind. In speculation, there is value in Mirabeau's dictum: Be bold, still be bold; always be bold.

4. Prudence: The power of measuring the danger, together with a certain alertness and watchfulness, is important. There should be a balance of these two, prudence and courage; prudence in contemplation, courage in execution. Connected with these qualities, properly an outgrowth of them, is a third, viz: promptness. The mind convinced, the act should follow. Think, act, promptly.

5. Pliability: The ability to change an opinion, the power of revision. 'He who observes,' says Emerson, 'and observes again, is always formidable.'

"The qualifications named are necessary to the makeup of a speculator, but they must be in well-balanced combination. A deficiency or an over plus of one quality will destroy the effectiveness of all. The possession of such faculties, in a proper adjustment is, of course, uncommon. In speculation, as in life, few succeed, many fail."[110]

Ultimately, people want to know why trend following keeps working. Livermore's words from another time answer that question for our time:

"Wall Street never changes, the pockets change, the suckers change, the stocks change, but Wall Street never changes, because human nature never changes."

Key Points

- Trend followers are not lucky. They are prepared for the unexpected.

- Trend followers take what the market offers in the moment. They don't predict the future.

- Making money requires that you be able to live with and accept volatility.

Part II

Performance
Data

3

"The criterion of truth is that it works even if
nobody is prepared to acknowledge it."
—Ludwig von Mises

"What we've got here is failure to communicate. Some men you just
can't reach, so you get what we had here last week, which is the way he
wants it. Well, he gets it. And I don't like it any more than you men."
—*Cool Hand Luke*

Any person can tell you that he has a successful trading method or system, but ultimately the only objective measurement that matters at the end of the day is raw performance. Consider the presented data in this text to be scientific proof of trend following. If a claim is to be made, it must be supported. The numbers in this chapter and Appendix B, "Performance Guide," don't lie.

In reviewing the performance histories from the trend followers profiled in Chapter 2, "Great Trend Followers," I zeroed in on five key concepts to help explain the data:

It is a capital mistake to theorize before one has data.

Sir Arthur Conan Doyle[1]

1. Absolute returns
2. Volatility
3. Drawdown
4. Correlation
5. Zero sum

Absolute Returns

An absolute return trading strategy simply means that you are trying to make the most money possible without being limited to a linkage to an index such as the S&P. Author Alexander Ineichen explains:

"An absolute return manager is essentially an asset manager without a benchmark—Bench marking can be viewed as a method of restricting investment managers so as to limit the potential for surprises, either positive or negative."[2]

Trend followers don't track or attempt to mimic any particular index in their trading—ever. If trend followers had a coat of arms, "Absolute Returns" would be emblazoned upon it. They thrive and profit from the "surprises" that benchmarking by its nature artificially stops.

This ain't clipping coupons. No risk, no return.

Anonymous

Are all trend followers shooting for absolute returns and the most amount of money possible? No, not all play the game full tilt. Jerry Parker, a good trend follower, purposefully aims for lower returns to cater to a different client base (those who want less risk and hence less return).

Trend trader John W. Henry has long made the case for his absolute return strategy:

"JWH's overall objective is to provide absolute returns. JWH is an absolute return manager, insofar as it does not manage against a natural benchmark. Relative return managers, such as most traditional equity or fixed income managers, are measured on how they perform relative to some pre-determined benchmark. JWH has no such investment benchmark, so its aim is to achieve returns in all market conditions, and is thus considered an absolute return manager."[3]

Shoot for a benchmark in return, and you run with the crowd. Benchmarks such as the S&P might make people feel safe, even when that feeling is clearly artificial. Trend followers, on the other hand, understand that trading for absolute returns and not from blind adherence to benchmarks is the best way to handle uncertainty.

The concept of indexing and benchmarking is very useful in the world of traditional, long-only investing, but it has limited usefulness for absolute return investing. Again, it gets back to the notion of what it takes to achieve an absolute return—portfolio managers need to have an enormous amount of latitude and freedom in the execution of their trading strategy to ensure capital preservation and achieve a positive return. At its core, the concept of absolute return investing is almost antithetical to benchmarking, which encourages traditional managers to have similarly structured portfolios and look at their performance on a relative basis.[4]

If you base your trading strategy on benchmark comparisons, it doesn't matter whether you are a talented trader or not because all decisions are made only with respect for what the averages are doing. Why is any trading skill relevant? It's not. That's why 80 percent of mutual funds don't beat the averages.

The class of those who have the ability to think their own thoughts is separated by an unbridgeable gulf from the class of those who cannot.

Ludwig von Mises[6]

Fear of Volatility and Confusion with Risk

There are organizations that rank and track monthly performance numbers. One organization gives a "star ranking" (like Morningstar):

> "The quantitative rating system employed ranks and rates the performance of all commodity trading advisors (CTA)…Ratings are given in four categories: a) equity, b) performance, c) risk exposure, and d) risk-adjusted returns. In each category, the highest possible rating is five stars and the lowest possible rating is one star. The actual statistics on which the percentiles are based as follows:
>
> 1. Performance: Rate of Return
> 2. Risk: Standard Deviation
> 3. Risk Adjusted: Sharpe Ratio
> 4. Equity: Assets"[5]

Volatility is the tendency for prices to change unexpectedly.[1]

Dunn Capital receives one star for "risk," the implication being that an investment with Dunn is risky. However, do these rankings give accurate information on Dunn's true risk? This rating group uses standard deviation as their measure of risk. But is this a measure of volatility and not necessarily risk. High volatility alone does not necessarily mean higher risk.

It's doubtful that Dunn is too concerned about being penalized with this measurement, but using standard deviation as a risk measurement simply distorts critical issues.

The ranking of infamous trader Victor Niederhoffer demonstrates a great example of the star system weakness. At the time of Niederhoffer's public-trading demise in 1997 (more on Niederhoffer in Chapter 4, "Big Events, Crashes, and Panics"), he was rated as four stars for "risk." Based on the past performance of Niederhoffer, the rankings were saying that he was a much "safer bet" than Dunn. Obviously, the star system failed for people who believed Niederhoffer was less "risky." Standard deviation as a risk measure has done trend followers an injustice. One of my goals is to dispel the simplistic notion that trend following is "just risky" or that they "all have high standard deviations," which means they are "bad."

Where does proper analysis begin? Examine the following chart of various trend following performances for 10 years (see Chart 3.1):

CHART 3.1: Absolute Return: Annualized ROR (January 1993–June 2003)

Trading Managers	Annualized ROR	Compounded ROR
1 Eckhardt Trading Co. (Higher Leverage)	31.14%	1622.80%
2 Dunn Capital Management, Inc. (World Monetary Asset)	27.55%	1186.82%
3 Dolphin Capital Management Inc. (Global Diversified I)	23.47%	815.33%
4 Eckhardt Trading Co. (Standard)	22.46%	739.10%
5 KMJ Capital Management, Inc. (Currency)	21.95%	703.59%
6 Beach Capital Management Ltd (Discretionary)	21.54%	675.29%

Trading Managers	Annualized ROR	Compounded ROR
7 Mark J. Walsh & Company (Standard)	20.67%	618.88%
8 Saxon Investment Corp. (Diversified)	19.25%	534.83%
9 Man Inv. Products, Ltd (AHL Composite Pro Forma)	17.66%	451.77%
10 John W. Henry & Company, Inc. (Global Diversified)	17.14%	426.40%
11 John W. Henry & Company, Inc. (Financial & Metals)	17.07%	423.08%
12 Dreiss Research Corporation (Diversified)	16.47%	395.71%
13 Abraham Trading Co. (Diversified)	15.91%	371.08%
14 Dunn Capital Management, Inc. (Targets of Opportunity System)	14.43%	311.66%
15 Rabar Market Research (Diversified)	14.09%	299.15%
16 John W. Henry & Company, Inc. (International Foreign Exchange)	13.89%	291.82%
17 Hyman Beck & Company, Inc. (Global Portfolio)	12.98%	260.18%
18 Campbell and Company (Fin. Met. & Energy—Large)	12.73%	251.92%
19 Chesapeake Capital Corporation (Diversified)	12.70%	250.92%
20 Millburn Ridgefield Corporation (Diversified)	11.84%	223.88%
21 Campbell and Company (Global Diversified—Large)	11.64%	217.75%
22 Tamiso & Co., LLC (Original Currency Account)	11.42%	211.29%
23 JPD Enterprises, Inc. (Global Diversified)	11.14%	203.03%

At some point, just saying a trader is volatile makes little sense if you examine absolute return performance (Chart 3.1). Raw absolute returns should count for something other than fear.

However, volatility (what standard deviation measures) is still a four-letter word for most market participants. Volatility scares people; even when a freshman student can quickly analyze any historical data series of any market or trend follower and see that volatility is normal, many investors run away from a hint of volatility (even when running is not even possible). Of course, some markets and traders are more volatile than others, but degrees of volatility are a basic fact of life. To trend followers, volatility is the precursor to profit. No volatility equals no opportunity for profit.

The press is just as confused with the concept of volatility as seen in this excerpt from *Business Week*:

> "Trend followers are trying to make sense out of their dismal recent returns. 'When you look past the superficial question of how we did, you look under the hood and see immense change in the global markets,' says John W. Henry's president. 'Volatility is just a harbinger of new trends to come.' Maybe. But futures traders are supposed to make money by exploiting volatility. Performance isn't a 'superficial question' if you were among the thousands of commodity-fund customers who lost money when the currency markets went bonkers."[8]

Focusing on one time period in isolation while ignoring a complete performance history does not present the full picture. I wondered if this reporter had written a follow-up article correcting his observations about trend following since the following year trend trader Dunn produced a 60.25 percent return and trend trader Parker produced a 61.82 percent return. It didn't surprise me when my search of all *Business Week* archives revealed nothing resembling a follow-up or correction.

Some people suggested a few years ago that trend following had been marginalized. The answer is we haven't been marginalized—[trend following] has played a key role in helping protect a lot of people's wealth this year.

Mark Rzepczynski, President and Chief Investment Officer (CIO) of John W. Henry & Co, 2003[9]

Volatility

Nicola Meaden, a hedge fund researcher, compared monthly standard deviations (volatility as measured from the mean) and semi-standard deviations (volatility measured on the downside only) and found that although trend followers arguably experience higher volatility, it is often concentrated on the upside (positive returns), not the downside (negative returns).

What does this mean? Trend following performance is unfairly penalized by performance measures such as the Sharpe ratio. The Sharpe ratio does not care whether volatility is on the plus or the minus side because it does not account for the difference between the standard deviation and the semi-standard deviation. The actual formula for calculating them is identical, with one exception, the semi-standard deviation looks only at observations below the mean. If the semi-standard deviation is lower than the standard deviation, the historical pull away from the mean has to be on the plus side. If it is higher, the pull away from the mean is on the minus side. Meaden points out the huge difference that puts trend following volatility on the upside if you compare monthly standard (12.51) and semi-standard (5.79) deviation.[10]

Here is another way of thinking about upside volatility: Ponder a market that is going up. You enter at $100 and the market goes to $150. Then the market drops down to $125. Is that necessarily bad? No. Because after going from $100 to $150 and then dropping back to $125, the market might then zoom up to $175. This is upside volatility in action.

Trading is a zero-sum game in an important accounting sense. In a zero-sum game, the total gains of the winners are exactly equal to the total losses of the losers.[12]

Trend followers have greater upside volatility and less downside volatility than traditional equity indices such as the S&P because they exit losing trades quickly with preset stop losses. This means they have many small losses as they constantly try to see if an entry into a market pans out into a big trend.

Michael Rulle, president of Graham Capital, helps to mitigate volatility fears:

> "A trend follower achieves positive returns by correctly targeting market direction and minimizing the cost of this portfolio. Thus, while trend following is sometimes referred to as being 'long volatility,' trend followers technically do not trade volatility, although they often benefit from it."[11]

The question, then, is not how to reduce volatility (you can't control the market after all), but how to manage it through proper position sizing or money management.

Bottom line, you have to get used to riding the bucking bronco. Great trend traders don't see straight up equity curves in their accounts, so you are in good company when it comes to the up and down nature of making money.

John W. Henry makes clear the distinction between volatility and risk:

"...Risk is very different from volatility. A lot of people believe there is no difference, but there's a huge difference and I can spend an hour on that topic. Suffice it to say that we embrace both volatility and risk and, for us, risk is that we're going to lose if we risk two tenths of one percent on a particular trade. That is, to us, real risk. Giving back a profit to you probably seems like risk, to us it seems like volatility."

Some people seem to like to lose, so they win by losing money.

Ed Seykota[14]

Henry's long-term world-view doesn't avoid high volatility. The last thing he wants to experience is volatility that forces him out of a major trend before he can make big profits. Dinesh Desai, a trend follower from the 1980s, was fond of saying that he loved volatility. Being on the right side of a volatile market was the source of his profits.

However, the skeptics mistakenly view high volatility, the engine that drives trend following's spectacular returns, as consistently negative. For example, a fund manager who manages $1.5 billion in assets remains on the sidelines refusing to believe in trend following:

"My biggest source of hesitancy about the asset class [trend following] is its reliance on technical analysis. Trading advisors do seem to profit, but because they rarely incorporate economic data, they simply ride price trends until they reverse. The end result of this crude approach is a subpar return to risk ratio." Another money manager opines: "Why should I give money to a AA baseball player when I can hire someone in the major leagues?"[13]

How can one look at the absolute performance of great trend traders and call it AA baseball? I wonder if this manager still exists following October 2008? Weren't the funds and banks that blew out all considered Major League? If you can get beyond the majority's irrational fear of volatility, you can learn how volatility really matters. Trend follower Jason Russell states for him when volatility starts:

"Volatility matters when you feel it. All the charts, ratios, and advanced math in the world mean nothing when you break down, vomit, or cry due to the volatility in your portfolio. I call this the vomitility threshold. Understanding your threshold is important for it is at this point that you lose all confidence and throw in the towel. Traders, portfolio managers, and mathematicians seem well equipped to describe risk with a battery of formulas and ratios they use to measure volatility. However, even if you can easily handle the math, it can be a challenge to truly conceptualize it. The simple fact is that for the investor, the act of truly working through the thoughts and feelings that accompany losing money is hard. It is about as enjoyable as working through the thoughts and feelings associated with your death when preparing a will. There is no mathematical formula for vomitility because it is different for each person…For the [trader] who wants anything other than an interest-paying deposit at the bank, I think I can sum it up as follows: Surrender to the reality that volatility exists or volatility will introduce you to the reality that surrender exists."

If you were to put all the trend following models side by side, you would probably find that most made profits and incurred losses in the same markets. They were all looking at the same charts and obtaining the same perception of opportunity.

Marc Goodman, Kenmar Asset Allocation[16]

Russell's comments, however, don't mean people easily accept his wisdom. Trend trader David Harding has seen the persistent confusion. He was recently asked: "You've attracted quite a lot of new money into the fund since you've launched, but particularly in the last couple of years. Why?"

Harding replied: "I think that the market has bought what actually is quite a complicated story. The Winton story [his firm] is not a simple story. In our early years, we were impeded by the terrific performance of dot-com stocks. Later people became very attracted to certain types of hedge funds, which produced very smooth and steady returns; something which we've never purported to do. And, to be honest, as I said before, the Winton story, obviously I believe in it, but it isn't simple and I'm not that surprised that it took the market some time to show considerable enthusiasm for it. But now that the story has been got across better, people are, I think, realizing that Winton is a good horse to back in the race…"

Drawdowns

With volatility comes the inevitable drawdown. What do I mean? A drawdown is any losing period during an investment record. It is defined as the percent retrenchment from an equity peak to an equity valley. A drawdown is in effect from the time an equity retrenchment begins until a new equity high is reached, i.e., in terms of time, a drawdown encompasses both the period from equity peak to equity valley (length) and the time from the equity valley to a new equity high (recovery).[15]

For example, if you start from $100,000 and drop to $50,000, you are in a 50 percent drawdown. You could also just say that you have lost 50 percent. Thus, the drawdown is just a reduction in account equity.

Dunn Capital Management's documents include a "summary of serious past losses." The summary explains that the firm has suffered through seven difficult periods of losses of 25 percent or more. Every potential investor receives a copy. Dunn says the summary communicates that this is what happened before and it will happen again. "If the investor is not willing to live through this, they are not the right investor for the portfolio," Dunn says.[18]

Unfortunately, many investors and regulators have made drawdown a dirty word. Trend traders are often forced to talk about their drawdowns in a negative way, as if to make excuses for taking smart losses in the context of an overall trading system. Consider this excerpt from Dunn Capital's marketing materials:

"Investors should be aware of the volatility inherent to [our] trading programs. Because the same portfolio risk profile is intrinsic to all...programs, investors in any... program can be expected to experience volatility similar to [our] composite record. During 26+ years of trading, the composite record, on a month-to-month basis, has experienced eight serious losses exceeding 25 percent. The eighth such loss equaled 40 percent, beginning in September 1999 and extending through September 2000. This loss was recovered in the three-month period ending in December 2000. The most serious loss in [our] entire history occurred over a four-month period, which ended in February 1976 and equaled 52 percent [Dunn did have a 57 percent loss in 2007, which it has nearly recovered from]. Clients should be prepared to endure similar or worse periods in the future. The inability (or unwillingness) to do so will probably result in serious loss, without the opportunity for subsequent recovery."[17]

Unless you truly understand how Dunn trades, you might refuse to consider investing with him, even though his 30-year plus track record is the envy of most.

Examine this drawdown history (see Chart 3.2):

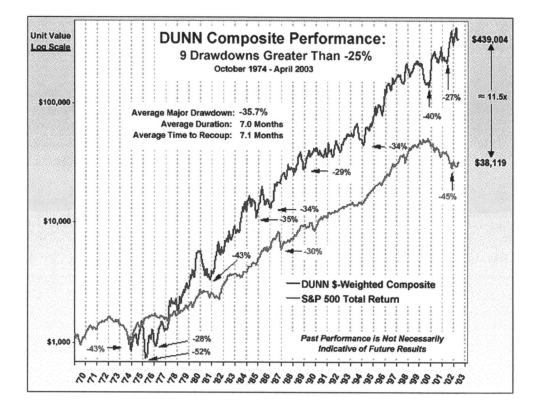

CHART 3.2: Dunn Drawdown Chart. Source: Dunn Capital Management

Imagine that the valleys between the peaks are filled with water. First, place a piece of paper over the chart and then slowly move the paper to the right and uncover the chart. Imagine that you have made a large investment in the fund. How do you feel as you move the page? How long can you remain underwater? How deep can you dive? Do you pull out the calculator and figure out what you could have earned at the bank? Do you figure out that you lost enough to buy a vacation, car, or house or perhaps solve the hunger crisis in a small country?

Obviously you don't want to overhaul a program in response to one year just because something didn't work. That's when you're almost guaranteed that it would have worked the next year had you kept it in there.

James Klingler, Eclipse Capital, MAR, April 2002, Issue No. 278

The 25 or 50 biggest trend followers are essentially going to make money in the same places. What differentiates them from one another are portfolio and risk management.[19]

To the smart investor, this drawdown chart (Chart 3.2) is acceptable because of the absolute returns over the long term, but of course that doesn't make those numbers necessarily easy to live with.

An accurate discussion of trend following drawdown inevitably leads to the recovery conversation, which simply means bringing capital back to the point where a drawdown began. Historically, trend followers quickly make money back during recovery from drawdowns.

However, you can't neglect the math associated with losing money and making it back. What if you start with $100 and it drops to $50? You are now in a 50 percent drawdown. How much do you have to make just to get back to breakeven (Chart 3.3)? One hundred percent. That's right, when you go down 50 percent, you need to make back 100 percent to get to breakeven again.

Notice that as drawdown increases (see Chart 3.3), the percent gain necessary to recover to the breakeven point increases at a much faster rate. Trend followers live with this chart daily. Their strategy is designed to deal with the following math:

CHART 3.3:   Drawdown Recovery Chart

Size of drawdown	Percent gain to recover
5%	5.3%
10%	11.1%
15%	17.6%
20%	25.0%
25%	33.3%
30%	42.9%
40%	66.7%
50%	100%
60%	150%
70%	233%
80%	400%
90%	900%
100%	Ruin

Unfortunately, the investment community uses drawdown numbers to paint an incomplete picture of trend following. Trend trader David Harding of Winton Capital offered insight:

"A key measure of track record quality and strategy 'riskiness' in the managed futures industry is drawdown, which measures the decline in net asset value from the historic high point. Under the Commodity Futures Trading Commission's mandatory disclosure regime, managed futures advisors are obliged to disclose as part of their capsule performance record their 'worst peak-to-valley drawdown.' As a description of an aspect of historical performance, drawdown has one key positive attribute: It refers to a physical reality, and as such, it is less abstract than concepts such as volatility. It represents the amount by which you are less well off than you were; or, put differently, it measures the magnitude of the loss an investor could have incurred by investing with the manager in the past. Managers are obliged to wear their worst historical drawdown like a scarlet letter for the rest of their lives."[20]

That said if the entire story of an absolute return trading strategy is revealed, fearing a drawdown is mitigated. For example, here is drawdown and recovery in action (Chart 3.4):

We have not made any changes because of a drawdown. While we have made minor changes since the program started trading in 1974, over the course of the years the basic concepts have never changed. The majority of the trading parameters and the buy and sell signals largely have remained the same.

Bill Dunn[21]

CHART 3.4: JWH Financial and Metals Portfolio, January 1, 1989 through October 31, 1999 Source: John W. Henry and Company[22]

	−10% or More	−15% or More	−20% or More	−25% or More	−30% or More
# Month-End Occurrences	28	18	10	7	3
Average Drawdown	−19.7%	−24.0%	−29.2%	−31.7%	−37.5%
# Profitable 12 Months Later	25	17	All	All	All
Average Profit 12 Months Later	+52.4%	+58.6%	+73.5%	+74.8%	+96.1%
Average Time to New Peak through Trough	4 months	4 months	4 months	4 months	4 months

You have to keep trading the way you were before the drawdown and also be patient. There's always part of a trader's psyche that wants to make losses back tomorrow. But traders need to remember you lose it really fast, but you make it up slowly. You may think you can make it up fast, but it doesn't work that way.

David Druz[23]

This historical recovery bolsters my words with cold, hard numbers. However, you can't eliminate catastrophic risk, much less drawdowns, from your trading. A great example of getting scared right at the wrong time during a drawdown can be seen in a story relayed to me by trend following trader Justin Vandergrift:

"In the summer of 2006, I opened an account for a client. At the time we were down 10–12 percent, and I explained the drawdown and our expectation for losses. Suddenly, when his account went down 20 percent, he became very anxious. He eventually closed his account. He made the business decision to stop trading because of the pain he was feeling from the drawdown. I continued to track his account hypothetically so I could see what would happen if he would have continued trading. As it turns out, he closed his account within 2 days of the drawdown low. Had he stayed invested he would be up +121.1 percent from his closing value, and +71.6 percent from his starting value (through October 2008). I am reminded of a statement quoted many times from Peter Lynch, the manager of the Fidelity Magellan Fund. In light of Lynch's trading success, he revealed that over 50 percent of the investors in his fund lost money. He explained the reason—most investors pulled out at the wrong time. They traded with their gut and treated drawdowns as a cancer, rather than the natural ebb and flow of trading."

Interestingly, there is another perspective on drawdowns that few people consider. When you look at trend following performance data—for example, Dunn's track record—you can't help but notice that certain times are better than others to invest with Dunn.

Smart clients of Dunn look at his performance chart and buy in when his fund is experiencing a drawdown. Why? Because if he is down 30 percent, and you know from analysis of past performance data that his recovery from drawdowns is typically quick, why not "buy" Dunn while he is on sale? This is commonly referred to as equity curve trading. Trend trader Tom Basso makes the case:

Correlation coefficient: A statistical measure of the interdependence of two or more random variables. Fundamentally, the value indicates how much of a change in one variable is explained by a change in another.[25]

"I haven't met a trader yet that wouldn't say privately that he would tend to buy his program on a drawdown, particularly systematic traders. But, investors seem to not add money when, to traders, it seems to be most logical to do so…Why don't investors invest on drawdowns? I believe the answer to that question lies in the investing psychology of buying a drawdown. The human mind can easily extrapolate three months of negative returns into 'how long at this rate will it take to lose 50 percent or everything?' Rather than seeing the bargain and the positive return to risk, they see only the negative and forecast more of the same into the future."[24]

Not only do trend followers tell clients to buy into their funds during a drawdown, but they also buy into their own funds with their own capital during the drawdowns. I know many employees at top trend who follow funds and are giddy when they are in a drawdown because they know they can buy their fund "cheap."

Do other trading styles have drawdowns? You bet. For example, look at the return you would have generated by buying and holding the NASDAQ index since 2000, a still 71 percent drawdown as of November 2008. Does it seem like a recovery is right around the corner? On top of that example, some of the best names on Wall Street (nontrend followers) have had tough sledding in 2008:

Warren Buffett (Berkshire Hathaway): –43 percent

Ken Heebner (CMG Focus Fund): –56 percent

Harry Lange (Fidelity Magellan): –59 percent

Bill Miller (Legg Mason Value Trust): –50 percent

Ken Griffin (Citadel): –44 percent

Carl Icahn (Icahn Enterprises): –81 percent

T. Boone Pickens: Down $2 billion since July 2008

Kirk Kerkorian: Down $693 million on Ford shares alone

Drawdowns happen. The key is to determine how quickly and successfully you can recover and get back to making new money again, but a comparison between trend trading drawdowns and buy and hold drawdowns doesn't seem to be much of a comparison.

Maryland-based Campbell and Co., a trend following managed futures firm with almost $3 billion in assets under management, has returned 17.65 percent since its inception in 1972, proving that performance can be sustainable over the long-term.[26]

The Millburn Diversified Portfolio has a 10 percent allocation which has historically exhibited superior performance characteristics coupled with an almost zero correlation of monthly returns to those of traditional investments. If an investor had invested 10 percent of his or her portfolio in the Millburn Diversified Portfolio from February 1977 through August 2003 he or she would have increased the return on his or her traditional portfolio by 73 basis points (a 6.2 percent increase) and decreased risk (as measured by standard deviation) by 0.26 of a percent (an 8.2 percent decrease).

www.millburncorp.com

Correlation

Correlation comparisons help to show that trend following is a legitimate style and demonstrate the similarity of performances among trend followers. Correlation is not only important in assembling the portfolio you trade (see Chapter 9, "Holy Grails"), but it is a critical tool to analyze and compare performance histories of trend followers. Unlike misguided comparisons, such as using standard deviation, I find correlation comparisons of performance data useful.

In a research paper titled "Learning to Love Non-Correlation," correlation is defined as "a statistical term giving the strength of linear relationship between two random variables. It is the historical tendency of one thing to move in tandem with another." The correlation coefficient is a number from –1 to +1, with –1 being the perfectly opposite behavior of two investments (for example, up 5 percent every time the other is down 5 percent). The +1 reflects identical investment results (up or down the same amount each period). The further away from +1 one gets (and thus closer to –1), the better a diversifier one investment is for the other. But because his firm is keenly aware of keeping things simple, it also provides another description of correlation: the tendency for one investment to "zig" while another "zags."[27]

I took the monthly performance numbers of trend followers and computed their correlation coefficients. Comparing correlations provided evidence that trend followers trade typically the same markets in the same way at the same time.

Look at the correlation chart (see Chart 3.5) and ask yourself: "Why do two trend followers who don't work in the same office, who are on opposite sides of the continent, have the same three losing months in a row with similar percentage losses?" Then ask: "Why do they have the same winning month, then the same two losing months, and then the same three winning months in a row?" The relationship is there because they can respond only to what the market offers. The market offers trends to everyone equally. They're all looking at the same market aiming for the same target of opportunity.

Does Chart 3.5 mean trend followers are using similar techniques? Absolutely.

CHART 3.5: Correlation Among Trend Followers

	AbrDiv	CamFin	CheDiv	DUNWor	EckSta	JohFin	ManAHL	MarSta	RabDiv
AbrDiv	1.00	0.56	0.81	0.33	0.57	0.55	0.56	0.75	0.75
CamFin	0.56	1.00	0.59	0.62	0.60	0.56	0.51	0.57	0.55
CheDiv	0.81	0.59	1.00	0.41	0.53	0.55	0.60	0.72	0.75
DUNWor	0.33	0.62	0.41	1.00	0.57	0.62	0.61	0.51	0.45
EckSta	0.57	0.60	0.53	0.57	1.00	0.57	0.58	0.74	0.71
JohFin	0.55	0.56	0.55	0.62	0.57	1.00	0.53	0.55	0.50
ManAHL	0.56	0.51	0.60	0.61	0.58	0.53	1.00	0.57	0.59
MarSta	0.75	0.57	0.72	0.51	0.74	0.55	0.57	1.00	0.68
RabDiv	0.75	0.55	0.75	0.45	0.71	0.50	0.59	0.68	1.00

AbrDiv: Abraham Trading Co.
CamFin: Campbell and Co.
CheDiv: Chesapeake Capital Corporation
DUNWor: DUNN Capital Management, Inc.
EckSta: Eckhardt Trading Co.
JohFin: John W. Henry & Company, Inc.
ManAHL: Man Inv. Products, Ltd
MarSta: Mark J. Walsh & Company
RabDiv: Rabar Market Research

Surprisingly, correlation can be a touchy subject for some trend followers. The Turtles (see Chapter 2) were all grateful to Richard Dennis for his mentoring, but some seemed to become ambivalent over time, obviously indebted to Dennis but struggling to achieve their own identity:

> "[One Turtle] says his system is 95 percent Dennis' system and the rest his 'own flair…I'm a long way from someone who follows the system mechanically…but by far, the structure of what I do is based on Richard's systems, and certainly, philosophically, everything I do in terms of trading is based on what I learned from Richard.'"[28]

Even when correlation data still shows similar patterns of trading among Dennis' Turtle students, the desire to differentiate themselves from each other is stronger than their need to honestly address obvious similarities in their return streams:

"There no longer is a turtle trading style in my mind. We've all evolved and developed systems that are very different from those we were taught, and that independent evolution suggests that the dissimilarities to trading between turtles are always increasing."[29]

A Turtle correlation chart paints a clear picture. The relationship is solid. The data (Chart 3.6) is the judge:

CHART 3.6: Correlation Among Turtle Traders

	Chesapeake	Eckhardt	Hawksbill	JPD	Rabar
Chesapeake	1	0.53	0.62	0.75	0.75
Eckhardt	0.53	1	0.7	0.7	0.71
Hawksbill	0.62	0.7	1	0.73	0.76
JPD	0.75	0.7	0.73	1	0.87
Rabar	0.75	0.71	0.76	0.87	1

Correlation coefficients gauge how closely an advisor's performance resembles another advisor. Values exceeding 0.66 might be viewed as having significant positive performance correlation. Consequently, values exceeding –0.66 might be viewed as having significant negative performance correlation.
Chesapeake Capital Corporation
Eckhardt Trading Co.
Hawksbill Capital Management
JPD Enterprises Inc.
Rabar Market Research

Of course, there is more to the story than just correlation. Although correlations show the Turtles trade in similar ways, their returns can also differ because of their individual leverage choices. Some traders use more leverage, whereas others, such as Jerry Parker, use less. Parker explains, "The bigger the trade, the greater the returns and the greater the drawdowns. It's a double-edged sword."[30]

Zero Sum Nature of the Markets

Zero-sum trading is arguably the most important concept in this chapter. Larry Harris, chair in Finance at the Marshall School of Business at University of Southern California, gets to the crux of the matter:

"Trading is a zero-sum game when gains and losses are measured relative to the market average. In a zero-sum game, someone can win only if somebody else loses."[31]

Another good explanation of zero sum is found in "The Winners and Losers of the Zero-Sum Game: The Origins of Trading Profits, Price Efficiency and Market Liquidity," a white paper authored by Harris. In speaking with Harris, he told me that he was amazed at how many people came from the TurtleTrader.com website to his site to download his white paper on zero-sum trading.

In brief, Harris examines what factors determine who wins and who loses when trading. He does this by categorizing traders by type and then evaluating their trading styles to determine whether the styles lead to profits or losses. Harris adds:

"Winning traders can only profit to the extent that other traders are willing to lose. Traders are willing to lose when they obtain external benefits from trading. The most important external benefits are expected returns from holding risky securities that represent deferred consumption. Hedging and gambling provide other external benefits. Markets would not exist without utilitarian traders. Their trading losses fund the winning traders who make prices efficient and provide liquidity."[32]

There are those who absolutely do not accept that there must be a loser for them to be a winner. They cannot live with the idea that everyone can't win. Although they want to win, many do not want to live with the guilt that by their winning, someone else has to lose. This is a poorly thought out, yet an all too common view of the mindset of a losing trader.

What separates winners from losers? Harris was clear: "On any given transaction, the chances of winning or losing may be near even. In the long run, however, winners profit from trading because they have some persistent advantages that allow them to win slightly more often (or occasionally much bigger) than losers win."[33]

For anyone who has ever played poker or studied "edges" in gambling, Harris' words ring true:

"To trade profitably in the long run, you must know your edge, you must know when it exists, and you must focus your trading to exploit it when you can. If you have no edge, you should not trade for profit. If you know you have no edge, but you must trade for other reasons, you should organize your trading to minimize your losses to those who do have an edge. Recognizing your edge is a prerequisite to predicting whether trading will be profitable."[34]

The noted finance professor Robert Samuelson adds, "For every trader betting on higher prices, another is betting on lower prices. These trades are matched. In the stock market, all investors (buyers and sellers) can profit in a rising market, and all can lose in a falling market. In futures markets, one trader's gain is another's loss."

In "The Gartman Letter," Dennis Gartman clarifies the situation even more: "In the world of futures speculation, for every long there is an equal and opposite short. That is, unlike the world of equity trading where there needn't be equal numbers of longs versus shorts, in the world of futures dealing there is. Money is neither made, nor lost, in futures; it is simply moved from one pocket to the next as margins are swapped at the close of trading each day. Thus, every time there is a buyer betting that prices shall rise in the future, there is an equal seller taking the very opposite 'bet,' betting that prices will fall."

These observations will save your skin if you're willing to accept them, but as you can see throughout this chapter and the next, many traders are either ignorant of zero-sum thinking, choose to ignore it, or refuse to believe it.

George Soros and Zero Sum

The success of famed trader George Soros is well known.

He is the best-known hedge fund manager. In 1992 he was called 'the man who broke the British Pound' for placing $10 billion in bets against the British pound that netted him at least $1 billion in profit.[35]

That said, even really smart guys sometimes miss the key point. Years back, Soros appeared on *Nightline*, the ABC news program.

The following exchange between Soros and then host Ted Koppel goes straight to the core of zero sum:

Ted Koppel: "...as you describe it, it [the market] is, of course, a game in which there are real consequences. When you bet and you win, that's good for you, it's bad for those against whom you have bet. There are always losers in this kind of a game?"

George Soros: "No. See, it's not a zero-sum game. It's very important to realize..."

Ted Koppel: "Well, it's not zero sum in terms of investors. But, for example, when you bet against the British pound that was not good for the British economy?"

George Soros: "Well, it happened to be quite good for the British economy. It was not, let's say, good for the British treasury because they were on the other side of the trade...It's not—your gain is not necessarily somebody else's loss."

Ted Koppel: "Because—I mean put it in easily understandable terms—I mean if you could have profited by destroying Malaysia's currency, would you have shrunk from that?"

George Soros: "Not necessarily because that would have been an unintended consequence of my action. And it's not my job as a participant to calculate the consequences. This is what a market is. That's the nature of a market. So I'm a participant in the market."

Soros opens a can of worms with his view on zero sum. Here's an online weblog post that incorrectly analyzes Soros' interview. The poster argues:

> "Cosmetically, Koppel wipes the floor with Soros. He's able to portray Soros as a person who destroys lives and economies without a second thought, as well as simplify, beyond belief, something that should not be simplified."[36]

This is nonsense. The fact that Soros is a player in the market does not establish him as a destroyer of lives. You might disagree with Soros' political ideology, but you can't question his morality for participation in the market. Do you have a 401k plan designed to generate profits from the market? Of course you do, just like Soros.

Others, such as Lawrence Parks, a union activist, correctly states that Soros is in a zero-sum game, but gets sidetracked by declaring zero sum unfair and harsh for the "working man":

What objectivity and the study of philosophy requires is not an "open mind," but an active mind—a mind able and eagerly willing to examine ideas, but to examine them critically.

Ayn Rand[37]

I believe the answer lies in coming to terms with what Heisenberg's research uncovered in the field of physics: that we cannot expect to accurately predict the future given this present environment. There are quite simply too many mixed signals, and too much uncertainty. In my view, we just cannot expect to understand the present situation with any exactness. Perhaps a more reasonable approach would be to embrace the uncertainty. Once we embrace the uncertainty, we may be able to use it to our advantage.

Jon C. Sundt, President,
Altegris Investments,
2nd Quarter 2004 Commentary

"Since currency and derivative trading are zero-sum games, every dollar 'won' requires that a dollar was 'lost.' Haven't they realized what a losing proposition this has been? What's more, why do they keep playing at a losing game? The answer is that the losers are all of us. And, while neither rich nor stupid, we've been given no choice but to continue to lose. And every time one of these fiat currencies cannot be 'defended,' the workers, seniors, and business owners of that country—folks like us—suffer big time. Indeed, as their currencies are devalued, workers' savings and future payments, such as their pensions, denominated in those currencies lose purchasing power. Interest rates increase. Through no fault of their own, working people lose their jobs in addition to their savings. There have been press reports that, after a lifetime of working and saving, people in Indonesia are eating bark off the trees and boiling grass soup. While not a secret, it is astonishing to learn how sanguine the beneficiaries have become of their advantage over the rest of us. For example, famed financier George Soros in his recent The Crisis of Global Capitalism plainly divulges: 'The Bank of England was on the other side of my transactions and I was taking money out of the pockets of British taxpayers.' To me, the results of this wealth transfer are inescapable."[38]

Parks argues that the only choice he has been given is to lose. He loses; his union loses. It seems everyone loses in the zero-sum game. Of course, there are winners and he knows that. The zero-sum game is, indeed, a wealth transfer. The winners profit from the losers. Parks correctly describes the nature of the zero-sum game, but positions the game in terms of morality. Life is not fair. If you don't like being a loser in the zero-sum game, perhaps it is time to consider how the winners play the game.

Although it might appear that I am defending Soros, I am not. The market is a zero-sum game. Trying to understand Soros' reasons for denying this would be speculation on my part. Soros is not always a zero-sum winner either. Soros was on the losing side of the zero-sum game during the Long Term Capital Management fiasco in 1998. He lost $2 billion. (I discuss this in more detail in Chapter 4.) He also had severe trouble in the 2000 technology meltdown:

"With bets that went sour on technology stocks and on Europe's new currency, the five funds run by Soros Fund Management have suffered a 20 percent decline this year and, at $14.4 billion, are down roughly a third from a peak of $22 billion in August 1998."[39]

It's all a matter of perspective. What some consider a catastrophic flood, others deem a cleansing bath.

Gregory J. Millman[42]

These wins and losses seem to have taken a toll on Soros: "Maybe I don't understand the market. Maybe the music has stopped but people are still dancing. I am anxious to reduce my market exposure and be more conservative. We will accept lower returns because we will cut the risk profile."[40]

I don't see evidence that the market has changed. Nor has the zero-sum game of the markets changed. However, something might have changed within George Soros.

Dot-Com Meets Zero Sum

Judge Milton Pollack's ruling a few years back that dismissed class action suits clearly illustrates the concept of zero sum. He minces no words in warning whiners about the game they are playing:

> "Seeking to lay the blame for the enormous Internet bubble solely at the feet of a single actor, Merrill Lynch, plaintiffs would have this Court conclude that the federal securities laws were meant to underwrite, subsidize, and encourage their rash speculation in joining a freewheeling casino that lured thousands obsessed with the fantasy of Olympian riches, but which delivered such riches to only a scant handful of lucky winners. Those few lucky winners, who are not before the Court, now hold the monies that the unlucky plaintiffs have lost, fair and square, and they will never return those monies to plaintiffs. Had plaintiffs themselves won the game instead of losing, they would have owed not a single penny of their winnings to those they left to hold the bag (or to defendants)."[41]

A 96-year-old judge bluntly telling the plaintiffs to take responsibility for their own actions might have been painful reading for investors who were following the case hoping for a bailout. Pollack nails the losers for trying to circumvent the zero-sum market process by using the legal process. He is basically saying that there would be no free lunch.

The harsh reality of the markets is that you only have yourself to blame for the decisions you make with your money. You can make losing decisions or winning decisions. It's your choice.

David Druz, a student of Ed Seykota and a longtime trend follower, takes Judge Pollack's ruling a step further and spells out the practical effects of the market's zero-sum nature:

If all it took to beat the markets was a Ph.D. in mathematics, there'd be a hell of a lot of rich mathematicians out there.

Bill Dries[43]

"Everyone who enters the market thinks they will win, but obviously there are losers as well. Somebody has to be losing to you if you are winning, so we always like to stress that you should know from whom you're going to take profits, because if you're buying, the guy that's selling thinks he's going to be right, too."

The market is a brutal place. Forget trying to be liked. Need a friend? Get a dog. The market doesn't know you and never will. If you are going to win, someone else has to lose. Don't like these survival-of-the-fittest rules? Then stay out of the zero-sum game.

Key Points

- Trend followers always prepare for drawdowns after strong periods of performance.
- An absolute return strategy means you are trying to make the most money possible.
- The fact that markets are volatile is not a problem. The problem is you if volatility scares you.
- Trading is a zero-sum game in an important accounting sense. In a zero-sum game, the total gains of the winners are exactly equal to the total losses of the losers.
- Trend followers go to the market to trade trends. However, not all market players are trying to do the same thing. Fannie Mae could be making a change in their bond portfolio. A major investment bank could be trading a strategy that will not tolerate volatility. The bottom line is that people trade for

different goals. George Crapple, a trend follower with 25+ years in experience, makes the point: "So while it may be a zero-sum game, a lot of people don't care. It's not that they're stupid; it's not speculative frenzy; they're just using these markets for a completely different purpose."

Big Events, Crashes, and Panics

4

"I have noticed that everyone who ever told me that the markets are efficient is poor." —Larry Hite, Mint Investment Management Company

"Rare events are always unexpected, otherwise they would not occur."
—Nassim Taleb[1]

To comprehend trend following's true impact, you have to look at trend followers' performance data—the returns they generate. Their performance data makes clear that they were the winners in the biggest trading events, bubbles, and crashes of the last 30 years. This chapter outlines high profile times where trend followers won huge profits in the zero-sum game.

An investment in DUNN acts as a hedge against unpredictable market crises.

Dunn Capital Management

Wall Street is famous for corporate collapses or mutual and hedge fund blow-ups that transfer capital from winners to losers and back again. However, interestingly, the winners always seem to be missing from the after-the-fact analysis of the mainstream media. The press is fascinated with losers. Taking their lead from the press, the public also gets caught up in the drama and narrative of the losers, oblivious to the real story: Who are the winners and why?

Occasionally, the right question is asked:

"Each time there's a derivatives disaster, I get the same question: If Barings was the loser, who was the winner? If Orange County was the loser, who was the winner? If Procter & Gamble was the loser, who was the winner?"[2]

I'd say that Procter & Gamble did what their name says, they proctored and gambled. And now they're complaining.

Leo Melamed

Prominent academics in finance searching for winners also come up short, as Christopher Culp of the University of Chicago laments:

"It's a zero-sum game. For every loser there's a winner, but you can't always be specific about who the winner is."[3]

When the big trading events happen, many people know the losses are going somewhere, but after time passes, they stop thinking about it. Reflecting on the unknown is not pleasant, as author Alexander Ineichen notes:

"Fear is still in the bones of some pension fund trustees—after Mr. Leeson brought down Barings Bank. The failure of Barings Bank is probably the most often cited derivatives disaster. While the futures market had been the instrument used by Nick Leeson to play the zero-sum game [and] someone made a lot of money being short the Nikkei futures Mr. Leeson was buying."[4]

It often seems that trends create events more than events create trends. The event itself is usually a reflection of everyone "getting it" as Ed [Seykota] calls it, "an aha."' By this time, the trend followers usually have well-established positions.

Jason Russell[6]

Someone did indeed make a lot of money trading short to Leeson's long, as I discuss later in the chapter. Perhaps Wall Street looks at the issue through the wrong lens. Michael Mauboussin and Kristen Bartholdson know that standard finance theory comes short when explaining the winners during high impact times:

"One of the major challenges in investing is how to capture (or avoid) low-probability, high-impact events. Unfortunately, standard finance theory has little to say about the subject."[5]

The unexpected events that everyone refers to are the source of big profits for trend followers. Big, unexpected events made David Harding, Christian Baha, Transtrend, Sunrise Capital, Michael Clarke, Bernard Drury, Paul Mulvaney, Bill Dunn, Salem Abraham, Bill Eckhardt, John W. Henry, and Jerry Parker (to name a few) rich. Trend trader Michael Rulle explains trend following's success during uncertain times:

"For markets to move in tandem, there has to be a common perception or consensus about economic conditions that drives it. When a major 'event' occurs in the middle of such a consensus, such as the Russian debt default of August

1998, the terrorist attacks of September 11, 2001, or the corporate accounting scandals of 2002 [and the 2008 equity market crash], it will often accelerate existing trends already in place…'events' do not happen in a vacuum… This is the reason trend following rarely gets caught on the wrong side of an 'event.' Additionally, the stop loss trading style will limit exposure when it does—When this consensus is further confronted by an 'event,' such as a major country default, the 'event' will reinforce the crisis mentality already in place and drive those trends toward their final conclusion. Because trend following generally can be characterized as having a 'long option' profile, it typically benefits greatly when these occurrences happen."[7]

However, big events also generate plenty of inane analysis by focusing on unanswerable questions such as those posed by Thomas Ho and Sang Lee, authors of *The Oxford Guide to Financial Modeling*:[8]

1. "What do these events tell us about our society?"

2. "Are these financial losses the dark sides of all the benefits of financial derivatives?"

3. "Should we change the way we do things?"

4. "Should the society accept these financial losses as part of the 'survival of the fittest' in the world of business?"

5. "Should legislation be used to avoid these events?"

It is not unusual to see people frame market wins and losses as a morality tale. These types of questions are designed to absolve the guilt of the market losers for their bad strategies (i.e. Amaranth, Bear Stearns, Bernard Madoff, etc.). The market is no place for political excuses or social engineering. No law changes human nature. If you don't like losing, examine the strategy of the winners.

The performance histories of trend followers during the 2008 market crash, 2000–2002 stock market bubble, the 1998 Long-Term Capital Management (LTCM) crisis, the Asian contagion, the Barings Bank bust in 1995, and the German firm Metallgesellschaft's collapse in 1993, answer that all important question: "Who won?"

On Saturday, February 25, 1995, Mike Killian, who almost single-handedly built Barings Far East customer brokerage business over the past seven years, was awakened at 4:30 a.m. in his Portland, Ore., home. It was Fred Hochenberger from the Barings Hong Kong office.

"Are you sitting down?" Hochenberger asked a sleepy Killian.

"No, I'm lying down."

"Have you heard any rumors?"

Killian, perplexed, said no.

"I think we're bust."

"Is this a crank call?" Killian asked.

"There's a really ugly story coming out that perhaps Nick Leeson has taken the company down."[9]

Event #1: 2008 Stock Market Bubble and Crash

*One reason for this
paucity of early
information is suggested
by the following part of
the term trend following.
The implication is one of
passivity, of reaction,
rather than of bold,
assertive action—and
human nature shows a
distinct preference for the
latter. Also, trend
following appears to be
too simple an idea to be
taken seriously. Indeed,
simple ideas can take a
very long time to be
accepted; think of the
concept of a negative
number, or of zero: simple
to us, but problematic to
our ancestors.*

Original Turtle Stig Ostgaard

The world changed in October 2008. Stock markets crashed. Millions of people lost trillions of dollars when their long-held buy and hold strategies imploded. The Dow, S&P, and Nasdaq fell like stones with the carnage carrying over into November 2008. Most everyone has felt the ramifications: jobs lost, firms going under, and fear all around. No one made money during this time. Everyone lost. Hold on, is that really true? It is not true. There were winners during October 2008, and they made fortunes ranging from +5 percent to +40 percent in that single month.

Who were the winners? Trend followers. How did they do it? First, let me state how they did not do it:

1. Trend followers did not know stock markets would crash in October 2008.

2. Trend followers did not make all of their money from shorting stocks in October 2008.

What did they do? Trend followers made money from many different markets from oil to bonds to currencies to stocks to commodities. Trend followers always seem to do particularly well in times of wild and extended price swings, in part because their trend following trading systems programmed into computers can make calculated, emotionless buys and sells that human traders might be slower to accept.

"We are not going to be the first to get in or the first to get out, but we are generally able to capture 80 percent of the trends," says Paul Wigdor of Superfund. For example, consider Superfund performance from January 2008 through October 2008 along with their annual performance figures from 1996 to 2008:

- January: –2.21%
- February: 14.17%
- March: 1.59%
- April: –1.23%
- May: 6.52%
- June: 9.88%
- July: –10.26%
- August: –8.36%
- September: 2.59%
- October: 17.52%

Superfund Annual Returns:

- 1996: –10.30%
- 1997: 20.70%
- 1998: 62.55%
- 1999: 25.39%
- 2000: 23.19%
- 2001: 18.82%
- 2002: 38.42%

- 2003: 24.33%
- 2004: 10.98%
- 2005: –3.30%
- 2006: 10.47%
- 2007: –1.81%
- 2008: 30.02%

Not only trend following trader Superfund won big. Consider other trend following traders during the same period:

1. One fund run by John W. Henry & Co., founded by Boston Red Sox baseball-team owner John W. Henry, was up 72.4 percent through October 2008.

2. TransTrend, a Dutch-based trend following trader managing more than $1 billion in assets, saw one of its funds go up +71.75 percent from January 2008 through November 2008.

3. Clarke Capital Management Inc., led by Michael Clarke, saw its $72.2 million fund gain 82.2 percent through October 2008. Clarke, as but one example of his winning bets, shorted crude oil when it was around $140, and then stayed with the trade down to $80 before exiting, thereby collecting the bulk of the trend. This is just one example of his winning bets.

4. Trend follower Bernard Drury started selling short S&P 500 index futures in November 2007. The index is down about 36 percent since and the largest Drury fund was up 56.9 percent through October 2008.[10]

5. Paul Mulvaney, another trend following trader who has used a much longer timeframe in his trading (weekly bars), saw his fund post a 45.49 percent return for the month of October 2008—yes, in one month.

How did these numbers happen? What is the source of these returns? For example, trend follower Superfund provided some insights into its 2008 trading performance:

"October 2008 provides a prime example of how [we] can produce gains in volatile and otherwise adverse market conditions. During this month and preceding months, [our] trading system not only profited from trends that were gaining momentum, but also responded to historic volatility by reducing or eliminating positions, and thus risk exposure, in markets in which trends were growing stale."

How did they do it? How did it work out like this? Superfund explained to me:

"In February 2008, a sustained downward trend in the U.S. dollar against various currencies accelerated. This coincided with a significant rally in gold and energy markets. Many trend following trading systems...profited from short positions in the U.S. dollar [see Chart 4.1] and long positions in gold and energies."

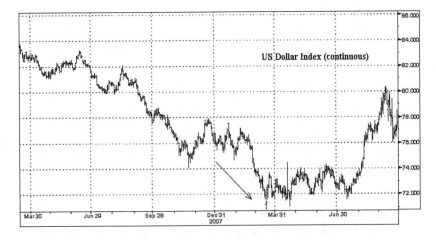

CHART 4.1: U.S. Dollar Short Trade

Superfund described the continuing unfolding market chaos:

"At the same time, several world stocks indices exhibited signs of weakness. By June, however, gold stumbled nearly $200 from recent highs above $1,000 per ounce [see Chart 4.2]. [We were able] to continue capturing gains in the U.S. dollar, energies, and stocks while reducing its long exposure to gold as returns in this market faltered."

CHART 4.2: Long Gold Trade with Exit

But how did these events lead to October 2008 gains? Superfund clarified:

> "During July and August, profitable trends in the U.S. dollar, energies, and grains exhausted themselves. It was at this juncture that the [our] system repositioned itself for results in October despite short-term drawdowns during these two months. While speculative traders may have viewed the precipitous drop in energies and other commodities as an opportunity to add to their long positions, [we] identified the end of sustained trends in these markets and significantly reduced its positions, and therefore its risk, particularly in the U.S dollar. Meanwhile, [our] system began identifying emerging trends in world treasury markets [see Chart 4.3], as well as meats and industrial metals."

Chart 4.3 shows the patience trend followers had to endure in the face of extreme volatility.

As the historic month of October 2008 arrived, Superfund offered a behind the scenes glimpse of their thinking:

> "Approaching October, [we were] ready to take advantage of changing market conditions both because of positions [we] no longer held as well as positions [we] had entered

But the other level of trend following is something else entirely. This is the meta-level, which sits above the tableau of material and psychological cause and effect, allowing participants to observe the behavior of the markets as a whole and to design intelligent, premeditated responses to market action. This is the level of trend following from which we as traders should—and usually do—operate.

Original Turtle Stig Ostgaard

during the subpar return periods of July and August. For example, [we] had avoided the potential for substantial losses from an 18.3 percent decline in gold futures and a 32 percent collapse in crude oil [see Chart 4.4] by reducing long exposure to these markets before their substantial October declines."

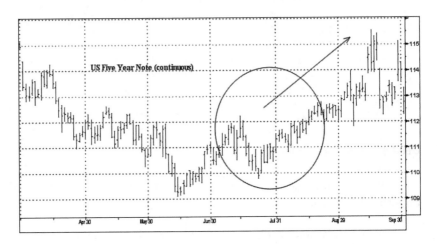

CHART 4.3: Long Five-Year Notes Trade

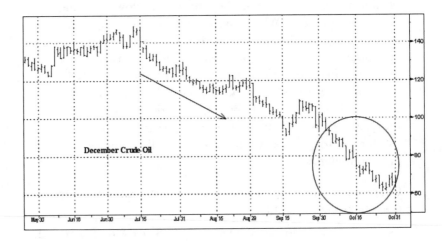

CHART 4.4: Crude Oil Winning Short Trade

Superfund, like other trend followers, captured a nice trend in the Nikkei 225 (see Chart 4.5):

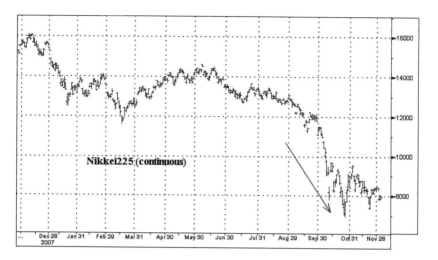

CHART 4.5: Nikkei Winning Short Trade

But this is not about predictions, so when trends changed, Superfund switched gears:

> "After having been short the U.S. dollar for most of the first half of 2008, by October, [we] had established positions designed to profit from the reversal of the U.S. dollar trend in July and August. At that point, currencies such as the British pound began to decline against the dollar [see Chart 4.6]."

It may surprise many to know that in my method of trading, when I see by my records that an upward trend is in progress, I become a buyer as soon as a stock makes a new high on its movement, after having had a normal reaction. The same applies whenever I take the short side. Why? Because I am following the trend at the time. My records signal me to go ahead!

Jesse Livermore (1940)

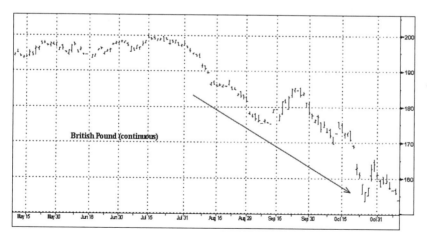

CHART 4.6: British Pound Winning Trade

Superfund, like most all trend followers, realized the bulk of their October profits as a result of the ability to capitalize on a variety of different market conditions while limiting losses based on a combination of diversification, flexibility, risk management, and discipline. While a substantial portion of trend following October profits were derived from short positions in the stock indices and world currencies, trend followers also realized profits from long bond positions. They also avoided major losses by reducing exposure to gold and energies.

Although not as large as more established trend following traders in terms of assets under management, Justin Vandergrift of Chadwick Investment Group offered insights into his 2008 performance. He took me through some of his trades where he saw monster returns at a time when buy and holders were all gasping for air.

Vandergrift first outlined a European interest trade (see Chart 4.7): "In the midst of the global financial crisis, we received signals on many short-term interest rates. The Euribor is a short-term interest rate futures contract traded at the EUREX. We bought on October 7 and are still long (through December 2008). Central banks around the globe began dropping interest rates to ward off equity market declines. Lower interest rates mean higher Euribor futures prices. That said, fundamentals did not drive our decisions."

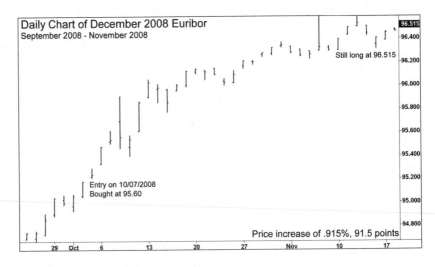

CHART 4.7: December 2008 Euribor

Vandergrift explained how he profited from another short term interest rate, the EuroSwiss (see Chart 4.8): "The EuroSwiss is another short-term interest rate futures contract. We entered this position well before the global equity market crash."

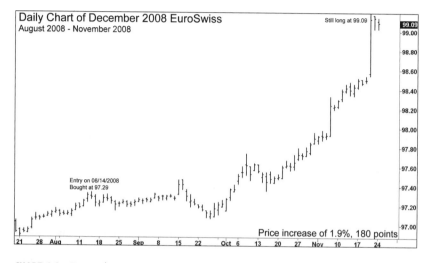

CHART 4.8: December 2008 EuroSwiss

I know I perhaps sound redundant about how trend followers don't even care what markets they make money in, but it is a critical point. Consider Vandergrift's explanation about trading "hogs" (see Chart 4.9): "The Hog position was one of the most beautiful trends that I've seen in years. As the U.S. dollar rallied, nearly every commodity tied to the dollar moved violently. Although our larger portfolio gains happened in October, this position profited throughout the fall of 2008."

Sure, we all focus on "stocks," but what about lumber? Vandergrift explained his lumber trade (see Chart 4.10): "Lumber was another great market over the fall of 2008. Lumber fell due to the housing crisis in the U.S. Lower demand means lower lumber prices. We sold the market short in the late summer and held the position until mid-November. However, it is important to keep in mind that we went short based off of price action, not fundamentals."

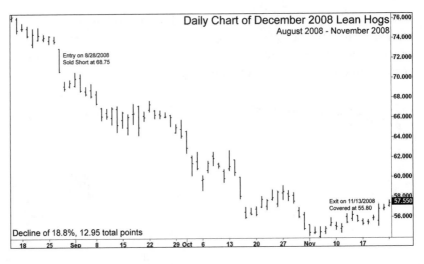

CHART 4.9: December 2008 Lean Hogs

This evidence of structure in stock prices suggests alluring possibilities in the way of forecasting. In fact, many professional speculators, including in particular exponents of the so-called Dow Theory widely publicized by popular financial journals, have adopted systems based in the main on the principle that it is advantageous to swim with the tide.

Alfred Cowles (1937)

CHART 4.10: January 2009 Lumber

Did you make money in "coffee" in the fall of 2008 (see Chart 4.11)? "Although traded in London, Robusta Coffee is denominated in U.S. dollars. The move up in Robusta Coffee was helped in large part from a strengthening U.S. dollar. A higher dollar means less purchasing power in other currencies, pushing Robusta lower. My fundamental views once again mean little, we just followed the trend."

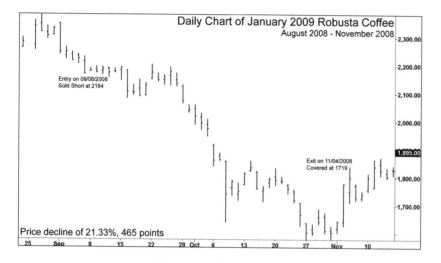

Daily Chart of January 2009 Robusta Coffee
August 2008 - November 2008

Entry on 09/08/2008
Sold Short at 2184

Exit on 11/04/2008
Covered at 1719

Price decline of 21.33%, 465 points

CHART 4.11: January 2009 Robusta Coffee

Perhaps no other market than the U.S. dollar was more important to trend followers. Once again, they did not care whether they made money in the dollar going long or going short—they were agnostic to the dollar's direction (see Chart 4.12): "The trend up in the U.S. dollar was cut into two segments. We saw more volatility in this contract than others, simply due to the U.S. equity markets. Although our entries and exits are tied to highs and lows in the U.S. dollar futures, moves in the U.S. equity markets influenced the price as well. The rise of this contract created opportunities in many of the other markets we trade, because they are so closely tied to the price of the dollar."

All you can do as a trend follower is take what is given. The goal is to make money in trending markets. The goal is not to fall in love with one particular market to the exclusion of another market, which is potentially a better opportunity.

Daily Chart of December 2008 US Dollar Index
September 2008 - November 2008

Entry #2 on 11/13/2008
Bought at 87.01

Exit #2 on 11/24/2008
Covered at 85.42

Exit #1 on 10/20/2008
Covered at 84.27

Entry #1 on 10/02/2008
Bought at 80.72

Trade #1
Price increase of 4.4%, 3.55 points

Trade #2
Price decline of 1.8%, (1.59) points

CHART 4.12: December 2008 U.S. Dollar

Day-by-Day Analysis

We think that forecasting should be thought of in the light of measuring the direction of today's trend and then turning to the Law of Inertia (momentum) for assurance that probabilities favor the continuation of that trend for an unknown period of time into the future. This is trend following, and it does not require us to don the garment of the mystic and look into the crystal balls of the future.

William Dunnigan (1954)

The market crash of 2008 offered fantastic data to see how trend following is so different than most of the investing world's mindset. Chart 4.13 shows daily data from trend follower Salem Abraham and lets you see the day-to-day performance differences between his trend following fund and the S&P. For those who hear about trend trading wins in October 2008 and who immediately want to scream "lucky," look closely at the Abraham data. It is a great proxy for the other trend following traders as well:

Even though gains by the likes of trend traders Abraham and Mulvaney (and the others) might make logical sense, their performance is not easy to accept for some. Consider feedback I received from a reader at my blog who was attempting to sell his firm on the benefits of trend following trading:

"Michael: I have been in discussions with [trend following trader] Mulvaney Capital Management since the summer for a company in which I was the COO. The board thought my ideas were too risky and that I tried to hit too many homeruns [by potentially hiring Mulvaney]. This particular [firm I was with] lost $30 million in September and October [2008]. I showed them the Mulvaney performance: $15 million invested in 1999 equated to $71 million today and

$30 million over the same period equated to $142 million. After my presentation at a board meeting, I returned to my office and was told [that] next week…I was being eliminated as I was too big of a risk taker. My only other investment in my short tenure was with Abraham Trading Co. and the returns equated to nearly positive 12 percent for the same time period. This was the only positive investment for the organization over that period. So much for my risk taking."

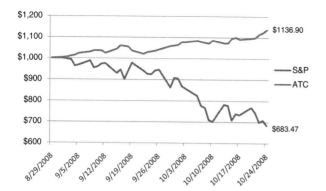

Abraham Trading Co.
vs.
S&P 500
Sept. 1, 2008 to Oct. 24, 2008

Sept. 1, 2008 to Oct. 24, 2008		
	S&P 500	ATC
Average	-0.87%	0.33%
Std. Dev.	4.08%	0.87%
Correlation	-0.39	

Daily ROR Comparison

Date	S&P	ATC	Date	S&P	ATC	Date	S&P	ATC	Date	S&P	ATC
9/1/2008	0.00%	0.32%	9/15/2008	-4.71%	1.95%	9/29/2008	-8.81%	1.56%	10/13/2008	11.58%	-1.16%
9/2/2008	-0.41%	0.26%	9/16/2008	1.75%	1.62%	9/30/2008	5.27%	0.24%	10/14/2008	-0.53%	-0.03%
9/3/2008	-0.20%	0.50%	9/17/2008	-4.71%	-0.33%	10/1/2008	-0.32%	0.33%	10/15/2008	-9.03%	2.06%
9/4/2008	-2.99%	0.33%	9/18/2008	4.33%	-0.25%	10/2/2008	-4.03%	1.23%	10/16/2008	4.25%	0.48%
9/5/2008	0.44%	0.86%	9/19/2008	4.03%	-1.78%	10/3/2008	-1.35%	0.06%	10/17/2008	-0.62%	-0.88%
9/8/2008	2.05%	0.67%	9/22/2008	-3.82%	-1.46%	10/6/2008	-3.85%	0.52%	10/20/2008	4.77%	0.44%
9/9/2008	-3.41%	0.62%	9/23/2008	-1.56%	0.83%	10/7/2008	-5.74%	-0.41%	10/21/2008	-3.08%	0.37%
9/10/2008	0.61%	0.05%	9/24/2008	-0.20%	0.26%	10/8/2008	-1.13%	-0.39%	10/22/2008	-6.10%	1.42%
9/11/2008	1.38%	-0.12%	9/25/2008	1.97%	0.35%	10/9/2008	-7.62%	-0.33%	10/23/2008	1.26%	0.78%
9/12/2008	0.21%	-1.09%	9/26/2008	0.34%	0.61%	10/10/2008	-1.18%	1.34%	10/24/2008	-3.45%	1.17%

CHART 4.13 Abraham Compared to the S&P

Logically, it is difficult to keep saying trend following is risky, especially in the face of "leveraged long only buy and hold" approaches that cratered in 2008, but then again who said most of Wall Street (what's left of it) is logical. I have these same conversations with many top trend followers. I sometimes think they scratch their heads that so many people don't take advantage of what they offer. For example, trend follower Christian Baha and

Conventional capital market theory is based on a linear view of the world, one in which investors have rational expectations; they adjust immediately to information about the markets and behave as if they know precisely how the structure of the economy works. Markets are highly efficient, but not perfectly so. Inefficiencies are inherent in the economy or in the structure of markets themselves...We believe inefficiencies in markets can be exploited through a combination of trend detection and risk management.

John W. Henry & Company, Inc.[11]

I have discussed the reasons why trend following is not accepted on multiple occasions. Maybe 2008 will be the tipping point for acceptance, but I would not bet on it!

Lastly, as you read the rest of this chapter, you will quickly find out that the fall 2008 performance of trend following traders was no aberration. It was business as usual.

Event #2: 2000–2002 Stock Market Bubble

The period from 2000–2002 was littered with volatile up-and-down markets. Although the prime story for that three-year period was the NASDAQ meltdown, several subplots also existed ranging from September 11 to Enron to trend following drawdowns and subsequent recoveries to new highs.

How did trend followers, for example, do compared to the S&P and NASDAQ for 2002 (see Chart 4.14)?

CHART 4.14: 2002 Performance Histories for Trend Followers

Bill Dunn: +54.23%

Salem Abraham +21.37%

John W. Henry: +45.06%

Jerry Parker: +11.10%

David Druz: +33.17%

Bill Eckhardt (Richard Dennis' Partner): +14.05%

Mulvaney Capital: +19.37%

S&P: –23.27

NASDAQ: –31.53%

Dow: –16.76

Charts 4.15 through 4.22 show what trends they were riding to produce this performance.

Drawdowns and Recoveries

It's no secret that for the majority of 2000, trend followers were in a nasty drawdown. They were down significantly heading into the last few months of the year. The press and skeptics were calling the strategy finished.

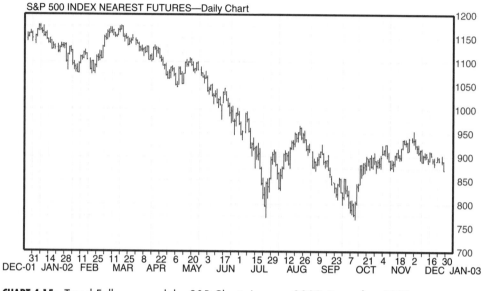

CHART 4.15: Trend Followers and the S&P Chart, January 2002–December 2002

Source: Barchart.com

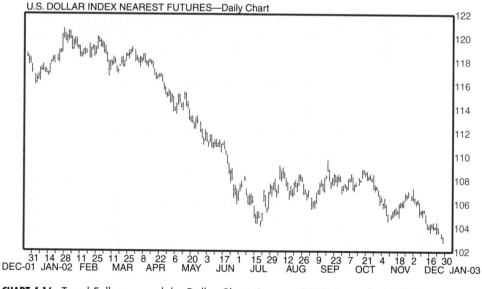

CHART 4.16: Trend Followers and the Dollar Chart, January 2002–December 2002

Source: Barchart.com

JAPANESE YEN NEAREST FUTURES—Daily Chart

CHART 4.17: Trend Followers and the Yen Chart, January 2002–December 2002

Source: Barchart.com

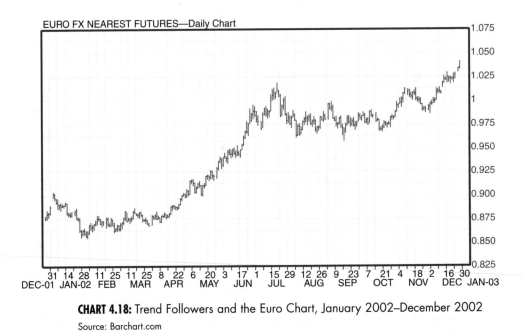

EURO FX NEAREST FUTURES—Daily Chart

CHART 4.18: Trend Followers and the Euro Chart, January 2002–December 2002

Source: Barchart.com

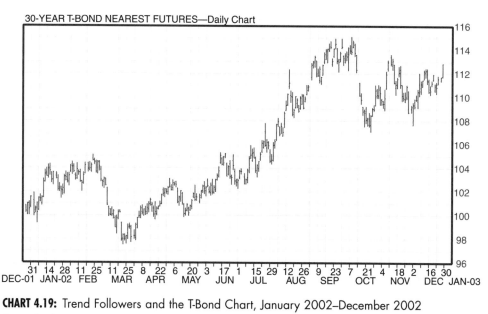

CHART 4.19: Trend Followers and the T-Bond Chart, January 2002–December 2002

Source: Barchart.com

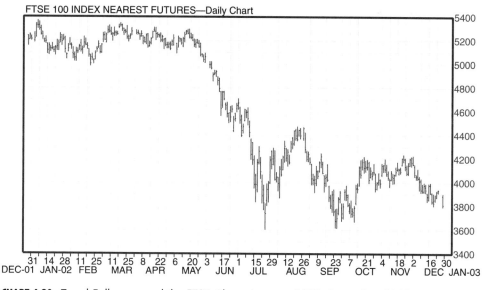

CHART 4.20: Trend Followers and the FTSE Chart, January 2002–December 2002

Source: Barchart.com

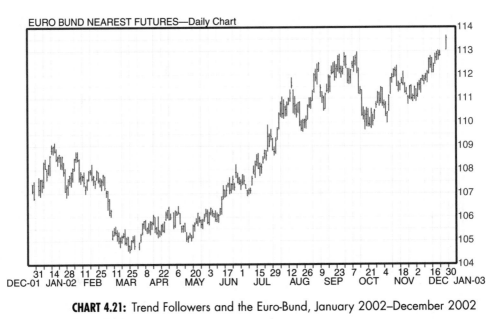

CHART 4.21: Trend Followers and the Euro-Bund, January 2002–December 2002

Source: Barchart.com

CHART 4.22: Trend Followers and the DAX, January 2002–December 2002

Source: Barchart.com

I was not surprised when a *Barrons* reporter contacted me via TurtleTrader.com for an opinion. She seemingly had it in for Henry and Dunn and was looking for confirmation that trend following was dead. I pointed out to her that drawdowns had occurred in the past and were not uncommon, but that over the long haul, trend followers made tremendous amounts of money trading for the absolute return. She ignored those facts. Here's an excerpt from the piece she wrote:

> "John W. Henry isn't alone in experiencing hard times. But the firm's losses are among the most staggering...The company's hardest-hit trend following trading program, called Financial & Metals, was down 18.7 percent in 1999...Henry, whom one rival calls 'our industry's Dave Kingman,' definitely swings for the fences. (Kingman hit 442 home runs during his 16 seasons in the majors, but he also struck out more than 1,800 times.) It's unclear whether John W. Henry will make changes to his trading program, one he cooked up decades ago while on a vacation to Norway."[13]

You have to wonder if this *Barrons'* reporter had taken the time to read Henry's speech from November of 2000 before writing her December article. Henry was hinting at success just around the corner:

> "Unfortunately, markets do not step to a drummer that we control. The period we have just been through has been terrifically painful for investors, brokers, general partners, and trading advisors. Drawdowns affect everyone emotionally, psychologically, and physically when they persist. It becomes very easy to envision a scenario in which things never get better. However, at JWH, experience tells us that things inevitably look bleakest before the tide turns."[14]

The tide was turning.

On January 10, 2001, this same reporter sent me an email stating that she was doing a follow-up story to the one in December and wanted a comment. I was impressed that she was essentially acknowledging her mistake and was even willing to set the record straight because, for the record, Dunn made 28 percent in November of 2000 and 29 percent in December of 2000. Henry

Convergent styles
- *World knowable*
- *Stable world*
- *Mean-reverting*
- *Short volatility*
- *Arbitrage-based*

Divergent styles
- *World uncertain*
- *Unstable world*
- *Mean-fleeing*
- *Long volatility*
- *Trend Following*

Mark S. Rzepczynski[12]

Don't be fooled by the calm. That's always the time to change course, not when you're just about to get hit by the typhoon. The way to avoid being caught in such a storm is to identify the confluence of factors and to change course even though right now the sky is blue, the winds are gentle, and the water seems calm...After all look how calm and sunny it is outside.

Thomas Friedman, *The World is Flat*

made 13 percent in November of 2000 and 23 percent in December. Here's an excerpt of her follow-up piece:

> "Wall Street's biggest commodity-trading advisers posted a dramatic turnaround in the fourth quarter, turning last year's heart-stopping losses into gains for the year. Will it last?...In the October–December period, CTAs benefited from pricing trends in global bond markets and rising prices in the natural-gas and oil sectors. Also, December's steady rise in the euro proved to be a boon for currency traders. 'This rebound is not a surprise,' says Michael Covel, of TurtleTrader.com, which tracks trend followers...Henry, a high-profile commodities-trading firm in Boca Raton, Florida, profiled by Barron's last month, posted a 20.3 percent return last year in its largest trading program which was down 13.7 percent for the first nine months of the year, powered back 39.2 percent in the fourth quarter."[15]

How was Henry able to "power back 39.2 percent" in the fourth quarter of 2000 after posting a loss of 13.7 percent for the first nine months of the year? What trends did he ride? Where was his target of opportunity? The answers can be found in Enron, California, and natural gas.

Enron, California, and Natural Gas

If you examine the natural gas market during the last few months of 2000 and almost all of 2001, you can see the trading opportunity. For trend followers, the natural gas market's great trend up and great trend down were sources of immense profit.

The losers were Enron and the state of California. Enron's collapse is a classic case of greed, fear, and ultimately, incompetence at work. From Enron's upper management's manipulation of the facts to the employees who purposefully ignored the manipulations to the state of California's inept attempts to play the energy markets, everyone was accountable. That said, in the zero-sum game, everyone is responsible, whether each person admits it or not.

The Enron debacle is stunning when you consider the losers. The number of investors who deluded themselves into thinking they were on a path to quick riches is incalculable. From the portfolio managers of pension funds and university endowments to individual investors, everyone was caught up in the exhilaration of

After having experienced a 40.0 percent decline through September 2000, Dunn Capital Management finished 2000 with a 17.3 percent asset weighted composite return. Dunn's 75.5 percent gain in the fourth quarter delivered $590 million to its investors; its annualized composite compound return since the firm's inception over 26 years ago is now 24.3 percent.[16]

a company that seemed to go in only one direction—up. Owners of Enron stock never stopped seeing the pot of gold. They were quite willing to look the other way and suspend their disbelief to celebrate a zooming share price guilt-free.

However, there was a problem: They had no strategy to sell when the time came and the trend turned. All good bulls die— whether people admit it or not. The Enron stock chart (see Chart 4.23) is now famous.

There was only one key piece of data needed to judge Enron: the share price. At its peak, the company's stock traded at $90 a share, but it collapsed to 50¢ a share. Why would anyone hold onto a stock that goes from $90 to 50¢? Even if Enron was the biggest scam ever propagated, must we not take to task the hopeful investors who held on all the way down to 50¢ a share? Don't blind investors bear responsibility for *not* selling? The chart was telling them the trend had changed.

Q: Why didn't Wall Street realize that Enron was a fraud? A: Because Wall Street relies on stock analysts. These are people who do research on companies and then, no matter what they find, even if the company has burned to the ground, enthusiastically recommend that investors buy the stock.

Dave Barry, humor columnist

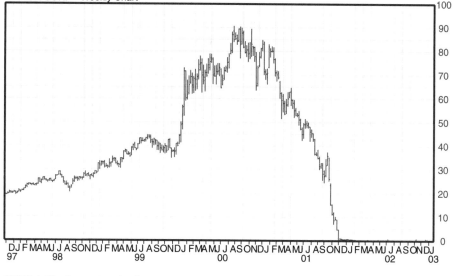

CHART 4.23: Enron Stock Chart Source: Barchart.com

Not only were there massive winners and losers in Enron stock, but the zero-sum game sprang into full force during the California energy crisis in late 2000 and during 2001. Enron was a primary supplier of natural gas to California. California, bound by its own flawed deregulation schemes, freely signed long-term contracts with

They say patience is a virtue. For me patience is synonymous with discipline. You must have the discipline to know that markets change and poor periods are followed by good periods. Longevity in this business—I have seen it again and again—is measured by discipline.

Among the hottest funds this year [2002] are Dunn Capital Management, which is up more than 50 percent. Daniel Dunn, who runs the firm from Stuart, Florida, profited on trades on Japan's Nikkei, Germany's DAX, and Britain's FTSE stock indexes, as well as on bond and eurodollar interest-rate futures offered on the Chicago exchanges.[18]

energy trading firms and bought natural gas from Enron to generate electricity.

Not surprisingly, with inexperienced players and bad agreements in place, Enron and the state of California all but forgot that natural gas was just another market. Like any market, it was subject to go up and down for any number of fundamental reasons. Eventually, natural gas spiked up and down in ferocious trends. Unfortunately, neither Enron nor California had a plan in place to deal with price changes.

Feeling abused, California complained loudly. California Senator Diane Feinstein maintained that they had no culpability in the game. In a press release, she argued:

> "I am writing to request an additional hearing to pursue what role Enron had in the California energy crisis with respect to market manipulation and price gouging. Enron's ability to deal in complex unregulated financial derivatives in the natural gas market while controlling a tremendous share of the gas trading market provided Enron the ability to manipulate market prices. This was very likely a key factor in driving up gas and electricity prices leading to the California energy crisis."

It has been said that the Enron crisis cost California $45 billion over two years in higher electricity costs and slowed economic growth. When you look at the charts of natural gas (see Chart 4.24) and Enron (see Chart 4.23), you have to question Feinstein's basic market understandings.

Why did California lock itself into stringent agreements with firms such as Enron? Why did California, through its own deals, trade outside typical market structures? Why couldn't they deal with a changing natural gas price? California must accept blame for its dumb decisions.

Anyone at any time can trade natural gas at the New York Mercantile Exchange. Anyone can hedge a natural gas position. The opportunity to speculate and hedge is there for everyone. It is not a novel concept. Of course, trend followers were playing the natural gas game too, riding it up and down for profit, as Chart 4.25 demonstrates.

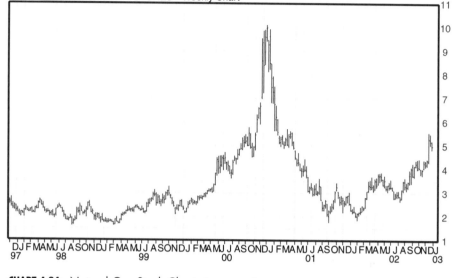

CHART 4.24: Natural Gas Stock Chart Source: Barchart.com

CHART 4.25: Trend Followers' Performance

Dunn Capital Management WMA

October 2000: +9.12%

November 2000: +28.04%

December 2000: +29.39%

January 2001: +7.72%

John W. Henry Financials and Metals

October 2000: +9.39%

November 2000: +13.33%

December 2000: +23.02%

January 2001: +3.34%

Graham Capital Management K4

October 2000: +1.44%

November 2000: +7.41%

December 2000: +9.37%

January 2001: +2.37%

Man Investments

October 2000: +4.54%

November 2000: +10.30%

December 2000: +10.76

January 2001: +1.49%

Campbell and Company Financials and Metals

October 2000: +3.19%

November 2000: +5.98%

December 2000: +2.38%

January 2001: −1.09%

Chesapeake Capital

October 2000: −0.62%

November 2000: +7.42%

December 2000: +8.80%

January 2001: −0.43%

Abraham Trading

October 2000: +9.51%

November 2000: +8.58%

December 2000: −0.18%

January 2001: +2.28

One Enron employee was frustrated by the entire sordid affair: "My fellow (former) colleagues have no one to blame other than themselves for allowing such disastrous losses to occur in their retirement accounts. An abdication of personal responsibility should not be rewarded. It is a sad consequence, but it is reality."[19]

From private mutual fund companies such as Janus, to retirement funds managed by state governments, no one had a plan for exiting Enron. They all bought the stock, but incredibly selling was never part of the plan. The Enron story is much more profound than a tale of one company's journey to disaster. It is the story of inept individuals managing billions of retirement wealth.

How much did the losers lose? Losses in Enron were staggering:

- Japanese banks lost $805.4 million.
- Abbey National Bank lost £95 million.
- John Hancock Financial Services lost $102 million.
- British Petroleum retirement lost $55 million on Enron debt.

David Brady, Stein Roe Focus Fund manager, admits to making a bad bet on Enron: "Where did I go wrong? If I learned anything, I learned the same old lessons…The numbers just didn't add up. If you had looked at the numbers, the balance sheet would have showed you the real problems."

Notice how he blames the balance sheets and not his decisions? Public retirement accounts recklessly bet on Enron to go up forever, too:

- The Kansas Public Employees Retirement System had about $1.2 million invested in about 82,000 shares of Enron stock, "It was based on (Enron's) spectacular earnings growth, and many analysts recommended it as a hot stock," said David Brant, Kansas securities commissioner.
- The retirement fund for the City of Fort Worth lost nearly $1 million in Enron.
- The Teacher Retirement System of Texas first invested in Enron in June 1994. It has realized a net loss of approximately $23.3 million from its Enron stock holdings and $12.4 million in net unrealized losses from its current bond holdings in Enron. Jim Simms of Amarillo, a board member for six years and chairman of the board, said: "We're human beings—when you're investing money, you'll have some winners and some losers…You can't protect yourself when you're being fed inaccurate information…We had all the precautions in place."

What precautions were in place? Come on! Enron's fall from grace is no different from other corporate implosions, although the losers (such as those in Chart 4.26) might need to call it "new" to rationalize their losses. However, the game doesn't change, even if the names of the companies do.

The best way I can explain it is that many investors believed that [our] returns were in some way inferior to the returns of many other hedge fund strategies, because of a perception of higher volatility, and lower absolute returns. The additional…benefits of low correlation, transparency, liquidity, and effective regulation somehow escaped their attention. What 2002 has demonstrated is that in fact the returns of many of those other strategies are not as "absolute" as had been perceived, and many of them appear to actually have a strong upside bias.

Bruce Cleland, Campbell and Co.[20]

[A]ll the intensive research these firms performed did not protect them, or their investors, from massive losses. It is particularly noteworthy [that] Janus, whose commercials tout their superior research efforts and skills, [held] over 16 million shares. On April 30, 2001, the last time it reported individual fund holdings, 11 Janus funds collectively owned more than 5 percent of Enron. As of Sept. 30, Janus still owned more than 5 percent of Enron. Another touter of their superior stock-picking skills is the Fidelity family of funds. As of September 30, 2001, together they owned 154 million shares. So much for the value or research [of Janus and Fidelity].

Larry Swedroe, Buckingham Asset Management[21]

CHART 4.26: Largest Shareholders in Enron (Percent Fund in Enron Shares)

Alliance Premier Growth (4.1%)
Fidelity Magellan (0.2%)
AIM Value (1%)
Putnam Investors (1.7%)
Morgan Stanley Dividend Growth (0.9%)
Janus Fund (2.9%)
Janus Twenty (2.8%)
Janus Mercury (3.6%)
Janus Growth and Income (2.7%)
Rydex Utility (8%)
Fidelity Select Natural Gas (5.7%)
Dessauer Global Equity (5.6%)
Merrill Lynch Focus Twenty (5.8%)
AIM Global Technology (5.3%)
Janus 2 (4.7%)
Janus Special Situations (4.6%)
Stein Roe Focus (4.2%)
Alliance Premier Growth (4.1%)
Merrill Lynch Growth (4.1%)

An interesting aspect of the Enron fiasco was the close relationship between the Enron share price and natural gas. To lose money in Enron stock was essentially to lose money in natural gas. They were connected at the hip. Enron acted like a derivative for natural gas. The company presented mutual funds and pension funds an opportunity to get into natural gas speculation even if their mission statement might have limited them to stock speculation. Using Enron as a proxy, mutual and pension funds were able to ride natural gas to the top. Not only was everyone buying and holding Enron, they were, for all intents and purposes, buying and holding natural gas. The data makes the case.

We don't see things as they are. We see things as we are.

Anais Nin

September 11, 2001

September 11, 2001 demonstrates the unpredictable on a grand scale. How could anyone know in advance where the safe place to be in the market was? Before considering September 11th specifically, consider Ed Seykota's words in general:

> "A surprise is an event that catches someone unaware. If you are already on the trend, the surprises seem to happen to the other guys."[22]

No one could have predicted that a terrorist attack would close Wall Street for four days. Although it was difficult to stay focused on the rigors of everyday life, trend followers maintained a sense of balance. Unlike those investors who made trading decisions they would not have made before September 11, trend followers confronted the market as always. They dealt with it as they always had—with a plan set in motion long before an unexpected event happened.

Trend followers were short stocks and long bonds ahead of the attack, because that was where those markets were already headed. For example, Marty Ehrlich of Sunrise Capital Partners said how lucky they were to be well positioned ahead of the September 11 attack. Jim Little, executive vice president for Campbell and Co. makes the case that currency markets also followed through with continued trends. "The (U.S.) dollar had already begun to weaken before the attacks, hence Campbell was short that market." He also noted that Campbell had been long bonds and short a number of global stock index futures contracts ahead of the attack because of established trends.[23]

Their entries into positions were not triggered by actions on September 11. Their decisions to be in or out of the market were set in motion long before the unexpected event of September 11 happened. Although Enron, the California energy crisis, and September 11 are vivid illustrations of the zero-sum game with trend followers as the winners, the story of Long-Term Capital Management in the summer of 1998 may be the best trend following case study.

Event #3: Long-Term Capital Management Collapse

Long-Term Capital Management (LTCM) was a hedge fund that went bust in 1998. The story of who lost has been told repeatedly over the years; however, because trading is a zero-sum game, exploring the winners was the real story. LTCM is a classic saga of the zero-sum game played out on a grand scale with trend followers as winners.

"Trillion Dollar Bet," a PBS special, described how LTCM came to be. In 1973, three economists—Fischer Black, Myron Scholes, and Robert Merton—discovered an elegant formula that revolutionized modern finance. This mathematical Holy Grail, the Black-Scholes Option Pricing Formula, was sparse and deceptively simple. It earned Scholes and Merton a Nobel Prize and attracted the attention of John Meriweather, the legendary bond trader of Salomon Brothers.

LTCM promised to use complex mathematical models to make investors wealthy beyond their wildest dreams. LTCM attracted the elite of Wall Street's investors and initially reaped fantastic profits managing their money. Ultimately, their theories collided with reality and sent the company spiraling out of control.[24]

Needless to say, this was not supposed to happen:

"They were immediately seen as a unique enterprise. They had the best minds. They had a former vice chairman of the Federal Reserve. They had John Meriwether...So they were seen by individual investors, but particularly by banks and institutions that went in with them, as a ticket to easy street."[25]

The most damaging consequence of the LTCM episode is, therefore, the harm done by the perception that Federal Reserve policy makers do not have the faith to take their own medicine. How can they persuade the Russians or the Japanese to let big institutions fail if they are afraid to do the same themselves?[26]

To understand the LTCM fiasco, we first need to take a quick look at the foundations of modern finance. Merton Miller and his colleague Eugene F. Fama, two scholars at the University of Chicago, launched what became known as the Efficient Market Hypothesis:

"The premise of the hypothesis is that stock prices are always right; therefore, no one can divine the market's future direction, which in turn, must be 'random.' For prices to be right, of course, the people who set them must be both rational and well informed."[27]

In other words, Miller and Fama believed that perfectly rational people would never pay more or less than any financial instrument was actually worth. A fervent supporter of the Efficient Markets Hypothesis, Myron Scholes was certain that markets could not make mistakes. His associate, Robert Merton, took it a step further with his continuous-time finance theory, which essentially wrapped the finance universe into a supposed tidy ball.[28]

Merton's markets were as smooth as well brewed java, in which prices would flow like cream. He assumed…that the price of a share of IBM would never plunge directly from 80 to 60 but would always stop at 79 3/4, 79 1/2, and 79 1/4 along the way.[29]

If LTCM's universe was supposed to be "in a tidy ball," it might have been because where Merton and Scholes pioneered their theories, academic life was tidy. LTCM's founders believed the market was a perfect normal distribution with no outliers, no fat tails, and no unexpected events. Their problems began the moment they accepted these assumptions.

After Merton, Scholes, and Meriwether had Wall Street convinced that the markets were a nice, neat, and continuous normal distribution, and there was no risk worth worrying about, LTCM began using mammoth leverage for supposedly risk-free big returns.

Approximately 55 banks gave LTCM financing, including Bankers Trust, Bear Stearns, Chase Manhattan, Goldman Sachs, J.P. Morgan, Lehman Brothers, Merrill Lynch, Morgan Stanley, and Dean Witter. Eventually, LTCM would have $100 billion in borrowed assets and more than $1 trillion worth of exposure in markets everywhere. This type of leverage was not a problem initially or so it seemed. Merton was even said to have remarked to Miller that you could think of LTCM's strategy as a gigantic vacuum cleaner sucking up nickels across the world.

UBS said last week it would take a SFr950m ($686m) charge reflecting losses relating to its equity investment in LTCM, which was linked to an options deal that the former Union Bank of Switzerland had done with the hedge fund before merging with Swiss Bank Corporation to create the new UBS.[30]

However, it was too complicated, too leveraged, and devoid of real risk management. The Organization for Economic Cooperation and Development described a single trade that exemplified LTCM's overall trading strategy. It was a bet on the convergence of yield spreads between French bonds (OATs) and German bonds (bunds). When the spread between the OATs and the bunds went to 60 basis points in the forward market, LTCM decided to double its position. That deal was only one leg of an even more complex convergence bet, which included hedged positions in Spanish peseta and Italian lira bonds.[31]

The result of all these complex convergences was that no one had a clue what LTCM was up to, risk-wise, including LTCM. The LTCM professors ran a secretive and closed operation so convoluted that regulators and investors had no idea what, when, or how much they were trading. Not being able to price an instrument or trade freely in and out of it on a daily basis ignores what Wall Street calls

Last month [August 1998], during one of the most stressful points in market performance, our largest portfolio, Financial and Metals, was up [an estimated] 17.7 percent. Of the $2.4 billion that we manage, I think just slightly over half of it is in the Financial and Metals Portfolio. This was not a direct result of the decline in the U.S. market—as I said we don't trade in the S&P 500—but rather an example of the typical predictable investor behavior in the face of trouble. In reverting to rules of thumb, in this case, the flight to quality, global bonds rose, global stock markets plunged, and a shift in foreign exchange rates occurred. However, the magnitude of the moves was the only real surprise for us. The trends which were demonstrated during late August had been in place for weeks or months beforehand.

John W. Henry[33]

"transparency." Trend follower Jerry Parker sees the differences in transparency between LTCM and his own trading:

> "We've always had 100 percent transparency...The good thing about CTAs is their strategies are usually straightforward, not something that only a few people in the world can understand. We're trend following and systems-based, something you can easily describe to a client...People who aren't willing to show clients their positions are in trouble...One of the problems was that people put too much money in these funds [such as Long-Term Capital]. We ask for just 10 percent of risk capital, and clients know they may make 10 percent one month and lose 10 percent the next month. The ultimate error is to put a ton of money with geniuses who never lose money. When all hell breaks loose, those guys lose everything."[32]

Even more than LTCM's lack of transparency, a bigger failure involved "lightning" as one critic noted:

> "I don't yet know the balance between whether this was a random event or whether this was negligence on theirs and their creditors' parts. If a random bolt of lightning hits you when you're standing in the middle of the field, it feels like a random event. But if your business is to stand in random fields during lightning storms, then you should anticipate, perhaps a little more robustly, the risks you're taking on."[34]

The Black-Scholes option pricing formula did not factor in the randomness of human behavior—only one example of the negligence that ultimately would cause the lightning bolts of August and September 1998. When lightning struck LTCM, trend followers were assessing the same markets—playing the zero-sum game at the same time. In hindsight, the old-guard Chicago professors were clearly aware of the problem as Nobel Laureate Professor Merton Miller pondered:

> "Models that they were using, not just Black-Scholes models, but other kinds of models, were based on normal behavior in the markets and when the behavior got wild, no models were able to put up with it."[35]

If only the principals at LTCM had remembered Albert Einstein's quote that elegance was for tailors, part of his observation about how beautiful formulas could pose problems in the real world. LTCM had the beautiful formulas; they were just not for the real world. Eugene Fama, Scholes' thesis advisor, had long held deep reservations about his student's options pricing model:

> "If the population of price changes is strictly normal [distribution], on the average for any stock...an observation more than five standard deviations from the mean should be observed about once every 7,000 years. In fact, such observations seem to occur about once every three to four years."[36]

LTCM lost 44% of its capital, or $1.9 billion, in August 1998 alone. In a letter to LTCM's 100 investors, dated September 1998, John W. Meriwether wrote:

For most investors, August was the month from hell. Not for William Dunn, though. His firm, Dunn Capital Management, with $900 million under management, had one of its best runs in years. He's up 25.4 percent so far this year, and 23.7 percent in August alone.[37]

> "As you are all too aware, events surrounding the collapse of Russia caused large and dramatically increasing volatility in global markets throughout August. We are down 44 percent for the month of August and 52 percent for the year to date. Losses of this magnitude are a shock to us as they surely are to you, especially in light of the historical volatility of the fund."[38]

At the time of Meriwether's letter, LTCM's history consisted of only four short years, and although its "losses of this magnitude" might have shocked LTCM, its clients, and the lender banks to whom it owed over $100 billion, those trading losses became the source of profits for trend followers. Amazingly, years later, Scholes still seemed to have a problem with accepting personal responsibility for his action in the zero-sum game:

> "In August of 1998, after the Russian default, you know, all the relations that tended to exist in a recent past seemed to disappear."[39]

Ultimately, the Fed, along with major world banks, most of which were heavily vested in LTCM, bailed the firm out. I believe that if this bailout was not allowed to happen, we might not have had the events of October 2008 unfold, which included bailouts that made LTCM look like a walk in the park. The LTCM bailout stopped normal market forces. It set in motion the events of the next 10 years, culminating in the fall of 2008.

Who Lost?

CNN Financial outlined the following LTCM losers:

- Everest Capital, a Bermuda-based hedge fund, lost $1.3 billion. The endowments of Yale and Brown Universities were invested in Everest.
- George Soros' Quantum Fund lost $2 billion.
- High Risk Opportunity Fund, a $450 million fund run by III Offshore Advisors, went bust.
- The Tiger Fund run by Julian Robertson lost $3.3 billion in August and September of 1998.
- Liechtenstein Global Trust lost $30 million.
- Bank of Italy lost $100 million.
- Credit Suisse lost $55 million.
- UBS lost $690 million.
- Sandy Weill lost $10 million.
- Dresdner lost $145 million.

"There are two kinds of people who lose money: those who know nothing and those who know everything." With two Nobel prize winners in the house, Long-Term Capital clearly fits the second case.[41]

Who Won?

As dramatic as the LTCM blowout story is, the real lessons we can learn are from the winners. Bruce Cleland, of trend follower Campbell and Company, candidly summed up LTCM and his firm's strategy:

"If you look back to the early part of 1998, you will see it was a similar period in terms of industry returns. It was a very sad time all the way through July. And then out of nowhere it came, the collapse or the near-collapse of Russia in August and the LTCM crisis. All of a sudden, August was up 10 percent and September and October were up 4 percent or 5 percent, and many CTAs pulled down an 18 percent or 20 percent year out of nowhere. It's very hard to put your head back where you were three months before that and say it looked like a very gloomy business without much of a future and all of a sudden we're the place it's all at. The hedge fund world had fallen apart, equities had gone into the toilet, and managed futures were king and on the front page of *The Wall Street Journal*. So some of this is the psychology of what we do."[40]

The performance data for trend followers in August and September of 1998 looks like one continuous credit card swipe from LTCM. During the exact same period that LTCM lost $1.9 billion in assets, the aggregate profits (see Chart 4.27) of five long-term trend followers; Bill Dunn, John W. Henry, Jerry Parker, Keith Campbell, and Man exceeded $1 billion in profit.

The Fed's intervention was misguided and unnecessary because LTCM would not have failed anyway, and the Fed's concerns about the effects of LTCM's failure on financial markets were exaggerated. In the short run, the intervention helped the shareholders and managers of LTCM to get a better deal for themselves than they would otherwise have obtained.[42]

CHART 4.27: Trend Following Profits August–September 1998

Dunn Capital Management WMA

July 1998: –1.37%, 575,000,000

August 1998: +27.51%, 732,000,000

September 1998: +16.8%, 862,000,000

Dunn Capital Management TOPS

July 1998: –1.08%, 133,000,000

August 1998: +9.48%, 150,000,000

September 1998: +12.90%, 172,000,000

John W. Henry Financials and Metals

July 1998: –0.92%, 959,000,000

August 1998: +17.50, 1,095,000,000

September 1998: +15.26, 1,240,000,000

Campbell and Company Financials and Metals

July 1998: –3.68, 917,000,000

August 1998: +9.23, 1,007,000,000

September 1998: +2.97, 1,043,000,000

Chesapeake Capital

July 1998: +3.03, 1,111,000,000

August 1998: +7.27, 1,197,000,000

September 1998: –0.59, 1,179,000,000

...[O]ne of the former top executives of LTCM [gave] a lecture in which he defended the gamble that the fund had made. What he said was, "Look, when I drive home every night in the fall, I see all these leaves scattered around the base of the trees...There is a statistical distribution that governs the way they fall, and I can be pretty accurate in figuring out what that distribution is going to be. But one day, I came home and the leaves were in little piles. Does that falsify my theory that there are statistical rules governing how leaves fall? No. It was a man-made event." In other words, the Russians, by defaulting on their bonds, did something that they were not supposed to do, a once-in-a-lifetime, rule-breaking event...[this] is just the point: In the markets, unlike in the physical universe, the rules of the game can be changed. Central banks can decide to default on government-backed securities.

Malcolm Gladwell[43]

Man Investments

July 1998: +1.06, 1,636,000,000

August 1998: +14.51, 1,960,000,000

September 1998: +3.57, 2,081,000,000

Note: Percent returns for each month and total money under management in that fund.

Crunch the numbers on Dunn Capital Management's World Monetary Assets (WMA) fund. Their fund made nearly $300 million for the months of August and September 1998 alone. What markets (see Charts 4.28–4.35), for example, did trend followers profit from?

CHART 4.28: Trend Followers and the 10 Year T-Note May 1998–December 1998 Source: Barchart.com

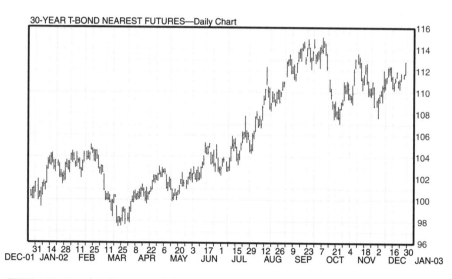

CHART 4.29: Trend Followers and the US T-Bond May 1998–December 1998

Source: Barchart.com

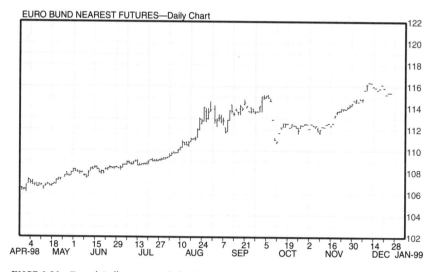

CHART 4.30: Trend Followers and the German Bund May 1998–December 1998

Source: Barchart.com

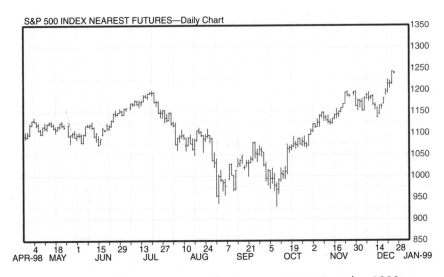

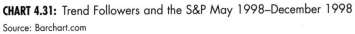

CHART 4.31: Trend Followers and the S&P May 1998–December 1998

Source: Barchart.com

CHART 4.32: Trend Followers and the Swiss Franc May 1998–December 1998

Source: Barchart.com

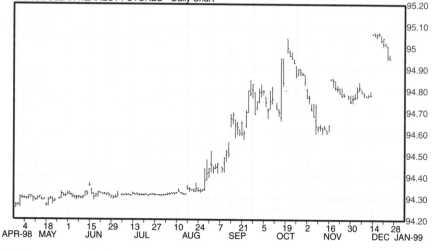

CHART 4.33: Trend Followers and the Eurodollar May 1998–December 1998

Source: Barchart.com

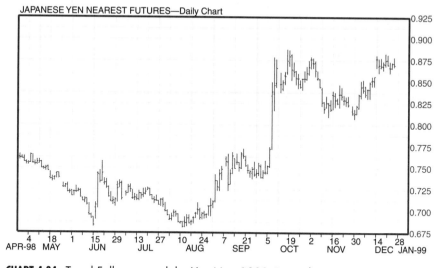

CHART 4.34: Trend Followers and the Yen May 1998–December 1998

Source: Barchart.com

CHART 4.35: Trend Followers and the Dollar Index May 1998–December 1998 Source: Barchart.com

It isn't that they can't see the solution. It is that they can't see the problem.

G. K. Chesterton[44]

What "lessons learned" do business school professors teach when analyzing LTCM's failure today? I am guessing that they don't teach the crucial points Jerry Parker made when he differentiated his firm from LTCM:

- **Transparent**—By and large, trend followers trade markets on regulated exchanges. They are not cooking up new derivatives in their basements. Trend followers typically trade on freely traded markets where a price that everyone can see enables anyone to buy or sell. Trend followers have nothing in common with the derivatives fiascos that damaged Orange County or Proctor and Gamble.

- **Understandable**—Trend following strategies can be understood by just about anybody. No high-level math that only PhDs can comprehend.

- **No rock stars**—There are individuals who not only want to make money, but also want a rock star as their portfolio manager. They want to think that the strategy being used to make them money is exciting and state-of-the-art. Trend followers are not in the game for notoriety, just to win.

Debate continues about whether it was proper for the government to step in and save LTCM. Indeed, what would have happened (and how much more money would trend followers have made) if LTCM had been allowed to properly implode?

I asked Dunn Capital Management whether they thought it was proper that the Fed helped bail out LTCM. Daniel Dunn replied with a one-word answer: "No." When I asked Bill Dunn, he opined:

"I believe the Long-Term Capital Management collapse was caused by:

1. Their trading approach was based on the theory that prices and relationships between prices tend to vary, but they also tend to return to their mean value over long periods of time. So in practice, they probably looked at a market (or a spread between markets) and determined what its mean value was and where the current price was in relation to their estimate of its 'true mean' value. If the current price was below the mean, a 'buy' was indicated, and if it was above the mean, a 'sell' was indicated. (I don't know what their exit strategy was.)

2. The main problem with the above is that as market prices move further against your position, you will be experiencing losses in your open positions and your above trading approach would suggest that adding to the current position will prove to be even more profitable than originally expected. Unless this market very quickly turns and starts its anticipated return to its mean, additional losses will be suffered and the potential for profit will seem to become even greater, although elusive.

3. This problem can only be overcome by either adopting a strict entry and exit strategy that is believed to promote survivability or by having a nearly unlimited amount of capital/credit to withstand the occasional extreme excursions from the mean, or better yet, adopt both of these ideas.

4. But the situation became even more unstable when LTCM ventured into highly illiquid investment vehicles and also became a very major part of these very thin markets.

5. In the end, they became overextended and they ran out of capital before any anticipated reversion to the mean could bail them out."

Investors who cannot or will not learn from the past could be setting themselves up for another August–September 1998. Another LTCM fiasco might be in the offing if the Black-Scholes way of life, where the world is a normal distribution, is still considered a viable approach to investing. Philip Anderson, a Nobel Prize Recipient in Physics, sees the dangers that come from thinking in terms of normal distributions:

> "Much of the real world is controlled as much by the 'tails' of distributions as by means or averages: by the exceptional, not the mean; by the catastrophe, not the steady drip; by the very rich, not the 'middle class.' We need to free ourselves from 'average' thinking."[45]

Breaking out from average thinking results in hitting home runs (trend followers) instead of attempting and failing to slap those supposed sure-fire singles (LTCM).

A footnote: Myron Scholes went on to form a new fund called Platinum Grove after LTCM's demise. With Scholes as Chairman, Platinum Grove lost $600 million dollars during 2007–2008 during the credit market meltdown. How many funds does this particular financial genius have to blow up before the genius tag should be taken away?

Event #4: Asian Contagion

The Asian crisis of 1997, also referred to as the Asian Contagion, was yet another big event where trend followers won. One of the biggest losers during the fall of 1997 was the infamous trader Victor Niederhoffer. Always opinionated, bombastic, and for most of his trading career, exceptionally successful, Niederhoffer's trading demise was swift.

Niederhoffer played a big game, whether at speculating, chess, or squash. He challenged grandmasters in chess, and he won repeated titles as a national squash champion. He regularly bet hundreds of millions of dollars and consistently won until Monday,

October 27, 1997. That day he lost an estimated $50 to $100 million, and his three hedge funds Limited Partners of Niederhoffer Intermarket Fund L.P., Limited Partners of Niederhoffer Friends Partnership L.P., and Niederhoffer Global Systems S.A. bellied up.[46]

Imagine receiving this letter, which was faxed to clients of Niederhoffer on Wednesday, October 29, 1997:

We make a lot more money trading at the level we do. The trade-off is volatility, but if it doesn't cause you to perish, then you're better off in the long run.

Dunn Capital[47]

To:

Limited Partners of Niederhoffer Intermarket Fund, L.P.

Limited Partners of Niederhoffer Friends Partnership, L.P.

Shareholders of Niederhoffer Global Systems, S.A.

Dear Customers:

As you no doubt are aware, the New York stock market dropped precipitously on Monday, October 27, 1997. That drop followed large declines on two previous days. This precipitous decline caused substantial losses in the fund's positions, particularly their positions in puts on the Standard & Poor's 500 Index. As you also know from my previous correspondence with you, the funds suffered substantial losses earlier in the year as a result of the collapse in the East Asian markets, especially in Thailand.

The cumulation [sic] of these adverse developments led to the situation where, at the close of business on Monday, the funds were unable to meet minimum capital requirements for the maintenance of their margin accounts. It is not yet clear what is the precise extent (if any) to which the funds' equity balances are negative. We have been working with our broker-dealers since Monday evening to try to meet the funds' obligations in an orderly fashion. However, right now, the indications are that the entire equity positions in the funds has been wiped out.

Sadly, it would appear that if it had been possible to delay liquidating most of the funds' accounts for one more day, a liquidation could have been avoided. Nevertheless, we cannot deal with "would have been." We took risks. We were successful for a long time. This time we did not succeed, and I regret to say that all of us have suffered some very large losses.[49]

On Wednesday Niederhoffer told investors in three hedge funds he runs that their stakes had been "wiped out" Monday by losses that culminated from three days of falling stock prices and big hits earlier this year in Thailand.[48]

Niederhoffer seems unable to acknowledge that he, alone, was to blame for his losses in the zero-sum game. He did it. No one else did it for him and he can't use the unexpected as his excuse.

I felt there were very definite economic trends that were established from knowledge and the ability to know what events meant. I was looking for a way to participate in [those] major trends when they occurred, even though they were unexpected.

Bill Dunn[51]

His trading performance was long heralded as low risk. He made money almost every month. Compared to trend followers, he was the golden boy. Who would want to place money with trend followers and potentially tolerate a bigger drawdown when they could put their money with Niederhoffer, who seemed to combine similar performance with what appeared to be far less risk and almost no drawdown?

The notion that Niederhoffer was devoid of risk sank with his trading firm in 1997. Examine his performance numbers during that year (Chart 4.36):

CHART 4.36: Niederhoffer 1997 Performance[50]

Date	VAMI	ROR	Quarter ROR	Yearly ROR	Amount Managed
Jan-97	11755	4.42%			
Feb-97	11633	−1.04%			
Mar-97	10905	−6.26%	−3.13%		$130.0M
Apr-97	11639	6.73%			
May-97	11140	−4.28%			
Jun-97	10296	−7.58%	−5.58%		$115.0M
Jul-97	11163	8.42%			
Aug-97	5561	−50.18%			
Sep-97	7100	27.67%	−31.04%		$88.0M
Oct-97	1	−99.99%			
Nov-97	1	0.00%			
Dec-97	1	0.00%	−99.99%	−99.99%	0

When reviewing Niderhoffer's 1997 performance meltdown (see Chart 4.36), keep in mind that in the last issue of The Stark Report where his performance was still listed, his ranking is as follows:

Return: four stars

Risk: four stars

Risk Adjusted: four stars

Equity: five stars[52]

These star rankings give the impression that Niederhoffer was risk-free. However, his trading, like LTCM's, was predicated on a world of normal distributions. Measuring him with standard deviation as the risk measure gave an imperfect view of what Niederhoffer's true risk actually was. Of course, some observers were well aware of the inherent problems in Niederhoffer's contrarian style long before his blowout. Frank J. Franiak spoke out six months earlier in spring 1997:

"It's a matter of time before something goes wrong."[53]

But Niederhoffer loyalists were concerned only with whether the profits were coming in, even if his strategy was deeply flawed and potentially dangerous. His clients were enamored with his ability to rebound: "Whatever voodoo he uses, it works," said Timothy P. Horne, chairman of Watts Industries Inc. (and a Niederhoffer customer since 1982).[54]

Unfortunately, the vast majority of Niederhoffer clients did not realize until after their accounts were toast that voodoo doesn't work.

Niederhoffer Confuses Trend Following

Oddly, five years after his blowout, Niederhoffer ripped trend following:

"Granted that some users of trend following have achieved success. Doubtless their intelligence and insights are quite superior to our own. But it's at times like this, when everything seems to be coming up roses for the trend followers' theories and reputations, that it's worthwhile to step back and consider some fundamental questions:

1. Is their central rule; is the trend is your friend valid?

2. Might their reported results, good or bad, be best explained as due to chance?

"But first, a warning: We do not believe in trend following. We are not members of the Market Technicians Association or the International Federation of Technical Analysts or the TurtleTrader Trend Followers Hall of Fame. In fact, we are on the enemies' lists of such organizations."[56]

[Victor Niederhoffer] looked at markets as a casino where people act as gamblers and where their behavior can be understood by studying gamblers. He regularly made small amounts of money trading on that theory. There was a flaw in his approach, however. If there is a...tide...he can be seriously hurt because he doesn't have a proper fail-safe mechanism.

George Soros[55]

In statistical terms, I figure I have traded about 2 million contracts—with an average profit of $70 per contract. This average profit is approximately 700 standard deviations away from randomness, a departure that would occur by chance alone about as frequently as the spare parts in an automotive salvage lot might spontaneously assemble themselves into a McDonald's restaurant.

Victor Niederhoffer[59]

I have a hard time understanding how, after reviewing the month-by-month performance histories of numerous trend following traders that Niederhoffer sees their returns as "due to chance."

Niederhoffer goes on to question trend following: "No test of 'the trend is your friend' is possible, because the rule is never put forward in the form of a testable hypothesis. Something is always slippery, subjective, or even mystical about the rule's interpretation and execution."[57]

Even though the performance data is clear, in his most recent book Niederhoffer still didn't "get it:"

> "In my dream, I am long IBM, or priceline.com, or worst of all, Krung Thai Bank, the state owned bank in Thailand that fell from $200 to pennies while I held in 1997. The rest of the dream is always the same. My stock plunges. Massive margin calls are being issued. Related stocks jump off cliffs in sympathy. Delta hedges are selling more stocks short to rebalance their positions. The naked options I am short are going through the roof. Millions of investors are blindly following the headlines. Listless as zombies, they are liquidating their stocks at any price and piling into money market funds with an after tax yield of −1 percent. 'Stop you fools!' I scream. 'There's no danger! Can't you see? The headlines are inducing you to lean the wrong way! Unless you get your balance, you'll lose everything—your wealth, your home!'"[58]

Most important, Niederhoffer is an inveterate contrarian. He feeds off panic, making short-term bets when prices get frothy. He condemns the common strategy of trend following, which helped make his buddy George Soros super-rich. "A delusion," he declares.[60]

Niederhoffer seems to have a difficult time accepting blame. He is one nontrend follower who should be profiled in two of my chapters. Not only does his zero-sum wealth transfer during the 1997 Asian Contagion make him critical to Chapter 4, but his inconsistent thinking and refusal to take responsibility place him squarely in Chapter 9, "Holy Grails."

Event #5: Barings Bank

The first few months of 1995 must go down as one of the most eventful periods in the history of speculative trading. The market events of that time period, by themselves, could be the subject of a graduate course in finance at Harvard Business School. Only a few years later, despite the significance of what happened, the events have been forgotten.

A rogue trader, Nick Leeson, overextended Barings Bank in the Nikkei 225, the Japanese equivalent to the American Dow, by speculating that the Nikkei 225 would move higher. It tanked, and Barings, the Queen's bank, one of the oldest, most well established banks in England, collapsed, losing $2.2 billion.

Who won the Barings Bank sweepstakes? That question was never asked by anyone—not *The Wall Street Journal* nor *Investor's Business Daily*. Was the world interested only in a story about failure and not the slightest bit curious about where that $2.2 billion went? Trend followers were sitting at the table devouring Leeson's mistakes. They saw, in Barings, an opportunity to win as Barings lost.

The majority of traders do not have the discipline to plan 3, 6, and 12 months ahead for unforeseen changes in markets. However, planning for the unexpected is an essential ingredient of trend following. Big moves are always on the horizon if you are simply reacting to the market and not trying to predict it.

Why do many people miss the big events and consequently the big trends? Most traders make decisions on their perceptions of what the market direction will be. After they make their directional choice, they become blinded to any other option. They keep searching for any type of validation to support their analysis even if they are losing money—just like Nick Leeson. Before the Kobe earthquake in early January 1995, with the Nikkei trading in a range of 19,000 to 19,500, Leeson had long futures positions of approximately 3,000 contracts on the Osaka Stock Exchange. After the Kobe earthquake of January 17, his build up of Nikkei positions intensified and Leeson just kept buying as the Nikkei sank.[62]

Despite his envy and admiration, he did not want to be Victor Niederhoffer—not then, not now, and not even for a moment in between. For when he looked around him, at the books and the tennis court and the folk art on the walls—when he contemplated the countless millions that Niederhoffer had made over the years—he could not escape the thought that it might all have been the result of sheer, dumb luck.

Malcolm Gladwell[61]

Who Won?

Observe the Nikkei 225 (see Chart 4.37) from September 1994 until June 1995. Barings' lost assets padded the pockets of disciplined trend following traders.

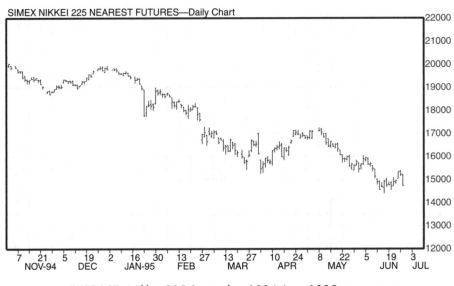

SIMEX NIKKEI 225 NEAREST FUTURES—Daily Chart

CHART 4.37: Nikkei 225 September 1994–June 1995   Source: Barchart.com

A few months after Barings, John W. Henry's performance (see Chart 4.38) makes the case clear:

CHART 4.38: John W. Henry Trading Programs

Name of Program	01-95	02-95	03-95
Financials and Metals	$648	$733	$827
	–3.8	15.7	15.3
Global Diversified	$107	$120	$128
	–6.9	13.5	8.5
Original	$54	$64	$73
	2.1	17.9	16.6
Global Financial	$7	$9	$14
	–4.1	25.6	44.4

All dollars are in millions under management.

Dean Witter (now Morgan Stanley) was Henry's broker at the time:

"I have over $250 million with Henry…I have been pleased to see how well the Original [Henry] Program has done so far in 1995: up over 50 percent through April 18 [1995]."[63]

Other trend followers brought home huge gains in February and March of 1995 (see Chart 4.39). However, their winnings arguably were more from the Japanese Yen trend up and down.

CHART 4.39: 1995 Trend Following Performance

Name	01-95	02-95	03-95
Chesapeake	$549	$515	$836
	–3.2	–4.4	8.6
Rabar	$148	$189	$223
	–9.4	14.0	15.2
Campbell Fin/Metals	$255	$253	$277
	–4.53	5.85	9.58
Mark J. Walsh	$20	$22	$29
	–16.4	17.0	32.3
Abraham	$78	$93	$97
	–7.9	1.2	6.6
Dunn (WMA)	$178	$202	$250
	0.5	13.7	24.4
Dunn (TOPS)	$63	$69	$81
	–7.6	9.9	22.7
Millburn Ridgefield	$183	$192	$233
	–6.5	8.7	19.4

Monthly percent returns with total money under management. All dollars are in millions under management.

What about luck? In my opinion, luck is far and away the most important determinant in our lives. Various events of infinitesimal probability—where you are born, to whom you are born, who you marry, where you take your first job, which school you choose—have enormous impact on our lives. People tend to deny that luck is an important determinant. We like explanations. For instance, during a basketball game, there are innumerable random events. If a guy hits three in a row, he's really hot. Most of the time, it's random. Of course, the announcer doesn't want to say, "Oh my! Another random event!" That's not exciting, so he'll give a reason. But it's just luck. Not all of our luck is good, but there is more good luck behind our performance than even I like to acknowledge.

James Simons, The Greenwich Roundtable, June 17, 1999

There might be slight differences in leverage and signal timing, but even from a quick glance it is clear: Big trends equaled big profits at the same time for all trend followers. Henry confirmed in 1998, albeit cryptically, his massive zero-sum Barings win:

"The inflation story, of course, is not the most dramatic example. More recently Asia is another example of how one-time big events can lead to trends that offer us opportunity, and really shape our world. Whether you believe the causal story of banking excesses in Asia or not,

There is no profit taking per se. We only exit on stop-losses, because profit taking would interfere with the unlimited upside potential we have, in theory, on every position. Our stop-loss policy is an actuarial model that analyzes the probability and consequences of hitting stops placed at various prices relative to the current market level. This allows us to estimate the expected loss associated with each possible exit point and hence to construct an optimal liquidation schedule.

Paul Mulvaney, CIO of Mulvaney Capital Management, Ltd.

there was a clear adjustment in the Asian economies that has been, and will continue to be, drawn out. Under these situations, it's natural that trends will develop, and recognizing these trends allows us to capitalize on the errors or mistakes of other market participants. Because, after all, we're involved in a zero-sum game."[64]

Henry and Leeson were involved in a zero-sum game. They both ponied up to the table. However, there was one big difference—Henry had a strategy. What Leeson had nobody really knows, but as long as Leeson was making money, his bosses and higher-ups in England did not much care. They surely cared after he destroyed their bank, but it was too late.

Event #6: Metallgesellschaft

Metallgesellschaft (MG) now has a new name and a new identity as a specialty chemicals plant and process-engineering concern. However, for 119 years, the German company was a metals, trading, and construction conglomerate, best known for the high-profile mess it was involved in after a New York arm, MG Refining Marketing Inc. (MGRM), produced what its chief lenders considered reckless losses in its energy-trading operations. In 1993, steep margin debt calls contributed significantly to MG's loss of $1.5 billion (2.3 billion Deutsche marks at the time). Just before collapsing, the company was bailed out by German banks.[65]

What happened?

MG was long crude oil futures on the New York Mercantile Exchange (NYMEX) through most of 1993. During that time period, MG lost, depending on the estimate or source, $1.3 to $2.1 billion. Because trading is a zero-sum game, those traders in short crude oil futures made the money MG lost. They were the winners, and they were trend followers.

During the course of 1993, crude oil futures (see Chart 4.40) slowly declined from May through December.

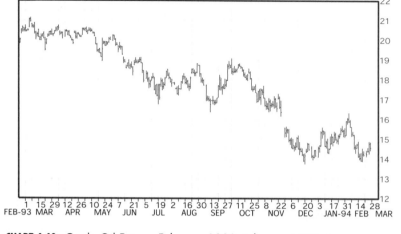

CHART 4.40: Crude Oil Futures February 1993–February 1994 Source: Barchart.com

There is always someone on each side of a trade. The difficulty lies in determining who is on the opposite side of a position if only one side is publicly known. The fact that MG lost was known, but who won and how? In the aftermath of the MG losses, a variety of explanations developed. The financial world was treated to academic mumbo jumbo from MBA students analyzing why MG lost money, as well as numerous articles condemning energy futures. The actual explanation is simply: MG had a bad plan and lost big.

Clearly, trend followers played a major role in MG's defeat. The job of explaining this is made easy by their performance data (see Chart 4.41):

But in the course of the next 12 months, it became more and more obvious that other traders were formulating trading strategies that exploited MG's need to liquidate its expiring long position. At the end of each trading month, as MG tried to liquidate its long positions by buying the offsetting shorts, other traders would add their short positions to MG's, creating the paper market equivalent of a glut in supply that initially exceeded the number of longs, driving prices down until the market reached equilibrium. The combined force of MG's selling its long position in the prompt contract and other traders increasing their short positions was severe downward pressure on crude prices as the prompt month contract neared expiration.[66]

One of the few things the post-mortems seem to have glossed over is the trap that MG had gotten itself into by becoming the dominant participant in the futures markets. By the fall of 1993, some traders had come to anticipate the rollovers of MG's positions. As long as its huge position was in the market, MG hung there like a big piñata inviting others to hit it each month. The self-entrapping nature of its positions is what is missing from Edwards and Canter's, and even Culp and Miller's, defenses of MG.[67]

CHART 4.41: Trend Followers' Performances June 1993–January 1994

	6-93	7-93	8-93	9-93	10-93	11-93	12-93	1-94
Abraham	–1.2	6.6	–5.3	1.2	–6.6	3.5	12.5	–1.45
Chesapeake	1.0	9.5	5.8	–2.7	–0.1	1.1	5.8	–3.33
JPD	–6.9	10.2	–2.1	–4.1	–2.0	2.7	8.6	–3.9
Rabar	–1.3	14.8	–3.9	–4.1	–6.0	5.6	10.1	–10.5
Saxon	–2.7	20.5	–14.3	–2.1	–1.1	6.6	17.1	–10.8

The key to explaining Chart 4.41 lies in the months of July 1993, December 1993, and January 1994. Those months do not require much more than a glance at the correlation data to confirm the similarity in strategies used by trend followers. Trend followers all made money in July and December, and they all lost money in January.

The academics, the media, and everyone, it seems, figured out that professional traders were shorting the energy market and putting extensive pressure on MG. What the academics never found out or never seemed to be interested in finding out was who those professional traders were. The performance data was out there for everybody to look at. It wasn't a secret.

Every day, trend followers knew how many contracts or shares to trade based on total capital at that time. For example, after they initiated positions and were rewarded with strong profits in July, they were willing to risk those profits again, which is what they did. In August, with nice profits in hand, they were willing to risk those profits and still lose a fixed percentage based on their original stops. They were willing to let profits on the table turn into losses. They let the market tell them when the trend was over (January 1994).

In the fall of 1993, trend followers continued to hold their established short positions in crude oil futures. MG was long crude oil futures and desperately trying to stay afloat while trend followers waited like predators. However, trend followers were not just short; they were aggressively short, reinvesting their profits back into additional short crude oil positions as the market decreased more and more.

On the losing side of this zero-sum game, MG had no apparent strategy. They refused to take a loss early on. In fact, the whole MG affair would have been a footnote in trading history if they had simply exited after the July price decline. However, instead, MG stayed in the game in hopes of an upward trend to make up for losses. But MG had no inkling of the steely discipline of their opponents. Not one of the trend followers was going to exit anytime soon. The price told them the trend was down. An exit would have violated one of their most fundamental rules: let winners run.

Crude oil began its final descent in late November into December. At this time, MG management liquidated all positions and further fueled the November and December crude price drop. Ultimately, all good trends must end. Trend followers would eventually begin their crude oil futures exit in January 1994. If you look at the performance of trend followers in January 1994 (see Chart 4.41), you can see what they lost for the month as they extricated themselves from their history-making profits of 1993 (see Chart 4.42).

According to the NYMEX, MGRM held the futures position equivalent of 55 million barrels of gasoline and heating oil.[68]

CHART 4.42: 1993 Trend Following Returns

Name	% Return
Abraham Trading	+34.29%
Chesapeake Capital	+61.82%
Man Investments	+24.49%
Rabar Market Research	+49.55%
Dunn WMA	+60.25%
John W. Henry Financials and Metals	+46.85%
Mark J. Walsh	+74.93%
Eckhardt Trading	+57.95%

"Can you do addition?" the White Queen asked. "What's one and one and one and one and one and one and one and one and one and one?" "I don't know," said Alice. "I lost count."

Lewis Carroll[69]

Final Thoughts

There is no shortage of big events in the past three decades to demonstrate how trend followers won big. However, there are still skeptics who think they have found the Achilles heel of trend following.

The 1987 Stock Crash

One of my favorite questions from skeptics is: "How did the trend followers do during the 1987 stock crash?" Their tone always gives away what they think the answer will be (or what they hope it will be). The fall of 1987, as the data proves (see Chart 4.43 and Chart 4.44), produced historic gains for trend followers:

CHART 4.43: October–November 1987 Stock Market Crash

Name	% Return
S&P 500	–28%
John W. Henry Original Investment Program	+58.2%
John W. Henry Financials and Metals Portfolio	+69.7%

CHART 4.44: Trend Following Performance 1987

Name	% Return
Chesapeake Capital	+38.78%
JPD	+96.80%
Rabar	+78.20%
John W. Henry Financials and Metals	+251.00%
Campbell and Company Financials and Metals	+64.38%
Millburn Ridgefield	+32.68%
Dunn Capital Management WMA	+72.15%
Mark J. Walsh	+143%
Man Investments	+42.54%

The First Gulf War

Skeptics also assume that the first Gulf War was probably a time period in which trend followers incurred losses. The data from John W. Henry shows otherwise.

During the 1990 market decline and subsequent recovery, Henry's Financials and Metals Portfolio generated returns of 38.1

percent against the S&P 500's 4.4 percent. While Jaguar [Julian Robertson] and Quantum [George Soros] performed better than the broad market, they did not perform as well as Financial and Metals Portfolio.[71]

Trend follower Jerry Parker outlined a clear and coherent view of why fundamental analysis played no role in the trading of trend followers:

> "Fundamental analysis that excluded the possibility of an Iraqi invasion of Kuwait in the summer of 1990 would have been incomplete and possibly unprofitable, or worse. This was the only 'fundamental' that was worth knowing, yet was the very one that almost no one could have known. Technical analysis relies upon the idea that smart money will move into a market and give advance warning that a position should be taken. This often occurs when the true major fundamentals are unknown."[72]

The events presented in this chapter should leave everyone with one inescapable conclusion: One of the main reasons that trend following trading does well is because it has no quarterly performance constraints. It is opportunistic. What do I mean? Both Wall Street and Main Street measure success on the artificial constraints of the calendar. For example, looking back at the end of 2000, you can see that without November and December offering such huge home runs, trend followers would have had a terrible year. For those people who judge trading success by "quarters," trend followers were dead the better part of 2000.

When you have eliminated the impossible, what ever remains, however improbable must be the truth.
Sir Arthur Conan Doyle[73]

The whole idea of quarterly performance reporting implies you can predict the market or successfully shoot for profit targets. Quarters as a measurement might not be real, but they provide a comfortable structure for investors who mistakenly believe they can demand nice, consistent profits. This demand for consistency has led to a constant search for the Holy Grail or "hot hand" to the detriment of ever winning consistently. It's a catch-22.

Imagine playing football where there are four quarters, and you have to score in each quarter to win. Imagine placing more importance on scoring in each quarter than winning the game. Now a great trend trader says, "I might score 28 points in any of the four quarters. I might score at any point in the game, but the object, at the end of the game is to win." So if a trend following trader scores

Blaming derivatives for financial losses is akin to blaming cars for drunk driving fatalities.
Christopher L. Culp[74]

28 points in the first quarter and no points in the next three quarters, and wins, who cares when he scored? Wall Street's misguided emphasis on quarterly performance puts more importance on scoring each quarter than it does on winning the game.

The alternative is to become a home run hitter and take what the market gives no matter when it arrives. Absolute return traders, trend followers, have no profit targets. They view their world as a "rolling return." I asked Bill Dunn how they address the quarterly performance measures so popular on Wall Street. I wanted to know how they educate clients to appreciate "big event hunting." The response was clear: "Clients must already have an appreciation for the pitfalls of relying on short-term performance data before they can appreciate us."

Blunt talk for a serious game. On the other hand, after he retired from trading, Julian Robertson publicly lamented his constraints, comparing them to a necessary but incompetent baseball umpire: "One of the great investors likened it to a batter not having an umpire. If you don't have an umpire, you can wait for the fat pitch. The trouble with investing for other people, particularly in a hedge fund, is that you do have an umpire—called quarterly performance."

If everyone knows the umpire of quarterly performance is ridiculous, why do we stick with it? The behavioral and psychological biases to examine to answer such a simple question would far exceed the few hundred pages of *Trend Following*!

The Always "New" Coming Storm

I added the following excerpt to my second edition of this book in the fall of 2005. It was from commentary from a February 2004 edition of *The Economist*:

"The size of banks' bets is rising rapidly the world over. This is because potential returns have fallen as fast as markets have risen, so banks have had to bet more in order to continue generating huge profits. The present situation "is not dissimilar" to the one that preceded the collapse of LTCM...banks are 'walking themselves to the edge of the cliff.' This is because—as all past financial crises have shown—the risk-management models they use woefully underestimate the savage effects of big shocks, when everybody is trying to wriggle out of their positions at the same time…By regulatory fiat, when banks' positions sour, they must either stump up more capital or reduce their exposures. Invariably, when markets are panicking, they do the latter. Because everyone else is heading for the exits at the same time, these become more than a little crowded, moving prices against those trying to get out, and requiring still more unwinding of positions. It has happened many times before with more or less calamitous consequences… There are any number of potential flashpoints: a rout in the dollar, say, or a huge spike in the oil price, or a big emerging market getting into trouble again. If it does happen, the chain reaction could be particularly devastating this time."[75]

I am no prophet, but I do feel satisfaction that I included that excerpt in this book more than three years ago, long before we ever got to the chaos that was October 2008. That excerpt unfolded just like a movie script with trend traders again winning big. My next prediction is that the excerpt will probably unfold again in the years to come just as it did in 2008. Will you be ready? Will you have a plan?

Or will you be sitting there, like so many, as Hunter S. Thompson once so sadly noted about the condition of human herds: "In a nation ruled by swine, all pigs are upwardly mobile and the rest of us are [screwed] until we can put our acts together: not necessarily to win, but mainly to keep from losing completely. We owe that to ourselves and our crippled self-image as something better than a nation of panicked sheep."

The success of options valuation is the story of a simple, asymptotically correct idea, taken more seriously than it deserved, and then used extravagantly, with hubris, as a crutch to human thinking.

Emanuel Derman[76]

It seems LTCM could have survived one Nobel prize-winner, but with two, they were doomed.

Frederic Townsend[77]

Key Points

- Seykota: "Trends become more apparent as you step further away from the chart."
- Trend followers are generally on the right side of big moves.
- The most interesting aspect of the Barings Bank blowout was who won. Everyone knew the Queen's bank lost, but the winners were trend followers in the zero-sum game.

Corporations make good and bad decisions every day offers one dealer. P&G made a bad decision. But if they came in with a Pampers line that flopped, you wouldn't have hearings in Congress, would you?[78]

When the mind is in a state of uncertainty the smallest impulse directs it to either side. [Lat., Dum in dubio est animus, paulo momento huc illuc impellitur.]

Terence (Publius Terentius Afer),
Source: Andria (I, 5, 32)

- People place too much emphasis on the short-term performance of trend followers. They draw conclusions about one month's performance and forget to look at the long term. Just like a batting average, which can have short-term streaks over the course of a season, trend followers have streaks. Trend following performance does deviate from averages, but over time there is remarkable consistency.

- Value-at-risk (VAR) models measure volatility, not risk. If you rely on VAR as a risk measure you are in trouble.

- Hunt Taylor, Director of Investments, Stern Investment Holdings, states: "I'm wondering when statisticians are going to figure out that the statistical probability of improbable losses are absolutely the worst predictors of the regularity with which they'll occur. I mean, the single worst descriptor of negative events is the hundred-year flood. Am I wrong? How many hundred-year floods have we lived through in this room? Statistically maybe we should have lived through one and we lived through seven now at this point."

Baseball: Thinking Outside the Batter's Box

5

> "How to hit home runs: I swing as hard as I can, and I try to swing right through the ball... The harder you grip the bat, the more you can swing it through the ball, and the farther the ball will go. I swing big, with everything I've got. I hit big or I miss big. I like to live as big as I can."
> —Babe Ruth

> "What is striking is that the leading thinkers across varied fields— including horse betting, casino gambling, and investing—all emphasize the same point. We call it the Babe Ruth effect: even though Ruth struck out a lot, he was one of baseball's greatest hitters."
> —Michael J. Mauboussin and Kristen Bartholdson[1]

The concepts that make up trend following need to be experienced to be understood completely, which is a tough prerequisite. I find it helpful to compare trend following to baseball, a sport we have probably experienced either passively or actively to one degree or another. Baseball has always been a passion of mine. My playing career went from Little League through college, and I've watched more baseball than I care to admit. I've always known that baseball and trend following have much in common, but it wasn't until the past few years that sportswriters and financial writers started acknowledging the similarities. Not surprisingly, this was

The point about Dykstra, at least to Billy, was clear: Dykstra didn't let his mind mess him up. Only a psychological freak could approach a 100-m.p.h. fastball aimed not all that far from his head with total confidence. "Lenny was so perfectly designed, emotionally, to play the game of baseball," Beane said. "He was able to instantly forget any failure and draw strength from every success. He had no concept of failure. I was the opposite."

Moneyball[2]

The general complacency of baseball people—even those of undoubted intelligence—toward mathematical examination of what they regard properly and strictly as their own dish of tea is not too astonishing. I would be willing to go as far as pretending to understand why none of four competent and successful executives of second-division ball clubs were most reluctant to employ probabilistic methods of any description…but they did not even want to hear about them!

Earnshaw Cook[6]

about the time that John W. Henry bought the Boston Red Sox. Henry makes the connection in the classic book *Moneyball*:

"People in both fields [stock market and baseball] operate with beliefs and biases. To the extent that you can eliminate both and replace them with data, you gain a clear advantage. Many people think they are smarter than others in the stock market and that the market itself has no intrinsic intelligence as if it's inert. Many people think they are smarter than others in baseball and that the game on the field is simply what they think through their set of images/beliefs. Actual data from the market means more than individual perception/belief. The same is true in baseball."[3]

If you could find data that would prove otherwise, but still enable you to win, would you be able to set aside your ego and play the game by a set of rules? If so, you might be on the same path as John W. Henry.

The Home Run

Clearly, David Harding, Bill Dunn, Salem Abraham, and John W. Henry to name a few trend followers swing for the fence. They hit home runs in their trading performance. They are the Babe Ruths of trend following. If any of them coached a baseball team, they would approach it like the former manager of the Baltimore Orioles:

"Earl Weaver designed his offenses to maximize the chance of a three-run homer. He didn't bunt, and he had a special taste for guys who got on base and guys who hit home runs."[4]

Ed Seykota uses a clever baseball analogy to explain his view of absolute returns (and home runs):

"When you're up to bat, it doesn't pay to hedge your swing…True for stocks and true for [Barry] Bonds."[5]

If you are going to play, you might as well play hard. Swing hard and if you miss, so be it.

Babe Ruth, hero of New York, hero of baseball, and arguably one of the greatest sports legends of all time, will always be known for his home runs. However, he had another habit that isn't talked about much: striking out. In fact, with a lifetime batting average of .342, the Babe spent almost two-thirds of his time trudging back to the dugout. From a pure numbers perspective, he saw more failure at the plate than success.

Life is too dynamic to remain static.

John W. Henry[7]

There's a reason why "Ruthian" is still a well-known adjective in sports writing that conveys the awe and power of a mighty blast that sails far over the fence. Ruth understood that the big hits help more than the strikeouts hurt. He summarized his philosophy in a nutshell: "Every strike brings me closer to the next home run."

Richard Driehaus, a hugely successful trader who has made millions trading trends, while physically no Babe Ruth, sure sounds like Ruth:

> "A third paradigm [pushed in the financial press] is don't try to hit home runs—you make the most money by hitting a lot of singles. I couldn't disagree more. I believe you can make the most money hitting home runs. But, you also need a discipline to avoid striking out. That is my sell discipline. I try to cut my losses and let my winners run."[8]

But swinging for the fence is often characterized as reckless by the uninitiated:

> "One competitor said Henry is our industry's Dave Kingman, referring to the ex-ballplayer famous for either hitting home runs or striking out. Henry says such talk is unfair. 'I've been doing this for 20 years, and every time there's a change in the market, they say I should change my ways. But every time there's a period when we don't do well, it's followed by one in which we do extraordinarily well.'"[9]

A competitor thinks Henry is Dave Kingman? Henry's performance is much closer to Babe Ruth's than Kingman's. Consider the actual hitting statistics of Ruth and Kingman (see Chart 5.1).

Even before he trained with commodities legend Richard Dennis, Jim DiMaria had learned an important trading principle in the less lucrative arena of baseball statistics: The players who score the most runs are home run hitters, not those with consistent batting records. "It's the same with trading," the 28-year-old DiMaria says. "Consistency is something to strive for, but it's not always optimal. Trading is a waiting game. You sit and wait and make a lot of money all at once. The profits tend to come in bunches. The secret is to go sideways between the home runs, not lose too much between them."[10]

And if you step back from American society and ask "What kind of people are getting rich these days?" the answer is increasingly "People like John W. Henry." That is, people on the nerdly end of the spectrum, who have a comfort with both statistical analysis and decision making in an uncertain environment. And these people, increasingly, will demand that their teams be run along rational lines.

Michael Lewis[11]

CHART 5.1: Babe Ruth Versus Dave Kingman

	Babe Ruth	Dave Kingman
At Bats	8399	6677
Hits	2873	1575
Runs	2174	901
Home Runs	714	442
Batting Average	.342	.236
Slugging	.690	.478

Compare the slugging percentages. There is no comparison. Kingman could not be considered a great run producer by any measure. On the other hand, John Henry's performance numbers are consistently out-sized. He had a great slugging percentage.

People want it both ways. Henry supposedly strikes out too much in his trading, but he's made himself enough money to buy the Boston Red Sox for $700 million. Where do you think he got the money? Henry knows numerous institutional investment managers have spent more than 20 years watching him and waiting for him to fail.

When John W. Henry purchased the Boston Red Sox, he understood that a combination of good management and hard science was the most efficient way to run a major league baseball team. As a trend follower, Henry had been exploiting market inefficiencies for decades.

Michael Lewis[12]

The lesson is this: If you have confidence in your method and yourself, temporary setbacks don't matter and strike outs don't matter because you will come out ahead in the long run if you keep swinging.

To further illustrate, consider a modern-day example: blue-collar Joe versus the entrepreneur. Blue-collar Joe is paid the same sum every two weeks like clockwork (with the occasional raise paced to keep up with inflation). In terms of winning percentage, blue collar Joe is king: His ratio of hours worked to hours paid is one to one, a perfect 100 percent. He has a steady job and a steady life. Of course, the security he feels is something of an illusion—his paycheck comes at the whim of his local economy, his industry, and even the foreman of his plant. The pay isn't exactly impressive; it gives him a solid, livable life, but not much more.

In contrast, consider the entrepreneur. His paydays are wildly irregular. He frequently goes for months, sometimes years, without seeing tangible reward for his sweat and toil. His winning percentage is, in a word, pathetic. For every 10 big ideas he has, 7 of them wind up in the circular file. Of the remaining three, two of those fizzle out within a year—another big chunk of time, money, and effort down the drain. However, I can't feel too sorry for the poor entrepreneur who spends so much time losing. He has a passion for life, he controls his own destiny, and his last idea paid off with a seven-figure check.

Moneyball and Billy Beane

Billy Beane is the General Manager of the Oakland A's baseball team. He does things differently than the stodgy old-line baseball managers. He makes his baseball decisions on the "numbers."

Beane doesn't have a fancy stadium or a wealthy owner. In fact, this small-market team's payroll is tiny compared to that of the New York Yankees. However, the Oakland A's are routinely among the best teams in major league baseball and have reached the playoffs four years in a row. What happened? Beane became the Oakland A's general manager. In a recent newsletter titled "The Buffett of Baseball," the old-school perspective on what constitutes a winning baseball team (familiar truisms about talent, character, and chemistry) is compared with the new scientific approach based on "numbers." This new approach is based on extensive scientific research into baseball statistics. It is often called sabermetrics, after SABR, the Society for American Baseball Research, and it has proved almost all of the old truisms to be false. The genius behind sabermetrics was a mechanical engineer named Earnshaw Cook, who, in the early 1960s, compiled reams of data that overturned baseball's conventional wisdom. However, when he presented the data to executives at a handful of struggling teams, they pushed him away. So Cook wrote a book called *Percentage Baseball,* based on statistics that were irrefutable.[13]

Beane-ball and trend following trading both use a scientific thinking (a precision with numbers) as opposed to using subjective "opinions" and "feelings."

What are some examples of Beane's "by-the-numbers" approach to baseball? He "uses actuarial analysis to figure out the odds of a high school pitcher becoming a major leaguer. And, in drafting and acquiring talent, he relies on those sabermetric truths. For instance, if a team draws a lot of walks and hits a lot of home runs while giving up few of each, it will win a lot of ballgames. Not

When I started writing I thought if I proved X was a stupid thing to do that people would stop doing X. I was wrong.

Bill James

You know, there are a core of institutional investment managers, primarily in Europe, who manage billions of dollars for clients, who have waited for me to fail for more than 20 years. They have an inherent bias against the notion that data or mechanical formulas can lead to success over time in markets. They have personally watched my success now for more than 20 years. Yet, if anything, they are now no more convinced than they were 20 years ago that I am going to be successful in the future using data over analysis. I am not legendary (on Wall Street or off). Bill [James] is, and I assume the inherent bias against him within baseball will increase now that he has taken sides.

John W. Henry[14]

Even while managing $1.1 billion using quantitative analysis, which he calls "quant," Henry knew that the same, dispassionate statistical investigation could be used to help shape a baseball team and its budget. "It is remarkably similar, I just happened to apply 'quant' to an area that's extremely lucrative."[15]

The nature of markets is to trend. The nature of life is to trend.

John W. Henry[18]

Usually when making investments, it is implicit that investors believe they have some degree of knowledge about the future. So Wall Street has more fortune tellers than any other industry. I feel I've had an advantage over the years because I am clear about a couple of things: 1) it is part of the nature of life itself (and markets are simply manifestations of people's expectations) to trend, and 2) I will never have a complete or full understanding of anything. Therefore, all investment decisions should be based on what can be measured rather than what might be predicted or felt.

John W. Henry[19]

surprisingly Beane has stocked his team with sluggers who take walks and control pitchers who rarely give up home runs."[16]

Beane opines, "Get me the runs." In his world, he neither wants nor needs a team full of singles hitters who never hit home runs.

John W. Henry Enters the Game

Many trend followers started trading on their own with small accounts. They grew slowly as independents. They were often renegades, unlike the more conventional traders on Wall Street who "earned their spurs" at Goldman Sachs or Morgan Stanley (well, not now that they are bank holding companies!). Their nature and their strategies were opposites of the traders who inhabit the world built on commissions. Similar to Beane's view of baseball players, trend followers realize that large amounts of cash do not guarantee wins. Strategy and smarts beats capital 9 times out of 10.

Trend following's connection with baseball and numbers picked up even more steam with John W. Henry's hiring of Bill James, the quintessential baseball "quant," or numbers guy, for more than 20 years. James, the consummate outsider, was brought on to enrich Henry's Red Sox club with his numbers-based view of baseball. James' views are harsh for the majority of baseball professionals. For example, he was excruciatingly blunt in his negative assessment of Don Zimmer, the loveable-looking former bench coach for the Yankees:

> "[A]n assortment of half-wits, nincompoops, and Neanderthals like Don Drysdale and Don Zimmer who are not only allowed to pontificate on whatever strikes them, but are actually solicited and employed to do this."[17]

Unfortunately, Zimmer added fuel to James' fire with his boneheaded attack on Pedro Martinez during the 2003 American League Championship Series with the Yankees. Zimmer might have exhibited a hint of Neanderthal behavior. However, the bad feelings James has about the establishment seem to be mutual:

> "'A little fat guy with a beard who knows nothing about nothing,' is how Hall-of-Fame manager Sparky Anderson once described James, who's neither short nor fat."[20]

How unique is the James perspective of baseball? Extremely:

"I keep thinking, however, about an e-mail that James sent me after I visited him in Kansas, in which he tried to explain the connection between his obsession with crime stories and baseball. 'I feel a need to be reminded, day in and day out, how easy it is for a fantasy to grab hold of your foot like a rope and dangle your life upside down while brigands go through your pockets,' he wrote. 'The essential message of crime books is: Deal with the life you've got. Solve the problems you have rather than fantasizing about a life without them.'"[21]

When James says solve the problems you have as opposed to fantasizing about what your life would be like without them, I am reminded of trend following traders' reliance on price as objective data. Price is a collective perception. You can accept it or ignore it. For example, even when he owned the Florida Marlins, John Henry knew he had to change.

By the time he sold the Marlins to buy the Red Sox, Henry was convinced that baseball was putting too much emphasis on tools—baseball jargon for athletic ability—and not enough on performance. The on-the-field success of the Oakland A's, then the only team using sabermetrics, confirmed Henry's view. "The Marlins would draft athletes," he says, "while the A's would draft baseball players."[22]

Part of the problem, from Henry's perspective, is the baseball old guard's love of the Adonis athlete over pure production—hitting, power, plate discipline. Would you rather have the ripped stud that looks the part, but swings and misses at every curveball, or do you notice that short fat guy who can't run and looks ridiculous, but never swings at a bad pitch and produces runs by the bushel? "Producing" is the Henry goal in both his baseball and trading. To reach that goal requires clarity. Henry was clear:

"People in both baseball and the financial markets operate with beliefs and biases. To the extent you can eliminate both and replace them with data, you gain a clear advantage. Many people think they are smarter than others in the stock market, and that the market itself has no intrinsic intelligence—as if it's inert. Similarly, many

For nearly 25 years, there's been a huge food fight in baseball. The argument was basic: How do you evaluate a player? On one side were general managers, scouts and managers. For the most part, they evaluated players the old-fashioned way—with their eyes, stopwatches, and radar guns and by looking at statistics which were popularized in the nineteenth century. Their mind-set was always, "How fast does he run? How hard does he throw? What's his batting average? Does he look like a major leaguer should look?" On the other side—led by statistical gurus such as Bill James and Pete Palmer, and assisted by countless lesser "seamheads" (including, at times, me)—were the geeks, the outsiders, mere fans, who thought they knew better.

Thomas Boswell,
The Washington Post[23]

people think they are smarter than others in baseball, and that the game on the field is simply what they think it is, filtered through their set of images and beliefs. But actual data from the market means more than individual perception/belief. And the same is true in baseball."[24]

Thinking about baseball in terms of "numbers" was not done when I played the sport, nor do I have any memory of my coaches preaching the Bill James gospel. It would have been nice to had played baseball at a time when stats were the ultimate judge.

It's like any field. There's a vested interest in maintaining the status quo so you don't have to learn anything new.

Robert Neyer, ESPN[25]

Red Sox 2003–2007

Red Sox Nation still debates whether Pedro Martinez should have been lifted in the eighth inning of Game 7 of the 2003 American League Championship Series against the Yankees. He was left in, and the Yankees rallied from three runs down to win the series. Grady Little, the Red Sox manager, was blamed for Boston's loss and fired soon thereafter. Many people wondered if he was unfairly scapegoated for a decision others would have possibly made too. After all, Martinez was his ace, and Little's gut told him to stay with his ace.

Perhaps in this situation, Martinez gets through the eighth 9 times out of 10. After all, the percentage of innings in which a pitcher gives up three or more runs is small, and Martinez was an exceptional pitcher. However, a look at the numbers says that leaving him in was the wrong decision. After 105 pitches in a given start, his batting average against rises to .370. He ended up throwing 123 pitches in Game 7.

By the end of the 2003 baseball season, I had learned something from publishing Moneyball. *I'd learned that if you look long enough for an argument against reason, you will find it.*

Michael Lewis[27]

Little's firing as manager was summed up in *The Brown Daily Herald*:

"Grady isn't a stats guy, plain and simple. He's an old school manager who goes with his gut and defers to his partially informed conscience when making decisions. Contrast this with the front office, which has transformed itself into a sabermetric, number-crunching machine, and the divide is clear as day—Fast forward to the eighth inning of Game 7 of the ALCS. Grady sends Pedro back onto the mound to the surprise of many who assumed he would be yanked after throwing exactly 100 pitches. Opponents hit .364 off Pedro this year after his 105th pitch—even Tony Clark could hit Pedro in the late innings."[26]

The late, great Stephen Jay Gould, a numbers man (and lifelong baseball fan), offered some insight into the decision-making process that might have left Martinez in the game:

"Everybody knows about hot hands. The only problem is that no such phenomenon exists. The Stanford psychologist Amos Tversky studied every basket made by the Philadelphia 76ers for more than a season. He found, first of all, that probabilities of making a second basket did not rise following a successful shot. Moreover, the number of 'runs,' or baskets in succession, was no greater than what a standard random, or coin-tossing, model would predict. Of course Larry Bird, the great forward of the Boston Celtics, will have more sequences of five than Joe Airball—but not because he has greater will or gets in that magic rhythm more often. Bird has longer runs because his average success rate is so much higher, and random models predict more frequent and longer sequences. If Bird shoots field goals at 0.6 probability of success, he will get five in a row about once every 13 sequences (0.6^5). If Joe, by contrast, shoots only 0.3, he will get his five straight only about once in 412 times. In other words, we need no special explanation for the apparent pattern of long runs. There is no ineffable 'causality of circumstance' (if I may call it that), no definite reason born of the particulars that make for heroic myths—courage in the clinch, strength in adversity, etc. You only have to know a person's ordinary play in order to predict his sequences."[28]

Gould's friend, Ed Purcell, a Nobel laureate in Physics, did research on baseball streaks. He concluded that nothing ever happened in baseball above and beyond the frequency predicted by coin-tossing models. The longest runs of wins and losses are as long as they should be.[29]

Had Grady Little played the numbers in 2003, the Red Sox might not have had to wait until 2004 to finally win the World Series (which they followed up and won again in 2007). There is little

When Grady Little let Pedro continue pitching into the eighth in Game 7 of the ALCS against the Yankees, he provided the perfect demonstrator of why the Red Sox fired him after his second winning season in Boston. Little explained his move (which allowed the Yankees to tie and eventually win) after the game: "We trained him to work just like that deep into a game. When he tells me he has enough in the tank to keep going, that's the man I want out there. That's no different than what we've done the last two years." In fact, the stats said just the opposite. Pedro pitched into the eighth only five times in his 29 regular-season starts, and simply didn't pitch well after he'd thrown 100 pitches, the number he'd tossed before taking the mound in the eighth. In fact, during 2003, opponents' batting averages went up .139 after Pedro tossed his 105th pitch—strong evidence that he'd continue to weaken. That it would turn out badly was likely, as most everyone knew—and as the Red Sox computers knew.[30]

The truth of a theory is in your mind, not in your eyes.

Albert Einstein[31]

doubt that an analysis of numbers to make baseball decisions, as evidenced by Bill James, Billy Beane, and John W. Henry, is smart business. It is a smart way to play the odds.

Key Points

- John W. Henry: "Life is too dynamic to remain static."
- If you have realistic confidence in your method and yourself, then temporary setbacks don't matter. Going for the home run can allow you to come out ahead in the long run.
- Thinking in terms of odds is a common denominator of baseball and trend following.

Part III

Human Behavior $\quad$ 6

"For me, intuition comes from experience. After years of experience, a
person will have, if they have been paying attention and revising their
thinking and behavior, intuitions about their area of experience."
—Charles Faulkner

"[W]e are not really interested in people who are experts at the French
stock market or German bond markets [due to the technical nature of
the trading]...it does not take a huge monster infrastructure: [neither]
Harvard MBAs [nor] people from Goldman Sachs...I would hate it if the
success of Chesapeake was based on my being some great genius.
It's the system that wins. Fundamental economics are nice
but useless in trading. True fundamentals are always unknown.
Our system allows for no intellectual capability."
—Jerry Parker[1]

Perhaps not surprising, trend followers have spent as much
time observing and understanding human behavior as they have
trading. Understanding human behavior and how it relates with
markets is commonly referred to as behavioral finance.

Behavioral finance evolved out of a contradiction between
classical economic theory and reality. Economic theory is based on
the assumption that people act rationally, have identical values and
access to information, and use rational decision making. The truth
is people are irrational and seldom make completely rational
decisions even if they think they do. I have had the good fortune to

*We understand the
distinction between simple
and easy. Simple, robust
solutions are easier to find
than robust people or firms
willing to apply them.*

Jason Russell[2]

History does not repeat itself; people just keep forgetting it. No matter how many stock market bubbles there have been, or will be, investors and their advisors always treat the current one as permanent, sometimes even calling it a "new era." In the meantime, others, myself included, have abandoned all hope of people permanently remembering the lessons of history.[3]

learn from some of the top minds in the field of behavioral finance. From Nobel Prize winner Vernon Smith to Charles Faulkner, my eyes have been opened. Faulkner outlined the core issues:

"The current proliferation of electronic technologies—computers, the Internet, cell phones, 24-hour news, and instant analysis—tend to distract us from the essentially human nature of markets. Greed, hope, fear, and denial, herd behavior, impulsiveness, and impatience with process ('Are we there yet?') are still around, and if anything, more intensely so. Few people have absorbed the hard neuroscience research that reasons arrive afterwards. That given the choice between a simple, easy-to-understand explanation that works and a difficult one that doesn't, people tend to pick the latter. People would rather have any story about how a series of price changes happened than that there is no rational reason for it. Confusing hindsight with foresight and complexity with insight are a few more 'cognitive illusions' of Behavioral Finance."

Faulkner is correct, but that doesn't make his words easy. The problem is that by not accepting that truth, you will get into trouble one way or another, as Carl Sagan reminds us:

"It is far better to grasp the universe as it really is than to persist in delusion, however satisfying and reassuring."

Prospect Theory

Investment bubbles have always been a part of market history. For example, seventeenth century speculators in the Netherlands drove up the prices of tulip bulbs to absurd levels. The inevitable crash followed. Since then, from the Great Depression to the dot-com implosion to October and November 2008, people can't seem to steer clear from manias. They repeatedly make the same mistakes.

Daniel Kahneman, a Princeton professor who was the first psychologist to win the Nobel Prize in Economics, attributed market manias to investors' "illusion of control," calling the illusion "prospect theory." He studied the intellectual underpinnings of investing—how traders estimate odds and calculate risks—to prove how often we act from the mistaken belief that we know more than we do.

Kahneman found that a typical person acts on what they christened the "law of small numbers"—basing broad predictions on narrow samples of data. For instance, if we buy a fund that's beaten the market three years in a row, we are convinced it's on a hot streak. People are simply unable to stop themselves from over-generalizing the importance of a just a few supporting facts. Limited statistical evidence satisfies no matter how inadequate the depiction of reality.[4]

He also determined that people dislike losses so much that they make irrational decisions in vain attempts to avoid them. This helps explain why some investors sell their winning stocks too early, but hold on to losers for too long. It is human nature to take the profit from a winner quickly on the assumption that it won't last for long, but stick with a loser in the futile hope it will bounce back.[5]

Knowing others is wisdom;

Knowing the self is enlightenment.

Mastering others requires force;

Mastering self needs strength.

Lao Tsu[6]

However, trend followers know if you don't cut your losses short, that if you don't exit with a small loss, there's a good chance losses will get much larger. The more you struggle with your small loss, the larger it might become and the harder it will be to deal with it later. The problem with accepting a loss is that it forces us to admit we were wrong. Human beings don't like to be wrong.

Not surprisingly, any discussion of why investors are their own worst enemies must start with the concept of a sunk cost. A sunk cost is simply a cost that has already been incurred that you can't recoup. Thinking in terms of sunk costs lets you see a loss for what it actually is—a loss. Although sunk costs must not influence our present decisions, we have a hard time forgetting the past. A person might buy more of a stock even though it is tanking simply because of the initial decision to buy it. The person can then say proudly, "I bought on a discount!" Of course if the price of the stock never goes up again, as is often the case, this theory implodes.

"Take your small loss and go home" is the trend following mantra. However, most of us are ambivalent when we have to deal with sunk costs. Although intellectually we know that there is nothing we can do about money already spent and we should move on, emotionally we dwell.

An experiment with a $10 theater ticket demonstrates the irrationality of sunk costs. Kahneman told one group of students to imagine they have arrived at the theater only to discover they have lost their ticket. "Would you pay another $10 to buy another ticket?" A second group was told to imagine that they are going to the play but haven't bought a ticket in advance. When they arrive at the theater, they realize they have lost a $10 bill. Would they still buy a ticket? In both cases, the students were presented with essentially the same simple question: Would you want to spend $10 to see the play? Eighty-eight percent of the second group, which had lost the $10 bill, opted to buy the ticket. However, the first group, the ticket losers, focusing on sunk costs, tended to ask the question in a different way: Am I willing to spend $20 to see a $10 play? Only 46 percent said yes.[7]

There are a number of behaviors that almost guarantee losses in the markets. These behaviors, the antithesis of the way trend followers operate, include:

- **Lack of discipline:** It takes an accumulation of knowledge and sharp focus to trade successfully. Many would rather listen to the advice of others than take the time to learn for themselves. People are lazy when it comes to the education needed for trading. Think about Bernard Madoff. People just wanted to believe.

- **Impatience:** People have an insatiable need for action. It might be the adrenaline rush they're after—their "gambler's high." Trading is about patience and objective decision making, not action addiction.

- **No objectivity:** We are unable to disengage emotionally from the market. We "marry" our positions.

- **Greed:** Traders try to pick tops or bottoms in the hope they'll be able to "time" their trades to maximize profits. A desire for quick profits blinds traders to the real hard work needed to win.

- **Refusal to accept truth:** Traders do not want to believe the only truth is price action. As a result, they follow other variables setting the stage for inevitable losses.

- **Impulsive behavior:** Traders often jump into a market based on a story in the morning paper. Markets discount news by the time it is publicized. Thinking that if you act quickly, somehow you will beat everybody else in the great day-trading race is a grand recipe for failure.

If there is one trait that virtually all effective leaders have, it is motivation. They are driven to achieve beyond expectations—their own and everyone else's. The key word here is achieve. Plenty of people are motivated by external factors such as a big salary or the status that comes from having an impressive title or being part of a prestigious company. By contrast, those with leadership potential are motivated by a deeply embedded desire to achieve for the sake of achievement.
Daniel Goleman[8]

- **Inability to stay in the present:** To be a successful trader, you can't spend your time thinking about how you're going to spend your profits. Trading because you have to have money is not a wise state of mind.

- **Avoid false parallels:** Just because the market behaved one way in 1995 does not mean a similar pattern today will give the same result.

If you try to bridge the gap between the present and the future with market predictions, you're guaranteed to be in a continual state of uncertainty whether you admit to it or not. Scientists have begun to investigate the impact of extended uncertainty on human beings. The conclusion? We react the same way to uncertainty that other animals do when faced with a threat, by shifting into "fight-or-flight" mode.

Unlike the animal's environment, where the threat passes quickly one way or another, our lives are spent in constant stressful situations, many of which never go away or never arrive. According to neuroscientist Robert Sapolsky, human beings, unlike other animals, can—and often do—experience stress simply by imagining stressful situations. "For 99 percent of the beasts on this planet, stressful situations include about three minutes of screaming terror, after which the threat is over or you are over. Humans turn on the exact same stress response thinking about 30-year mortgages. Yet, while thinking about a mortgage is not life-threatening, the stress is probably going to last much longer than three minutes. So what will the biggest public health problem be in the developed world 50 years from now? Depression."[9]

Traders also get depressed when they lose. Usually, they look everywhere else, blaming others or events to avoid taking responsibility for their actions. Instead of understanding their own emotions to understand why they make the decisions they do, they chase after Holy Grails to hopefully find an ironclad "winning" strategy.

Another reason our uncertainty looms so large is because we are ambivalent about money to begin with. Some of us would like to have more money, but feel guilty about admitting that. A few of us have lots of money, but want even more and still feel guilty. Take a moment to think through your motivations for trading. If you have

NLP is short for Neuro-Linguistic Programming. The name sounds high tech, yet it is purely descriptive. Neuro refers to neurology, our nervous system—the mental pathways our five senses take which allow us to see, hear, feel, taste, and smell. Linguistic refers to our language ability; how we put together words and phrases to express ourselves, as well as how our "silent language" of movement and gestures reveals our states, thinking styles and more. Programming, taken from computer science, refers to the idea that our thoughts, feelings and actions are like computer software programs. When we change those programs, just as when we change or upgrade software, we immediately get positive changes in our performance. We get immediate improvements in how we think, feel, act and live.

Charles Faulkner[10]

Fat, drunk, and stupid is no way to go through life, son.

Animal House[12]

Self-Knowledge Keys

1. Know what you want. Know who you are, not who you think you should be. Self-awareness gives you the power to pursue what really feeds your soul and the belief that you deserve it.

2. Know the cost of getting what you want. Realize the trade-offs of every choice. People often think if they are clever they can make choices without experiencing any downside. Any road you choose means there is a road you won't experience.

3. Be willing to pay the cost. People often try to negotiate to win a choice without cost. Every choice involves a price; we get to decide what cost we want to pay.[13]

any reason for trading other than to make money, find something else to do and avoid the stress from the beginning. There is nothing good or bad about money. Money is just a tool—nothing more, nothing less.

Is money a legitimate reason to feel anxious or guilty? Ayn Rand articulates a nonjudgmental and rational attitude about money in her classic *Atlas Shrugged*:

> "'So you think that money is the root of all evil? Have you ever asked what is the root of money? Money is a tool of exchange, which can't exist unless there are goods produced and men able to produce them. Money is the material shape of the principle that men who wish to deal with one another must deal by trade and give value for value. Money is not the tool of the moochers, who claim your product by tears, or of the looters, who take it from you by force. Money is made possible only by the men who produce. Is this what you consider evil?'"[11]

According to any number of economic theories, conflicted feelings about money shouldn't exist, but clearly they do. Human behavior should reflect a rational approach to money. We are supposed to refuse to pay too much for a watch because of the social cache of a label, but we still pay. We are supposed to make intelligent objective choices that maximize our wealth and financial security, but we don't.

Then what is the motivation behind the person who runs up credit card debt at 14 percent interest, but would never think of dipping into his savings account to pay off that debt? What is the explanation for people who spend time researching a new car or designer kitchen, but when it comes time to invest, refuse to learn or engage in any research? Charles Faulkner thinks there is more at play in these situations:

> "Some problems run deeper, springing from limiting, unconscious beliefs. For instance, a trader who has labeled himself a one-for-trader, or who learned as a child the biblical story it's easier for a camel to pass through the eye of a needle than for a rich man to enter the kingdom of God, may subconsciously sabotage his trading to respect his

beliefs. They're deeply ingrained in us…but if all the ethical people think money is bad, who's going to get the money?"[14]

Building off Faulkner's comments, David Harding (Winton Capital) is focusing on the need for proper thinking across all areas of life when it comes to money and risk. At the University of Cambridge, Harding created a new professorship designed to help improve people's understanding of the mathematics of risk. The idea is to help individuals, institutions, and governments refine their decisions in the middle of risky situations.

A recent Harding press release was clear: "Risk is a factor in all human activity and different people react to risks in very different ways. Questions requiring a scientific ability to assess the chances of something happening—or not happening—arise all the time. Here are some examples:

- Following the poisoning of the Russian ex-spy Alexander Litvinenko, traces of polonium-210 were found at various locations in London that he had visited. Statistically, how probable is it that someone who visited the same locations at a later stage would contract radiation poisoning?

- An apparently healthy woman is judged to be at risk of breast cancer and is advised to undergo mastectomy. Should she do so?

- A person has to cross a main road to reach a few shops. Should he walk straight across the road, or use an available footbridge instead?

- How sensible would it be for me to invest in the stock market today? Might delaying improve my prospects greatly?

- A 29-year-old man decides to marry his girlfriend of three years. What is the chance that he will meet a more suitable partner at a later stage?"

As these examples show, risks need to be considered in both the most ordinary of situations, and in high-pressure environments. But always be careful to not abuse the statistics.

It may readily be conceived that if men passionately bent upon physical gratifications desire greatly, they are also easily discouraged; as their ultimate object is to enjoy, the means to reach that object must be prompt and easy or the trouble of acquiring the gratification would be greater than the gratification itself. Their prevailing frame of mind, then, is at once ardent and relaxed, violent and enervated. Death is often less dreaded by them than perseverance in continuous efforts to one end.

Alexis de Tocqueville[15]

Emotional Intelligence: Daniel Goleman

Many traders mindlessly repeat the same actions, day after day, hoping for better results. They want to believe that if they are able to discern patterns, they will win. As a result, they are continually making connections and drawing parallels that are not valid. They miss seeing the differences. Ironically, the real pattern they miss is the pattern of acting with complete confidence to make decisions, right or wrong, in the face of the unknown.

The less confident we are, the more frustrating and demoralizing the experiences will be. The more you learn about the markets and yourself, the more confident you become. The more confident you become, the more effective you become as a trader.

In 1995, psychologist Daniel Goleman published his best-seller *Emotional Intelligence*, a powerful case for broadening the meaning of intelligence to include our emotions. Drawing on brain and behavioral research, Goleman demonstrated why people with high IQs often flounder, while people with modest IQs often do extremely well. The factors that influence how well we do in life include self-awareness, self-discipline, intuition, empathy, and an ability to enter the flow of life, character traits most traders would not consider particularly useful for garnering profits from the markets.[16]

You see, Dr. Stadler, people don't want to think. And the deeper they get into trouble, the less they want to think. But by some sort of instinct, they feel that they ought to and it makes them feel guilty. So they'll bless and follow anyone who gives them a justification for not thinking.

Ayn Rand[19]

Being self-aware also means understanding what you want out of life. You know what your goals and values are and you are able to stick to them. For instance, if you're offered a high-paying job that doesn't square with your values or your long-term goals, you can turn it down promptly and without regret. If one of your employees breaches corporate ethics, you deal with it instead of either ignoring it or worse yet making a half-hearted response because you pretend to yourself it won't happen again.[17]

Emotional self-control makes anyone more productive. However, Goleman is not saying we should repress our feelings of anxiety, fear, anger, or sadness. We must acknowledge and understand our emotions for what they are. Like animals, biological impulses drive our emotions. There is no way to escape them, but we can learn to self-regulate our feelings and, in so doing, manage them. Self-regulation is the ongoing inner conversation that emotionally intelligent people engage in to be free from being prisoners of their feelings. If we are able to engage in such a conversation, we still feel bad moods and emotional impulses just as everyone else does, but we can learn to control them and even to channel them in useful ways.[18]

A trend follower's ability to delay gratification, stifle impulsiveness, and shake off the market's inevitable setbacks and upsets, makes him not only a successful trader, but also a leader. Goleman found that effective leaders all had a high degree of emotional intelligence along with the relevant IQ and technical skills. While other "threshold capabilities" were entry-level requirements for executive positions, emotional intelligence was the "sine qua non" of leadership. Without emotional intelligence, someone can have superior training, an incisive and analytical mind, and infinite creativity, but still won't make a great leader.[21]

If you look at how trend followers develop, you'll see that they are often self-starters, motivated from the beginning to achieve. However, perfecting the strategy of trend following, applying it to new markets, teaching others how to trend follow, and expanding their own knowledge of trading is what keeps the great trend traders motivated to pursue the game.

Just as important as managing feelings is being able to recognize the feelings of others. Few of us live, or trade for that matter, in a vacuum. The sense of being cut off from the world, of being isolated with no one to turn to, is a common consequence for traders. This doesn't necessarily mean you need a group of colleagues to hang out with around the water cooler every couple of hours, but objectivity most definitely comes from having a balanced life, so make sure you don't sit at a computer 24/7!

Charles Faulkner

Why have men like Richard Donchian and Ed Seykota (see Chapter 2, "Great Trend Followers") been able to teach trend following? One answer is found in the field of Neuro-Linguistic Programming (NLP). One of the top teachers of NLP is Charles Faulkner who speaks with an authority and clarity gained from having taught hundreds of traders how to gain the "mental edge":

"NLP's techniques involve moving out negative mental beliefs and replacing them with positive ones. Think of an

Over-familiarization with something—an idea, say or a method, or an object—is a trap… Creativity requires something new, a different interpretation, a break from the twin opiates of habit and cliché.

Denise Shekerjian[20]

When popular opinion is nearly unanimous, contrary thinking tends to be most profitable. The reason is that once the crowd takes a position, it creates a short-term, self-fulfilling prophecy. But when a change occurs, everyone seems to change his mind at once.

Gustave Le Bon[23]

Walk into the college classroom, and you will hear your professors teaching your children that man can be certain of nothing; that his consciousness has no validity whatsoever; that he can learn no facts and no laws of existence; that he's incapable of knowing an objective reality.

Ayn Rand[24]

unpleasant trade…As you do that, what happens if you take a breath and go 'aaah,' push it out and then trade with it? Much better. People go through fifths of scotch trying to get that feeling. When you get agitated, go 'whoosh' and just step out of it that way and you'll find that it's less. Do it again and you'll be at zero real fast."[22]

I first met Charles Faulkner at a trading seminar years back. It was easy to see that people are immediately drawn to him. I also saw this trait again in my recent interview of him for my documentary film *Broke: The New American Dream*. Faulkner just has a natural gift for teaching how to see the big picture. He always urges traders to take matters into their own hands.

He wants traders to believe that, "I am competent to be confident. I know what's going on in these markets. If I don't know, I get out."[26]

Like many teachers, Faulkner uses simple stories to illustrate complex lessons. I found, for instance, Faulkner's "Swiss skiing" example from *The New Market Wizards* to be especially insightful. He used skiing to explain NLP. He pointed out that until the 1950s, most people thought skiing was a matter of natural talent that you had or you didn't have. Then, films were made of some of Europe's greatest skiers to identify all the movements that characterized them. It was found that they all had certain techniques in common. All kinds of people could learn to be good skiers if the movements that made a great skier, the essence of their skills, could be identified so they could be taught to others. Faulkner observed that this essence of skills was called a model, and that the model (or set of basic principles) could be applied to any endeavor.[27]

Ed Seykota's Trading Tribe

Ed Seykota has long served as a mentor to traders. His natural inclination to teach and mentor has evolved into his Trading Tribe, a global network of groups of traders who meet monthly to work through challenges:

"The trading tribe is an association of traders who commit to excellence, personal growth, and supporting and receiving support from other traders."[28]

"I model human excellence."
Charles Faulkner[25]

Reason is the main resource of man in his struggle for survival.
Ludwig von Mises[29]

What feels good is often the wrong thing to do.
William Eckhardt[30]

When the market is moving and money is flying, it's easy to forget that it's the basics that ultimately produce success. Even after trading everything from exotic over-the-counter options to plain vanilla Dow stocks, I still need to constantly and obsessively evaluate every single trade, every single day.
Jonathan Hoenig,
Portfolio Manager,
Capitalistpig Hedge Fund LLC

Seykota's tribe works on the psychological and emotional issues that he believes are crucial for successful trading (and life for that matter). Faulkner tells a story about Seykota's finely honed intuition when it comes to trading:

"I am reminded of an experience that Seykota shared with a group. He said that when he looks at a market, that everyone else thinks has exhausted its up trend, that is often when he likes to get in. When I asked him how he made this determination, he said he just put the chart on the other side of the room and if it looked like it was going up, then he would buy it...Of course this trade was seen through the eyes of someone with deep insight into the market behavior."[31]

Seykota doesn't pretend to have all the answers, but he is extremely good at turning the mirror back to students so they focus on where issues really lie. His precision with language, like Faulkner's, makes one pay attention. One of Seykota's students, Chauncey DiLaura, broke down Seykota's teachings:

"The mind is a filter, letting only some information in...When you're designing systems or setting stops, it's an ever-present part of what you do. My goal is to get in touch with those subconscious processes. A lot of what [Seykota does is] a breathing technique to achieve an altered state of consciousness where you somehow relax your conscious filters. We did it both unstructured and in a structured way, with ideas to concentrate on, such as, 'Why do I always do this when I'm trading?'"[32]

Here are some of my favorite insights from my conversations with Seykota:

- One use of the Trading Tribe Process (TTP) is to locate and dissolve the feelings that stand between you and following your system.

- When you notice all things happen now, and when you take responsibility for your experience, you notice that even "noise" results from your intention. At that point, you can clarify your intention and remove the noise. The entire length of the chain

"My life has stopped, but I continue to age," deadpans Karen Levine, a Wharton School MBA who has worked at General Mills (GIS), Unilever, Deloitte Consulting, Condé Nast, and Hearst. But in real terms, Levine made more in 1988 fresh out of Harvard College than she earns today. During her two years of battling unemployment, Levine has worked for $8 an hour at Pottery Barn and for $18 an hour as a temp for a Wall Street trading firm. "I can't even afford a dog," she says.[33]

The illiterate of the twenty-first century will not be those who cannot read and write, but those who cannot learn, unlearn, and relearn.

Alvin Toffler

Human beings never think for themselves, they find it too uncomfortable. For the most part, members of our species simply repeat what they are told—and become upset if they are exposed to any different view. The characteristic human trait is not awareness but conformity...Other animals fight for territory or food; but, uniquely in the animal kingdom, human beings fight for their 'beliefs'...The reason is that beliefs guide behavior, which has evolutionary importance among human beings. But at a time when our behavior may well lead us to extinction, I see no reason to assume we have any awareness at all. We are stubborn, self-destructive conformists. Any other view of our species is just a self-congratulatory delusion.

Michael Crichton[36]

of events exists in the ever evolving moment of now—and at all points of now, you might choose to see your result equals your intention. Alternatively, you might choose to avoid responsibility, especially for the noise, and then try to find exogenous "causes."

- Analysis leads to solving and fixing. TTP leads to dissolving and noticing things already work right. Incontrovertible solvers tend to use TTP as an analytical tool—until they happen to experience a desire to solve things.

- Take responsibility for your experience and see that intentions equals result. Deny responsibility and a delta between intentions and results may appear.

- Your real trading system is the set of feelings you are unwilling to experience.

- In tracking your feelings and in tracking the markets, take whatever comes up and go with it. Trying to force a feeling is like trying to force a market. You might find some joy in the process of allowing feelings and markets to come and go as you experience them.

Why does a trader as successful as Seykota spend time delving into the subject of feelings? He has said: "It is a dominant idea in Western society that we should separate emotion and rationality. Advances in science show that such a separation is not only impossible but also undesirable."[34]

Seykota has known about the "advances in science" for 30 years.

Curiosity Is the Answer, Not Degrees

Can you remember how to experience simple childlike curiosity with no agenda other than simply to know? The curiosity I am talking about is open-ended and enthusiastic. Kids have the same wide-eyed wonderment when they take apart their first toy to figure out how it works.

Emotional issues aside, many traders remain fixated on academic intelligence as their only decision-making tool. William Eckhardt, a longtime trend follower, sees the issue:

"I haven't seen much correlation between good trading and intelligence. Some outstanding traders are quite intelligent, but a few are not. Many outstandingly intelligent people are horrible traders. Average intelligence is enough. Beyond that, emotional makeup is more important."[35]

Having an education is one thing, being educated is another.

Lee Kuan Yew, former Prime Minister of Singapore[37]

When it comes to being an outstanding trader, emotional intelligence is as important as IQ. Because we are conditioned to appear "book smart," we are often afraid to be curious. We think that by asking questions, we'll be perceived as ignorant; although in truth, by not questioning the world, we get into more trouble. Still others might not fear the question, but instead fear the answer, which might be the piece of information that requires integration into your life or worse, information that proves you wrong. Open-ended curiosity lets you take a step back and see everything for what it is right now.

For most of our lives, many of us spend our time listening to someone else feed us information. Then we are judged on how well we can regurgitate that information back to whomever offered it in the first place. When it comes time to taking responsibility for our decision making, we are constantly waiting for someone else to tell us what to do or checking to see what others are doing. Curiosity has been pulled from us.

For example, Alan "Ace" Greenberg, former CEO of Bear Stearns (before it imploded), in his book *Memos from the Chairman*, told his employees that, "Our first desire is to promote from within. If somebody with an MBA degree applies for the job, we will certainly not hold it against them, but we are really looking for people with PSD ("a poor, smart, and deep desire to be rich degree") degrees. They built this firm and there are plenty around because our competition seems to be restricting themselves to MBAs."[38]

Greenberg "gets" the need for passion and curiosity, but many would-be traders pursue pleasing others. They have spent their lives delivering the "right" answer to their teachers to please them. Eventually they equate pleasing people with being right. Ironically, after they leave the academic world and are out on their own, their need to be right often backfires.

When teaching children, a good chess teacher devises ways to get students through the pain of losing, since they lose a lot when first learning the game. One teacher describes how there is a "hot corner." Students sit with the teacher at the board and talk chess. They cannot move the pieces physically, but instead must tell the teacher their moves. They must play the game in their heads. In the beginning, the students hate a visit to the "hot corner." However, gradually they discover that they can, in fact, play a game of chess in their head. More important, what seems like difficult mental work requiring deep concentration and focus becomes intuition after a while. By learning how to handle defeat, the young students can learn how to win.[39]

Anyone with average intelligence can learn to trade. This is not rocket science.

William Eckhardt

Look at Wall Street in 2008. All of the so-called best and brightest traders, the ones armed with the Ivy League educations and Goldman Sachs pedigrees, now what do they do? They played by the rules their whole life. They went to the right schools. They were at the right investment banks. They were quickly rewarded for playing the part, then the 2008 crash hit. Now what? Back to school for an MBA in the hope that if they follow more rules it will all work out right?

Ignoring the opinions and contributions of others to be "right" is not particularly "pleasing" behavior as Faulkner points out:

> "One doesn't have to be a student to want to please people or want to be right. I would claim that serious students (and professors) know there is much they don't know, and are less interested in what is right. On the other hand, those that know little often feel the need to be in the right about it. People pleasing is an entirely different dimension, though people that need to be right are usually experienced at ignoring others, and therefore, failing to please them."

Never call on intuition. It calls on you.[40]

Sigmund Freud gets right to heart of the problem when it comes to our lack of curiosity:

> "What a distressing contrast there is between the radiant intelligence of the child and the feeble mentality of the average adult."

A top CEO recently spoke before a Harvard MBA class. After his presentation, the students asked questions. One of the questions was, "What should we do?" The CEO replied, "Take the rest of the money you have not spent on tuition and do something else." This isn't to say that people with advanced degrees cannot be successful trend followers, but it does say that relying solely on your degree for success in the markets, or in life, for that matter, is not a wise strategy.

As simplistic as it sounds, maintaining childlike wonder and enthusiasm keeps the mental doors open. Is it possible to disengage your ego and think of yourself as still evolving? Don't answer "no."

Commitment to Habitual Success

Simply reading trading philosophies and rules alone is not going to make you hungry. It's not going to make you want to succeed at trading. You must be committed to winning. Because if you don't want to win, if you don't have it in your gut, there's a good chance you won't win.

Commitment to trend following trading is the same commitment you would make to anything new in life. If you're committed, you will figure it all out one way or another.

Commitment to trend following is also similar to the commitment needed to be a top athlete. If you're going to be a fantastic baseball player, you keep pushing. You never give up. By the time you get to the big leagues, you have what you want. However, the only reason you have those things is because you made the commitment at the outset to be a winner. Everyone wants the big leagues and big money, but are they committed to making it happen with relentless drive? Faulkner sees it a bit differently, as he explained to me:

> "I see it more as a matter of choosing between what is in accord with your nature or changing your nature to accord with your dreams. Most people don't recognize this as a choice point. They get praised into a career, 'You're good with people; you should be a sales person' or 'You're good at math; you should be a computer programmer.' Few realize that it is possible to hold their dreams constant and vary their behavior until they are good at what they need to be good at. And usually, there is a bit of both."

If you're going to chase success, the basic principles, the basic psychological requirements are the same, no matter what you do in life. You still have to wake up every day with a deep desire to be successful. You have to be consistently focused every day. You can't just wake up and say, "Hey, I'm going to give a little bit of effort today and see what happens. If it doesn't work out for me, I can say I tried and complain to my wife or girlfriend." You can't just jump around because the newspaper or some TV analyst says, "Here's some get rich quick scheme or Holy Grail."

That's not the way it works. Act like that and you will fail. Doubt me? Consider some very simple trading "do nots" from Amos Hostetter, the wise sage of famed trend following incubator Commodities Corporation:

- Don't sacrifice your position for fluctuations.
- Don't expect the market to end in a blaze of glory. Look out for warnings.
- Don't expect the tape to be a lecturer. It's enough to see that something is wrong.
- Never try to sell at the top. It isn't wise. Sell after a reaction if there is no rally.

We sometimes delude ourselves that we proceed in a rational manner and weight all of the pros and cons of various alternatives. But this is seldom the actual case. Quite often 'I decided in favor of X' is no more than 'I liked X'...We buy the cars we 'like,' choose the jobs and houses we find 'attractive,' and then justify these choices by various reasons.[41]

- Don't imagine that a market that has once sold at 150 must be cheap at 130.
- Don't buck the market trend.
- Don't look for the breaks. Look out for warnings.
- Don't try to make an average from a losing game.
- Never keep goods that show a loss, and sell those that show a profit. Get out with the least loss, and sit tight for greater profits.

Hostetter also saw the dangers in trading caused by human nature:

- Fearful of profit and one acts too soon.
- Hope for a change in the forces against one.
- Lack of confidence in one's own judgment.
- Never cease to do your own thinking.
- A man must not swear eternal allegiance to either the bear or bull side.
- An individual fails to stick to facts!
- People believe what it pleases them to believe.

Think about how simple Hostetter's wisdom appears on the surface. However, how many investors adhere to these basics? Imagine that those simple rules were handed out in January 2008 to every investor with their life savings in mutual funds. How much money would they have saved?

The strategies of human reason probably did not develop, in either evolution or any single individual, without the guiding force of the mechanisms of biological regulation, of which emotion and feeling are notable expressions. Moreover, even after reasoning strategies become established in the formative years, their effective deployment probably depends, to a considerable extent, on the continued ability to experience feelings.[42]

Key Points

- Faulkner: "All of the successful traders I have met are consciously aware that their lives are bigger than their trading. They are very interested in the money and they are very interested in what they get to do to get it. They embrace their pasts, as well as who they are. Whether it's mathematics or music, philosophy or psychology, or baseball, their interests in the world around them help carry them through the market, and equity, changes. Every day, whether they make money or not, they get to do what they want. I hear it really helps with sitting with positions, too."

- Seykota: "To freshen a room, open a window. Works for minds, too, and for hearts."

- Seykota: "Sometimes people gamble and lose to cover up some other feelings they wish to avoid experiencing…guilt, for example."

- Seykota: "Some like to search, some like to find and some realize they already have it."

- If you want to be a successful trader, you must be passionate about the learning process.

- Let the hype, crowd emotion, and "I must be right attitude" be someone else's problem.

- Winners take responsibility. Losers place blame.

- You have to believe from the start that you can do it. It takes courage to do what the majority is not doing.

- Who is John Galt?

- Atul Gawande speaks directly to the importance of practice: "There have now been many studies of elite performers— concert violinists, chess grandmasters, professional ice-skaters, mathematicians, and so forth—and the biggest difference researchers find between them and lesser performers is the amount of deliberate practice they've accumulated. Indeed, the most important talent may be the talent for practice itself…the most important role that innate factors play may be in a person's willingness to engage in sustained training."

- Online personality testing can be purchased at www.knowyourtype.com.

We know of "traders" whose public image "looks pristine," but their personal lives, mental health, and balance are in such dire straights— they are not capable of any type of real success or achievement. They might get "the numbers," but their problematic mental health keeps them back. Bottom line—they never get to where they want to go. Life becomes one big rationalization (or excuse) for them.

If you try to impose a rigid discipline while teaching a child or a chimp, you are working against the boundless curiosity and need for relaxed play that make learning possible in the first place…learning cannot be controlled; it is out of control by design. Learning emerges spontaneously, it proceeds in an individualistic and unpredictable way, and it achieves its goal in its own good time. Once triggered, learning will not stop—unless it is hijacked by conditioning.

Roger Fouts
2think.org

Decision Making　7

Trend followers approach their trading decisions in a distinctly different way from most traders. They keep it simple. For example, each day thousands of traders attempt to evaluate a relentless onslaught of confusing, contradictory, and overwhelming market information to hopefully make profitable trading decisions (the type of information on CNBC for example). Although they know the right decisions should be educated and based on factual data, they often do things they *think* are required for proper decision-making, even when they are not. Confronted by deadlines and other demands on their time, they either end up paralyzed making no decision, or they let someone else decide for them. It's a vicious circle.

Any individual decisions can be badly thought through, and yet be successful, or exceedingly well thought through, but be unsuccessful, because the recognized possibility of failure in fact occurs. But over time, more thoughtful decision-making will lead to better overall results, and more thoughtful decision-making can be encouraged by evaluating decisions on how well they were made rather than on outcome.

Robert Rubin[3]

People who make decisions for a living are coming to realize that in complex or chaotic situations—a battlefield, a trading floor, or today's brutally competitive business environment—intuition usually beats rational analysis. And as science looks closer, it is coming to see that intuition is not a gift but a skill.[6]

Terrence Odean, a researcher in the field of behavioral finance, uses a roulette wheel to illustrate the issue. He postulates that even if you knew the results for the last 10,000 roulette spins, knew what materials the roulette wheel was made of, and whatever hundred other pieces of information you could dream up as possibly being useful, you still wouldn't know what really matters, which is where the ball will land next. Ed Seykota takes Odean's thought a step further in poking holes in fundamental analysis:[4]

"While fundamental analysis may help you understand how things work, it does not tell you when, or how much. Also, by the time a fundamental case presents, the move may already be over. Just around the recent high in the Live Cattle market, the fundamental reasons included Chinese Buying, Mad Cow Disease, and The Atkins' Diet."[5]

Trend followers control what they know they can control. They know they can choose a certain level of risk. They know they can measure volatility. They understand the transaction costs associated with trading. However, there is still plenty they know they do not know, so in the face of uncertainty, what do they do? They swing the bat. Their ability to decide is core to their trading philosophy—that is their swinging the bat. Their decision-making skills might seem not worthy of much discussion, but the philosophical framework of their decision making is critical to understanding how they trade successfully.

If I were to put their style into a baseball analogy I would ask: Do you want to play ball or do you not want to play ball? The pitch is coming across the plate. Decide whether to swing the bat. Know how you will decide in advance. When the pitch comes—if it's your pitch, swing the bat. You want to wait for more information before you swing? No time. Because in an uncertain world, if you wait until the data is clear (or the ball has crossed the plate), you miss the pitch.

Occam's Razor

Nature operates in the shortest way possible.
Aristotle

Tackling the challenge of making smart decisions in a real and complicated world is hardly new. As far back as the fourteenth century, when medieval life was as rigidly complex as its cathedrals, philosophers grappled with how to make simple decisions when time was pressing. In any scientific realm, when a new set of data requires the creation of a new theory, many hypotheses are proposed, studied, and rejected. Yet, even when all unfit hypotheses are thrown out, several might remain, in some cases reaching the same end, but having different underlying assumptions. To choose among similar theories, scientists use Occam's razor.

Occam's razor is a principle attributed to logician and Franciscan friar William of Occam. The principle states that entities must not be multiplied unnecessarily. In its original Latin form, Occam's razor is *"Pluralitas non est ponenda sine neccesitate."* This underlies all scientific modeling and theory building. A common interpretation of the principle is that the simplest of two or more competing theories is preferable.[7] Occam's razor does not guarantee that the simplest solution will be correct, but it does focus priorities.

> *We could still imagine that there is a set of laws that determines events completely for some supernatural being who could observe the present state of the universe without disturbing it. However, such models of the universe are not of much interest to us mortals. It seems better to employ the principle known as Occam's razor and cut out all the features of the theory which cannot be observed.*
>
> Stephen Hawking[9]

Fast and Frugal Decision Making

In the field of cognitive science, economics, and trading, it has always been assumed that the best decision makers have the time and ability to process vast amounts of information. However, we are finding out that is not true. The field of heuristics explores how to make constructive, positive choices by simplifying the process. Gerd Gigerenzer and Peter Todd's *Simple Heuristics That Make Us Smart* shows how we can cope with the complexities of our world using the simplest of decision-making tools. Their premise is as follows:

> *Heuristic: Serving to discover; using trial and error; teaching by enabling pupil to find things out.*
>
> Oxford Dictionary

> "Fast and frugal heuristics employ a minimum of time, knowledge, and computation to make adaptive choices in real environments."[8]

For example, a component of fast and frugal heuristics is one-reason decision making. This sounds remarkably like what trend followers do when faced with a trading decision:

> "One reason decision makers use only a single piece of information for making a decision—this is their common building block. Therefore, they can also stop their search as soon as the first reason is found that allows a decision to be made."[10]

I'm increasingly impressed with the kind of innovation and knowledge that doesn't come from preplanned effort, or from working towards a fixed goal, but from a kind of concentration on what one is doing. That seems very, very important to me. It's the actual process, the functioning, the going ahead with it.

J. Kirk T. Varanedoe,
Director of Painting and Sculpture,
Museum of Modern Art, New York City,
MacArthur Award Recipient

In other words, whether your decisions are about life in general or trading in particular, your decision-making process doesn't have to be complex for the sake of complexity. You can make a trading decision, buy or sell, on the single piece of information of 'price'. However, can you allow yourself to be that confident in simplicity? Charles Faulkner, backing the point, found that great traders he has studied share many character traits with other successful people, such as quick reactions or, said another way, being able to turn a position on a dime.[11]

Think about it this way. When we are faced with a decision, going with our first instinct is often the right choice. If we reflect, consider our options and alternatives, or try to second-guess ourselves, we might end up making the wrong decision or the same right decision but only after taking valuable time to get there.

Gigerenzer and Todd elaborate: "[T]hat fast and frugal heuristics can guide behavior in challenging domains when the environment is changing rapidly (for example, in stock market investment), when the environment requires many decisions to be made in a successively dependent fashion. These particular features of social environments can be exploited by heuristics that make rapid decisions rather than gathering and processing information over a long period during which a fleeter-minded competitor could leap forward and gain an edge."[12]

Heart, guts, attitude, and the ability to tolerate uncertainty are core to long-term winning.

To be uncertain is to be uncomfortable, but to be certain is to be ridiculous.

Gigerenzer makes another analogy with the simple act of catching a baseball: "Consider how players catch a ball—in baseball, cricket, or soccer. It may seem that they would have to solve complex differential equations in their heads to predict the trajectory of the ball. In fact, players use a simple heuristic. When a ball comes in high, the player fixates the ball and starts running. The heuristic is to adjust the running speed so that the angle of gaze remains constant—that is, the angle between the eye and the ball. The player can ignore all the information necessary to compute the trajectory, such as the ball's initial velocity, distance, and angle, and just focus on one piece of information, the angle of gaze."[13]

Former baseball catcher, now announcer, Tim McCarver drew the same conclusion, and he is by no means a scientist: "Before each delivery, the catcher flashes a hand signal to the pitcher indicating the best pitch to throw. Imagine that a strong batter faces a count of three balls and two strikes, with runners on first and third. What should the hurler serve up, a fastball high and inside, a slider low and away, or a change-up over the heart of the plate? By the way, Mark McGwire's up next. You have to put down a sign quickly. The first one is going to be the right one. For most baseball decisions I think you can train yourself to be right quicker than in five seconds."[14]

McCarver is talking about bare-bones decision making. Be quick is his message. The transitioning from fast and frugal decision making by a baseball player, McCarver, to fast and frugal decision-making by a baseball team owner and trader, John W. Henry, is remarkably smooth. Henry was one of the first to publicly focus on the use of heuristics in his trading. Traders after Henry, like David Harding of Winton Capital, have taken heuristic decision making to even higher levels of understanding.

But it was at a speech before the New York Mercantile Exchange that the president of John W. Henry and Co. talked about why fast and frugal decision making was core to their trading: "We're a trend follower; we use just price information and volatility in order to make decisions. The reason why we do that is because we don't think that we can predict the future...[Further] I can't be an expert in every one of them [markets]. In fact I can't be an expert in any of them, so what I have to do is be able to be expert at being able to move faster when I see information that's important...So my way in which I can move faster is to just use the price information that's the aggregation of everyone's expectation...What we try to do is extract the appropriate signals as quickly as possible so we can act fast to limit our risk and also create opportunities...we're frugal in the senses that we use...very simple recognition heuristics...the price information itself...what could be an example of this? We like to think of those as non-linear models. But it's no different than what some people describe as breakout systems."[15]

His simple heuristic for making trading decisions was no surprise: price action. The truth is that the less traders involve themselves in complicated analysis—the fewer trading decisions they allow themselves to make—the better off they are. Many people mistakenly think simple means unsophisticated. However, simple methods of decision-making are more successful than more complicated alternatives. This may seem counter-intuitive, but in a complex world where decisions have to be made with limited information and real-world time constraints, time to consider all possible alternatives may not be an option."[17]

There are lots of misperceptions that influence how people think about and play chess. Most people believe that great players strategize by thinking far into the future, by thinking 10 or 15 moves ahead. That's just not true. Chess players look only as far into the future as they need to, and that usually means thinking just a few moves ahead. Thinking too far ahead is a waste of time: The information is uncertain. The situation is ambiguous. Chess is about controlling the situation at hand.[16]

Leaving the trees could have been our first mistake. Our minds are suited for solving problems related to our survival, rather than being optimised for investment decisions. We all make mistakes when we make decisions.

James Montier
Global Equity Strategy
Dresdner Kleinwort Wasserstein
Securities Limited

Sporting events, which are played out step by step in the most public of settings, allow the researchers to determine the precise moment that somebody veers from good sense. The professors say that coaches and managers often go awry when faced with a decision involving an obvious, yet ultimately sensible, risk. They seem to focus too much on the worst-case scenario: the Bonds home run, the game-ending brick, the failed fourth down. Travelers who drive hundreds of miles because they are afraid of a plane crash make the same mistake. "It has to be the case that sound knowledge will win out eventually," Thomas Gilovich, a psychology professor at Cornell, said. "But the path is tortuous and slow."[20]

Trend following inherently is very simple, but nobody wants to believe—especially investors—that something that simple can make money. The reason they have done well is they have been able to stay focused and stay very disciplined. They execute the game plan—that is their real strength.[18]

However, not everyone agrees with the science of fast and frugal heuristics as Gigerenzer states: "One group said this can't be true, that it's all wrong, or it could never be replicated. Among them were financial advisers, who certainly didn't like the results. Another group of people said, 'This is no surprise. I knew it all along. The stock market's all rumor, recognition, and psychology.'"[19]

That being said, staying exclusively with a simple heuristic such as price is not easy. Traders often can't help themselves from trying to improve their trading. They become impatient, greedy, lazy, or even bored. Far too many simply like to make decisions even if those decisions only suit short-term emotional needs that have nothing to do with making a profit. It happens all the time.

For example, let's say you have a trading signal to buy Google. You buy the stock if it follows your philosophy and rules. You trust your rules and your decision making, right? Then don't try to make it more complicated than it is—buy it when you get the signal. That's not to say that trend following is simple. However, the decisions that go along with being a successful trend trader must be.

The Innovator's Dilemma

Clayton M. Christensen, author of *The Innovator's Dilemma*, understands trend following. What Christensen understands, like trend followers, are the concepts of odds and reactions. He saw this as people attempted to decipher his writing:

"They were looking at my book [*Innovator's Dilemma*] for answers rather than for understanding. They were saying 'tell me what to do' as opposed to 'help me understand so I can decide what to do.'...[Wall Street analysts] are theory-free investors. All they can do is react to the numbers. But the numbers they react to are measures of past per-formance, not future performance. That's why they go in big herds. Wall Street professionals and business consultants have enshrined as a virtue the notion that you should be data-driven. That is at the root of the inability of companies to take action in a timely way."[21]

What Christensen is driving at is that you must be able to make decisions without having all the facts, because you cannot foresee how a changing market will look until the change has taken place and then it's too late. Take, for example, an up and down stock such as Yahoo! You probably said to yourself, "I should have bought here and sold there." But there was no way you could have predicted the future of Yahoo! You could only act early before the direction of the trend was obvious. You must be in "ready, set, go" mode long before the CNBC talking heads start telling you the hindsight 20/20 story when the move is clear to everyone. Those people are the herders and herds Christensen alludes to.

Here is another decision-making story similar to the pitcher & catcher relationship in Tim McCarver's earlier story. Years ago in baseball, the catcher and the pitcher called the pitches. Today you still have a catcher and a pitcher, but the coaches in the dugout are usually calling the pitches. Why? So the pitcher can execute exactly what he's told to do. When the typical Major League pitcher gets a signal to throw a curveball, he doesn't stand out there on the mound debating it. He says to himself, "This is the system we're using. I have a coach on the sidelines with a computer. He's charted everything. He knows I should throw a curve ball. The only thing I'm going to worry about right now is throwing a curveball to the precise location that I'm supposed to throw it." The pitcher than can concentrate solely on execution—the best pitch possible he can throw.

Likewise, as a trend follower, you wake up and see the market move enough to cause you to take action (such as buy signal). For example, the rule says buy at price level 20. You do it. You don't debate it or second guess it. Sure, that might feel boring and it might feel like you're not in control. It might feel like there should be something more exciting, more glamorous, more fun to do in which case you might consider a trip to Las Vegas. If you want to win, you execute the signal as prescribed. That means you trade at price level 20, and you throw the curve ball when called for by the coach. What do you want? Fun, excitement and glamour? Or do you want to execute correctly and possibly win?

Charles Faulkner quotes Ed Seykota as saying, "I've made phenomenal amounts of money for very simple decisions but I was willing to make them. Somebody had to." Faulkner then comments, "Others are looking for highly complex ways of interacting with the markets, when most of the time it's only the simple ones that are going to work."[22]

Everything should be made as simple as possible, but not simpler.
Albert Einstein

Process Versus Outcome

The decision-making process is just that—a process. You can't make decisions based on what you want the outcome to be. Michael Mauboussin and Kristen Bartholdson have presented a compelling argument for "process":

"In too many cases, investors dwell solely on outcomes without appropriate consideration of process. The focus on results is to some degree understandable. Results—the bottom line—are what ultimately matter. And results are typically easier to assess and more objective than evaluating processes. But investors often make the critical mistake of assuming that good outcomes are the result of a good process and that bad outcomes imply a bad process. In contrast, the best long-term performers in any probabilistic field—such as investing, sports team management, and pari-mutuel betting—all emphasize process over outcome."[23]

Building on those observations, Edward Russo and Paul Schoemaker, professors in the field of decision making at the Wharton School, presented a simple yet effective tool (see Chart 7.1) to map out the process versus outcome conundrum:

		Outcome	
		Good	Bad
Process Used to Make the Decision	Good	Deserved Success	Bad Break
	Bad	Dumb Luck	Poetic Justice

CHART 7.1: Process Versus Outcome[24]

The process versus outcome shown in Chart 7.1 is a simple tool trend followers intuitively use within their trading systems every day. For example, imagine the trading process you used to make a decision is a good one. If your outcome is also good, you can view your trading result as deserved. On the other hand, if you use a good process, but your outcome is bad, you take solace and view your trading failure as a bad break, but achieved with a good process. Trend trader Larry Hite said it another way to me:

"There are just four kinds of bets. There are good bets, bad bets, bets that you win, and bets that you lose. Winning a bad bet can be the most dangerous outcome of all, because a success of that kind can encourage you to take more bad bets in the future, when the odds will be running against you. You can also lose a good bet, no matter how sound the underlying proposition, but if you keep placing good bets, over time, the law of averages will be working for you."

Smart advice.

Key Points

- Seykota: "Gigerenzer's 'fast and frugal heuristics' is another name for 'rules of thumb.' One pretty good one is: Trade with the Trend."

- Do not equate simplicity with unsophisticated thinking.

- As science looks closer, it is beginning to acknowledge that intuition is not a gift, but a skill. Like any skill, it is something you can learn.

- Occam's razor: If you have two equal solutions to a problem, pick the simplest.

- Fearless decision makers have a plan and execute it. They don't look back. Along the way if something changes, their plan has flexibility built into it so they can adjust.

- Murray N. Rothbard, of Mises.org, states: "...if a formerly good entrepreneur should suddenly make a bad mistake, he will suffer losses proportionately; if a formerly poor entrepreneur makes a good forecast, he will make proportionate gains. The market is no respecter of past laurels, however large. Capital does not 'beget' profit. Only wise entrepreneurial decisions do that."

- Mark Cuban: "With every effort, I learned a lot. With every mistake and failure, not only mine, but of those around me, I learned what not to do. I also got to study the success of those I did business with as well. I had more than a healthy dose of fear, and an unlimited amount of hope, and more importantly, no limit on time and effort...The point of all this is that it doesn't matter how many times you fail. It doesn't matter how many times you almost get it right. No one is going to know or care about your failures, and neither should you. All you have to do is learn from them and those around you because...All that matters in business is that you get it right once. Then everyone can tell you how lucky you are."

Science of Trading

8

An interviewer asked Ann Druyan (Carl Sagan's wife),
"Didn't [Sagan] want to believe?" She responded,
"He didn't want to believe. He wanted to know."

"First principles, Clarice. Read Marcus Aurelius. Of each particular
thing ask, 'What is it in itself? What is its nature?'"
—Hannibal Lector[1]

Trend followers approach trading as a science. They view the world like a physicist. The following 'physics' definition is critical to trading success:

> "The science of nature, or of natural objects; that branch of science which treats of the laws and properties of matter, and the forces acting upon it; especially, that department of natural science which treats of the causes that modify the general properties of bodies; natural philosophy."[2]

Physics and trend following are both grounded in numbers. Both work off models that describe relationships. Physics, like trend following, works best when it constantly tests models with real-world applications.

Managing money, just like a physics experiment, means dealing with numbers and varying quantities. And the connection goes

If you can't measure it, you probably can't manage it... Things you measure tend to improve.

Ed Seykota[3]

From error to error, one discovers the entire truth.

Sigmund Freud

deeper. Physics is actually about developing general descriptions—mathematical models—of the world around us. The models may describe different types of complexity, such as the movement of molecules in a gas or the dynamics of stars in a galaxy. It turns out that similar models can just as well be applied to analogous complex behavior in the financial markets.[4]

When I use the term "science of trading," that is not a reference to engineers and scientists who develop elegant and complex academic models, but sometimes to their disadvantage, forget to keep things simple. Keeping it simple is hard, because it is hardest to do what is obvious. By no means will I cover a complete undertaking of the philosophy behind the science of trading, but I have tried to offer an overview of the scientific perspective taken by trend followers.

Critical Thinking

It is remarkable that a science which began with the consideration of games of chance should have become the most important object of human knowledge...The most important questions of life are, for the most part, really only problems of probability.

Pierre Simon,
Marquis de LaPlace[5]

Trend followers, like physicists, approach their world with an open mind. They examine and experiment. Like physicists, they think critically and ask smart questions. The skill of asking objective and focused questions (and then finding the answers) is a key reason why trend followers excel. To be successful as a trader, to be successful in life, you need to develop an ability to ask those right questions, those smart questions. Examples of those include:

- Questions that come from digging deep to face the real problem, instead of mindlessly going for an easy superficial query.

- Questions that make clear why they are being asked. We need to be completely honest with ourselves regarding the real reason we want an answer.

- Questions that are not hypocritical, but instead help us discover how we interpret the information before we ask the question—in other words, questions that offer us the opportunity to make a midcourse correction.

- Questions that enable us to face the cold facts about who we are.

- Questions that enable us to face the reality of where the answer leads us.

- Questions that enable us to face our subjective take on the world and factor in new objective data.

- Questions that enable us to see what is relevant in asking them in the first place.

- Questions that engender important details we might have missed had we not asked them.[6]

When I spoke with Charles Faulkner about the importance of critical thinking and the questions surrounding it, he prioritized favorites:

> "I think the questions that are most critical—in both senses of that word—are the ones that question our assumptions, our assumptions of what is or is not a fact or a truth or possible. After this comes questions that assist statistical thinking through. Finally, are those directed to checking logic and consistency, which are important, but only if applied to worthwhile assumptions and viable probabilities."

Trend followers are insatiably curious about what is real. They do not avoid asking a question if they're suspicious that they might not like the answer. They do not ask self-serving questions that reinforce an opinion they might already have. They do not ask mindless questions, and do not accept mindless answers. They are content to ask questions knowing that there might not be an answer. This is not easy.

Unfortunately, most people do not ask critical questions when it comes to money and markets. (Bernard Madoff is the great example I will never stop coming back to.) The questions they do ask tend to be superficial and ill-informed because they have not taken ownership of the issue. Instead they ask dead-end questions such as, "Is this going to be on the test?" Their questions demonstrate a complete lack of desire to think. They might as well be sitting in silence; their minds on pause and mute. To think critically, we want to stimulate our intellect with questions that lead us to more questions, of course. We want to undo the damage previous traditional "rote memorization" schooling has done to our manner of learning. We want to resuscitate minds that are "dead" with the intellectual equivalent of artificial respiration to make dead minds come to life again.[7]

Probability theory is the underpinning of the modern world. Current research in both physical and social sciences cannot be understood without it. Today's politics, tomorrow's weather report, and next week's satellites depend on it.[8]

Do not believe in anything simply because you have heard it. Do not believe in anything simply because it is spoken and rumored by many. Do not believe in anything simply because it is found written in your religious books. Do not believe in anything merely on the authority of your teachers and elders. Do not believe in traditions because they have been handed down for many generations. But after observation and analysis, when you find that anything agrees with reason and is conducive to the good and benefit of one and all, then accept it and live up to it.

Buddha

I hope investors who have asked few questions so far and, as a result, been beaten down by their rote memorization of the mantra "buy-and-hold is good for you" will finally ask critical questions and scientifically examine data for themselves.

Chaos Theory: Linear Versus Nonlinear

Everyone's entitled to their own opinion, but they're not entitled to their own facts.
Donald Rumsfeld,
Secretary of Defense 2003[10]

Chaos theory dictates that the world is not linear. The unexpected happens. Spending your time looking for "perfect" is an exercise in futility. The future is unknown no matter how educated a fundamental forecast. Manus J. Donahue III, author of *An Introduction to Chaos Theory and Fractal Geometry*, addressed a chaotic, nonlinear world:

> "The world of mathematics has been confined to the linear world for centuries. That is to say, mathematicians and physicists have overlooked dynamical systems as random and unpredictable. The only systems that could be understood in the past were those that were believed to be linear, that is to say, systems that follow predictable patterns and arrangements. Linear equations, linear functions, linear algebra, linear programming, and linear accelerators are all areas that have been understood and mastered by the human race. However, the problem arises that we humans do not live in an even remotely linear world; in fact, our world must indeed be categorized as nonlinear; hence, proportion and linearity is scarce. How may one go about pursuing and understanding a nonlinear system in a world that is confined to the easy, logical linearity of everything? This is the question that scientists and mathematicians became burdened with in the nineteenth century; hence, a new science and mathematics was derived: chaos theory."[9]

Although acceptance of a nonlinear world is a new concept for many, it is not a new proposition for trend followers. The big events described in Chapter 4, "Big Events, Crashes, and Panics," such as the 2008 market crash, are nonlinear events. Trend followers won those events because they expected the unexpected. Lack of linearity, or cause and effect, was not something unanticipated because their trading models were built for the unexpected. How did they do this? Trend followers are statistical thinkers. Gerd

Gigerenzer, featured in Chapter 7, "Decision Making," is a proponent of the power of statistical thinking:

> "At the beginning of the twentieth century, the father of modern science fiction, Herbert George Wells, said in his writings on politics, 'If we want to have an educated citizenship in a modern technological society, we need to teach them three things: reading, writing, and statistical thinking.' At the beginning of the twenty-first century, how far have we gotten with this program? In our society, we teach most citizens reading and writing from the time they are children, but not statistical thinking."[11]

I have no special talents. I am only passionately curious.

Albert Einstein

One of my favorite examples of statistical thinking is very simple. It is a case study regarding the birth ratio of boys and girls.

Consider that there are two hospitals. In the first one, 120 babies are born every day; in the other, there are only 12. On average, the ratio of boys to girls born every day in each hospital is 50/50. However, one day, in one of those hospitals twice as many girls are born as boys. In which hospital was it more likely to happen? The answer is obvious for a good trader, but as research shows, not so obvious for a lay person: It is much more likely to happen in the small hospital. The reason for this is that technically speaking, the probability of a random deviation of a particular size (from the population mean) decreases with the increase in the sample size.[12]

What do statistics about birth and gender have to do with trend following trading? Take two traders who, on average, win 40 percent of the time with their winners being three times as large as their losers. One has a history of 1,000 trades and the other has a history of 10 trades. Who has a better chance in the next 10 trades to have only 10 percent of their total trades be winners (instead of the typical 40 percent)? The one with the 10-trade history has the better chance. Why? The more trades in a history, the greater probability of adhering to the average. The less trades in a history, the greater probability of deviation from the average.

Standard deviation measures the uncertainty in a random variable (in this case, investment returns). It measures the degree of variation of returns around the mean (average) return. The higher the volatility of the investment returns, the higher the standard deviation will be.

National Institute of Standards and Technology[13]

Consider a friend who receives a stock tip and makes some quick money. He tells everyone about his new found trading prowess. You are impressed and think he must really know his trading. You would be less impressed if you were a statistical thinker because you would realize immediately that his "population" of tips was extremely small. He could just as easily follow the next great stock tip and lose it all. One tip means nothing. The sample is too small.

The difference between these two views is why great trend followers have grown from one-man shops to hugely successful firms that routinely beat the so-called Wall Street powerhouses. Why did Wall Street sit by and allow trend traders to enter and then dominate arenas they could, and perhaps should, have controlled? The answer lies in Wall Street's fascination with benchmarks. Wall Street is after index-like performance ("benchmarks"), whereas trend followers are after absolute performance not hinged to benchmarks.

Large, established Wall Street firms, many of which blew out in 2008 (unlike trend followers who made money in 2008), judge success with measures of central tendency, not absolute return. The large banks and brokerages view an average measure (mean) and the variation from that average to determine whether they are winning or losing. They are beholden to irrational desires of investors. Thinking in terms of a trend following mindset would be too hard.

Where do they all go wrong? Volatility around the mean (standard deviation) is the standard Wall Street definition of risk (see Chapters 3 and 4). Wall Street types, long-only types, aim for consistency instead of absolute returns, and, as a result, Wall Street returns are typically average. How do you free yourself from averages? It is difficult. We are influenced heavily by standard finance theory that revolves almost entirely around normal distribution worship. Michael Mauboussin and Kristen Bartholdson see clearly the state of affairs:

"Normal distributions are the bedrock of finance, including the random walk, capital asset pricing, value-at-risk, and Black-Scholes models. Value-at-risk (VaR) models, for example, attempt to quantify how much loss a portfolio may suffer with a given probability. While there are various forms of VaR models, a basic version relies on standard deviation as a measure of risk. Given a normal distribution, it is relatively straightforward to measure standard deviation, and hence risk. However, if price changes are not normally distributed, standard deviation can be a very misleading proxy for risk."[14]

Mathematics and science are two different notions, two different disciplines. By its nature, good mathematics is quite intuitive. Experimental science doesn't really work that way. Intuition is important. Making guesses is important. Thinking about the right experiments is important. But it's a little more broad and a little less deep, So the mathematics we use here can be sophisticated. But that's not really the point. We don't use very, very deep stuff. Certain of our statistical approaches can be very sophisticated. I'm not suggesting it's simple. I want a guy who knows enough math so that he can use those tools effectively but has a curiosity about how things work and enough imagination and tenacity to dope it out.

Jim Simons[15]

The problem with using standard deviation as a risk measurement can be seen with the example where two traders have similar standard deviations, but might show entirely different distribution of returns. One might look like the familiar normal distribution, or bell curve. The other might show statistical characteristics called kurtosis and skewness. In other words, the historical pattern of returns does not resemble a normal distribution.

Trend followers never have and never will produce returns that exhibit a normal distribution. They never produce consistent average returns that hit benchmarks quarter after quarter. When trend followers hit home runs in the zero-sum game and win huge profits from the likes of Barings Bank, Long-Term Capital Management, and the 2008 market crash, they are targeting the edges or those fat tails of our non-normally distributed world. Jerry Parker, the most successful of Richard Dennis' trained turtle traders, states this outright:

> "The way I describe it is that overlaying trend following on top of markets produce a non-normal distribution of trades. And that's sort of our edge—in these outlier trades. I don't know if we have an inherent rate of return, but when you place this trend following on top of markets, it can produce this distribution—the world is non-normal."[17]

Jean-Jacques Chenier, like Parker, believes that the markets are far less linear and efficient than Wall Street does. We all forget this, but not everyone in the market plays to win the game. Some might be hedging, such as central banks commonly do. Chenier points out that, as a result, they regularly lose:

> "The Bank of Japan will intervene to push the yen lower…a commercial bank in Japan will repatriate yen assets overseas just to window dress its balance sheets for the end of the fiscal year. These activities create liquidity but it is inefficient liquidity that can be exploited."[18]

To make accurate judgments about trend following and better understand Parker's words, it helps to break down the statistical concepts of skew and kurtosis. Skew, nicely summarized by Larry Swedroe of Buckingham Asset Management, measures the statistical likelihood of a return in the tail of a distribution being

Luck is largely responsible for my reputation for genius. I don't walk into the office in the morning and say, "Am I smart today?" I walk in and wonder, "Am I lucky today?"

Jim Simons[16]

Investment manuals suffer another deficiency, which is that expert (and I use the term advisedly) opinion in the field tends to be cyclical, not cumulative. One would not expect to see a home-improvement volume with the title The New Reality of Plumbing. But the science of investing, at least as it is propagated by financial writers, undergoes a seeming revolution every couple of thousand points on the Dow.[19]

Two lessons from the St. Petersburg Paradox. The risk-reducing formulas behind portfolio theory rely on a number of demanding and ultimately unfounded premises. First, they suggest that price changes are statistically independent from one another...The second assumption is that price changes are distributed in a pattern that conforms to a standard bell curve. Do financial data neatly conform to such assumptions? Of course, they never do.

Benoit B. Mandelbrot[20]

higher or lower than that commonly associated with a normal distribution. For example, a return series of –30 percent, 5 percent, 10 percent, and 15 percent has a mean of 0 percent. Only one return is less than 0 percent, whereas three are higher but the one that is negative is much farther from the mean (0 percent) than the positive ones. This is called negative skewness. Negative skewness occurs when the values to the left of (less than) the mean are fewer, but farther from the mean than the values to the right of the mean. Positive skewness occurs when the values to the right of (more than) the mean are fewer, but farther from the mean than the values to the left of the mean.[21]

Trend followers, as you might have guessed, exhibit a positive skew return profile. Kurtosis, on the other hand, measures the degree to which exceptional values, much larger or smaller than the average, occur more frequently (high kurtosis) or less frequently (low kurtosis) than in a normal (bell-shaped) distribution. High kurtosis results in exceptional values called "fat tails." Fat tails indicate a higher percentage of very low and very high returns than would be expected with a normal distribution.[22]

The president of John W. Henry and Co. clarified:

"Skew may be either positive or negative and affects distribution symmetry. Positive skew means that there is a higher probability for a significant positive return than for a negative return the same distance from the mean. Skew will measure the direction of surprises. Risk management should minimize the number of negative surprises. Outliers, or extremes in performance not normally associated with a distribution, will clearly affect skewness. The crash of 1987 is usually considered an extreme outlier. For example, a positive outlier will stretch the right hand tail of the distribution. Because JWH's trading methodology eliminates losing positions and holds profitable positions, historically there has been a tendency for positive outliers and a higher chance of positive returns. A negative skew results in a higher probability of a significantly negative event for the same distance from the mean."[23]

Skewness is a measure of symmetry, or more precisely, the lack of symmetry. A distribution, or data set, is symmetric if it looks the same to the left and right of the center point.

National Institute of Standards and Technology[24]

As important as these concepts are to making money, they are typically ignored by many. They are not as sexy as listening to Jim

Cramer hoot and holler each night. Few people see the use for statistical thinking in their trading. They either don't understand or dismiss skew, kurtosis, and upside/downside volatility (see Chapter 3, "Performance Data"). If you avoid these concepts, you will never see the reality that great trend following traders see every day—the reality of a nonlinear world.

Compounding

One of the first Wall Street books I read was Jim Rogers *Investment Biker*. It had a huge influence on me because Rogers brought so much passion and common sense to the table. Nearly 14 years later, in early 2008, I had the good fortune to interview Rogers for my first documentary film (*Broke: The New American Dream*) at his home in Singapore. Even though I had been up for nearly 48 hours straight (I did have to go around the world to see him) when I did the interview, it was a fantastic experience. Rogers, who is not a technical trend following trader, but who has made a fortune off trading trends, put the importance of compounding at the top of his list for anyone trying to make money:

"One of the biggest mistakes most investors make is believing they've always got to be doing something…the trick in investing is not to lose money…the losses will kill you. They ruin your compounding rate; and compounding is the magic of investing."[26]

You can't get rich overnight, but with compounding, you at least have a chance to make big money. For example, if you manage to make 50 percent a year in your trading, you can compound an initial $20,000 account to over $616,000 in just seven years. Is 50 percent unrealistic? Perhaps! However, do the math again using 25 percent. In other words, compounding is essential. You can be a trend follower, make 25 percent a year, and spend all your profit each year. Or you can trend follow and compound your 25 percent a year for 20 or more years and become rich.

Consider a hypothetical investment of $20,000 (see Chart 8.1):

Kurtosis is a measure of whether the data are peaked or flat relative to a normal distribution. That is, data sets with high kurtosis tend to have a distinct peak near the mean, decline rather rapidly, and have heavy tails. Data sets with low kurtosis tend to have a flat top near the mean rather than a sharp peak. A uniform distribution would be the extreme case.

National Institute of Standards and Technology[25]

For such a long time we thought that most data must have a normal distribution and therefore that the mean is meaningful. With the perfect vision of hindsight, this is a bit odd. Much of the world around us is not normal…The point is that it is so difficult to see the simplest things as they really are. We become so used to our assumptions that we can no longer see them or evidence against them. Instead of challenging our assumptions, we spend our time studying the details, the colors of the threads that we tear from the tapestry of the world. That is why science is hard.[27]

Say goodbye to a nice, steady, equilibrium perspective, says Professor Bak. Equilibrium equals death. Things do not rock along smoothly, change in small increments. Change is catastrophic. We must learn to adapt because we cannot predict.[28]

CHART 8.1: Compounding Example

	30%	40%	50%
Year 1	$26,897	$29,642	$32,641
Year 2	$36,174	$43,933	$53,274
Year 3	$48,650	$65,115	$86,949
Year 4	$65,429	$96,509	$141,909
Year 5	$87,995	$143,039	$231,609
Year 6	$118,344	$212,002	$378,008
Year 7	$159,160	$314,214	$616,944

Another great compounding example? In October 1997, David Harding launched the Winton Futures Fund, which has provided investors with annualized returns of over 21 percent per year. To put that in context, if you had been the buyer of Vincent van Gogh's "Irises" in 1947, you would have paid $80,000. The next time it changed hands, in 1987, it was bought for $53.9 million. This seems like a huge increase in value, but mathematically it shows a compound average annual growth rate of 17.7 percent, which is less than the annualized returns from Harding's fund.

Compounding is not easy to do in a society forever focused on instant gratification. However, if some trend following traders can thrive and flourish in a compounded world, we all can.

Key Points

- Defining risk in terms of a number is critical. If you can't think in terms of numbers, don't play the game.
- To be successful as a trader and to be successful in life, you need to develop the ability to ask the right questions.
- Trend following strategies make money on the edges of the bell curve.
- Act as a devil's advocate. Question assumptions. Check your inferences. Consider the improbable or the unpopular.
- People mistakenly see a regular event and think it rare. They think chance will correct a series of rare events. They see a rare event and think it regular.
- People tend to regard extremely probable events as certain and extremely improbable events as impossible.

Holy Grails

9

Another psychological aspect that drives me to use timing techniques on my portfolio is understanding myself well enough to know that I could never sit in a buy and hold strategy for two years during 1973 and 1974, watch my portfolio go down 48 percent and do nothing, hoping it would come back someday.

Tom Basso

Most of Wall Street died in 2008. The big names, the brokerage firms, the banks, and hedge funds were permanently exposed as con artists. You say harsh language? Well, look at all of the fees Wall Street collected for the last decade to deliver a performance that was abysmal. How did this happen?

The single biggest mistake traders make is thinking that investing and trading is "easy." They allow themselves to fall for advertisements promising, "You can get rich by trading" or "Earn all the income you've ever dreamed of" or "Leave your day job forever and live off your day-trading profits." Wall Street compounds the problem with analysts constantly screaming, "Buy" or with their nearly fanatical pitching of buy and hold as a legitimate trading strategy. It's not legitimate. It's a criminal, inane approach to trying to make money.

In *Buy and Hold: A Different Perspective*, Richard Rudy explains how we always seek simple solutions to intricate problems. In response to the messy and frustrating reality, we often develop "rules of thumb" that we use in our decision making. Whenever we see evidence that our "rules" are even remotely correct, our sense of security is boosted and our simplistic decision-making mechanism is validated. If we are faced with evidence contrary to our "rules," we quickly rationalize it away.[3]

With the title alone causing hysterics, placing this on your coffee table will elicit your guests to share their best dot-com horror story. How they invested their $100,000 second mortgage in Cisco Systems at $80 after reading about it, waiting for it to become $500 (as predicted in this very book) only to see it dive to $17. Just the thought of this book gives me the chuckles.

Amazon.com Review of *Dow 36,000*[4]

These simplistic, irrational "security blankets" are often referred to as Holy Grails. Grail legends have their origins in Celtic paganism, but they became increasingly more Christian in theme. In medieval times, the Holy Grail was the cup used at the Last Supper of Christ. Holy Grail stories are always filled with mystery and hint at some secret that is never completely revealed. Although the Grail itself, unimaginably precious, might be found, only the holiest of holy can experience it, and they can never, ever bring it back. The markets have always overflowed with Holy Grails—those systems, strategies, secret formulas, and interpretations of fundamentals that promise riches to whomever trades with them. Today, in 2009, it is no different.

Buy and Hold

After the stock market bubble burst in spring 2000 and after the crash of October and November 2008, the concept of buy and hold as a trading strategy should have been shown as the failure it is once and for all. Yet, I doubt that has happened. Investors still obey mantras such as, "Buy and hold for the long term." "Stay the course." "Buy the dips." "Never surrender." Buy-and-hold mantras are junk because they never answer the basic questions: Buy how much of what? Buy at what price? Hold for how long? Jerry Parker gives a strong rationale for choosing trend following over buy and hold:

"Trend following is [similar] to a democracy. Sometimes it doesn't look so good, but it's better than anything else out there. It's a worse investment now, let's say, than it was in the '70s or '80s. But so what? What other choice do we have? Are we going to buy market breaks? Are we going to rely on buy and hold? Buy and hope, that's what I call it. Are we going to double up when we lose money? Are we going to do all these things that everyone else does? Eventually people will come to understand that trend following works in other markets, markets that produce trends."[5]

Consider the NASDAQ market crash of 1973–1974. The NASDAQ reached its high peak in December 1972. It then dropped by nearly 60 percent, hitting rock bottom in September 1974. We did not see the NASDAQ break permanently free of the 1973–1974 bear market until April 1980. Buy and hold did nothing for investors from December 1972 through March 1980. Investors would have made more money during this period in a 3 percent savings account. History repeated itself with the more recent 77 percent drop in the NASDAQ from 2000–2002. Now we have October and November 2008, which makes the dot-com bubble look like a picnic with Grandma.

Making matters worse is that a pure buy-and-hold strategy during an extended drop in the market makes the recovery back to breakeven difficult (if not impossible).

The "buy-and-hold" investor has been led to believe (perhaps by an industry with a powerful conflict of interest) that if he has tremendous patience and discipline and "stays with it," he will make a good long-term return. These investors fully expect that they will make back most, if not all, of recent losses soon enough. They believe that the best place for long-term capital is the stock market and that if they give it 5 or 10 or 20 years they will surely do very well. Such investors need to understand that they can go 5, 10, and 20 years and make no return at all and even lose money.[6]

To compound problems even more, buy-and-hold panders to a kind of market revenge. Investors who bought and lost want their money back. They think, "I lost my money in Sun Microsystems, and I'm going to make my money back in Sun Microsystems come hell or high water." They can neither fathom the concept of sunk costs nor admit that buy-and-hold might not work. So they buy and hold no matter what happens in the mean time.

You will run out of money before a guru runs out of indicators.

Neal T. Weintraub

There is the old trading parable about fishing and revenge. You are out at the fishing hole. The big one gets away, and you throw

There is little point in exploring the Elliott Wave Theory because it is not a theory at all, but rather the banal observation that a price chart comprises a series of peaks and troughs. Depending on the time scale you use, there can be as many peaks and troughs as you care to imagine.[1]

your hook back in. Are you only after the one that got away? Of course not, you throw the hook back in to catch a big fish—any big fish. Ed Seykota has always said to catch more fish, go where the fish are. Jonathan Hoenig puts the emphasis where it must be:

"I am a trader because my interest isn't in owning stocks per se, but in making money. And while I do trade in stocks (among other investments), I don't have blind faith that stocks will necessarily be higher by the time I'm ready to retire. If history has demonstrated anything, it's that we can't simply put our portfolios on autopilot and expect things to turn out for the best. You can't be a trader when you're right and an investor when you're wrong. That's how you lose."

Warren Buffett

Warren Buffett has long been positioned as the single biggest proponent of buy-and-hold. Like Sir Galahad, he has achieved his Holy Grail, and I salute his success. However, can you achieve what he has? Doubtful. He is the exception to the rule. There is only one Buffett. Unfortunately, many people mistakenly assume Buffett is just a buy-and-hold investor. It is more complex than that.

SUNW probably has the best near-term outlook of any company I know.

James Cramer
September 7, 2000[9]

For example, in an interview in *Forbes*, Buffett was squarely against derivatives:

"'Things are less lucrative in the stock market. We have more money than ideas,' he said, adding that 6 percent to 7 percent was a fair rate of return in the current environment. The company has more than $37 billion in cash to invest. One place the money certainly won't go is derivatives. 'There's no place with as much potential for phony numbers as derivatives,' he said. Buffett's 78-year-old billionaire vice chairman, Charlie Munger, couldn't resist chiming in. 'To say that derivative accounting is a sewer is an insult to sewage.'"[8]

Sixteen days later, Buffett was saying something different:

"Berkshire Hathaway issues first ever-negative coupon security: Omaha, Nebraska, May 22, 2002. Berkshire Hathaway Inc. (NYSE: BRK.A and BRK.B), announced today that it has sold $400 million of a new type of security, named 'SQUARZ,' in a private placement to qualified institutional investors...'Despite the lack of precedent, a negative coupon security seemed possible in the present interest rate environment,' said Warren E. Buffett, chairman of Berkshire Hathaway. Mr. Buffett added, 'I asked Goldman Sachs to create such an instrument and they responded promptly with the innovative security being announced today.'"[10]

If Buffett was being forthright the first time he spoke on the subject what made him change his mind two weeks later and create an investment instrument so complicated and secretive that not even his press release could explain it? Even more confusing is that Buffett contradicted himself again a year later, going against his financial creation:

> "Derivatives are financial weapons of mass destruction, carrying dangers, while now latent, are potentially lethal... We view them as time bombs, both for the parties that deal in them and the economic system."[11]

Now in 2008 Buffett has once again been caught in the headlines for trading derivatives. The Buffett legend of buy-and-hold as his one and only strategy has permeated the public consciousness with literally books by the dozens. But when he launches a new derivatives strategy that goes against his legend, either no one notices or those who do notice are reluctant to criticize in public.

Losers Average Losers

There's a famous picture of Paul Tudor Jones, the great macro trader first profiled in Jack Schwager's *Market Wizards*, relaxing in his office. Tacked up on the wall behind him on loose-leaf sheet of paper is the simple phrase in black magic marker, "Losers Average Losers." Jones' wisdom was obviously lost on James K. Glassman, judging from the following excerpt from a Glassman *Washington Post* stock-picking column:

> "If you had Enron in your portfolio and didn't sell it at $90 or even at $10, don't feel embarrassed. As Alfred Harrison,

When people say the market is over-valued and there's a bubble, whatever that means, they're talking about just a handful of stocks. Most of these stocks are reasonably priced. There's no reason for them to correct violently anytime in the year 2000.

Larry Wachtel, Market Analyst,
Prudential Securities
December 23, 1999[13]

Imagine you are at a car auction hoping to buy a beautiful red '66 Corvette. Imagine the car that is being auctioned before the Corvette is a 1955 Mercedes Gull Wing Coupe that sells for $750,000. The Corvette is up next and the Blue Book price is $35,000. What would you bid? Now imagine the car before yours was a 'kit' car replica of the Gull Wing Mercedes that sold for $75,000. What would you pay now? Research has shown that incidental price data can affect what you are willing to pay. We have a tendency to pay more if the preceding price is considerably higher!

Jon C. Sundt, President,
Altegris Investments
1st Quarter 2004 commentary

a money manager at Alliance Capital Management Holding LP, which owned a ton of Enron, put it, 'On the surface it had always seemed to be a fairly good growth stock. We bought it all the way down.'"[12]

Glassman and Harrison are both dead wrong. What they call dollar-cost averaging is really averaging a loser (Enron in this example) all the way down. Traders should feel sick if they average losers, not just embarrassed. When you have a losing position, it must tell you something is wrong. As unbelievable as it seems to the novice investor, the longer a market declines, the more likely it is to continue declining. Falling markets must never be viewed as places to buy cheap.

Harrison violated a cardinal rule of trading. In the zero-sum world of trading, if the trend is down, it is not a buying opportunity; it is a selling opportunity—a "time to go short" opportunity. Even worse, as an active money manager for clients, he admitted to averaging losers as a strategy. To top it off, Glassman later adds:

> "Could the typical small investor have discovered a year ago that Enron was on the brink of disaster? It's highly unlikely. Still, if you looked for the right thing, you would have never bought Enron in the first place."[14]

Actually, there was a way to spot Enron's problems. The price going from $90 to 50 cents was a pretty clear clue that the brink of disaster was just around the corner. Jesse Livermore knew nearly 80 years earlier how to spot losers:

> "I have warned against averaging losses. That is a most common practice. Great numbers of people buy a stock, let us say at 50, and two or three days later if they can buy it at 47 they are seized with the urge to average down by buying another hundred shares, making a price of 48.5 on all. Having bought at 50 and being concerned over a three-point loss on a hundred shares, what rhyme or reason is there in adding another hundred shares and having the double worry when the price hits 44? At that point there would be a $600 loss on the first hundred shares and a $300 loss on the second shares. If one is to apply such an

Jan, the bottom line is, before the end of the year [2000], the NASDAQ and Dow will be at new record highs.

Myron Kandel,
Financial Editor and Anchor
CNNfn/Cofounder, CNN
April 4, 2000[15]

unsound principle, he should keep on averaging by buying 200 at 44, then 400 at 41, 800 at 38, 1,600 at 35, 3,200 at 32, 6,400 at 29, and so on. How many speculators could stand such pressure? So, at the risk of repetition and preaching, let me urge you to avoid averaging down.'"

Other traders have seen their once great empires scuttled by averaging losers as well. Julian Robertson ran one of the biggest and profitable hedge funds ever. However, things ended badly. On March 30, 2000, CNN excerpted a letter Julian Robertson wrote to Tiger's investors blaming the fund's problems on the rush to cash in on the Internet craze:

> "As you have heard me say on a number of occasions, the key to Tiger's success over the years has been a steady commitment to buying the best stocks and shorting the worst. In a rational environment, this strategy functions well. But in an irrational market, where earnings and price considerations take a back seat to mouse clicks and momentum, such logic, as we have learned, does not count for much. The result of the demise of value investing and investor withdrawals has been financial erosion, stressful to us all. And there is no real indication that a quick end is in sight."[16]

The story of Tiger resembles a Greek tragedy, where the protagonist is the victim of his own self-pride. Tiger's spiral downward started in the fall of 1998 when a catastrophic trade on dollar-yen cost the fund billions. An ex-Tiger employee was quoted as saying: "There's a certain amount of hubris when you take a position so big you have to be right and so big you can't get out when you're wrong. That was something Julian never would have done when he was younger. That isn't good risk-return analysis."[17]

The problem with Tiger was its philosophically shaky foundation. Robertson stated: "Our mandate is to find the 200 best companies in the world and invest in them, and find the 200 worst companies in the world and go short on them. If the 200 best don't do better than the 200 worst, you probably should go into another business."

If you want a guarantee, buy a toaster.

Clint Eastwood

I am of the belief that the individual out there is actually not throwing money at things that they do not understand, and is actually using the news and using the information out there to make smart investment decisions.

Maria Bartiromo,
Anchor, Reporter, CNBC
March 2001[18]

Assimilating and sifting through vast quantities of information was Robertson's forte. According to one associate, "He can look at a long list of numbers in a financial statement he'd never seen before and say, 'that one is wrong,' and he's right." Although that talent is impressive, being able to read and critique a balance sheet doesn't necessarily translate into knowing when and how much to buy or sell as trend following trader Richard Donchian pointed out (see Chapter 2, "Great Trend Followers").

Crash and Panic

What do Julian Robertson, the concept of losers average losers, the dot-com stock crash, and October 2008 have in common? Bubbles. The 2008 crash is no different from the tulip bubble made famous in Holland. In 1720, when the south sea bubble was at its height, even the greatest genius of his time, Sir Isaac Newton, got sucked into the hysteria. Investing as if his brilliance in science carried over to his finances, Newton eventually lost £20,000.

Although bubbles might appear as short-term blips in economic history, more often the aftermath is long term, resulting in severe recessions and government intervention that usually makes the situation worse. The collapse of bubbles of the past 400 years threw each nation into a recession lasting a decade or longer. What lesson can we learn from bubbles? Human nature continues to be the way it has always been and probably always will be.[19]

You have to say, "What if?" What if the stocks rally? What if they don't? Like a catcher, you have to wear a helmet.

Jonathan Hoenig, Portfolio Manager, Capitalistpig Hedge Fund LLC

Today, especially after the October/November 2008 crash, investors must do more than simply trust someone else for their financial decision making or glance at their pension statement once a quarter. They can no longer pretend it is just "retirement" and that their nest egg will go back up. Take a quick view of the Japanese Nikkei 225 stock index (see Chart 9.1).

The index reached nearly 40,000 in 1989. Now, 19 years later, it hovers around below 10,000. Do you think the Japanese still believe in buy and hold? Another example reveals a chart (see Chart 9.2) of the hot tech stocks of 1968.

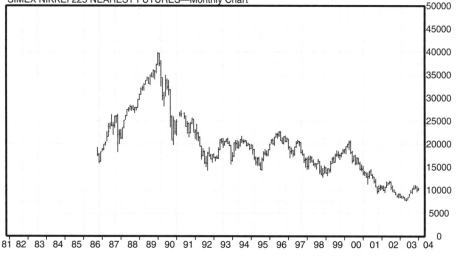

SIMEX NIKKEI 225 NEAREST FUTURES—Monthly Chart

CHART 9.1: Weekly Chart Nikkei 225 1985–2003 Source: Barchart.com

CHART 9.2: 1968 Tech Stocks

Company	1968 High	1970 Low	% drop	P/E at High
Fairchild Camera	102.00	18.00	−82	443
Teledyne	72.00	13.00	−82	42
Control Data	163.00	28.00	−83	54
Mohawk Data	111.00	18.00	−84	285
Electronic Data	162.00	24.00	−85	352
Optical Scanning	146.00	16.00	−89	200
Itek	172.00	17.00	−90	71
University Computing	186.00	13.00	−93	118

Who cares what year it is? Bubbles and busts come and go and they all look the same. Unfortunately for investors, financial writers such as Alan Sloan are often too quick to use good metaphors to describe bad predicaments, which only further damages one's ability to ever retire:

What makes the Dow at 10,000 particularly noteworthy for us is that it means that the index has to rise a mere 26,000 more points to vindicate the prophecy of those two jokers who achieved 15 seconds of fame when we were in full bubble by predicting it would hit 36,000. We kind of miss them; they were always good for comic relief. Another 500 points and we've a hunch they'll be back peddling the same old moonshine.

Alan Abelson,
Barrons
December 20, 2003[21]

"So now, with your portfolio trashed and Social Security looking insecure, you may be having nightmares about spending your retirement haunting the mac-and-cheese, early-bird specials, or about not being able to retire until six years after you've died. With the bull market gone, will the impending retirement of the post-World War II generation be the Boomer Bust?—If you work hard, save and adopt more realistic expectations, you can still retire rather than die in the harness. Earning maybe 9 percent on stocks isn't as good as the 20 percent that you might have grown used to. But it's not bad."[20]

Saying 9 percent compounded is not bad compared to 20 percent compounded, ignores the pure math. Imagine the last 25 years and two investments of $1,000 each. The first investment generated 9 percent for 25 years, and the second investment generated 20 percent for 25 years.

- $1,000 compounded at 9% for 25 years = $8,600.
- $1,000 compounded at 20% for 25 years = $95,000.

Here are two examples of frustration exhibited by not having a real compounding plan, but rather just trusting buy-and-hold as the only strategy:

- "What do you do if you find yourself at retirement age without enough to retire on? You keep working."—John Rother, AARP's policy director.
- "I've worked hard all my life and been a responsible citizen and it's not supposed to be threatened at this point."—Gail Hovey, 62, who works for nonprofit groups in Hawaii.

No one wants to see Gail homeless. On the other hand, do we want to live in a society that rewards one group's mistakes with government assistance paid for by a second group who did not make the same mindless mistakes? Look at all of the bailouts of 2008! Life must not be contorted into being fair when it isn't. It is fine for us to compound our trading gains, but it's not fine for the government to compound idiocy. Even the top well-paid professionals in charge of pension assets were just buy-and-holders:

"Every major investor in the nation was heavily invested in WorldCom. They were one of the largest corporations in America." New York State Comptroller[22]

What was their plan? Their plan was the same as the state retirement plans of Michigan, Florida, and California that also lost in WorldCom:

• The State of Michigan reported an unrealized loss of about $116 million on WorldCom.

• The State of Florida's reported an unrealized loss of about $90 million on WorldCom.

• The California Public Employees Retirement System (CalPERS) reported an unrealized loss of about $565 million on WorldCom.

Referring to $8.4 million in WorldCom stock now worth only about $492,000, Robert Leggett of Kentucky Retirement Systems said, "Until you actually sell it, you haven't lost it."

Thanks, Bob. Helluva plan you got there. Ed Seykota philosophically summed up nicely these results:

"The best measure of your intention is the result you get."[24]

There is no greater source of conflict among researchers and practitioners in capital market theory than the validity of technical analysis. The vast majority of academic research condemns technical analysis as theoretically bankrupt and of no practical value...It is certainly understandable why many researchers would oppose technical analysis: the validity of technical analysis calls into question decades of careful theoretical modeling [Capital Asset Pricing Model, Arbitrage Pricing Theory] claiming the markets are efficient and investors are collectively, if not individually, rational.[23]

Analysis Paralysis

In 2000, there were 28,000 recommendations by brokerage-house analysts. At the start of October 2000, 99.1 percent of those recommendations on U.S. companies were either strong buy, buy, or hold. Just 0.9 percent of the time, analysts said sell. Listening to these analysts for guidance was the public's conscious decision not to think for themselves.

A study at Dartmouth College by Kent Womack observed that analysts often comment on and recommend companies that their firms have recently taken public. The research shows that stocks recommended by analysts perform more poorly than "buy" recommendations by unaffiliated brokers prior to, at the time of, and subsequent to the recommendation date.

However, it seems many ignore the data. Analysts still go on TV, and viewers think to themselves, "She sounds bright; she works for JP Morgan or Morgan Stanley, and she's using a lot of financial jargon that I don't understand, so she must know something I don't." She doesn't. The fact that so many analysts told you that you could buy so many stocks in the middle of the dot-com bubble and over 2008—and were entirely wrong—must be permanent proof that analysts' insight is not the answer. On top of that, the performance of most of Wall Street's advice-givers is closely tied to current market movement anyway. What are you listening for?

Even though there was never any rationale for listening to these analysts, many people did and became angry when the advice proved disastrous. At one point, one discredited analyst became a favorite whipping boy for those investors who refused to accept responsibility for their losses:

- "Every time my broker mentions […], I get nauseous."
- "For the past few years, every time I'd call them, they'd say, '[…] likes WorldCom' or '[…] really likes Global Crossing.' As a result, I now own hundreds of shares of these duds."
- "So now when it comes to investment research, we need to think twice about the veracity of top-rate advice and stock picks from someone earning $20 million a year."
- "[…] should have warned that this epochal bubble was doomed to burst. After all he was the industry's greatest seer."
- "However unfair it is to blame just […], here's a situation when one person's contribution to wholesale disaster is impossible to overlook."
- "In the late 1990s, telecommunications stocks were explosive. New companies went public, old companies saw spectacular growth, and […] never once warned us that this was all a mirage."

Does anyone think this analyst had knowledge that the telecom bubble was about to burst? I am not defending him, but if investors had their life savings tied up in the opinion of one man, they were bound to be in trouble no matter what happened in the market. If one stock tanks or an entire sector implodes, who was supposed to warn them? No one was forced to listen to anyone. Anyone who held Fannie, Freddie, AIG, Bear Stearns, or Lehman Brothers all the way down over the course of 2008 had no one to blame except the person staring back at them in the mirror.

Yet, people are still unwilling to take responsibility for their own decisions. Although they might have lost more than half their portfolio in the past decade, they eagerly accept invitations like this one from a brokerage firm that imploded in 2008:[25]

"Merrill Lynch cordially invites you to an educational workshop...Topics discussed:

* Merrill Lynch Stock Market Forecast for [...].
* When will the recession end?
* What do I do now?
* What are the factors of a good stock market?
* How did this bear market compare to others?"

Forecasts are financial candy. Forecasts give people who hate the feeling of uncertainty something emotionally soothing.

Thomas Vician, Jr., student of Ed Seykota's

If Merrill Lynch produced useless forecasts for the last decade and had basically gone under in 2008 (they would have folded if not for a last minute Bank of America buyout), why would they assume anyone would believe their forecast for "whatever" year? Why would you ever want to trust a group like this?

Never let the fear of striking out get in your way.

Babe Ruth

Final Thoughts

The Nasdaq bubble popped. The real estate bubble popped. The credit bubble popped. The Dow bubble popped in 2008. Will there be another bubble anytime soon? No one knows. What you can do is ride trends up and down using a precise set of rules to get in and out. If you are watching CNBC for prediction of a trend change, you are in trouble, 'Casey Jones,' as Jerry Garcia of The Grateful Dead reminds:

"Trouble with you is the trouble with me

Got two good eyes but you still don't see

Come round the bend, you know it's the end

The fireman screams and the engine just gleams..."[26]

The Henry theory— statistically corroborated, of course—is that assets, once in motion, tend to stay in motion without changing direction, and that turns the old saw— buy low, sell high—on its ear.[27]

Enron stock was rated as "Can't Miss" until it became clear that the company was in desperate trouble, at which point analysts lowered the rating to "Sure Thing." Only when Enron went completely under did a few bold analysts demote its stock to the lowest possible Wall Street analyst rating, "Hot Buy."

> Dave Barry
> February 3, 2002[28]

After breaking down a number of wrongheaded trading beliefs and actions in which, like Casey Jones, investors "still don't see," it makes sense to break down the daily strategy of a trend follower. The following chapter looks at what makes a trend following trading system work.

Key Points

- Wall Street works hard to make what they do, which is nothing more than buying and holding, appear complex and sophisticated.

- Why would you be a buy-and-holder when the best in the business don't do it that way?

- Stop your search for "value." Even if you locate value, that alone does not ensure your ability to make money in the market.

- The buy-and-hold dream as a retirement solution is toast.

- Stock tips don't work. They are incomplete. They indicate only the buy side of the equation. When do you sell?

- Trend trader Charlie Wright states: "It took me a long time to figure out that no one really understands why the market does what it does or where it's going. It's a delusion to think that you or any one else can know where the market is going. I have sat through hundreds of hours of seminars in which the presenter made it seem as if he or she had some secret method of divining where the markets were going. Either they were deluded or they were putting us on. Most Elliott Wave practitioners, cycle experts, or Fibonacci time traders will try to predict when the market will move, presumably in the direction they have also predicted. I personally have not been able to figure out how to know when the market is going to move. And you know what? When I tried to predict, I was usually wrong, and I invariably missed the big move I was anticipating, because it wasn't time. It was when I finally concluded that I would never be able to predict when the market will move that I started to be more successful in my trading. My frustration level declined dramatically, and I was at peace knowing that it was okay not to be able to predict or understand the markets."

Part IV

Trading Systems 10

I think it's much too early to tell. I think all we've learned is what we already knew, is that stocks have become like commodities, regrettably, and they go up to limit and they go down to limit. And we've also known over the years that when they go down, they go down faster than they go up.

Leon Cooperman[3]

Trend followers take a specific philosophy rooted in crowd behavior and reduce it to rules to guide them in daily decision making of when to buy and when to sell. These rules comprise what are commonly called trading systems. There is no limit to the number of different types of trading systems. That being said, most trend following systems are similar as they seek to capture the same trends.

Unlike Holy Grails, such as buy and hold or subjective fundamentals, trading systems must be quantified with rules that govern your decision making. Bill Dunn, for example, says his trading system has a "programmed risk of a 1 percent probability of suffering a monthly loss of 20 percent or more."[2] That's what I mean by quantifying. That's what the pros do.

The best place to live on this curve is the spot where you can deal with the emotional aspect of equity drawdown required to get the maximum return. How much heat can you stand? Money management is a thermostat—a control system for risk that keeps your trading within the comfort zone.

Gibbons Burke[5]

Risk, Reward, and Uncertainty

Trend followers understand that life is a balance of risk and reward. If you want the big rewards, take the big risks. If you want average rewards and an average life, take average risks. Charles Sanford gave a commencement address that is timeless. It said in part:

"From an early age, we are all conditioned by our families, our schools, and virtually every other shaping force in our society to avoid risk. To take risks is inadvisable; to play it safe is the counsel we are accustomed both to receiving and to passing on. In the conventional wisdom, risk is asymmetrical: it has only one side, the bad side. In my experience—and all I presume to offer you today is observations drawn on my own experience, which is hardly the wisdom of the ages—in my experience, this conventional view of risk is shortsighted and often simply mistaken. My first observation is that successful people understand that risk, properly conceived, is often highly productive rather than something to avoid. They appreciate that risk is an advantage to be used rather than a pitfall to be skirted. Such people understand that taking calculated risks is quite different from being rash. This view of risk is not only unorthodox, it is paradoxical—the first of several paradoxes which I'm going to present to you today. This one might be encapsulated as follows: Playing it safe is dangerous. Far more often than you would realize, the real risk in life turns out to be the refusal to take a risk."[4]

Life is fraught with risk. There is no getting away from it. However we try to control the direction of our lives, there are times when we fail. Therefore, we might as well accept that life is a game of chance. If life is a game of chance, to one degree or another, we must be comfortable with assessing odds in the face of risk.

Bottom line, there is no way to avoid making choices, and those choices create risk. Money under a mattress is no good. Buy a house? The house could burn down or the real estate market might tank like it did in 2007–2008. Invest in your company? If the company fails, you lose your employment and your nest egg at the same time. Buy mutual funds? Pray that the empty mantra of "buy and hold" works for you, and that you do not face a bear market at the age of 65? 2008 burned down that idea!

How should we proceed in the face of risk? We should begin by accepting the fact that markets do not reward stupidity in the long run. They reward those with the brains, guts, and determination to find opportunity where others have overlooked it and to press on and succeed where others have fallen short and failed.

Think about your money from a business perspective. Every business is ultimately involved in assessing risk. Putting capital to work in the hopes of making it grow is the goal. In that sense, all businesses are the same. The right decisions lead to success and the wrong ones lead to bankruptcy (Bear Stearns, Lehman Brothers, AIG, IndyMac, and so on). Here are key issues that are addressed in a good business plan:

- What is the market opportunity in the market niche?
- What is our solution to the market need?
- How big is the opportunity?
- How do we make money?
- How do we reach the market and sell?
- What is the competition?
- How are we better?
- How will we execute and manage our business?
- What are our risks?
- Why will we succeed?

Those same questions must be answered by a good trading system as well. It is important to answer those questions to assess the risk of a business venture, and it is equally important to answer them if you are going to trade.

Bright minds know that the amount of risk we take in life is in direct proportion to how much we want to achieve. If you want to live boldly, you must make bold moves. If goals are meager and few, they can be reached easily and with less risk of failure, but with greater risk of dissatisfaction once you have achieved them. One of the saddest figures is the person who burns with desire to live big, but to avoid risk chooses to embrace fear and lives lost instead. He

> *[I]f you're trying to reduce the volatility or uncertainty of your portfolio as a whole, then you need more than one security. This seems obvious, but you also need securities which don't go up and down together [reduced correlation]... It turns out that you don't need hundreds and hundreds of securities [to be diversified]. Much of the effective diversification comes with 20 or 30 well-selected securities. A number of studies have shown that the number of stocks needed to provide adequate diversification are anywhere from 10 to 30.*
>
> Mark S. Rzepczynski
> John W. Henry & Co.[6]

is worse off than someone who tries and fails or someone who never had any desire in the first place.

But there is hope. If you study risk, you will find there are two kinds: blind risk and calculated risk. The first one, blind risk, is suspect. Blind risk is the calling card of laziness, the irrational hope, something for nothing, the cold twist of fate. Blind risk is the pointless gamble, the emotional decision, and the sucker play. The man who embraces blind risk demonstrates all the wisdom and intelligence of a drunk stepping into traffic.

However, calculated risk builds fortunes, nations, and empires. Calculated risk and bold vision go hand in hand. To use your mind, to see the possibilities, to work things out logically, and then to move forward in strength and confidence is what places man above the animals. Calculated risk lies at the heart of every great achievement and achiever since the dawn of time. Trend followers thrive on calculated risk.

People tend to use discretion or gut feeling to determine the trade size.

David Druz[7]

Trend followers don't worry about what the markets are going to do tomorrow. They don't concern themselves with forecasts, fundamental factors, or technological breakthroughs. They can't undo the past and can't predict the future. Does a 50 percent drop in stocks mean the bull has finally run its course? No one knows.

Think about it this way. Most traders focus only on how to enter a market. Many will say, "Hey, I've got a way to beat the markets because this trading system I have, it's right 80 percent of the time. It's only wrong 20 percent of the time." They need to take a step back for a second and say, "Okay. What does 80 percent right mean?" If 80 percent of the time you don't win much, but 20 percent of the time you lose a lot, your losses can far outweigh your gains even though you're right 80 percent of the time. You must take the magnitude of wins and losses into account.

Lotteries, for example, can reach jackpots of hundreds of millions of dollars or more. And as the jackpot gets bigger, more people buy tickets in the buying feeding frenzy. But as they buy more tickets, the odds of winning do not increase in any appreciable fashion. The ticket buyers still have a better chance of being struck by lightning as they leave the convenience store.

For example, the odds of winning the California Super Lotto Jackpot are 1 in 18 million. If one person purchases 50 Lotto tickets each week, he will win the jackpot about once every 5,000 years. If a car gets 25 miles per gallon, and a gallon of gas is bought for every Lotto ticket bought, there will be enough gas for about 750 round trips to the moon before the jackpot is won. If you know the odds are against you why would you even play?

Likewise, if your trading system says that you have a 1 in 30,000 chance of winning, or roughly the same chance as being struck by lightning, you might not want to bet everything on that trade. When you trade, you must have a mathematical expectation, or "edge," or you can't win. For example, consider a coin-flipping game.

Imagine for a moment a coin toss game with an unbiased coin. Suppose also that we are offered the opportunity to bet that the next flip will be heads and the payoff will be even money when we win (we received a $1 profit in addition to the return of the wager). The mathematical expectation in this example is:

Volatility, risk, and profit are closely related. Traders pay close attention to volatility because price changes affect their profits and losses. Periods of high volatility are highly risky to traders. Such periods, however, can also present them with opportunities for great profits.[9]

$$(.5) (1) + (.5) (-1) = 0$$

The mathematical expectation of any bet in any game is computed by multiplying each possible gain or loss by the probability of that gain or loss and then adding the two figures. In the preceding example, you can expect to gain nothing from playing this game. This is known as a fair game, one in which a player has no advantage or disadvantage. Now, suppose the payoff was changed to 3/2, a gain of $1.50 in addition to a $1 bet—the expectation would change to:

$$(.5) (1.5) + (.5) (-1) = +.25$$

Playing this game 100 times would give us a positive expectation of .25.[8]

This is the kind of edge cultivated and honed daily by trend followers. You might ask, "If everyone knows about expectation, how can I ever find my edge?"

Think about it this way. Consider a scene from the movie *A Beautiful Mind*, the biography of mathematician John Nash. Nash and some of his mathematician buddies are in a bar when a sexy blonde and four brunettes walk in. After they admire the new arrivals, Nash and his friends decide to compete for the blonde. However, Nash has reservations, correctly observing that, if everyone goes for the same woman, they will just end up blocking each other out. Worse, they will offend the rest of the women. The only way for everyone to succeed is to ignore the blonde and hit on the brunettes. The scene dramatizes the Nash Equilibrium, his most important contribution to game theory. Nash proved that in any competitive situation—war, chess, even picking up a date at a bar—if the participants are rational and they know that their opponents are rational, there is only one optimal strategy. That theory won Nash a Nobel Prize in economics and transformed the way we think about competition in both games and the real world.[10]

Building off Nash's general thoughts, Ed Seykota lays out a basic risk definition from a trading perspective: "Risk is the possibility of loss." That is, if we own some stock, and there is a possibility of a price decline, we are at risk. The stock is not the risk, nor is the loss the risk. The possibility of loss is the risk. As long as we own the stock, we are at risk. The only way to control the risk is to buy or sell stock. In the matter of owning stocks, and aiming for profit, risk is fundamentally unavoidable and the best we can do is to manage the risk. To manage is to direct and control. Risk management is to direct and control the possibility of loss. The activities of a risk manager are to measure risk and to increase and decrease risk by buying and selling stock. In general, good risk management combines several elements:

1. Clarifying trading and risk management systems until they can translate to computer code.

2. Inclusion of diversification and instrument selection into the back-testing process.

3. Back-testing and stress-testing to determine trading parameter sensitivity and optimal values.

4. Clear agreement of all parties on expectation of volatility and return.

5. Maintenance of supportive relationships between investors and managers.

6. Above all, stick to the system.

7. See #6, above.

As you navigate this chapter, keep in mind Seykota's wisdom.

Five Questions for a Trading System

Answer the following five questions and you have the core components of a trend following trading system and you are on your way to having your edge:

1. How does the system determine what market to buy or sell at any time?

2. How does the system determine how much of a market to buy or sell at any time?

3. How does the system determine when you buy or sell a market?

4. How does the system determine when you get out of a losing position?

5. How does the system determine when you get out of a winning position?

Although these five questions are seminal to trend following, no less critical is your attitude. Don't forget to ask yourself:

"What do you really want? Why are you trading? What are your strengths and weaknesses? Do you have any emotional issues? How disciplined are you? Are you easily convinced? How confident are you in yourself? How confident are you in your system? How much risk can you handle?"

When I discussed trend following with Seykota and Charles Faulkner, they both said that the first thing any person should do before trading is to complete a personal inventory by asking:

• What is my nature and how well am I suited to trading?

• How much money do I want to make?

• What level of effort am I willing to make to reach my goals?

• What, if any, is my investing/trading experience?

• What resources can I bring to bear?

• What are my strengths and weaknesses?

Sound investment policy is really about intelligent risk management. There is no such thing as a risk free investment. The real issue is not whether you want to take risk, but which risks and how many of them you are willing to accept.

Jim Little and Sol Waksman[11]

If you have a $100,000 account and you're going to risk 5 percent, you'd have $5,000 to lose. If your examination of the charts shows that the price movement you're willing to risk equals $1,000 per contract, then you can trade five contracts. If you want to risk 10 percent, then do 10 contracts.

Craig Pauley[12]

Answering these questions in advance helps when you are in the middle of the zero-sum game and the adrenaline and sweat are flowing.

What Market Do You Buy or Sell at Any Time?

One of the first decisions any trader makes is what to trade. Will you trade stocks? Currencies? Futures? Commodities? What markets will you choose? While some people might focus on limited, market-specific portfolios, such as currencies or bonds, others pursue a more widely diversified portfolio of markets. For example, The Adam, Harding, & Lueck (AHL) Diversified Program (the largest trend following fund in the world now run by Man Financial) trades a diversified portfolio of over 100 core markets on 36 exchanges. They trade stock indices, bonds, currencies, short-term interest rates, and commodities (energy, metal, and agricultural contracts):

CHART 10.1: AHL Portfolio

Currencies: 24.3%

Bonds: 19.8%

Energies: 19.2%

Stocks: 15.1%

Interest rates: 8.5%

Metals: 8.2%

Agriculturals: 4.9%

AHL does not have fundamental expertise in all of these markets. I know of no trend follower who keeps fundamental experts on staff. They do not have in-depth understanding of each of the companies that comprise whatever stock index. Their expertise is to take these different markets and "make them the same" through price analysis.

When you look at a breakdown of performance at any given time, losses are typically negated by winners. This is by design because no one ever knows which market will be the one to take off with a big trend that pays for all of the losses—hence the need for diversification. AHL is even more precise about its need for diversification in an uncertain world: "The cornerstone of the AHL investment philosophy is that financial markets experience persistent anomalies or inefficiencies in the form of price trends. Trends are a manifestation of serial correlation in financial markets—the phenomenon whereby past price movements inform about future price behavior. Serial correlation can be explained by factors as obvious as crowd behavior, as well as more subtle factors, such as varying levels of information among different market participants. Although they vary in their intensity, duration, and frequency, price trends are universally recurrent across all sectors and markets. Trends are an attractive focus for active trading styles applied across a diverse range of global markets."

How can AHL's words act in practice? Trend following trader Justin Vandergrift of Chadwick Investments spoke to me about diversification and his lessons:

> "Portfolio diversification is often said to lose its importance after you have 7–10 different instruments in your portfolio. We found this simply not to be the case. Pre June 2007, we traded with 18 major markets in the program and we were in 7–8 of them most of the time. In short, our exposure was 7–8 markets at any one time, while signals in 18 were possible. After evaluating the program we discovered that most of our losses [at the time] were coming from one or two sectors that hit their maximum loss at roughly the same time. A breakout in the Ten Year Notes was most likely followed by a breakout in the Five Year Notes. Trading several highly correlated markets had led to exaggerated losses because these markets triggered a larger drawdown as they were stopped out together."

Vandergrift went on to explain that in June 2007 he increased his portfolio to over 40 markets with the goal of being in 15+ markets most of the time. He kept his core trading system (entry and exits) the same. The turnaround in results for his firm was dramatic and it was from simply changing his portfolio diversification.

Paul Mulvaney (Mulvaney Capital) is a more established trend follower based in London. Mulvaney made over 40% for the single month of October 2008. What performance did he generate from what markets? Consider:

The most important aspect of any trading decision is never the condition of the market, but rather that of your own position. The trick is to be constantly moving toward a position of strength, both within an individual trade and within the marketplace at large. Just like basketball, chess or any other activity that requires focus, you know you're in the "zone" of trading when you start playing for position, not for points.

Jonathan Hoenig, Portfolio Manager, Capitalistpig Hedge Fund LLC

Currency: 8.91%

Interest Rates: 2.78%

Stocks: 14.59%

Metals: 9.83%

Energy: 3.43%

Crops: 7.84%

Livestock: 4.51%

Is that one great outlier month? Yes. Will all sectors always be positive? Of course not, but Mulvaney's performance during one of the worst months ever for most investors should be a wake up call.

Is there a perfect portfolio composition? No. Many traders trade many different portfolios. That said, generally speaking, trend followers trade the same markets. However, although larger trend following funds might avoid smaller markets, such as pork bellies or wheat, other trend followers might trade currency or bond only portfolios. Salem Abraham (profiled in Chapter 2, "Great Trend Followers"), for example, made a killing off cattle a few years back. Whatever markets trend followers choose to trade, they must remain open to opportunity when it arrives. Author Tom Friedman gives a strong argument for sound strategy in a complex world:

> "If you can't see the world, and you can't see the interactions that are shaping the world, you surely cannot strategize about the world. And if you are going to deal with a system as complex and brutal as globalization, and prosper within it, you need a strategy for how to choose prosperity for your country or company."[13]

Friedman knows that the real power brokers in today's world are traders, not politicians.

How Much of a Market Do You Buy or Sell at Any Time?

The question investors typically avoid at all costs is the question of money management. Money management is also called risk management, position sizing, or bet sizing, and it is the critical component to trend following success as Gibbons Burke observes:

There is a random distribution between wins and losses for any given set of variables that defines an edge. In other words, based on the past performance of your edge, you may know that out of the next 20 trades, 12 will be winners and 8 will be losers. What you don't know is the sequence of wins and losses or how much money the market is going to make available on the winning trades. This truth makes trading a probability or numbers game. When you really believe that trading is simply a probability game, concepts like "right" and "wrong" or "win" and "lose" no longer have the same significance. As a result, your expectations will be in harmony with the possibilities.

Mark Douglas
Trading in the Zone

"Money management is like sex: Everyone does it, one way or another, but not many like to talk about it and some do it better than others. When any trader makes a decision to buy or sell (short), they must also decide at that time how many shares or contracts to buy or sell—the order form on every brokerage page has a blank spot where the size of the order is specified. The essence of risk management is making a logical decision about how much to buy or sell when you fill in this blank. This decision determines the risk of the trade. Accept too much risk and you increase the odds that you will go bust; take too little risk and you will not be rewarded in sufficient quantity to beat the transaction costs and the overhead of your efforts. Good money management practice is about finding the sweet spot between these undesirable extremes."[14]

When you look at a trading strategy, you must ask, "I've only got a certain amount of money. How much do I trade?" If you have $100,000 and you want to trade Microsoft, well, how much of your $100,000 must you trade on Microsoft on your first trade? Must you trade all $100,000? What if you're wrong? What if you're wrong in a big way, and you lose your entire $100,000 on one bet?

How do you determine how much to bet or trade each time? Trend followers make small bet sizes initially. So, if you start at $100,000, and you're going to risk 2 percent, that will be $2,000. You might say to yourself, "Oh my gosh, I've got $100,000, why am I only risking $2,000? I've got $100,000. $2,000 is nothing." That's not the point. You can't predict where the trend is going to go. One trend follower presented a view on the initial risk decision:

"There are traders who are unwilling to risk more than 1 percent, but I would find it surprising to hear of any trader who risks more than 5 percent of assets per trade. Bear in mind that risking too little doesn't give the market the opportunity to allow your profitable trade to occur."[15]

Think about money management as you would about getting into physical shape. Let's say you're a male athlete and you want to get into great shape. You weigh 185 pounds, and you're six foot one. Well guess what? You can't lift weights six times a day for 12 hours a day for 30 straight days without hurting yourself sometime during

If you look at the past 30 years, there is only one fundamental investor who has consistently produced huge absolute returns—Warren Buffet. Compare that, however, with countless trend following traders who have outperformed throughout bull and bear market cycles. One of the keys to our success is to have a huge diversification of over 100 financial and commodity markets. A systematic, mechanical approach is the only way to successfully trade so many markets...every decision...from market entry, position sizing, stop placement...must be fully automated.

Christian Baha
CEO Superfund

those 30 days. There's an optimum amount of lifting that you can do in a day that gets you ahead without setting you back. You want to be at that optimal point just as you want to get to an optimal point with money management. There indeed is just such a number. Ed Seykota describes that optimal point with the concept of "heat":

> "Placing a trade with a predetermined stop-loss point can be compared to placing a bet: The more money risked, the larger the bet. Conservative betting produces conservative performance, while bold betting leads to spectacular ruin. A bold trader placing large bets feels pressure—or heat—from the volatility of the portfolio. A hot portfolio keeps more at risk than does a cold one. Portfolio heat seems to be associated with personality preference; bold traders prefer and are able to take more heat, while more conservative traders generally avoid the circumstances that give rise to heat. In portfolio management, we call the distributed bet size the heat of the portfolio. A diversified portfolio risking 2 percent on each of five instruments has a total heat of 10 percent, as does a portfolio risking 5 percent on each of two instruments."[16]

Chauncy DiLaura, a student of Seykota's, adds to the explanation, "There has to be some governor so I don't end up with a whole lot of risk. The size of the bet is small, around 2 percent." Seykota calls his risk-adjusted equity "core equity" and the risk tolerance percentage "heat." Heat can be turned up or down to suit the trader's pain tolerance—as the heat gets higher, so do the gains, but only up to a point. Past that point, more heat starts to reduce the gain. The trader must be able to select a heat level where he is comfortable.[17]

Also critical is how you handle your capital as it grows or shrinks. Do you trade the same with $100,000 as you would $200,000? What if your $100,000 goes to $75,000?

Trend follower Tom Basso knows traders usually begin trading small, say with one contract and as they get more confident they might increase to 10 contracts. Eventually they attain a comfort level of 100 or 1,000 contracts, where they may stay. Basso counsels against this. He stresses that the goal is to keep things on constant leverage. His method of calculating the number of contracts to trade keeps him trading the same way even as equity increases.[18]

One of the reasons traders sometimes can't keep trading proportional as capital increases is fear. Although it might feel comfortable when the math dictates that you trade a certain number of shares or contracts at $50,000, when the math dictates to trade a certain amount at $500,000, people might become risk-averse. So instead of trading the optimal amount at whatever capital you have, people trade less. How can this be avoided? Create an abstract money world. Don't think about what the money can buy, just look at the numbers like you would when playing a board game, such as Monopoly or Risk.

However, because capital is always changing, it's critically important to keep trading consistent. A description of Dunn Capital's trading echoes Basso's view: "Part of [Dunn's] approach is adjusting trading positions to the amount of equity under management. He says if his portfolio suffers a major drawdown, he adjusts positions to the new equity level. Unfortunately, he says not enough traders follow this rather simple strategy."[19]

If you start with $100,000 and you lose $25,000, you now have $75,000. You must make your trading decisions off $75,000, not $100,000. You don't have $100,000 any more. However, Paul Mulvaney felt I was missing a critical final aspect of money management:

> "Trend following is implicitly about dynamic rebalancing, which is why I think successful traders appear to be fearless. Many hedge fund methodologies make risk management a separate endeavor. In trend following it is part of the internal logic of the investment process."

When Do You Buy or Sell a Market?

When do I buy? When do I sell? These are the questions that keep people up at night. Yet there is no reason why the buy and sell process should become a melodrama. Obsessing about when to buy or sell, keeps your limited time on things you can't control. Needless to say, trend followers apply a precise method to the buy and sell process.

In limiting risk, people also limit the opportunity for gain. It is common, today, for investors to own six or eight mutual funds, each of which is likely to be invested in hundreds of stocks. This will, they hope, assure that no little bump, no little meltdown, overly upsets their portfolios. But since when was investing about avoiding the bumps?

"The Way We Live Now;
See a Bubble?"
Roger Lowenstein
June 5, 2005

What are the three best market indicators? In order they are:

1. Price
2. Price
3. Price

When do trend followers enter? After a trend has begun. As I mention in Chapter 1, trend followers have no ability to predict when a trend will start. The only way to know that a trend has started is when it starts to move either up or down. For example, let's say Apple is trading between 100 and 120 for six months. All of a sudden Apple jumps, or breaks out, to a price level of 130. That type of upward movement from a range is a trigger for trend followers. They say, "I might not know that Apple is going to continue upward, but it's been going sideways for a while, and all of a sudden, the price has jumped to 130. I'm not in this game to try and find bargains or cheap places to buy. I'm in this game to follow trends, and the trend is up." This approach is counterintuitive for many. One trend trader outlined the simplicity:

"As our systems are designed to send a buy or sell signal only when a clear trend develops. By definition, we never get in at the beginning of a trend or get out at the top."[20]

If your goal is to ride a trend that starts at 50 and perhaps goes to 100, does it really make a difference whether you got in at 52 or 60 or 70? Even if you got in at 70 and the trend went to 100, you still made a lot, right? Of course if you got in at 52 (and how you think you might predict the bottom, I will never know), you made more money than if you got in at 70. There are plenty of traders out there who think, "Oh, I couldn't get in at 52, so I don't get in at all, even if I have the chance to get in at 70." Richard Dennis elaborates:

You've got to think about big things while you're doing small things, so that all the small things go in the right direction.
Alvin Toffler

"Anytime the market goes up a reasonable amount—say a strong day's work—after you've put on a position, it's probably worth adding to that position. I wouldn't want to wait for a retracement. That is everyone's favorite technique—to buy something strong that retraces. I don't see any justification in the statistics for that. When beans are at $8.00 and go to $9.00, if the choice is to buy them at $9.00 or buy them if they retrace to $8.80, I'd rather buy them at $9.00. They may never retrace to $8.80. Statistics would show that you make more money buying them and not waiting for a retracement."[21]

Even if people are familiar with Dennis' approach to trading, they still focus on entry—a misdirection of energy and focus.

Seykota dead-panned: "The entry is a big concern before it happens, a small concern thereafter."[22]

He is saying that after you are in a trade, the entry price isn't important. You have no idea how high the market is going to go, right? You should be concerned about protecting your downside in case the market goes against you as opposed to creating dramas associated with entry. How long can trend following trades last? Another trend trader opined:

> "Positions held for two to four months are not unusual, and some have been held for more than one year, says a spokesman. Historically, only 30–40 percent of trades have been profitable."[23]

The words of great baseball player Ted Williams immediately come to mind: "Hitting a baseball, I've said it a thousand times, is the single most difficult thing to do in sport. If Joe Montana or Dan Marino completed 3 of every 10 passes they attempted, they would be ex-professional quarterbacks. If Larry Bird or Magic Johnson made 3 of every 10 shots they took, their coaches would take the basketball away from them."[24]

However analogous it is to baseball, only 40 percent winners is hardly a percentage worth most people would think wise to emulate. So how is it possible to make money with 40 percent of your trades winners? Jim Little of trend follower Campbell and Company was clear:

> "Say, for example, on the 60 percent, you lose 1 percent of your capital, but on the 40 percent winning trades you make 2 percent. Over longer periods of time, say a year or more, this would net 20 percent on a broadly diversified program."[25]

In other words, winning and losing trades over time are blended together. Winners make up for small losers. Trend followers' rules to enter and exit are driven by what many call technical indicators. The technical indicator for trend followers is price action. However, most traders remain preoccupied with the hundreds upon hundreds of other indicators that promise "prediction." They discuss and debate which is better—MACD or Bollinger Bands? Which is more profitable—ADX or Williams %R?

"I didn't necessarily have system creation as a goal...What I did have as a goal was supplementing my fundamental trading with some technical insights." What resulted was his long-term technical system that he realized worked well for diverse markets, not just grains. He says that moving away from fundamentals made it easier to create something that held true for a variety of markets.

Bernard Drury
Drury Capital
Futures Magazine, August 2001

Of course the answer is: none of them. Technical indicators are small components of an overall trading system and are not a complete system. They are like a couple of tools in a toolkit, not the kit itself. A technical indicator accounts for typically 10 percent of the overall trading success of a trend following system. When traders say, "I tried Indicator X and found it was worthless" or "I tried Indicator Y and found it useful," they make no sense. These statements imply that an indicator is the actual trading system. By itself, a technical indicator is meaningless.

Bottom line, because trend followers never know which trend will be their big winner, they accumulate small losses trying to find it. It's like sticking the toothpick in the cake to find out if it's done. They are testing the market to find out if the little trend will grow into a big trend. Hence, you can end up with the 60-percent losing trades.

When Do You Get Out of a Losing Position?

The time to think most clearly about why and when to exit is before getting in. In any trading system, the most important thing is to preserve your capital. A sell strategy gives the opportunity to not only preserve capital, but to also redeploy into more opportune markets. When do trend traders actually get out of a losing position? Fast! This is a fundamental element of trend following. The logic of cutting your losses and then cutting them even more has been around far longer than trend following as Bernard Baruch reminds:

I learned you are not trading a commodity— you are buying and selling risk. As a technical trader, that's the only way to look at it.

Mark van Stolk[26]

"If a speculator is correct half of the time, he is hitting a good average. Even being right 3 or 4 times out of 10 should yield a person a fortune if he has the sense to cut his losses quickly on the ventures where he is wrong."

For example, you enter GOOG with a 2-percent stop loss. This means if you lose 2 percent, you exit. Period. Get out. Don't debate it. Look back at the British pound trade in the Dunn profile. That chart (see Chart 2.4) shows the constant starts and stops. Dunn keeps receiving entry signals and then exit signals. The trend is up, and then it is down. He enters and then exits. Dunn knows he can't predict the direction of the British pound. He only knows that he has received an entry signal, so he gets on board. Then he receives an exit right after that, so he gets out. Then another entry signal, then another exit comes. Dunn did say he "rides the bucking bronco."

Traders call these back and forth swings "whipsaws." Whipsaws are quick ups and downs that go nowhere. Your trade is jerked, or whipsawed, back and forth. Seykota has said that the only way to avoid whipsaws is to stop trading (see Seykota's "Whipsaw" song on YouTube). He is saying that whipsaws are part of the game. Live with them. Don't want to live with them? Don't trade.

Before you ever start trading as a trend follower, you should already know you will have small losses, but that is easier said than done. An old pro trader sent in a funny story about his days at trend following incubator Commodities Corporation:

> "Back in the early '90s, Commodities Corporation (CC) brought a few Japanese traders in for some in-house 'training.' Of course the ultimate and true goal was to capture some big Japanese money. I was still in their good graces and [CC] asked me to have lunch with a couple of these gentleman. They were new to the program, and I hoped to give them some insight into how I handled the process of trading. I told them they had to come up with a method or system that fitted who they were. Then I told them I thought it was great to find a mentor and I was available anytime they had questions or issues and that is still me today. I then began to discuss how important risk management was and that I was willing at that time to risk only 1 percent per bet in dealing with public money. I am more aggressive today, but that was then. I told them that losses were part of the process in finding winners. I will never forget as long as I shall live the youngest trader looked me square in the eye and with a very puzzled look asked 'You have losses?' I knew right then these birds had a very long way to go and I often wonder what happened to them."

From the beginning of my investigation, it became evident that the most direct way to make money and the one most compatible with my strengths was to be a position trader using computer models to develop the entry and exit points.

Michael J. Clarke
Clarke Capital Management, Inc.

When Do You Get Out of a Winning Position?

You have seen the headline hype: "Use Japanese candlesticks to spot reversals" or "Determine support and resistance" or "Learn proper profit-taking." Stop. You can't spot reversals until they

Reason's biological function is to preserve and promote life and to postpone its extinction as long as possible. Thinking and acting are not contrary to nature; they are, rather, the foremost features of man's nature. The most appropriate description of man as differentiated from nonhuman beings is: a being purposively struggling against the forces adverse to his life.

Ludwig von Mises[27]

Evaluating quantitative traders is much more about understanding their research process than looking at the last few years of a track record. The firmest grasp of all the individual, specific risks involved; the most critical and accurate analysis of the inherent underlying assumptions of their research; the knowledge of which statistical measurements are applicable or not; the creation of the purest mathematical descriptions of price structures, moves, and volatility...these abilities will determine the trader most likely to deliver the highest reward-to-risk in the future.

Mark Abraham
Quantitative Capital Management, L.P.

happen. There is no way to define the concept of support and resistance, as 100 people could have 100 different definitions. These ideas all try to do the impossible—predict. Tom Basso pointed out the futility of profit objectives:

> "A new trader approaches an old trend follower and asks, 'What's your objective on this trade?' The old trend follower replies that his objective is for the position to go to the moon."

Exiting a winning position can be a challenge because you have to be comfortable with letting a trend run as far as it can, crest, and then begin to decline before considering an exit with profits. Say you are up 100 percent in paper profits. If you cash in, those paper profits become real. However, the trend is still up. You have just made a big mistake because you limited yourself in how much you could make. If you are long several positions, there are huge open profits on the table, and the trend is still up—that is not time to get out of your winning position.

Because trend followers do not play the game with the belief that picking tops and bottoms is feasible, they do not have profit targets generally. Profit targets cap profits. If you have a profit target, you will stop trading after a set amount of profit. For example, you enter at 100 and before you ever enter you establish that you will exit if the price reaches a 25 percent gain, or 125. The idea of a profit target sounds secure and wise at first blush. However, if you have the experience of top trend traders, you know profit targets are not the way to big wins. If you are riding a trend, you have to let it go as far as it can go. You need to fully exploit the move. You don't want to exit at 125 and watch the trend go to 225.

Although profit targets keep you from getting to 225, they also play a damaging role in the overall portfolio of a trend follower. Trend followers need those home runs to pay for all their whipsaw losses. If you are artificially creating a profit target for no other reason than to be comfortable, you might be limiting the potential for those big trends. This, in turn, limits your ability to cover all the small losses you've incurred. If, as a trader, you had used profit targets, how would you have ever been around to win the huge profits from the big unexpected events I describe in Chapter 4?

So where in a trend do trend followers earn their profits? They capture the meat, or middle, of a trend. They never get in at the bottom, and they don't get out at the top (see Chart 10.2).

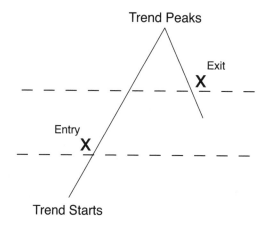

Trend Peaks

Exit

X

Entry

X

Trend Starts

CHART 10.2: Trend Following Entry/Exit Example: The Middle

Your Trading System

When you mechanize a trend following trading system, you take all your discretionary judgments and build them into the rules. For example, if you know you are uncomfortable with a high level of risk, you make a rule that sets a tolerable level of risk. If you want to trade a currency-only portfolio, you make that a part of the rules from the beginning. The idea is to "hardwire" all scenarios that you could see in daily trading in advance across a portfolio. If a market rises 100 percent in a day, you have rules that tell you what to do. If a market loses 10 percent, follow your rules.

When you are in the heat of the trading battle, your rules for entry or exit or how much you should buy must be precise. You cannot afford to think about the rules as the situation unfolds. You must have an unambiguous plan established in advance. It also helps to be on the defensive as Larry Hite reminds:

"We approach markets backwards. The first thing we ask is not what can we make, but how much can we lose. We play a defensive game."[28]

I have included a sample trend following trading system in Appendix F, "Trading System Example from Mechanica," from Bob Spear of Mechanica software.

The peripheral mishigas, your attitude, wardrobe, education, and expertise mean nothing to the market. From old-timer to first-timer, it will chew up a doctorate just as easily as a drug addict...in the markets and indeed in life, success starts with realizing that one's opinion means nothing. The market will move as life will move, perfectly unpredictable and with the best laid plans going horribly awry. We can't control the market just as we can't control the future. So the winners are simply those best-positioned to benefit from a future not yet seen.

Jonathon Hoenig, Portfolio Manager,
Capitalistpig Hedge Fund LLC

Frequently Asked Questions

FAQ #1: How Much Money?

Ed Seykota was once asked how much money someone should have before starting to trade. He responded, "Good money management is equity invariant. I'd ask a trader who thinks he needs a certain amount before he can trade exactly what amount he would need to stop trading." His point is that there is no dollar amount too little or too big that allows you to sit back and assume that your starting capital alone is some secret key to success.

Numerous factors related to the correct amount of starting capital exist, not least of which is the personal discipline and ability to stick with it. Anyone who promises a magic starting capital number of how much is needed to "win" is not truthful. No one can guarantee you profits. However, what if you have unlimited resources? That should be to your advantage, right? However, unlimited starting capital can be a benefit or a strike against you. Jaromir Jagr, the famous hockey player, and William Eckhardt, Richard Dennis' longtime partner, have contradicting views on how much is enough starting capital. Jagr sounds like a riverboat gambler:

> "Jaromir Jagr does not do moderation. This is a man who doesn't just play the stock market but romps through it; last year, published reports estimated he took a hit [loss] of anywhere from $8 million to $20 million in the dot-com market. He doesn't just have a girlfriend who is pretty and bright; he has a girlfriend who is a former Miss Slovakia and a second-year law student."[29]

Jagr might be a great hockey player, but his trading approach is leading him straight to the trading poor house. Backed by the millions he made playing hockey, Jagr is exactly the type of trader William Eckhardt avoided:

> "I know of a few multimillionaires who started trading with inherited wealth. In each case, they lost it all because they didn't feel the pain when they were losing. In those formative first years of trading, they felt they could afford

to lose. You're much better off going into the market on a shoestring, feeling that you can't afford to lose. I'd rather bet on somebody starting out with a few thousand dollars than on somebody who came in with millions."[30]

FAQ #2: Trend Following for Stocks

One of the great myths regarding trend following is that it does not work with stocks. That is wrong thinking. Trends in stocks are no different than trends in currencies, commodities, or futures. Chesapeake Capital, Jerry Parker's trend following firm, for example, has adapted its system to stock trading. Parker says his system works well with stocks, particularly stocks in outlier moves that are in single industries. He adds:

> "Our expertise [is] in systematic trend following or model development. So maybe we trend follow with Chinese porcelain. Maybe we trend follow with gold and silver, or stock futures, or whatever the client needs. We're trading these great systems, and testing, and making sure what we do has worked in the past. And being disciplined, and unemotional, and applying our methods to the futures markets, but limiting our trading to this one group of markets. We need to look at the investment world globally and communicate our expertise of systematic trading."[31]

Bruce Terry, president of Weston Capital Investment Services and a disciple of Richard Donchian, dismisses out of hand that trend following is not for stocks:

> "Originally in the 1950s, technical models came out of studying stocks. Commodity Trading Advisors (CTA) applied these to futures. In the late 1970s and early 1980s, stocks were quiet and futures markets took off. That is how the CTA market started. It has come full circle. People are beginning to apply these models to stocks once again."[32]

I am reminded of the opening line from a 1979 article from "Managed Account Reports" that I found in research: "Trading stocks and commodity futures by means of trend following techniques is an art with a long history."[33]

Robert Hormats, the vice chairman of Goldman Sachs International, observed that to understand and explain globalization, it is useful to think of yourself as an intellectual nomad. In the world of the nomad, there is no carefully defined turf.

Thomas Friedman[36]

Finally, for this edition of *Trend Following*, I am including extensive research materials that justify the use of trend following techniques on stocks. Cole Wilcox and Eric Crittenden of Blackstar Funds, LLC contributed this research. See Appendix A, "Trend Following for Stocks."

FAQ #3: Insight on Computers and Curve Fitting

Larry Hite has said that a computer can't get up on the wrong side of the bed in the morning, which is why he relies on computers for his decision making and for his implementation of his trading rules:

> "If your boyfriend or girlfriend breaks up with you, you'll feel one way; if you get engaged, you'll feel another way."[34]

Hite said he would much rather have one smart guy working on a lone Macintosh than a team of well-paid timekeepers with an army of supercomputers. At the same time, however, Hite was adamant that the real key to using computers successfully was the thinking that went into the computer code. When someone asked why even go the computer route if people power is so important. Hite responded:

> "[B]ecause it works—it's countable and replicable. I'm a great fan of the scientific method. And the other things are not scientific. If I give you the algorithms, you should be able to get the same results I did. That to me means a great deal."[35]

Whales only get harpooned when they come to the surface, and turtles can only move forward when they stick their neck out, but investors face risk no matter what they do.

Charles A. Jaffe

However, challenges go along with back testing. Computer technology can be easily used to over optimize or curve fit a trading system and produce a system that looks good on paper alone. By testing thousands of possibilities, anyone can create a system that works in theory, as Barbara Dixon warns:

> "When designing a system, I believe it's important to construct a set of rules that fit more like a mitten than like a glove. On the one hand, markets move in trends, but on the other hand, past results are not necessarily indicative of future performance. If you design a set of rules that fit the curve of your test data too perfectly, you run an enormous risk that it will fizzle under different future conditions."[37]

A robust trading system, one that is not curve fit, must ideally trade all markets at all times in all conditions. Trend following parameters or rules should work across a range of values. System parameters that work over a range of values are considered robust. If the parameters of a system are slightly changed and the performance adjusts drastically, beware. For example, if a system works great at 20, but does not work at 19 or 21, that system is not robust. On the other hand, if your system parameter is 50 and it also works at 40 or 60, your system is much more robust (and reliable).

Trend trader David Druz has long championed robustness in trading systems. He dismisses trades of short-term traders, who fight for quick hitting arbitrage style profits, as noise. Traders who focus on short-term trading often miss the longer-term trends—those areas where long-term trend followers wait patiently for their opportunities. To "wait," you need complete faith in your trading system. However, you are in serious trouble if all you think you need is the latest hardware and software to succeed at trading. Once again, Dixon makes it clear:

> "Contemporary databases, software, and hardware allow system developers to test thousands of ideas almost instantaneously. I caution these people about the perils of curve fitting. I urge them to remember that one of their primary goals is to achieve discipline, which will enable them to earn profits. With so many great tools, it's easy to change or modify a system and to develop indicators rather than rules, but is it always wise?"[38]

It is hard *not* to get caught up in the hype of computer programs for trading. They are advertised nonstop today on TV, from ads on CNBC to dedicated half-hour infomercials promising the world ("Investools," "Trend Trading to Win," etc.). You can spend several thousand dollars to purchase fancy charting software that makes you feel like you are the trader of your own fund, and it might turn out great, but make sure you don't fall into a false sense of security. When describing his early trading successes, John W. Henry made clear the key was philosophy, not technology:

> "In those days, there were no personal computers beyond the Apple. There were few, if any, flexible software packages available. These machines, far from being the ubiquitous tool seen everywhere in the world of finance and the world

I heard this story and I think it's true. Anyway, it's a pretty good story. It's about how the Air Force trains pilots. When a trainee made a good landing, he would be praised. When a trainee made a bad landing, he would be ridiculed. Well, it was perfectly clear to the general that the first approach was lousy and the second approach was good. He had statistics demonstrating that when you praised a pilot who made a perfect landing, his next landing was not likely to be as good. Whereas, if you berated a pilot who made a bad landing, his next landing was likely to be much better. However, if you think about it, it doesn't matter what you do because landings are most likely to be average. If a pilot had an exceptional landing, his next landing was likely to be average. If he had a poor landing, his next landing was likely to be average, also. By slicing the data and only looking at what follows good landings and praise, you only see part of the picture. You must consider how data was selected before you can draw conclusions.

James Simons
The Greenwich Roundtable
June 17, 1999

at large today, were the province of computer nerds...I set out to design a system for trading commodities. But things changed quickly and radically as soon as I started trading. My trading program, however, did not change at all. As I said, it hasn't changed even to this day."[39]

One of Henry's associates elaborated: "Originally all of our testing was done mechanically with pencil and graph that turned into lotus spreadsheets, which was still used extensively in a lot of our day to day work. With the advent of some of these new modeling systems like system writer, day trader and some of the other things, we've been able to model some of our systems on these products. Mostly just to back test what we already knew, that trend following works."[40]

Tom Basso sees the benefit: "You'll find that the more you're computerized, the more markets you'll be able to handle. Computers leverage your time if you know how to use them."[41]

Further, Richard Donchian's timeless wisdom should give many pause:

> "If you trade on a definite trend following, loss-limiting method, you can [trade] without taking a great deal of time from your regular business day. Because action is taken only when certain evidence is registered, you can spend a minute or two per [market] in the evening checking up on whether action-taking evidence is apparent, and then in one telephone call in the morning, place or change any orders in accord with what is indicated. [Furthermore] a definite method, which at all times includes precise criteria for closing out one's losing trades promptly, avoids... emotionally unnerving indecision."

The obvious is always least understood.
Prince Klemens von Metternich

Of course to reach the "minute or two" Donchian refers to takes preparation time. After you test your system and are satisfied enough with the results to begin trading, your work is not done. System results must be periodically compared to actual results to ensure that your testing closely reflects what is happening in real time. It is also helpful to keep a journal to record how well you stick to the processes of executing your system.

One trend trader, who was trained at Commodities Corporation, wrote me: "Early in my trading career I found myself hung up on the 'need' to be right rather than the 'desire' to make money. I learned early that being 'right,' of having a high percentage of winners, had very little to do with my overall trading success. Those who have a need to be right with a high percentage of winners will find themselves passing on their best trading opportunities, assuming they use some degree of discretion in their trade selections. One of my trading buddies enjoys a trading success rate annually of around 15 percent winners with 50 percent losers and 35 percent breakeven trades. In 2005, he made over 300 percent on his initial beginning of year trading capital [of] a seven-figure account. This is a risk-reward numbers game and most who think it is something else usually face a 'forced awareness' at some point in their trading careers. To further emphasize my point, everyone has seen ads on the Internet for systems being promoted for say a 90 percent accuracy. I bet 3/4 of these systems are based on a set of past criteria that have very little to do with their future performance. Let's say we do 100 trades in a calendar year. The average winning trade makes a net $100 so we make a net $9,000 in the 'winners.' Now the bad news is the 10 losing trades are for $1,000 so we lose a total of $1,000 for the year in a system that had 90 percent winners. Now, I realize this is a stretch from reality, but mathematically this is what happens once a trader commits capital to the so-called 'sure thing' trading systems!"

Trend follower Ken Tropin was even more specific: "In order for a system to be successful, it has to be what I call robust. Robust means that I can test that system in a market I designed it around. Say I'm using it in the treasury bonds, and then if I switch that market and I try that system in the Euro, it still works. And if I change its parameters, it still works. And if I switch it over to corn—something totally different than treasury bonds—it still works. And if I look at some data that was out of sample from what I designed it around, it still works. Then I have something that might be interesting and have a chance of living in the future. Because the nature of data is it changes a little all the time. And so the key to success in systems trading is to have what I call a loose fitting suit. I can't have a suit that's so tight and perfectly proportioned to me that if I gain two pounds, it won't fit the data anymore."

Andrew Lo brings it back to simplicity: "The first [rule of thumb] being that no matter how complex and subtle a strategy is and no matter how sophisticated it might be, it has to be possible to describe that strategy in relatively simple and intuitive terms to a sophisticated investor. In other words, regardless of how subtle and impressive and sophisticated the strategy is, I've never come across anything that couldn't be described in relatively straightforward terms as to what the value added of that strategy was, whether it was risk transfer, superior information, better executions, mean reversion, and so on. So, I think that's the first principle that I think is obvious to many investors; but to some who are not as familiar with quantitative methods, they may feel that they're just not really smart enough to understand. But, I think that's just not the case. The second rule of thumb is that you'll never see a bad back test. Now, again, this may be obvious to the experienced investor, but there's a very specific set of quantitative models that you can use to be able to gauge the bias that comes about from selection. The fact is that when I've talked with investors about doing due diligence, I've often said that, you know, whatever back test you'd like to see, I can certainly produce it for you. If you torture the data long enough, it will basically tell you anything you want..."

Day trading is emotional anesthesia—the frenetic pace works well to keep people preoccupied from feelings they do not wish to experience.

Thomas Vician, Jr.,
student of Ed Seykota's

FAQ #4: Limitations with Day Trading

When you trade with higher frequency, the profit that you can earn per trade decreases, whereas your transaction costs stay the same. This is not a winning strategy. Yet, traders still believe that short-term trading is less risky. Short-term trading, by definition, is not less risky, as evidenced by the catastrophic blowout of Victor Niederhoffer and Long Term Capital Management (LTCM). Do some short-term traders excel? Yes. However, think about the likes of whom you might be competing with when you are trading short term. Professional short-term traders, such as Jim Simons, have hundreds of staffers working as a team 24/7. They are playing for keeps, looking to eat your lunch in the zero-sum world. You don't stand a chance.

Unfortunately, the flaws in day trading are often invisible to those who must know better. Sumner Redstone, CEO of Viacom, was interviewed recently and talked of constantly watching Viacom's stock price, hour after hour, day after day. Although Redstone is a brilliant entrepreneur and has built one of the great media companies of our time, his obsession with following his company's share price is not a good example to follow. Redstone might feel his company is undervalued, but staring at the screen will not boost his share price.

FAQ #5: A Good Example of the Wrong Way to View a Trade

I wanted to end this chapter with a mini-case study about a prominent player in the Chicago futures markets: Leo Melamed. Melamed is Chairman Emeritus and senior policy advisor to the Chicago Mercantile Exchange. He is recognized as the founder of financial futures. At the close of 1999, he was named to the top 10 most important Chicagoans in business of the twentieth century. Yet, with this tremendous resume and success, he is clearly not a trend following trader as evidenced by excerpts from his book:

"The Hunt silver debacle also provided the setting for my worst trade. My company partner George Fawcett and I had become bullish on silver beginning in June 1978, when it was trading around $5.00 an ounce level. We were right in the market, and silver prices moved higher. In September 1979, silver reached the high price of $15.00 an ounce, and the profit we were each carrying was substantial. George and I had never before made that kind of money, it was truly a killing. How much higher would silver go? Wasn't it time to take the profit? Large profits, as I learned, were even more difficult to handle than large losses. I had a very good friend…with special expertise in the precious metals markets.…Since he knew I was long silver, I ventured to ask him his opinion. 'Well, Leo,' he responded, 'you have done very well with your silver position and I really can't predict how much higher silver will go. But I'll tell you this, at $15.00, it is very expensive. On the basis of historical values, silver just doesn't warrant much higher prices.' I never doubted that he gave me his honest and best opinion. I transmitted this information to George and we decided that if nothing happened by the end of the week, we would liquidate our positions and take our profits. That's exactly what we did. This was in late October 1979. So why was this my worst trade when in fact it was the biggest profit I had ever made up to that time? Because, within 30 days after we got out of our position, the Hunt silver corner took hold. It did not stop going higher until it hit $50.00 an ounce in January 1980. George and I had been long silver for nearly two years, and had we stayed with our position

…it is important to understand that in trading, as in real life, risk is an integral part of the process and one that deserves great respect. To earn a considerable return, one must take a comparable risk. It is essential, therefore, to have accurate measures of both risk and reward.

Alejandro Knoepffler
Cipher Investment Management

Life shrinks or expands in proportion to one's courage.

Anais Nin

"The computer model tells us when to get in and when to get out," he says. "The computer understands what the price is telling us about the trend of the market." What does the software look at, exactly? "Volatility, price behavior. How much does it change every day? We're trying to use as much data as we can get to interpret potential future price." Successful positions remain in place for about six months; Ken Tropin's programs bail out of unsuccessful trades after a month. "All of the systems are designed to risk modest amounts of capital and to stay with winners as long as possible."

Ken Tropin: Programmed to Succeed
Institutional Investor, June 2003

for just another 30 days, we would have been forced to take a huge profit. We both vowed never to calculate how many millions we left on the table."[42]

If I critique how Melamed traded from a trend following point of view, I can see why his 1979 silver trade was his "worst trade." To begin with, he had no predefined entry criteria. He never gives a reason why he and his partner were bullish on silver in 1978, nor does he explain why he entered the silver market other than because it was trading at such a low price ($5.00). When the price of silver started to increase, he attempted to find out how high it would go, which, as all trend followers know, is impossible. However, because he had no clearly defined exit rationale, he was uncertain when to get out, unlike trend followers, who know how they will handle their profits before they ever enter a trade. Without a strategy, Melamed fell back on conventional trading wisdom that buying higher highs is wrong. Melamed used fundamentals to determine that the price of silver would not continue to increase and set a profit target to get out of the trade. By having a profit target, instead of an exit plan, Melamed lost out on millions of dollars of potential profit.

What is a lesson learned? Rob Romaine, a long-time trend follower, notes:

> "The value of a disciplined trading [systems] approach is that it allows you to design your strategy during nonstressful times. Then, when the markets are tough, you need only to execute your plan rather than being forced to face difficult decisions under pressure when you are most likely to make mistakes."

Key Points

- Trend followers are right for the trend and wrong at each end.
- Seykota: "A system should support and reflect the attitude of a trader."
- Seykota: "There is no best system any more than there is a best car. There might however be a best car for you."
- Seykota: "If you can't afford to lose, you can't afford to trade."
- Money is only a means of keeping score.

- Taking losses should be easy. You should have them quantified before ever entering the market.

- Trust your trade. If you can't trust it, don't trade.

- The exact turning point, the top or bottom, can't be known until it is over and a matter of record.

- After you take your signals and enter, trading becomes a waiting game.

- The more volatile the market, the less you risk. The less volatile the market, the more you risk.

The Game

11

"Trends come and go. Trend followers do too.
Some stay longer than others."
—Ed Seykota[1]

In the book *Absolute Returns*, Alexander Ineichen stresses that trading is a "game." He sees no rules for the game except the constant of change, but more importantly, he reminds us that it is crucial to avoid becoming the "game." There are three types of players in the game:

- Those who know they are in the game.
- Those who don't know they are in the game.
- Those who don't know they are in the game and have become the game.[2]

If, within a half of an hour of playing poker (or trading for that matter), you don't know who the patsy is, you're the patsy, or as Ineichen calls it "the game." I have introduced those traders who didn't know they were in the game and therefore became the game in the big events of the Long Term Capital Management hedge fund implosion, the Barings Bank collapse, and the October 2008 market crash. I introduced those traders and investors who did not know

Larry Hite described his conversation with a friend who couldn't understand his absolute adherence to a mechanical trading system. His friend asked, "Larry, how can you trade the way you do? Isn't it boring?" Larry replied, "I don't trade for excitement; I trade to win."

they were in the game pursuing Holy Grails that never panned out. And I introduced trend followers who knew they were in a game and brought an edge to the table every time they played. If you know trading is a game and you want to be a part of it, these are stark choices.

Slow Acceptance

Many turtles claim the biggest reason they no longer tolerate immense drawdowns or strive for colossal returns is because customers want a more conservative approach. Most say striving to meet this request has been the biggest change.[4]

In case you're concerned that my writing will create a whole new generation of trend followers and their impact in the markets will negatively affect the frequency, direction, and intensity of trends (as well as an ability to make money), take note of wisdom from long-time trend follower Keith Campbell:

> "We are trend followers, not trend generators. At the beginning or end of a major trend, we may provide a little bump or a minor goose, but it will be an extremely superficial, temporary effect …"[3]

Campbell is correct. Trend followers don't generate trends. In Chapter 3, "Performance Data," recall professor Larry Harris' point: Traders play zero-sum games for many reasons. Not all play to win. However, trend followers do play the zero-sum game to win. And let's face it, this attitude can cause people to feel intimidated or defensive. At the end of the day, for trend following trading to lose its effectiveness, intimidated, defensive-minded investors would have to make dramatic changes in behavior, including the following:

…a CTA [trend following] investment is an investment like any other investment. Periods of above-average performance are alternated with periods of below-average performance. As soon as the inevitable, less attractive market environment commences, investors with wrong expectations are likely to become disgruntled. They will start complaining and with good reason: They will not understand why they lose money.

Harold M. de Boer, director of research, Transtrend B.V.
AIMA Journal, December 2003

- **People would no longer buy and hold:** Those believing in fundamental analysis (the vast majority of market participants) would have to switch how they trade. They would need to cease buy-and-hold long-only approaches and start trading as trend followers. Do they change now even after 2008? Doubtful.

- **People would start trading long and short:** Most do not sell "short" because of fear, ignorance, or confusion. They trade long only. That changes when?

- **People would dump mutual funds:** That will be hard to do with retirement programs literally mandating the average Joe be 100 percent invested in mutual funds.

- **People would embrace money management:** Most traders don't think about how much to buy or how much to sell. They only worry about when to buy and rarely think about when to sell. The "how much" question is not even on the table.

- **People would disengage their emotions and egos from trading:** As long as there are human beings involved in the trading process, there will be excessive reactions and trends to exploit.

Let's be honest, the majority of investors are more comfortable with the status quo—even if that means losing their life savings. Sustaining the focus, self-discipline, and recognition of the reality that almost all of their market knowledge is faulty is overwhelming. Millions would rather simply watch CNBC and Cramer or chat online than learn how to trade correctly for profit.

The broad application of these principles globally in markets all around the world, Chinese porcelain, gold, silver, markets that exist, that don't exist today, markets that others are making lots of money in that we're not trading. We will eventually start broadening out and realizing that trend following is a great way to trade. What other way can you trade and get a handle on risk?

Jerry Parker[5]

Blame Game

Not surprisingly, trend followers are sometimes accused of throwing the markets into disarray. Whenever a stock tanks, a bubble bursts, or a scandal hits, winning traders catch blame. The blame is never affixed to the little old lady in Omaha, who thought that some dotcom-invented web site would replace Walmart, and consequently lost her life savings gambling on dotcom stocks. The blame is never placed on the masses who were gambling that the Dow would go up forever only to see it crater in October/November 2008. No one wants to take responsibility for their losses, and who better to target than the winners when the mob is feeling uneasy and panicky. Here are some of my favorite misconceptions that purportedly make trend followers the bad guys:

- **They trade futures:** The vast majority of trend following traders trade on regulated exchanges. We can all trade there. If we can all trade there, why are trend followers singled out?

- **They use leverage:** Great traders use the tools at their disposal, one of which is leverage. The key is not to overdo it like so many on Wall Street did.

- **They cause worldwide panics:** Trend followers do not generate trends or cause worldwide panics; they react to unexpected events. They have no crystal ball.

Future shock [is] the shattering stress and disorientation that we induce in individuals by subjecting them to too much change in too short a time.

Alvin Toffler

- **They don't invest, they just trade:** Reality? The markets are for trading, not for investing. The markets reward winners, not losers. We can all choose, so if we choose wrong, it's time to look in the mirror.

- **Long Term Capital Management (LTCM):** The LTCM hedge fund (like the many more that failed in the 10 years after its death) proved that bad traders with bad strategy fail. Trend following has not failed.[6]

Trend followers have also been condemned for making money on the downside:

> "[Traders] have always been an easy target for the press whenever the public is looking for someone to blame for volatile markets, [and] ... the press have singled out 'the short sellers'... Perception or reality, many will now picture [traders] as bad boys, or 'boys having a bit of fun'... Making money in downside markets is portrayed as obscene and to blame for additional turbulence. The industry is not about 'bad boys' manipulating the market and gambling; it is about specific trading skills practiced by highly experienced [traders] who are rewarded on performance alone."[7]

Most battles are won before they are ever fought.

General George S. Patton

The attitude that "making money in down markets" is "obscene" is in itself obscene. The market has rules. You can go long or you can go short. All serious players trying to make a dollar should know the rules and if you don't know the rules, whose fault is that?

Understand the Game

Whether you want to trade for yourself, place money with a trend follower, manage money for clients, or whether you are an established trend follower with clients, trading for other people presents challenges both trader and client must deal with. Original turtle trader Jerry Parker, for one, thinks trend followers could do better at explaining their skill set:

> "I think another mistake we made was defining ourselves as managed futures, where we immediately limit our universe. Is our expertise in that, or is our expertise in systematic

trend following or model development. So maybe we trend follow with Chinese porcelain. Maybe we trend follow with gold and silver, or stock futures, or whatever the client needs. We need to look at the investment world globally and communicate our expertise of systematic trading…People look at systematic and computerized trading with too much skepticism. But a day will come when people will see that systematic trend following is one of the best ways to limit risk and create a portfolio that has some reasonable expectation of making money…I think we've miscommunicated to our clients what our expertise really is."[8]

In an unpredictable world, trend following is one of the best tools to manage risk and, ultimately, uncertainty. Although that is true, it doesn't make it easy to teach. Richard Dennis, for example, had some difficult times during his career and, as a result, is often blamed for perceived failures of trend following. However, to dismiss trend following based on Dennis' managed money attempts alone discounts the performance data of David Harding, Bill Dunn, Jerry Parker, Keith Campbell, and other trend followers such as Christian Baha, Bernard Drury, Michael Clarke, TransTrend, Sunrise Capital, and Larry Hite over the past 30 years. That said, Dennis was honest about his lesson learned about clients:

> "I certainly learned customers have a lower appetite for risk than I might … and that is probably incorporated into my risk appetite today. It's easier to trade for one's self than it is to trade for other people."[9]

The Sharpe ratio appears at first blush to reward returns (good) and penalize risks (bad). Upon closer inspection, things are not so simple. The standard deviation takes into account the distance of each return from the mean, positive or negative. By this token, large positive returns increase the perception of risk as though they could as easily be negative, which for a dynamic investment strategy may not be the case. Large positive returns are penalized and therefore the removal of the highest returns from the distribution can increase the Sharpe ratio: a case of "reductio ad absurdum" for Sharpe ratio as a universal measure of quality.

David Harding, Winton Capital, www.hedgefundsreview.com

Decrease Leverage; Decrease Return

Richard Dennis' Turtle students (see my second book, *The Complete TurtleTrader*) were originally instructed to make as much money as possible. They had no restrictions except to shoot for home runs. They were absolute return traders while under Dennis' guidance. However, later on, when they went out on their own to manage money for clients, some changed how they traded. Many of them accepted clients who demanded less leverage and ultimately less return. As a result, their performance records have sometimes been far less impressive than the old pro trend followers.

Everyone wants to invest when you're at new highs and making 50 percent a year. Everyone says they want to get in at a 10 percent drawdown or a 20 percent, or whatever, and no one ever does it. I just want to point out that right now, here is another chance to do just that—buy us at historical lows—and very few people are thinking in those terms. They want to buy the lows, but never seem to.

Richard Dennis[10]

Traders such as Bill Dunn, Keith Campbell, Millburn Ridgefield, Bruce Kovner, John Henry, and Ed Seykota know that in order to aim for and win big profits, trader and client must be aligned. Dunn is adamant about that alignment:

"Now there is, of course, the possibility of turning down the leverage and trading more capital, but with less leverage. That works fine if the client will go along with you and you're charging management fees because you're charging management fees on the capital and then incentive fees on the profit. Dunn Capital Management does not charge any management fees to any of its clients. So we care about the numbers that are generated."[11]

There might be safety with watered down trend following from a low-risk, low-reward standpoint, but the true way to win the big money is through Dunn's approach of higher risk, higher reward. And when you shoot for higher risk, higher reward, you're less inclined to worry about management fees from your clients because incentive fees on only profits earned can be fantastic paydays. The key is to be in concert as trend trader Jason Russell notes:

Some turtles won. Some were dismal failures. There were reasons for this.

"Managers often say that they are managing to long-term objectives but act to meet short-term objectives of clients who have not spent the time understanding what trend following means to them. As much as the managers, industry, and regulators try to educate and illustrate, the ultimate responsibility lies in the hands of the client."

For example, today is in the middle of June and there is a lot of talk about the weather, the grain situation, and whether it rains or snows or is dry. I have no idea. It's not the kind of thing I deal with. I don't have any way to use information like that. I don't think anyone else really does either ... If I think it is going to rain, perhaps it's an indication of how I should dress for the day, but little else.[12]

Of course, you might opt to trade as a trend follower for your own account and never hire one of the professional trend following traders. In that instance, you can pay fees to yourself for a job well done.

Fortune Favors the Bold

Trend following, like any entrepreneurial endeavor, demands you be responsible for yourself. Charles Faulkner emphasized the point:

"Trend trading and even trading in general isn't for everyone. As too few people check out what the day-to-day life of a trader is like, and trend trading specifically, I strongly recommend they find out before making a life-changing commitment."

What does "life-changing commitment" involve? You commit to not wanting to be right all of the time. Most people, let's face it, must be right. They live to have other people know they're right. They don't even want the success. They don't want to win. They don't want money. They just want to be right. The winners, on the other hand, just want to win.

What else can you do? You commit to patience and faith in a trading system that is not structured on quarterly performance or some other artificial measure of the "mass." You work hard to gain experience. Great experience leads to great intuition. You commit to thinking for the long term and not feeling insecure if you don't have a steady earnings stream of 1–2 percent a month. You might have one year where you are down 10 percent. The following year you might be down 15 percent. The next year you might be up 115 percent. If you quit at the end of the second year, you will never get to the third year. That's reality.

Trend following trader Larry Hite once passed a note to me about "bets" that hints at that very reality:

"Life is nothing more than a series of bets and bets are really nothing more than questions and their answers. There is no real difference between, "Should I take another hit on this Blackjack hand?" and "Should I get out of the way of that speeding and wildly careening bus?" Each shares two universal truths: a set of probabilities of potential outcomes and the singular outcome that takes place. Every day, we place hundreds, if not thousands, of bets—large and small, some seemingly well considered, and others made without a second thought. The vast majority of the latter, life's little gambles made without any thought, might certainly be trivial. "Should I tie my shoes?" Seems to offer no big risk, nor any big reward. While others, such as the aforementioned "speeding and wildly careening bus" would seem to have greater impact on our lives. However, if deciding not to tie your shoes that morning causes you to trip and fall down in the middle of the road when you finally

Optimism means expecting the best, but confidence means knowing how to handle the worst.

Max Gunther[13]

Although this may seem a paradox, all exact science is dominated by the idea of approximation.

Bertrand Russell[14]

decide to fold your hand and give that careening bus plenty of leeway, well then, in hindsight the trivial has suddenly become paramount."

As a trend follower, you commit to a choice that is anything but trivial: Trade yourself or let a trend following trader trade for you. There are pros and cons to both choices and you won't determine your best direction until you get in the game and stop with the "buy-and-hold long-only everything will be alright" nonsense. 2008 was a sea change. It was a turning point. The big question, "Will your behavior change now that you know better?"

Afterword

"If you can find someone who is really open to seeing anything,
then you have found the raw ingredient of a good trader,
and I saw that in Bruce right away."
—Michael Marcus on Bruce Kovner

Acceptance

*Success and happiness—
the conditions needed to
thrive on this earth—are
reflections of the choices
we make.*

Brett N. Steenbarger

The first edition of *Trend Following* hit the streets in April 2004. Almost immediately, the book made a splash landing in the top 100 of all books available at Amazon.com. One hedge fund that I had never heard of bought 1,000 copies because they liked the message and wanted to use it as an educational tool. Another fund bought 3,000 copies. Quickly, the success of the book brought me in contact with an assortment of Wall Street professionals.

Much of that recognition started in Baltimore at Legg Mason's headquarters. Richard Cripps, the Chief Market Strategist at Legg Mason, wrote a review of *Trend Following*. Following his review, he invited me to Legg Mason's headquarters for lunch with his colleague Timothy McCann. We talked about my book and the Legg Mason Equity Compass, a systematic trading model for stocks. After our conversation, Cripps escorted me up a flight of stairs to a nondescript door. I had no idea where we were headed. Upon entering the room, it was a surprise to find it filled with young banking associates listening to a speaker at a podium. Michael Mauboussin, Legg Mason's Chief Investment Strategist, motioned for me to sit down to the side. I recognized that the speaker was Bill Miller, the fund manager of Legg Mason Value Trust. At the time Miller had beaten the S&P 500 Index for 14 straight years. (He has since had a steep drawdown along with the likes of Warren Buffett and Ken Heebner.)

Most of the Ivy League guys I know are so used to being "right" they get very uncomfortable dealing with uncertainty—when there is no right answer. Their egos often make them so afraid of being "wrong," that they're unable to make good bets. They aren't comfortable with the idea of risk, because they don't know how to assess it or measure it. [They have been] taught to absorb knowledge, not what to do with it.

Larry Hite, Hite Capital

Miller spoke for a few more minutes, and then introduced me to the audience inviting me to the podium. Until that moment, I had no idea I was going to speak. For the next hour, Miller, from one side of the room, and Mauboussin, from the other side, alternately peppered me with questions about trend following, risk management, and technical analysis. As I continued to field questions, it was clear that the audience was primarily fundamentally trained but curious and open to hearing about new ideas and concepts such as trend following.

After the presentation, I thanked Miller for the opportunity to make my case and was curious how he found out about *Trend Following*. He said: "I read a lot. I surf Amazon.com for all types of books. I came across yours, bought it, liked it, and told all my people at Legg Mason that they should read it."

At that moment, I knew *Trend Following* was catching on. Forget sales (which were very good)—I knew that if the book's message had struck a chord with a long-ime mutual fund manager, not trading as a trend following trader, I was on to something, but acceptance did not stop there.

The same curiosity that would ultimately push me to write *Trend Following* motivated me to seek out and interview even more trend following traders in person. I interviewed, either in their offices or homes, many of the world's best performing trend following traders (Bernard Drury, Michael Clarke, and Grant Smith of Millburn Ridgefield to name a few), collectively managing over $10 billion USD. I also sat down with short-term systematic trader Toby Crabel of Crabel Capital at his home in St. Thomas overlooking Magen's Bay. They all liked *Trend Following*.

Not long after those initial meetings, I had the opportunity to sit down with Larry Hite at his home in Manhattan and at his office on Park Avenue. In the 1990s, Hite was instrumental in transforming a sleepy, 200-year-old London-based sugar-trading firm known as

ED & F Man into The Man Group, now the largest hedge fund manager in the world with over $40 billion USD under management. The fundamental driver of Man's growth was the application of a risk-management concept developed by Hite that he calls Asymmetrical Leverage (ASL). For The Man Group, Hite devised a "guaranteed fund" that offered investors above-market rates of return while setting aside a portion of the money in zero-coupon bonds to protect the principal.

Chatting in Hite's living room, eating sushi at one of his favorite New York City spots, and talking about the joys of entrepreneurship was great. However, it was later in his office, as Hite stood at the chalkboard explaining some of the basic concepts of asymmetrical leverage that I really "got" him. He point blank said it was impossible to predict the movement of any market. Then he asked me, "What is the value of perfect knowledge?" "What if we knew the ending prices at the end of the year across a portfolio of markets?" And that was when he told me about his experiment: "In an attempt to answer these questions, we went to our databases and looked up the prices on December 31st of a given year. We asked ourselves: 'With this knowledge, how much leverage could we have used to get the maximum advantage at the beginning of that same year on January 1st?' We found that even with perfect foresight of the ending price, we could not sustain more than three to one leverage because we could not predict the path it took to get there."

Luckily, I had a gut feeling where he was headed, but I am sure he stumps many people. The big lesson from Hite, however, was "bets." And it was an excerpt from one of his speeches that really struck the chord:

> "Life is nothing more than a series of bets, and bets are really nothing more than questions and their answers. There is no real difference between, 'Should I take another hit on this Blackjack hand?' and 'Should I get out of the way of that speeding and wildly careening bus?' Each shares two universal truths: a set of probabilities of potential outcomes and the singular outcome that takes place. Everyday we place hundreds if not thousands of bets—large and small, some seemingly well considered, and others made without a second thought. The vast majority of the latter, life's little gambles made without any thought, might certainly be trivial. 'Should I tie my shoes?' seems to offer no big risk,

Our response to this environment has to be disciplined. If disagreement of opinions leads to trends, we need to maintain our positions. Similarly, we must be willing to close or change positions without ambiguity if called for. Risk management is especially opportune at this time. Will Rogers summed it up succinctly: "Even if you are on the right track, you'll get run over if you just sit there."

Mark S. Rzepczynski
President, John W. Henry & Company

nor any big reward. While others, such as the aforementioned 'speeding and wildly careening bus,' would seem to have greater impact on our lives. However, if deciding not to tie your shoes that morning causes you to trip and fall down in the middle of the road when you finally decide to fold your hand and give that careening bus plenty of leeway, well then, in hindsight the trivial has suddenly become paramount."

While putting together a documentary film (*Broke: The New American Dream*) over the course of 2007-2008 I saw exactly what Hite was speaking about first hand. From people tied up in exotic mortgages facing foreclosure to people playing the lottery every day using "systems," the ability to think in terms of odds is just not natural for most people.

Inefficient Markets

As every author knows, especially first-time unknown authors writing about relatively obscure subjects such as trend following trading, you spend a significant amount of your time promoting your book. Because I fit the definition of "first-time unknown author" to a tee, that's exactly what I did, with no idea whether *Trend Following* would sell 10 or 10,000 copies. Thankfully, the book has sold over 100,000 copies and has been translated into German, Korean, Japanese, Chinese (traditional and simplified), French, Russian, and Turkish. As a result of the book's success, I soon found myself point person for trend following. With each forecast of trend following doom and gloom, usually in the form of book review, column, or interview, I would "set the record straight."

I'd usually start by addressing the assumption that generates much of the confusion in the first place—the efficient market hypothesis. The hypothesis essentially says that you can't find an edge to beat the market, and simply sticking with a benchmark or index is the best path to take for profit (believe that still after 2008?). Proponents of the efficient market hypothesis argue that because markets are efficient and prices fully reflect all information, traders who consistently outperform the market do so out of luck, not skill. Of course, in the real world, markets are both efficient and inefficient, some more than others. In the real world, there are traders who do beat the market by a wide margin, and many of them are trend followers.

> *Even more disturbing are the extreme lies in your "approach." Trend followers use "systems" and "money management" to make money based on momentum. They buy high and hope that there are enough suckers to buy higher. How can you describe that as sound investing? You make it sound like this is some form of intelligent investing. Like there is some rhyme or reason. There are no sound principles behind it. No intelligence. No reason. Just hold and hope and hope you get out before the crowd. Trend following depends on someone else being dumber than you.*
>
> Trend Following *book critic*

What accounts for the patience, discipline, and commitment to long-term success as a trend follower? It might ultimately be about making a profit, but it is also an understanding and keen appreciation for the scientific method. Just as scientists start with a hypothesis, trend followers start with a certain view of the world. Their divergent view sees the world in trends. Facing the reality of any market environment head on is the philosophical foundation of trend following. Yet, if the approach is that simple (and profitable), then why does trend following continue to be ignored or confused by so-called bright and market-wise people?

A recent email from one skeptic confessed that, "...the consistent volatility [and drawdown] of [trend following] makes it an untenable strategy, at least for me."

Hendrik Houthakker, a prominent Harvard economist, ran a test on trend following...he ran it on one contract. I believe it was wheat. Well some years it made money, some years it didn't make money. Houthakker... didn't try to trend follow across the board [just one market]. He came to the conclusion that trend following did not work.

Larry Hite, Hite Capital

Trend following is, indeed, untenable for those who cannot stand the feelings of being in a drawdown or who can't stand dealing with volatility. Trend followers understand that if you avoid volatility and drawdown, you will avoid large profits as well, a mindset that can be threatening to those who feel safest when they think they are pursuing supposedly low-risk trading methods. In my interviews with many of the great traders, we wondered why so many criticize trend following for drawdowns (which they typically recover from rather quickly), but seemingly ignore stock market drawdowns like those in 2008. This focus on trend following drawdowns probably accounts for *The Financial Times'* Philip Coggan's tentative review:

"It is possible that momentum-based strategies might work. Academic studies have suggested some success in the short term, although mean reversion occurs over longer periods."

"It is possible that momentum-based strategies might work?" Don't the results of Sunrise Capital, TransTrend, John W. Henry, David Harding, Jerry Parker, Larry Hite, George Crapple, Ken Tropin, Salem Abraham, Christian Baha, Dinesh Desai, Paul Rabar, Tom Shanks, Louis Bacon, Bruce Kovner, Bernard Drury, Michael Clarke, William Eckhardt, Liz Cheval, and Bill Dunn, to name just a few, count for something beyond "might work"? I'll trust the actual trading results of these traders over the "academic studies" and "suggestions" that Coggan relies on.

I get the same sort of value from these books [Trend Following] as I do from studying the Keech cult, supernatural operators such as Uri Geller and horoscope readers.

Victor Niederhoffer
See page 164 for more on Niederhoffer.

Bottom line, no one can make an intellectually honest argument against the hard performance data of trend followers—even though many people try. To that end, to quell naysayers, I have added performance reports on multiple trend-following trading traders to Appendix B, "Performance Guide." These month-by-month performance data histories should be an "aha" moment for people who did not know about it and an irritant for those who want to pretend it doesn't exist. Are you prepared to honestly deal with the reality of what the performance data shows?

Take, for example, the following from trend follower Salem Abraham's commentary to investors:

I decided almost 20 years ago that rather than become an expert trend follower I could better leverage my time by becoming an expert at identifying other trend followers. The decision has been very rewarding. Having placed over a billion dollars with trend followers over the years, I have become increasingly convinced that the level of passion, discipline, intelligence and hard work to become a long term success at trend following is enormous.

Jon C. Sundt, President, Altegris Investments

"Our research allows us to select trades that put the odds in our favor. However, it takes time to prove that the odds truly are in our favor. The statistics that follow demonstrate this truth:

- Percentage of time we make money in any day:
  54 percent
- Percentage of time we make money in any month:
  56 percent
- Percentage of time we make money in any 3 months:
  64 percent
- Percentage of time we make money in any 6 months:
  77 percent
- Percentage of time we make money in any 12 months:
  92 percent
- Percentage of time we make money in any 24 months:
  100 percent

"We do not have a crystal ball, so we do not know when this current losing period will end. However, we can look in the rear view mirror and see that when we experienced periods like this before, not only did we survive, but we thrived."

Those are the facts of life as long-time trend following traders deal with daily. Wouldn't it be nice if the roller-coaster ride were smoother? Perhaps, but you have to deal with the real world, and the real world is uncertain. Ride the bucking bronco, baby...or you can always accept the fake security of buy and hold investing.

Trend Following Critics

My interviews with the top traders confirmed what I have always believed and repeatedly say to be the primary reason people are confused about trend following. Their confusion is linked directly to a trading and investing culture familiar and therefore comfortable with only one approach to the markets: fundamental analysis (buy and hold, long only, etc.). Fundamental traders and investors think the only way to beat the market is to gather all the information you can find. They want news, they want CNBC, they want Jim Cramer, they want crop reports, they want OPEC rumors, they want Bernanke's shoe size—they believe extraneous information will help them to make profitable trading decisions. Trend followers, on the other hand, say, "Enough!" They know the market price is the best source of information about the market direction because the market price is the aggregate vote of everyone. Think about it—what else can you truly believe in except the market price? The market price can't be fixed or doctored. It is real.

What are some of the arguments put forth by trend following critics? When Peter Deoteris at Welling@Weeden reviewed *Trend Following*, he diminished the trend following community by mistakenly referring to trend followers as "a couple of commodities traders." The universe of trend following traders is hardly a party of two traders alone. Clearly there are many successful trend followers, and the majority of them trade stocks, currencies, bonds, and commodities. What is the implication of the word "commodity?" by Deoteris. Many people assume the term "commodity" means "risky." That criticism conveniently ignores the fact that all trading is risky. The trick is to understand the risk in any trading approach and to know what to do with it on a daily basis.

Deoteris also perpetuated the myth that trend followers attempt to forecast significant market events:

> "…there clearly is a strong element of revisionist history at work here…looking back and using subsequent events to justify various traders' positions. When those positions were established, however, they were based on logic and assumed risks that were often entirely different."

As any reader of *Trend Following* knows, trend followers take trading positions with no knowledge that an event or crisis will occur. They take their positions as markets move. With price leading the way, they follow along. The fact that these particular small, initial price trends lead to big trends that lead to big events is not something anyone can predict. Do you think trend followers

The market serves a valuable function in our economy not often talked about: It provides an efficient mechanism for transferring precious capital from those who are ill-equipped to steward its growth to those who are adept. A variety of market participants provide this service up and down the food chain. The financial markets are voluntary arrangements. No one is compelled to purchase a piece of trading software. No guns are involved in herding investors into seminars. Advisory letters are sent to those who willingly subscribe to them, and may be cancelled at will. Investors who avail themselves of these services without exercising due diligence and taking responsibility for their own actions are the true dangerous lot— they are a danger to themselves. They blame others for their bad decisions and misfortunes; they delude themselves about the true nature of their problem, so the solution remains ever beyond their ken.

Gibbons Burke, MarketHistory.com

predicted October 2008? No, they did not, but they sure made fortunes in October 2008.

Another common source of confusion stems from not understanding trend following's reliance on reactive technical analysis. For example, one form of technical analysis attempts to "read" charts to divine the market direction. The second form of technical analysis, practiced by trend followers, is based on reacting to market movements whenever they occur. Although I make this distinction clear in Chapter 1 of *Trend Following*, I still find myself explaining the difference to bewildered investors and traders. Trend followers are perfectly happy to accept the fact that their method of price analysis never allows them to enter at the exact bottom or exit at the exact top of a trend.

However, this particular concept is hard to fathom for many market players. For example, when Citigroup fired their entire technical analysis group as a cost-cutting measure and replaced it with more fundamental analysis, media coverage jumped all over the idea that technical analysis was dead. Immediately I started receiving emails asking if trend following was dead.

The real question with the Citigroup firings is not why they were replacing technical with fundamental analysis, but what kind of technical analysis were they using in the first place. It certainly wasn't the price-based analysis used by trend followers. Yet the only conclusion most people drew from Citigroup's actions was that technical analysis was now discredited. Did the performance data of trend followers matter to the story? No, the reporters had to put a story out and accuracy was not the issue.

Inaccurate media reports are encouraged by so-called financial "experts" whose reputations hinge on making fundamental predictions about market direction. James Altucher, a disciple of Victor Niederhoffer and, these days, a popular financial writer, posted an article on trend following. The article elicited an abundance of feedback. One trend follower wrote me saying:

> "John W. Henry and his peers advertise the riskiness of their investments on their sleeve, while some of the mean reversion hedge fund boys spend sleepless nights hoping no one ever figures out how much risk they are really taking. Most of those guys won't even admit to themselves how much risk they are taking!"

I mean, look at the concept of price targets. Someone—analyst, mutual fund manager, whoever—will come on and say, "I have a price target for this stock of XXX—which is up 30pct from here." I see it getting there over the next six months. Yeah right. When someone tells me they know where a stock is going, I can only laugh and ask them why they haven't mortgaged the house and put it all in the stock. Of course I know the answer. They don't want to put their money in the stock; they want YOU to put YOUR money in the stock so the price of the stock they own goes up. Get long and get loud. Why can't we just admit they are pitching a stock and treat it like a trinket on QVC?

Mark Cuban, www.blogmaverick.com

What about supposed "lower-risk" strategies such as PIPEs or other arcane forms of arbitrage trading? One trend follower emailed me an observation:

> "What a novel way to avoid being in a drawdown: Trade an instrument that is so illiquid that there is no market for it except under special circumstances. That makes it a lot more convenient to pretend that there is very little risk. If I get to make up my own price quote for an instrument on every day between my buy and sell points, then I can create an infinite Sharpe ratio as long as I sell it for more than I buy it. The only case where I ever have to face up to the big risks I really take is if the asset goes to a level that forces me to liquidate at a big loss. In that case, my strategy does not appear quite so risk free."

As I accumulated reader feedback, it became clear that some people thought that I had not accentuated the drawdowns of trend followers enough. Yet, I am clear in this book. There are no free lunches. You can make money, and you can lose money. To get the big gains—there will be periods of pain and drawdown. No risk, no return. However, how often do you hear about the Nasdaq being in a –60 percent drawdown almost 10 years after that bubble burst?

If further proof was needed, it occurred when I picked up the phone and called a top trend follower. His firm no longer reports their performance data, but they continue to trade billions. I had never talked with this man before, and he is not mentioned in this book. At first, he was uneasy talking with me. "How did you find me?" "Why are you calling?" However, he had a good sense of humor, even though he quickly said that he did not want to be quoted on the record. We talked for 45 minutes. His insights:

- He backed that many more Long Term Capital Managements (LTCMs) are ready to implode. He said to look at the numbers of the arbitrage guys. He pointed out that for the last four years, the arbitrage ("stat arb., convertible arb., etc.") guys are using more leverage to generate less return ("too much gearing"). He added, "They think they have found the Key to Rebecca and they have not found anything."

- He acknowledged that his billion dollar plus fund was on the other side of LTCM's losses in the zero-sum game: "We were the

If you have the good fortune to make some money in this world, you will always have detractors. John W. Henry, the owner of the Red Sox baseball team and one of the best trend followers ever, is no exception. Spring 2005 has seen the catcalls for John's head in some investment circles. Why is this? You have a choice of answers: John's success or his critic's ignorance. It's probably both. And for those who think Henry's trading prowess has diminished, check out his approximate +9 percent return for May 2005 and for good measure his +9 percent for June 2005.

other side...they were an accident waiting to happen...now seven years later, the risks for these types of strategies are just as great."

- Wall Street investment banks only want 35-year-old traders. You get to be 50 and they don't want you. What's his point here? Wall Street ignores experience like Richard Donchian trading into his nineties. I know great trend followers ranging in age from age 40 to 70.

Critic Geetesh Bhardwaj

Let us believe that it is possible to profit through economic changes by following today's trend, as it is revealed statistically day-by-day, week-by-week, or month-by-month. In doing this we should entertain no preconceived notions as to whether business is going to boom or bust, or whether the Dow-Jones Industrial Average is going to 500 or 50. We will merely chart our course and steer our ship in the direction of the prevailing wind. When the economic weather changes, we will change our course with it and will not try to forecast the future time or place at which the wind will change.

William Dunnigan (1954)

In the fall of 2008 I noticed an academic paper right at the time trend followers were having some of their best performance ever. The title of the paper, taking a stab at trend traders (commonly referred to by the regulatory name of Commodity Trading Advisor), was:

"Fooling Some of the People All of the Time: The Inefficient Performance and Persistence of Commodity Trading Advisors"

The author Geetesh Bhardwaj wrote that paper while working at AIG Financial Products. So Bhardwaj was part of a firm that took $150 billion of taxpayer dollars to stay afloat, but rips a strategy (trend following) that actually makes money without the government propping it up? The irony to me was inescapable.

Shortly after my criticism, Bhardwaj left AIG and joined index mutual fund company, Vanguard. This whole episode generated great feedback on my blog at michaelcovel.com, with Bhardwaj joining in to make his defense:

"If my affiliation is the only criticism that you have of the results, I am vindicated. So stop taking about who I work for and start justifying the industry wide Sharpe Ratio of 0.09 to your invstors [sic]. You have been stealing investor money for too long, 2-20 for trend following really?????"

Performance data for trend following traders, month-by-month performance, is there for all to see (Appendix B and Iasg.com). If those numbers are considered "stealing" to Bhardwaj, I can't convince him to see another light.

Further, Bhardwaj thinks the Sharpe ratio is an appropriate measure of trend following traders. It is not (see Chapter 3, "Performance Data"). Trend following trader David Harding has written on the Sharpe ratio: "The Sharpe ratio appears at first blush to reward returns (good) and penalize risks (bad). Upon closer inspection, things are not so simple. The standard deviation takes into account the distance of each return from the mean, positive or negative. By this token, large positive returns increase the perception of risk as though they could as easily be negative, which for a dynamic investment strategy [like trend following] may not be the case. Large positive returns are penalized, and thus the removal of the highest returns from the distribution can increase the Sharpe ratio: a case of reductio ad absurdum for Sharpe ratio as a universal measure of quality!"

Other readers on my blog responded to Bhardwaj:

"Of course Geetesh Bhardwaj's affiliation is significant. Vanguard is famous for taking the position that actively managed funds are a waste of time. That is why the vast majority of their assets under management are in indexed funds. So is it surprising that their marketing department hired an economics major to write reports that show active management in a bad light? Don't hold it against Geetesh. His previous job being a vice president of a disaster like AIG can't look good on a resume. He's probably lucky to be working at all."

Another reader responded:

"The Sharpe ratio of CTAs [trend following traders] does not need to be 'explained.' Most investors want the investment to be profitable. The Sharpe ratio does not measure 'risk' as it is commonly understood. Even Sharpe, in his original paper, wrote about 'variability' not 'risk.' The Sharpe ratio punishes a spike up in the same way as a spike down. Many managers have strategies that produce a good average profit over a long period, but require the investors to accept some gyration in the mean time. If you want highly predictable earnings, invest with Madoff, who, if news reports are correct, claimed to produce the same one percent return every month. I'm sure Geetesh would have loved his Sharpe ratio."

All trends are historical; none are in the present. There is no way to determine the current trend, or even define what current trend might mean; we can only determine historical trends. The only way to measure a now-trend (one entirely in the moment of now) would be to take two points, both in the now and compute their difference. Motion, velocity, and trend do not exist in the now. They do not appear in snapshots. Trend does not exist in the now, and the phrase, "the trend" has no inherent meaning…There is no such thing as a current trend. When we speak of trends, we are necessarily projecting our own definitions. With that in mind, we can proceed to examine ways to define, compute, and use trends.

Ed Seykota
Seykota.com

I met with a near billion-dollar hedge fund in their Texas office in Spring 2005. Funded primarily from the principals' personal wealth (they hit it big with one of the top technology firms of all-time), their firm was seeking insights into trend following. They want to invest with trend following traders, but they are having a hard time wrapping their arms around a strategy (trend following) not rooted in fundamentals. The three executives I met with were more comfortable with a trader who traded one market alone. They liked the idea that a trader might be able to fundamentally know everything he could about that one market. They liked the idea of that type of skill compared to trend following skill. The trend following skill of reducing all markets to the common denominator of price just did not connect with them. This group is very bright and they are doing extreme due diligence on trend following trading. Unlike some who dismiss trend following, these folks will get it since they are willing to learn something new.

Yet another reader added:

"Ahhh, now I get it. The buy and hold crowd justifies their 50% drawdowns and 0% 10 year total return by the Sharpe ratio, of course! I can hear the funds on the phone with their investors now, 'Yes, you've lost half your money in the last year and you have made nothing in 10 years but don't worry, the Sharpe ratio was good!' Is this what Vanguard means by 'sensible buy and hold'? If the Sharpe ratio is good then it must be sensible, returns and drawdowns be damned!"

Bhardwaj is a pawn of the mutual fund industry. The mutual fund industry spends millions through lobbying in Washington and propaganda (i.e 'academic research') to keep trend following traders from advertising their performance. Why do this? The mutual fund industry (i.e. Vanguard) has a stranglehold on the average investor that they don't want to lose. They keep the average guy stuck in 'long only' dead-end strategies to spin off their massive fees. Bhardwaj is no prophet. His attack is transparent and ignorant. When the immediate retort back is, 'Sharpe ratio', you know the dice were loaded.

Worse for Bhardwaj? Witnessing this interchange online happened to be a firm who manages money for AIG. This firm happens to be a trend following trader (CTA):

"Great stuff with Geetesh. Very entertaining reading. Off the record, here's a bit of irony for you, we manage a significant amount of money for AIG and have done so for several years!"

I am not surprised that a trend following critic like Bhardwaj, while working at AIG, failed to note that AIG actually had investments with trend followers.

Final Thoughts

An associate of mine in fund management approached me about attending an Altegris investment conference. Altegris has placed over $1 billion of client assets with assorted fund managers including significant placements with trend followers. Upon my arrival at the conference, I was introduced to the president of Altegris, Jon Sundt. Sundt's presentation at the conference hit home. He postulated:

> "Can a great trader have great skill and no opportunity to make money? Can a bad trader have no skill and tons of opportunity to make money? The answer is yes to both questions. Luck is at play in the short-term for most traders. There will always be 'some guy' with a great one-year return, but the sustained edge appears only over time."

What's Sundt's big picture point? He wants you to think about what happens when the bad trader with no skills finally finds himself with no opportunity. If you don't want to embrace his wisdom, you will eventually feel massive pain in your trading account.

There will always be critics, and there will always be cheerleaders. I, however, find solace in performance numbers and trend following performance numbers are the real story, the truth if you will. Bottom line, no matter how many people agree or disagree with the content of this book, and I know there are big fans and big critics, positive performance numbers from trend followers, especially from historic months like October 2008, paint a picture you either accept or reject—it's your choice. Although this is the third edition of *Trend Following* since 2004, I have a feeling it will not be the last. Some big, unexpected event will unfold in the future, some event where trend followers make a killing, and I will drive myself crazy until I get that "next" event profiled in these pages. *Trend Following* is on its way to becoming an ongoing blog, just like on the Web, except this one is in hard-copy format available at Amazon, Borders, and Barnes and Noble.

When you strip away all the noise, we see that long-term price movements, bull and bear markets, are a function of fear and greed. These human emotions, reacting to shifts and imbalances of supply and demand…will always exist. Superfund employs a disciplined, systematic approach and profits from investor emotion by harnessing clear price trends. Human emotion does not impact the positions we take or the open risk that we allow in our trades…

Christian Baha, CEO Superfund

Now, there's one thing that you men will be able to say when you get back home, and you may thank God for it. Thirty years from now when you're sitting around your fireside with your grandson on your knee, and he asks you, "What did you do in the great World War Two?" You won't have to say, "Well, I shoveled shit in Louisiana." Alright now, you sons of bitches, you know how I feel. I will be proud to lead you wonderful guys into battle anytime, anywhere. That's all.

General George S. Patton, 3rd Army speech — May 31, 1944

Foreword to the First Edition by Charles Faulkner

If you are browsing through this in a bookstore, you are most likely in the investments section. Look around. All of the people near you are also looking for an investing edge. If you are online, you can see by the ratings and recommendations that many other people have been here before you. The other titles in front of you, whether they are actual or virtual, all claim to represent an opportunity to enrich you. Whether you know it or not, you are in a market. You are looking for a winning trade—the information, the edge—that will put you ahead in the markets of stocks, bonds, real estate, or commodities.

When I first modeled the trading strategies of J. Peter Steidlmayer, CBOT trader and the originator of the Market Profile, I had a narrow notion of what makes a market, or how to make money in one. I had heard of George Soros, Jim Rogers, Peter Lynch, and a few others. When I heard the phrase, "buy low and sell high," it made sense to me. It also happened to appeal to me as a former antiques dealer and all-round bargain hunter.

I didn't know how little I knew. Somehow I traded my model of the Market Profile—despite my utter ignorance of risk and money management—into a tidy profit. A colleague pointed out to me, "So you're betting on your opinion of other people's opinions." The reality of W.C. Fields' famous retort to Mae West's question (in *My Little Chickade*) sunk in. "Is poker a game of chance?" "Not the way I play it." I was concerned only with market signals—I had a stretch of what you'll learn was "Dumb Luck," instead of the "Poetic Justice" usually dealt to traders with such a lack of preparation. I got out to trade another day.

My chapter in Jack Schwager's *The New Market Wizards* made it possible for me to meet top traders across the industry. Sometimes we appeared on professional panels together. Other times, it was a private conversation. I want to share some of what I learned with you. Before I do, though, I want you to take out a dollar bill. Turn it over. You will see two seals. Look at the one on the left. The one with the words "THE GREAT SEAL" inscribed underneath it, the one with an unfinished pyramid of 13 steps with an eye in a glowing triangle floating above it. It is a wonderful symbol for a successful trader and represents a trading tool as well.

The stones of the pyramid represent the ways a trader can make money. There's intermediation (brokerage charges), aggregating clients (reducing costs), carry trades, privileged information (insider trading), assessing asset flows (an institutional advantage), advanced technology (particularly for option pricing), models of economic actors and data (fundamentals), models of historical price data (technicals), and others. Some of these are basic—those near the base of the pyramid—and so they offer low returns. Other methods offer high returns. Naturally, as you make your way up on the pyramid, there are fewer stones. No one should be surprised by this. Neither was I.

What did surprise me when meeting and modeling these market wizards was that despite their outward, often dramatic, differences in trading and life style, their thinking about their trading principles was extremely similar. It was like they were floating above the world, seeing it from a different perspective than the rest of the market participants. What are these differences? Here are a few from the eye of the pyramid:

- It doesn't matter what you think, it's what the market does that matters.
- What matters can be measured, so keep refining your measurements.
- You don't need to know when something will happen to know that it will.
- Successful trading is a probabilistic business, so plan accordingly.
- There is an edge to be gained in every aspect of your trading system.

- Everyone is fallible, even you, so your system must take this into account.
- Trading means losing as well as winning, something you must learn to live with.

Now, you might say to yourself, "Where's the secret sauce in that?" In one sense, you're right. These are extremely simple principles. At the same time they are counterintuitive and take a focused effort to apply. Let me give you an example: I was attending the trading system conference where I first met market wizard Ed Seykota. His table was talking about how successful trading systems could, and should, be simple enough that they could fit on a bumper sticker. Of course, skepticism emanated from other tables. "What about the complexities of the markets?" Their response was that they weren't interested in the markets' complexities; simply in making money on changes in price. Ed and his traders saw through the smokescreen of untested assumptions and beliefs about what you need to know about a market and what it takes to make a successful trading system. This is the difference between knowing a principle and making its market application. Think about adding to a position—also known as "pyramiding." Adding less with each addition to a position actually creates more gain than adding equal amounts each time. It's simple and it's counterintuitive. Another way that image on the dollar is a trading tool.

The book you have in front of you bridges this gap between trading principles and their market application like no other. It may look like a book, but it is really a set of trading tools—a complete and detailed application of these principles and others to the method of trading known as *Trend Following*.

Author and trader Michael Covel has arranged these master lessons so that you can approach them according to your personal preference, or as they call them these days, biases.

The Personalities—In the chapters on great trend followers, you can read the personal histories of leading traders. You'll find there isn't just one type of successful personality; they range from college students to real scientists.

The Performance—For the factually minded, in the chapters on ferformance data and big events in trend following, there is a succinct summary of historical data from several trend following funds, along with parallel events in the world.

The Psychology—For those who think human behavior and decision making make the difference, there are chapters on each of these, as well as on emotional intelligence—and how to get it—followed by the dangers of Holy Grails.

The Trading Systems—The risk, the reward, the key questions to ask, and the questions Michael is most often asked, along with commentary from the master trend followers themselves, encompass these chapters.

The remarkable thing is not that you are looking at this book, but that it exists at all. Conventional wisdom says buy low and sell high. Each of us got our education in bargain hunting somewhere along the line. But what do you do now that your favorite market—be it a stock, bond, or commodity—is at an all-time high...or low? For a completely different perspective, from people who actually make money at this business, take a look inside. Michael Covel has written a timely and entertaining account of trend following—how it works, how to do it, and who can do it.

About Charles Faulkner

Charles Faulkner is an international NLP modeler and trainer who has worked with traders since 1986. The coauthor of NLP: The New Technology of Achievement, *he was interviewed on* The Psychology of Trading *by Jack Schwager for his book* The New Market Wizards: Conversations with America's Top Traders, *with other interviews appearing in Robert Koppel's* The Outer Game of Trading *and* The Intuitive Trader *and articles in* Futures Magazine *and* Stocks, Futures, and Options Magazine. *A speaker at the F.I.A., The Market Timers Association, the Chicago Board of Trade's Members Only program, and other professional conferences, Charles conducts seminars on the emotions, strategies, beliefs, and design of trading systems.*

Charles consults on human factors in financial risk management to asset management and commodity firms and works with Ed Seykota contributing to his Trading Tribe Process (TTP). He trades stocks and futures when his system signals and divides his time between the U.S. and the U.K. where his wife and stepdaughter reside.

Appendices

Introduction to Appendices

The following appendices are not just "extra" material. They are not just research notes. Each appendix adds additional value and clarification to the main book text. A careful consideration of all eight appendices will provide an even greater trend following education.

- Appendix A, "Trend Following for Stocks": Cole Wilcox and Eric Crittenden of Blackstar Funds have generously provided unique research explaining the use of trend following strategies on stocks.

- Appendix B, "Performance Guide": Historical performance data from professional trend followers provides concrete results, not just theory.

- Appendix C, "Short-Term Trading": Short-term trading is hard, but not impossible. Market Wizards Jim Simons and Toby Crabel do win as short-term traders, but Ed Seykota offers good insight on the difficulty.

- Appendix D, "Personality Traits of Successful Traders": Understanding the role of personality and temperament in great trading can be critical.

- Appendix E, "Trend Following Models": Paul Mulvaney of Mulvaney Capital Management presents a useful visual model for trend following trading.

- Appendix F, "Trading System Example from Mechanica": Bob Spear of Trading Recipes Software presents a sample trend following trading system.

Mean reversion works almost all the time, and then it stops and you are kind of out of business. So the market is always reverting to the mean except when it doesn't, and then we [trend followers] are on board this big huge trend and these people lose a lot of money. There are two competing philosophies [trend following versus mean reversion]...then every eight years you [mean reversion] are out of business because when it doesn't revert to the mean, your philosophy loses...mean reversion is somewhat uninformed.

Jerry Parker, Chesapeake Capital
Futures Industry Association
Presentation

- Appendix G, "Critical Questions for Trading Systems": Understand critical questions that must be answered to have a successful trend following trading system.

Trend Following for Stocks

A

Cole Wilcox and Eric Crittenden of Blackstar Funds, LLC graciously supplied all of the research in this appendix about trend following success on stocks. I view this appendix as a twelfth chapter, even though it is not labeled that way.

Does Trend Following Work on Stocks?

Introduction

Our firm Blackstar Funds, LLC manages a multi-advisor commodity pool that invests primarily in systematic[1], long volatility[2] programs. We focus mainly on trend following programs from the commodities, financial futures, and currency trading arenas, as they tend to be the most systematic in terms of trading and portfolio management. Years of searching for systematic trend following programs that focus on stocks, however, have left us empty handed. Having spent literally thousands of man hours performing due diligence on trend following funds, along with years of personal experience trading proprietary capital in stocks, we feel uniquely qualified to tackle the question, "Does trend following work on stocks?"

To evaluate the effectiveness of trend following on stocks we must first determine:

- What stocks will be considered?
- When and how will a stock be purchased?
- When and how will a stock be sold?

Data Integrity

Data Coverage

The database used included 24,000+ individual securities from the NYSE, AMEX, and NASDAQ exchanges. Coverage spanned from January 1983 to December 2004.

Survivorship Bias

The database used for this project included historical data for all stocks that were delisted at some point between 1983 and 2004. Slightly more than half of the database is composed of delisted stocks.

Corporate Actions

All stock prices were proportionately back adjusted for corporate actions, including cash dividends, splits, mergers, spin-offs, stock dividends, reverse splits, and so on.

Realistic Investable Universe

A minimum stock price filter was used to avoid penny stocks.[3] A minimum daily liquidity filter was used to avoid stocks that would not have been liquid enough to generate realistic historical results from. Both filters were evaluated for every stock and for every day of history in the database, mimicking how results would have appeared in real time.

A complete discussion of these data integrity issues can be found at the end of this appendix.

The following chart shows how many stocks would have passed the previously mentioned filters for each year of historical testing:

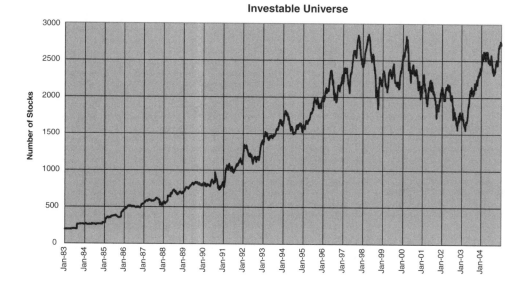

Entry and Exit

Entry

For the purposes of this project, the entry method chosen was the all-time highest close. More specifically, if today's close is greater than or equal to the highest close during the stock's entire history, then buy *tomorrow on the open.* We chose this method to avoid ambiguity. A stock that is at an all time high must be in an uptrend by any reasonable person's definition. This is a trend following entry in its purest form.

The following *weekly* charts illustrate what would have been notable trade entries for the system presented in this appendix. The green dots denote instances where the closing price for the week was at a new all time high. The horizontal pink line represents the previous all time high that would have triggered the initial entry:

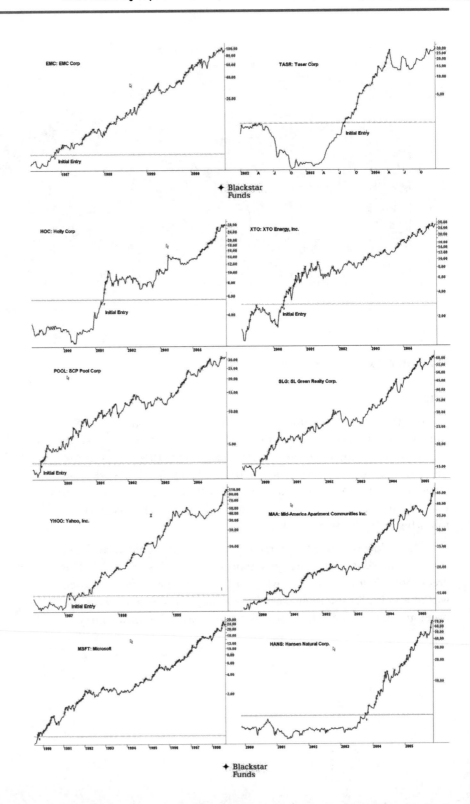

Exit (Stops)

Exits are essential to any trend following strategy. We decided to use average true range trailing stops because they are universally applicable and commonly used by trend following programs. The average true is a derivative of the true range indicator, which measures the daily movement of a security by calculating the greater of:

- Today's high minus today's low
- Today's high minus yesterday's close
- Yesterday's close minus today's low

The true range illustrates the maximum distance the security's price traveled from the close of one business day to the close of the next business day, capturing overnight gaps and intraday price swings. The average of this value can be used to integrate the volatility of a security into a universally applicable trailing stop. Average true range stops effectively account for volatility differences between individual securities.

For example, a 10 ATR stop on a volatile Internet stock might be 55 percent away from the stock price:

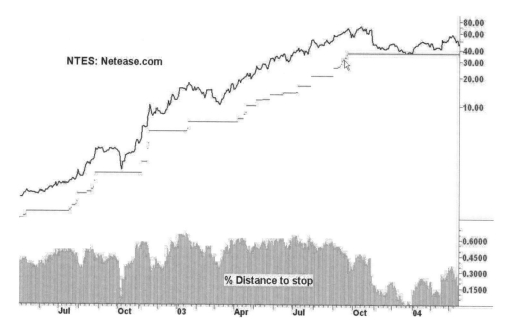

Alternatively, a 10 ATR stop on a quiet utility stock might only be 15 percent away from the stock price:

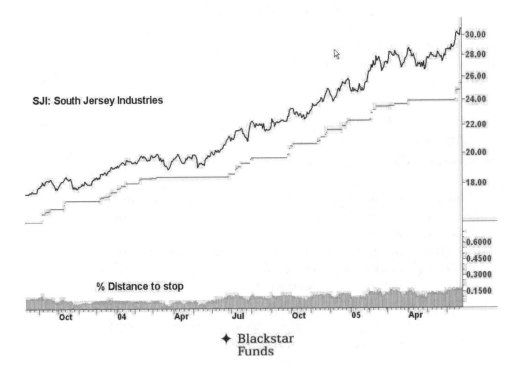

✦ Blackstar
   Funds

For the purposes of this project, we chose to exit a stock on the open *the day after the exit level was breached.* The following charts illustrate how a 10 ATR stop would have looked on some well known stocks from the past:

Many more graphical illustrations of the stops we used can be found at the end of this appendix.

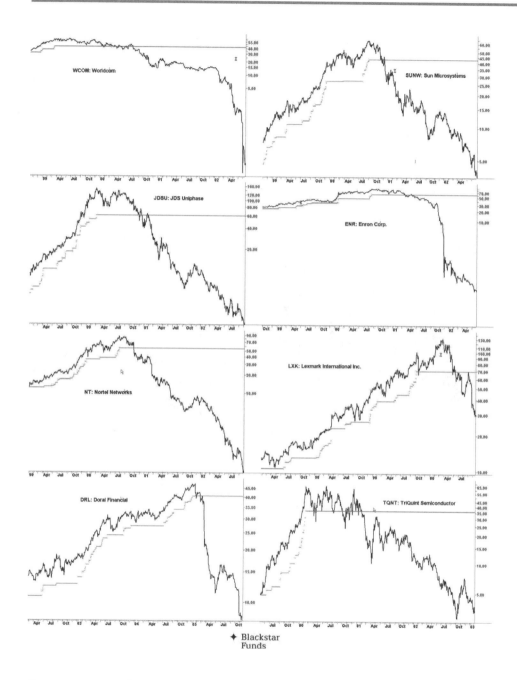

✦ Blackstar Funds

Expectancy Studies

To determine how well these entries and exits would have worked in the past, it was necessary to test the combination against the historical database, while honoring the previously mentioned data integrity issues.

The following distribution shows the results from using an all time high entry along with a 10-unit ATR stop. There were 18,000+ trades during the 22 year test period. Transaction costs of 0.5 percent round-turn were deducted from each trade to account for estimated commission and slippage.

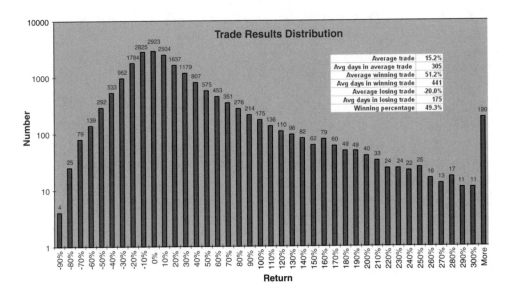

The X-axis represents the net return from the trade. The Y-axis indicates how many trades would have achieved the indicated net return. The long volatility component resulting from the combination of a trend following entry and trailing volatility stop is immediately recognizable by the significant right skew of the distribution. Seventeen percent of trades would have gained 50 percent or more while less than 3 percent of trades would have registered a loss equal to or worse than −50 percent.

At first glance, a winning percentage of 49.3 percent might seem less than impressive, but it is relatively high for a trend following system. Trend following systems can be very effective with much lower winning percentages if the profitable trades are significantly larger than the more frequent unprofitable trades. In the case of this system, the ratio between average winning trade and average losing trade is 2.56; a healthy number in our experience.

A positive mathematical expectancy is the bare minimum needed to justify the use of or further research of an investing or trading system. In the case of this system, the weighted average of the trade results distribution yields an expectancy of approximately 15.2 percent with an average holding period of 305 calendar days. Considering the significance of the sample size, depth of the sample period, realistic assumptions used, and the right skewed return distribution, we felt this was a very solid foundation to build from.

Other settings for the ATR stop were tested, the range spanned from 8 to 12 with a step increment of 0.5. The middle setting of 10 was chosen for illustration purposes. There were no material differences in results among the various settings. Higher ATR levels (looser stops) resulted in slightly higher winning percentages and slightly lower win/loss ratios. The inverse was true of lower ATR levels (tighter stops).

The next distribution illustrates a collection of all trades, each normalized for its own risk. This concept typically requires some explanation. Every trade ultimately has a recorded percent return.[4] Every trade also has a recorded percent initial risk[5] from the day of entry. The result is that we know what the percent return of each trade would have been and we know how much risk each trade would have subjected us to. The *ratio* between these two numbers is the focus of this section.

The simplest way to interpret the following distribution is to focus on a couple of specific numbers on the X-axis. First the –100 percent column contains trade results where the absolute value of the *net loss* approximately equaled the initial risk (lost the full amount that was expected). Likewise, the 100 percent column contains trades where the *net gain* approximately equaled the initial risk. Results worse than –100 percent represent trades where we would have lost more than what was budgeted for on the trade (negative outlier trades). This is usually the result of a large, overnight price decline. Results greater than 100 percent represent trades where we would have gained more than what was initially risked (positive outlier trades). Consider the following two scenarios:

- We purchase XYZ stock at $15.50. The 10 ATR stop is $11.32. Initial risk in this case is 27 percent. Two years later, we sell XYZ at $30.75 for a gain of 98 percent. The ratio between gain and initial risk is 3.63 or 363 percent. This data point would therefore go in the 350 percent column in the following distribution. The return would have been 363 percent the size of the initial risk.

- We purchase ABC stock at $32.35. The 10 ATR stop is $26.53. Initial risk in this case is 18 percent. Three months later the company misses its earnings estimate and gaps down well below the stop. We sell ABC at $21.15 for a loss of –35 percent. The ratio between gain and initial risk is –1.94 or –194 percent. This data point would therefore go in the –200 percent column. The loss would have been almost double what was budgeted for.

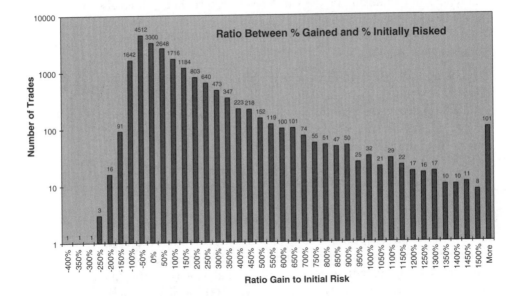

From the above distribution, one can get a feel for how realistic a 10 ATR stop is for real-world trading. Data points to the left of –100 percent reflect trades that couldn't be controlled. There were less than 400 trades that caused worse than expected losses. This amounts to approximately 2 percent of all historical trades.

In some ways, this second distribution is more important than the first. Normalizing each trade by its own risk reduces the possibility that highly volatile stocks will unjustifiably dominate the results.

Having a low number of negative outlier trades can lead to a false sense of security. If all or most of the negative outlier trades come in one year, the results can be far worse than what was expected. The following chart shows how negative outlier trades, as a percentage of total trades for the year, would have been distributed through time:

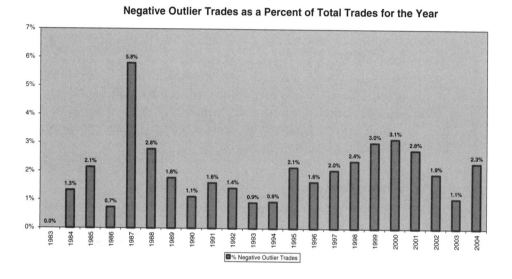

The next chart illustrates how positive outlier trades would have been distributed throughout time. These are trades that resulted in a net gain that exceeded estimated initial risk. Studies such as these provide insight into how effective a system is in different market environments.

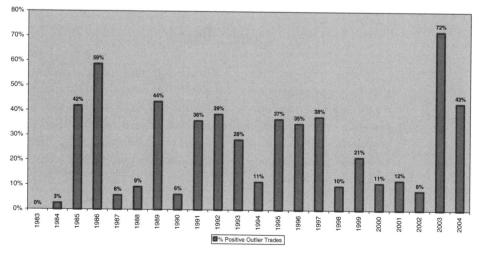

Short Selling

For the purposes of this project, we decided against testing short-selling[6] strategies. Our reasons for this have to do with the following issues.

Forced Buy-Ins

A short seller has to borrow shares before they can short sell them. Likewise, the short seller must return (deliver) the shares should the brokerage firm call them back. From the historical data available, there is no way to know *when or if* a short seller would have been subject to a forced buy-in.[7]

Borrowing Shares

Short selling a security requires borrowing shares from an investor who holds them in a margin account. Not all stocks meet these criteria all the time; some never meet these criteria at all. There is no reliable method to determine what stocks from the investable universe would have been realistically shortable in the past.

Limited Expectancy

With respect to long-term trend following, short selling offers a severely limited mathematical expectancy. The price of a stock can decline only by a maximum of 100 percent. However, it can rise by an infinite amount. This is a significant disability to overcome.

Tax Efficiency

The average hold time for the average trade came in lower than the 12 months necessary to qualify for long-term capital gains treatment. However, due to the nature of trend following systems in general, this statistic is misleading. There was a significant correlation between trade length and profitability, showing that the vast majority of historical profits would have qualified for long-term capital gains treatment.

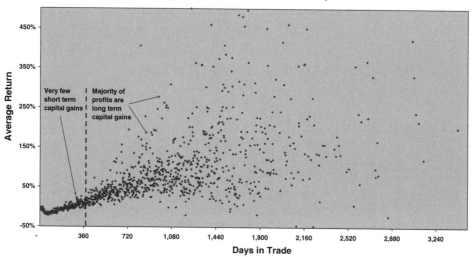

Average Trade Result Relative To Days in Trade

Diversification

The following table shows how many positions would have resulted from entering stocks at all time highs and exiting with a 10 ATR stop while honoring all data integrity and realistic universe issues. The resulting average number of positions per year exceeds that of most mutual funds.

Year	Average Number of Positions	Year	Average Number of Positions
1983	148	1994	808
1984	74	1995	1078
1985	215	1996	1455
1986	336	1997	1668
1987	319	1998	1305
1988	150	1999	983
1989	439	2000	970
1990	299	2001	722
1991	634	2002	607
1992	782	2003	708

(continues)

Year	Average Number of Positions	Year	Average Number of Positions
1993	1046	2004	1197
		2005	1779
		2006	1767
		2007	1854
		2008	750

Conclusions

The evidence suggests that trend following can work well on stocks. Buying stocks at new all time highs and exiting them after they've fallen below a 10 ATR trailing stop would have yielded a significant return on average. The evidence also suggests that such trading would not have resulted in significant tax burdens relative to buy-and-hold investing. Test results show the potential for diversification exceeding that of the typical mutual fund. The trade results distribution shows significant right skew, indicating that large outlier trades would have been concentrated among winning trades rather than losing trades. At this stage, we are comfortable answering the question, "Does trend following work on stocks?" The evidence strongly suggests that it does.

Further Research

The research described so far in this appendix was only a small initial step in a complex process. Portfolio level money management is absolutely essential to the success of a trend following system. Controlling risk at the portfolio level encompasses initial position sizing, scaling into and out of individual positions, total open risk constraints, and so on.

Having determined that a significant positive mathematical expectancy does exist for long-term trend following on stocks, we took the next step and implemented our proprietary portfolio and risk management process.

Portfolio Simulation[8]

Although a complete discussion is beyond the scope of this appendix, the following hypothetical returns reflect the application of the portfolio management system we use to manage client and proprietary capital.

The mechanics behind our portfolio management system are not disclosed; however, the system strictly adheres to the following principles:

- Losing trades are never added to.
- Winning trades are reduced only to alleviate risk concentrations.
- New entries are never skipped.
- Stop losses are always honored.
- Total open risk at the portfolio level is always *limited* to a specific number.

Hypothetical Equity Curve

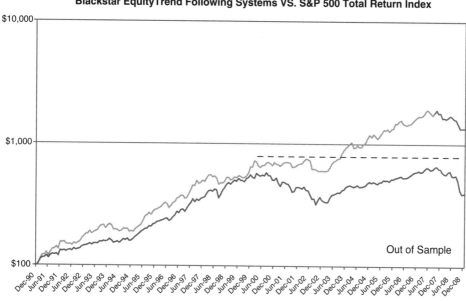

Hypothetical Monthly Returns

	Jan	Feb	Mar	Apr	May	Jun	Jul	Aug	Sep	Oct	Nov	Dec	Blackstar	S&P 500	+/-
1991	4.7%	9.3%	6.4%	0.0%	5.1%	-6.3%	7.4%	5.3%	1.2%	3.5%	4.3%	14.3%	55.2%	30.5%	24.7%
1992	-0.7%	1.3%	-4.0%	-1.0%	1.0%	-2.5%	4.6%	-2.1%	2.5%	1.9%	6.3%	4.9%	12.4%	7.6%	4.8%
1993	3.6%	0.5%	5.3%	-4.5%	2.7%	1.9%	1.6%	6.4%	2.7%	1.0%	-6.2%	5.5%	21.5%	10.1%	11.4%
1994	2.8%	-2.3%	-7.7%	0.3%	-1.1%	-2.9%	2.1%	4.0%	-1.2%	0.8%	-5.5%	1.5%	-9.3%	1.3%	-10.6
1995	-1.6%	4.8%	3.7%	2.2%	3.5%	7.1%	8.9%	2.1%	4.3%	-3.1%	5.6%	3.5%	48.9%	37.6%	11.3%
1996	1.0%	2.4%	2.3%	3.9%	4.0%	-2.0%	-7.8%	5.0%	5.1%	2.2%	6.3%	2.0%	26.2%	23.0%	3.2%
1997	3.5%	0.0%	-5.2%	1.3%	7.8%	7.6%	9.3%	-1.2%	10.4%	-5.6%	1.9%	4.1%	37.7%	33.4%	4.3%
1998	-2.0%	7.0%	6.1%	0.0%	-3.8%	1.8%	-4.1%	-10.9%	3.3%	-0.9%	3.1%	8.1%	6.1%	28.6%	-22.5%
1999	-0.2%	-4.7%	2.3%	3.7%	-1.6%	4.3%	-1.5%	-2.3%	0.1%	3.4%	5.4%	12.8%	22.6%	21.0%	1.6%
2000	-0.7%	12.8%	-2.1%	-7.7%	-2.4%	4.1%	0.2%	4.9%	0.9%	-2.6%	-3.8%	6.7%	9.0%	-9.1%	18.1%
2001	-3.2%	-1.4%	-2.3%	4.0%	2.5%	0.8%	-0.4%	-1.1%	-7.4%	0.5%	1.7%	3.0%	-3.8%	-11.9%	8.1%
2002	1.1%	0.9%	4.8%	4.0%	-1.2%	-2.1%	-15.0%	0.9%	-1.5%	-2.6%	-0.2%	0.3%	-11.4%	-22.1%	10.7%
2003	-0.6%	0.0%	1.2%	6.2%	8.0%	3.8%	1.9%	3.0%	1.2%	9.7%	5.4%	5.6%	55.5%	28.7%	26.8%
2004	2.8%	4.3%	3.0%	-9.6%	0.3%	4.2%	-3.2%	0.2%	5.2%	2.9%	9.6%	5.5%	26.7%	10.9%	15.8%
2005*	-3.57%	5.35%	-3.79%	-4.21%	5.24%	4.68%	7.10%	-1.02%	2.86%	-5.15%	5.33%	1.09%	13.6%	4.8%	8.7%
2006*	9.62%	-0.26%	4.47%	2.35%	-6.44%	-1.69%	-1.04%	1.97%	0.69%	4.85%	4.17%	2.59%	22.4%	15.2%	7.2%
2007*	3.33%	-1.43%	2.47%	5.04%	5.68%	-1.52%	-5.10%	-3.17%	4.84%	5.22%	-6.14%	0.66%	9.3%	5.1%	4.1%
2008*	-9.11%	0.32%	-1.54%	2.50%	3.50%	-2.34%	-3.86%	-1.55%	-7.58%	-7.92%	0.12%	-0.07%	-25.0%	-36.8%	11.8%

Annual Compounded Return	**15.5%**	**7.9%**
Annual Standard Deviation	**15.6%**	**14.3%**
Maximum Drawdown	**-29.3%**	**-44.9%**

*Out of sample years
Hypothetical portfolio returns are net of all trading costs including estimated commissions, slippage and margin expense.

Appendix 1: Examples of Recent Winning Trades

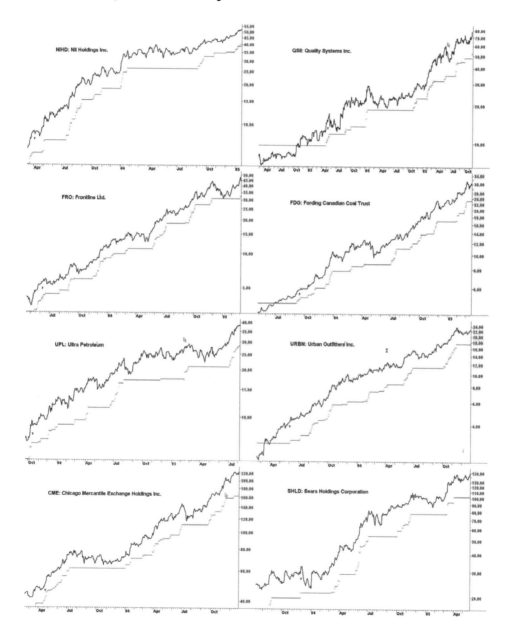

Appendix 2: Examples of Stocks That Were Entered, Exited, and Then Re-Entered

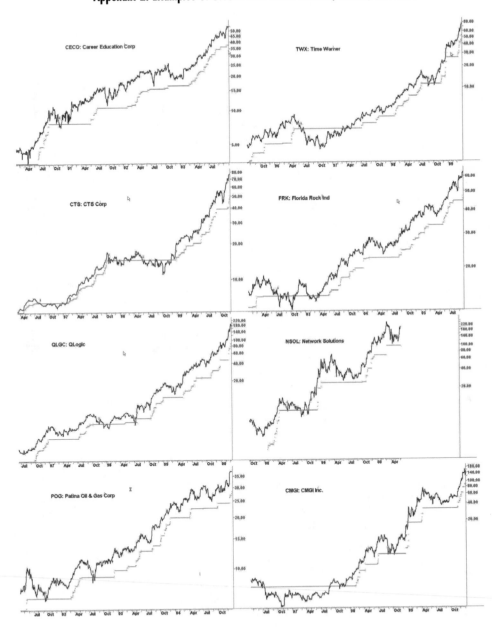

Appendix 3: Examples of Boom/Bust Stocks from the Past

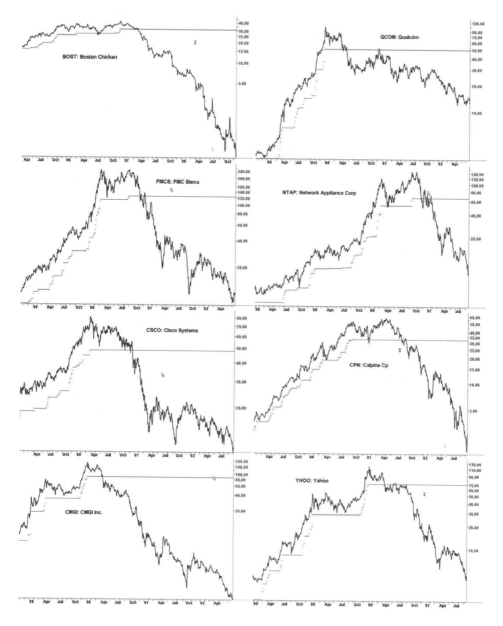

Appendix 4: Data Integrity Issues

The scope of this project included all stocks that traded on U.S. exchanges (AMEX, NYSE, and NASDAQ) from 1983 to year end 2004. This amounted to more than 24,000 securities spanning 22 years.

Delisted Stocks, Symbol Overlap, and Unique Identifiers

In our experience, a very common mistake made in testing stock trading strategies is the failure to understand and deal with the reality that actively traded securities existed for companies that have since gone out of business or have been acquired by other companies. These securities will *not* show up in most databases. Only the securities of "surviving" companies will show up in the typical database or charting service. To account for this survivorship bias, delisted companies were included in our universe. Because current companies sometimes use ticker symbols that were previously used by former (since delisted) companies, a unique serial number was necessary to identify each stock.

At the time of this writing, the entire database showed 24,057 individual securities. However, only 11,384 securities were active on U.S. exchanges. This left 12,673 securities that did exist historically but do not exist now. Most databases will omit these 12,673 securities, leading to erroneous results from any kind of historical testing. In the interest of accuracy, we chose to include these data in our testing.

The following illustrations are examples of companies whose shares became worthless and are thus not reflected in most of today's databases:

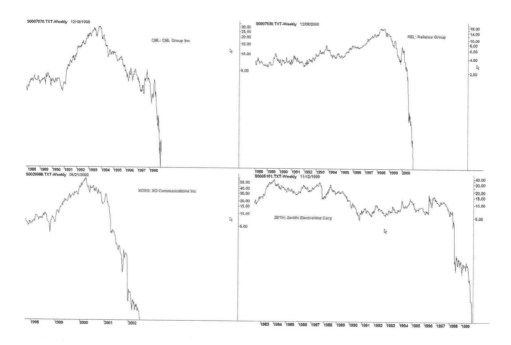

Adjustments for Corporate Actions (stock-splits, dividends, mergers, and so on)

Another common mistake made in testing stock-trading strategies is the failure to understand and deal with corporate actions. Most notably, databases and charting services often ignore cash dividends. This is unfortunate because a cash dividend is part of a shareholder's return on investment. Stocks almost always "gap down" by the amount of the dividend on the ex-dividend date.[9] The following illustrations show two different charts for the same security over the same time frame. The first is *not* adjusted for dividends and shows that Cousins Properties gapped down $6.65 on November 19, 2004, resulting in a one-day loss of 19.5 percent.

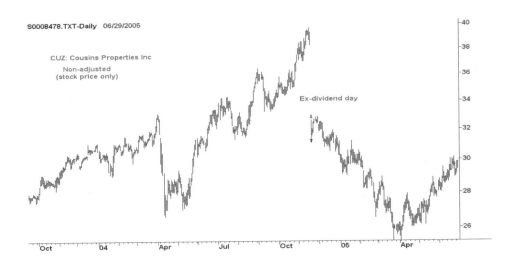

The second chart is adjusted for dividends and shows that Cousins Properties finished the day with a mild loss of only –1.3 percent. It turns out that November 19, 2004 was the ex-dividend date, the day after the owner of record has been determined regarding the $7.15 dividend.

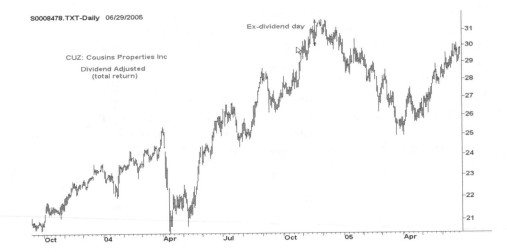

In reality, the security did gap down $6.65 and did trade even lower to close down –$7.66 for the day. But the owner of the security did *not* incur a 19.5 percent loss. Rather, the owner of the security became the beneficiary of a $7.15 dividend, and thus his/her return on investment should be calculated as a loss of 1.3 percent for the day. For the purposes of historical testing, this can be done by proportionally back adjusting previous price data down by a value equal to the amount of the dividend divided by the close on the day preceding the ex-dividend date.

Failure to adjust for dividends causes more than just erroneous profit and loss results. If you are using mathematically derived entries and exits for trading purposes, non-adjusted data will corrupt the logic of your system. For example, consider two investors starting their programs in December 2004. Both investors utilize the same strategy where a stock is purchased if it breaks out to a new 5-year high. Investor A is not using dividend-adjusted data and must wait for Cousins Properties to break out above $39.81. Investor B is using dividend-adjusted data and thus would be buying on a breakout above $31.62.

We will argue that Investor A is unnecessarily waiting for a price of $39.81. Investor B is correct to use a price of $31.62 as a key breakout point because it is not possible for any investor to have a loss in the investment above this price level. Any investor who purchased at higher prices and still owns the stock would have also been the shareholder of record prior to the ex-dividend date and would have received the $7.15 dividend.

The following illustrations highlight the significance of failure to adjust for dividends in high yielding stocks:

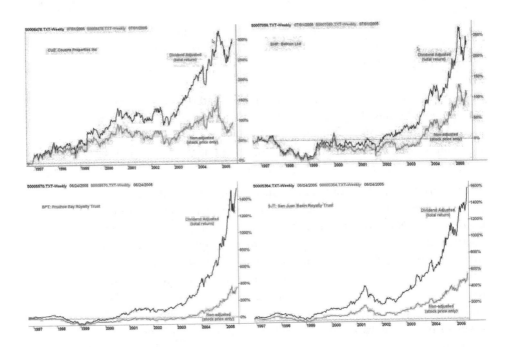

The same error impacts exits (stops) in a similar manner. A casual glance at the first chart of Cousins Properties clearly shows significant volatility that is a function only of a corporate action, not of monetary losses. This "phantom" volatility can result in your exit price being breached when it otherwise would not have been, as well as negatively impacting risk-adjusted return metrics.

A price chart supplied by the typical database or charting service often does not tell the whole story. Failure to adjust for cash dividends will result in an understatement of the profitability of owning dividend paying stocks. This error is a direct function of the dividend yield of the security in question; the higher the yield, the greater the error. Failure to adjust for cash dividends will also overstate the profitability of any short-selling strategies because the short seller (who must borrow shares to short) is responsible for compensating the actual owner of the shares for any dividends paid. Entries, exits, and subsequent profitability estimates are all impacted by any failure to properly adjust for cash dividends.

For the previous reasons, we have proportionately back adjusted our entire database for cash dividends, stock dividends, stock splits, reverse splits, and various other types of corporate actions.

Realistic Universe of Tradable Securities

A database consisting of all stocks that traded on U.S. exchanges since 1983 will include thousands of penny stocks and securities that were simply too illiquid to generate trustworthy historical test results from. For this reason, we created "minimum stock price" and "minimum average daily dollar volume" filters to limit our trading universe. Non-adjusted historical closing price and volume data are required to calculate both. If you'll recall from the last section on dividend adjusted data, the adjustment process artificially deflates historical prices in order to keep daily percent changes in line with what an investor would have realized. The higher the dividend yield, the more deflated the price series becomes during proportional back adjustment.

Having non-adjusted price information available makes it possible, through the use of formulas, to utilize "minimum stock price" and "minimum average daily dollar volume" filters historically *as the trades actually would have been executed or rejected.*

We chose $15 as the "minimum stock price." It was not a scientific decision. Rather, it was based on our current policy to avoid very low priced stocks. Low priced stocks tend to have relatively high statistical volatility and little institutional following. That being said, the "minimum stock price" filter was made to be dynamic, accepting stocks that climbed higher than $15 and rejecting stocks that fell to below $15. The "minimum average daily dollar volume" was chosen, in current terms, to be $500,000 for NYSE and AMEX listed securities; $1,000,000 for NASDAQ securities. This minimum value was back adjusted, in terms of time, with a decay rate equal to that of inflation, as defined by the consumer price index. For example, the "minimum average daily dollar volume" for an NYSE or AMEX security would have been $270,000 in 1983.

The Capitalism Distribution: Observations of Individual Common Stock Returns, 1983–2006

When most people think of the stock market they do so in terms of index results such as the S&P 500 or Russell 3000. They are unaware of the massive differences between successful stocks and failed stocks "under the hood" of their favorite index.

- 39 percent of stocks were unprofitable investments.
- 18.5 percent of stocks lost at least 75 percent of their value.
- 64 percent of stocks underperformed the Russell 3000.
- 25 percent of stocks were responsible for all of the market's gains.
- High performance stocks all tended to have one thing in common.

We make the case for the Capitalism Distribution, a nonnormal distribution with very fat tails that reflects the observed realities of long-term individual common stock returns.

Our database covers all common stocks that traded on the NYSE, AMEX, and NASDAQ since 1983, including delisted stocks. Stock and index returns were calculated on a total return basis (dividends reinvested). Dynamic point-in-time liquidity filters were used to limit our universe to the approximately 8,000 (due to index reconstitution, delisting, mergers, and so on) stocks that would have qualified for membership in the Russell 3000 at some point in their lifetime. The Russell 3000 Index measures the performance of the largest 3,000 U.S. companies representing approximately 98 percent of the investable U.S. equity market.

Total Lifetime Returns for individual U.S. stocks 1983-2006

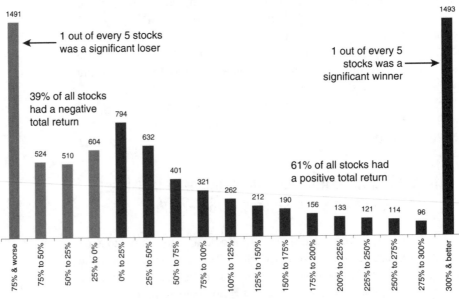

Stock's lifetime total return

The following chart shows the *lifetime* total return for individual stocks relative to the *corresponding* return for the Russell 3000. (Stocks return from X-date to Y-date minus index return from X-date to Y-date.)

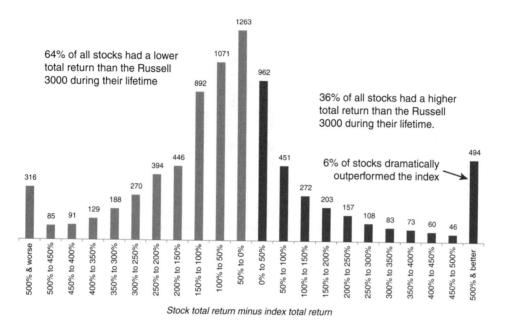

Total returns of individual stocks VS. Russell 3000 index, 1983 to 2006

64% of all stocks had a lower total return than the Russell 3000 during their lifetime

36% of all stocks had a higher total return than the Russell 3000 during their lifetime.

6% of stocks dramatically outperformed the index

Stock total return minus index total return

The fat tails in this distribution are notable. 494 (6.1 percent of all) stocks outperformed the Russell 3000 by at least 500 percent during their lifetime. Likewise, 316 (3.9 percent of all) stocks lagged the Russell 3000 by at least 500 percent.

The next chart shows the *lifetime* annualized return for individual stocks relative to the *corresponding* return for the Russell 3000.

Annualized Returns Individual Stocks VS. Russell 3000, 1983 to 2006

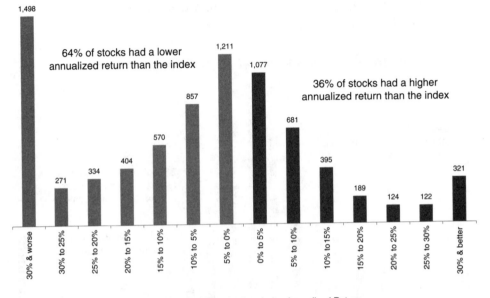

Stock Annualized Return minus Index Annualized Return

The left tail in this distribution is significant. 1,498 (18.6 percent of all) stocks dramatically underperformed the Russell 3000 during their lifetime.

The next chart shows the cumulative distribution of the annualized returns of all stocks.

You may be wondering how the Russell 3000 index can have an overall positive rate of return if the average annualized return for all stocks is negative. The answer is mostly a function of the index construction methodology. The Russell 3000 is market capitalization weighted. This means that successful companies (rising stock prices) receive larger weightings in the index. Likewise, unsuccessful companies (declining stock prices) receive smaller weightings. Eventually unsuccessful companies are removed from the index (delisted), making way for growing companies. In this way, market capitalization weighted indexation is like a simple trend following system that rewards success and punishes failure.

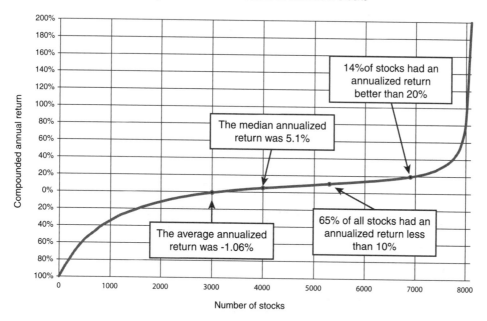

Compounded Annual Returns for Individual Stocks

It's also important to point out that stocks with a negative annualized return had shorter life spans than their successful counterparts. The average life span of a losing stock was 6.85 years versus 9.23 years for winning stocks (many of which are still living right now), meaning that losing stocks have shorter periods of time to negatively impact index returns. For these reasons, the average annualized return is probably a somewhat deceptive number for the purposes of modeling the "typical" stock, but interesting nonetheless.

The astute reader, at this point, is probably wondering if outperforming large capitalization stocks explain the observed distributions. Mathematically this would make sense. Small cap stocks certainly outnumber large cap stocks, while large cap stocks dominate the index weightings. However, while large cap stocks (Russell 1000) have outperformed small cap stocks (Russell 2000) over the long term, it has been by less than 1 percent per year, certainly not enough to explain our observations.

The next chart shows how stocks, when sorted from least profitable to most profitable, contributed to the total gains produced from all stocks. The conclusion is that if an investor was somehow unlucky enough to miss the 25 percent most profitable stocks and instead invested in the other 75 percent, his/her total gain from 1983 to 2007 would have been 0 percent. In other words, a minority of stocks are responsible for the majority of the market's gains.

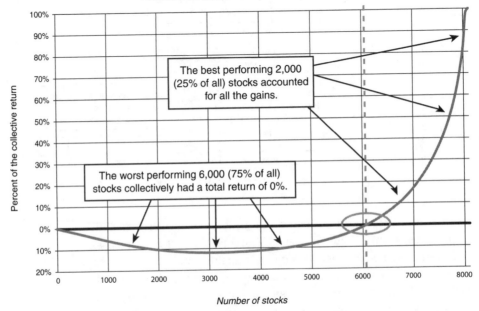

Attribution of collective total return 1983 - 2006

We identified the best performing stocks on both an annualized return and total return basis and studied them extensively. The biggest winning stocks on an annualized return basis had a moderate tendency to be technology stocks and most (60 percent) were bought out by another company or a private equity firm; not surprising.

Some of the biggest winners on a total return basis were companies that had been acquired. Examples include Sun America, Warner Lambert, Gillette, Golden West Financial, and Harrah's Entertainment. However, most (68 percent) are still trading today. Not surprisingly, they are almost exclusively large cap companies.

However, further research suggests that they weren't large companies when they were enjoying the bulk of their cumulative returns. Becoming a large cap is simply the natural result of significant price appreciation above and beyond that of the other stocks in the market. We were not able to detect any sector tendencies. The biggest winners on a total return basis were simply the minority that outperformed their peers.

Both the biggest winners on annualized return and total return basis tended to have one thing in common while they were accumulating market beating gains. Relative to average stocks, they spent a disproportionate amount of time making new multi-year highs. Stock ABC can't typically travel from $20 to $300 without first crossing $30 and $40. Such a stock is going to spend a lot of time making new highs. Likewise, the worst performing stocks tended to spend zero time making new multi-year highs while they were accumulating losses. Instead, relative to average stocks, they tended to spend a disproportionate amount of time at multi-year lows.

Mathematically, it makes perfect sense. Stocks that generate thousands of percent returns will hit new highs hundreds of times, usually over the course of many years.

	On the Way Up Number New Highs	Gain	After the Peak Number New Highs	Loss
Cisco Systems	488	99975%	0	−81%
General Electric	1011	25316%	0	−71%
Ford Motor	348	5484%	0	−94%
General Motors	384	3151%	0	−95%
Citigroup	353	5519%	0	−90%
Microsoft	424	62188%	0	−61%
Fannie Mae	342	8531%	0	−99%
Intel Corp.	304	16898%	0	−81%
American Intl Group	348	3974%	0	−98%
Bear Stearns	285	4691%	0	−95%

Charts

Winners

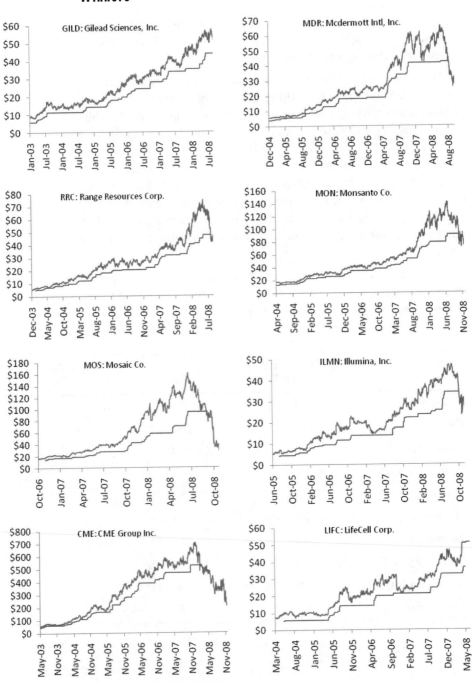

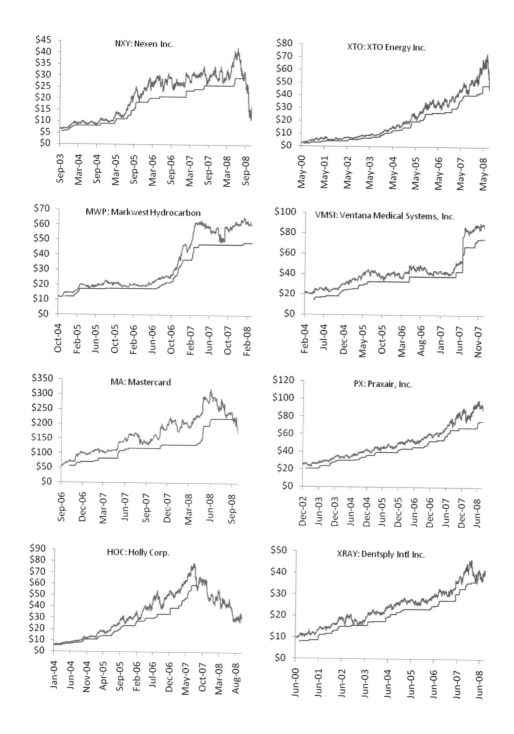

Big Historical Winners

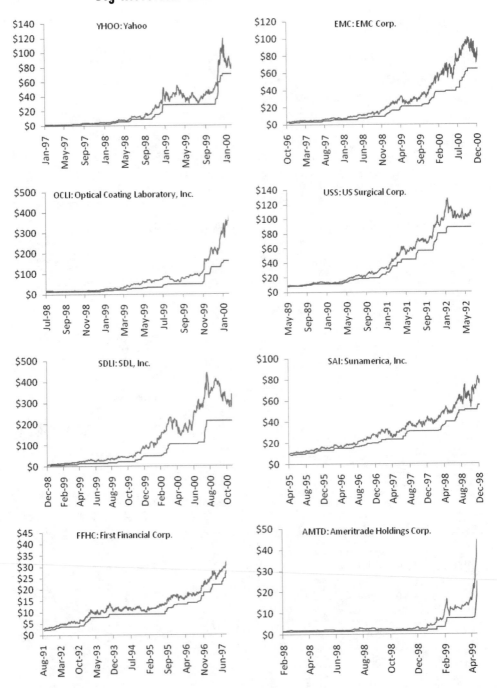

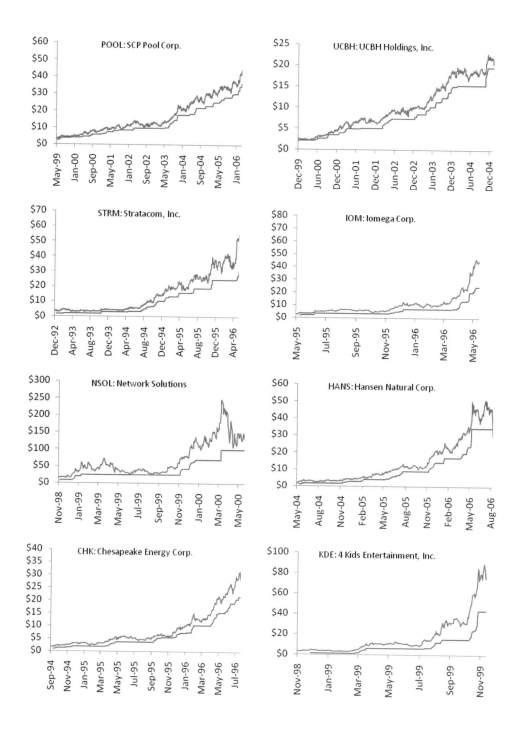

Failed Companies

ENR: Enron Corp.

ADE: Adelphia Communications Corp.

ULTE: Ultimate Electronics, Inc.

WCOM: Worldcom

CNC: Conseco, Inc.

XOXO: XO Communications, Inc.

LNX: Lenox Group, Inc.

CPN: Calpine Corp.

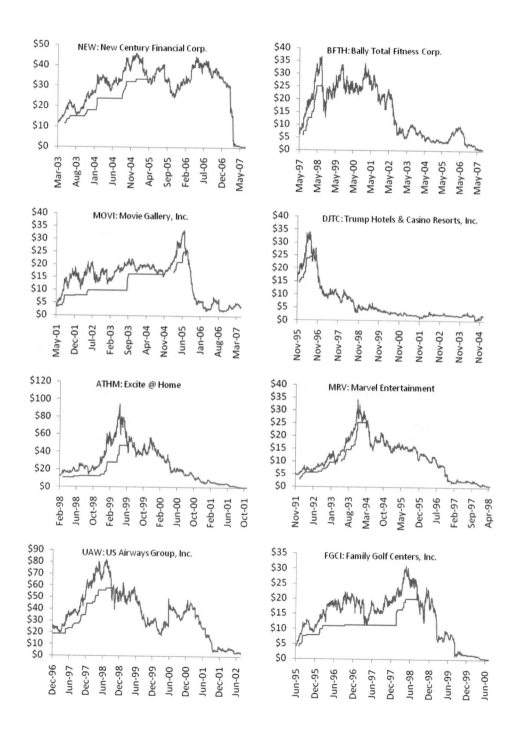

Blowups

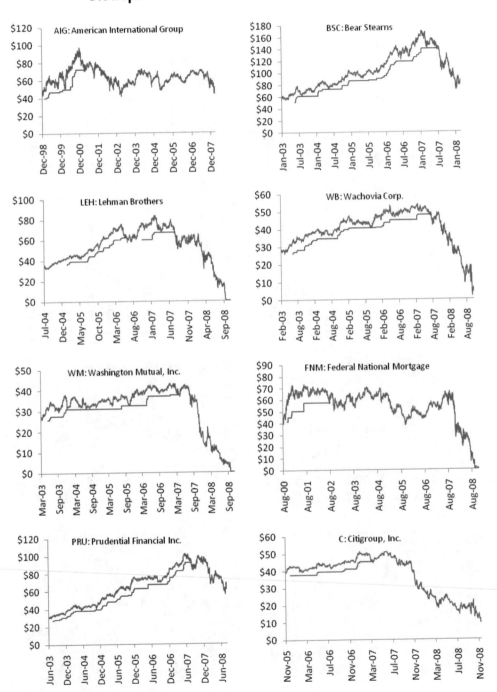

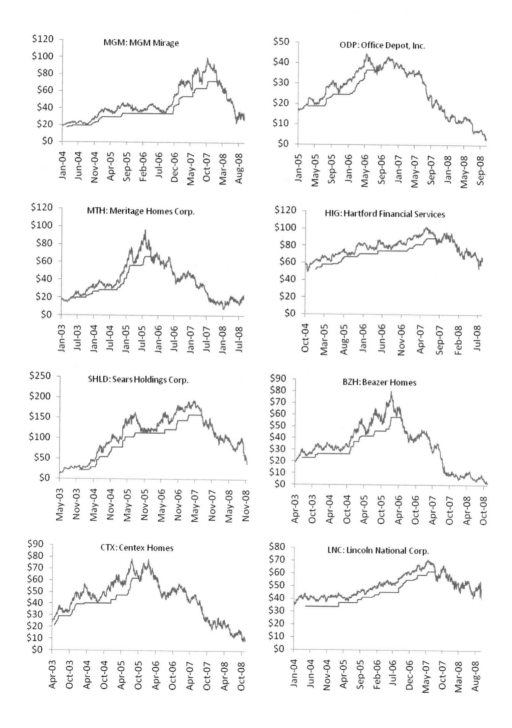

Current Long Position

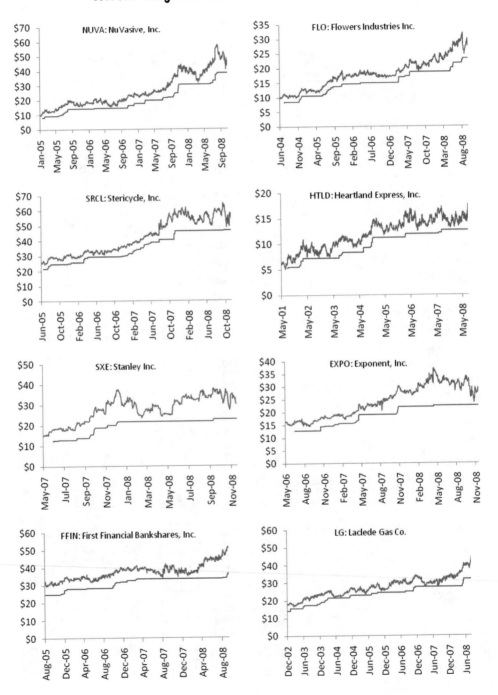

Performance Guide

B

Trend Following Historical Performance Data

Appendix B contains historical performance data from professional trend followers, so that you can see the concrete results for yourself. I had planned to include this data in the first release of the book, but editors thought it would be too much information. As you might have guessed, some readers questioned whether the performance numbers I gave were real, which made me realize how important it was to add the performance data back in for this edition. If you have questions about any trader or track record that I mentioned, feel free to contact me at my blog at www.michaelcovel.com.

Abraham Trading Company

Annual Performance Breakdown

	Yearly Statistics	
Year	**Return**	**Drawdown**
2008	28.77%	
2007	19.20%	−7.24%
2006	8.93%	−9.03%
2005	−10.95%	−26.80%

(continues)

Yearly Statistics		
Year	Return	Drawdown
2004	15.38%	–12.25%
2003	74.66%	–14.71%
2002	21.51%	–11.81%
2001	19.50%	–14.11%
2000	13.54%	–17.00%
1999	4.76%	–15.17%
1998	4.39%	–14.34%
1997	10.88%	–12.05%
1996	–0.42%	–19.69%
1995	6.12%	–21.02%
1994	24.22%	–10.99%
1993	34.29%	–10.50%
1992	–10.50%	–26.55%
1991	24.39%	–27.01%
1990	89.95%	–7.90%
1989	17.81%	–31.96%
1988	142.04%	–22.12%

Month by Month Returns

Month by Month Returns											
Year	Jan	Feb	Mar	Apr	May	Jun	Jul	Aug	Sep	Oct	Nov	Dec
1988	4.17	–2.59	–8.78	–12.35	32.34	71.99	–2.82	3.45	–1.98	8.01	17.83	4.51
1989	–8.05	–12.64	13.91	–20.08	38.65	–4.4	16.08	–13.84	–7.75	–14.40	10.30	39.52
1990	3.65	1.81	9.45	12.90	–7.90	2.49	20.08	18.54	8.57	–0.36	0.31	–0.09
1991	–15.94	1.30	2.43	–13.70	2.94	2.11	–1.52	–6.33	11.61	16.61	–2.09	33.75
1992	–12.60	–6.00	–5.47	0.31	–5.71	6.58	16.52	1.92	–0.34	–3.31	4.65	–4.54
1993	–4.21	6.10	4.57	9.24	4.88	–1.22	6.60	–5.28	1.16	–6.59	3.71	12.83

					Month by Month Returns							
Year	Jan	Feb	Mar	Apr	May	Jun	Jul	Aug	Sep	Oct	Nov	Dec
1994	−1.45	−4.16	2.87	−8.39	15.01	1.47	0.98	−7.38	5.05	5.43	14.24	1.06
1995	−7.91	1.24	6.63	4.73	8.22	0.11	−8.75	−5.34	−1.84	−6.67	−0.19	19.11
1996	−6.85	−13.78	9.66	14.27	−9.41	1.52	−6.30	−3.34	6.03	16.84	2.45	−6.41
1997	5.28	9.15	−1.50	−5.16	−1.32	0.38	4.11	−8.08	4.95	−5.37	2.10	7.46
1998	−0.90	4.09	−4.45	−4.45	2.61	−2.34	−0.83	23.24	−3.33	−11.39	0.94	4.67
1999	−11.56	13.35	−9.43	7.52	−6.09	−0.68	−0.83	3.12	0.99	−9.57	13.64	8.41
2000	8.02	−9.05	−4.16	5.48	−2.58	−2.19	−5.26	11.76	−4.53	9.51	8.58	−0.18
2001	2.28	2.99	15.17	−10.20	5.13	4.47	−2.58	4.89	9.28	4.13	−13.68	−0.50
2002	−1.73	1.33	−6.62	4.99	1.51	7.75	−3.97	9.86	3.29	−10.19	−1.80	18.41
2003	24.18	13.18	−4.73	2.02	5.59	−7.06	−4.86	−3.54	7.02	22.09	−0.03	8.69
2004	0.47	8.38	0.88	−6.22	2.53	1.37	6.74	−12.25	7.84	4.32	2.79	−0.51
2005	−5.48	−8.95	−1.00	−10.04	1.93	6.66	−12.16	15.74	−5.79	−5.98	14.15	3.96
2006	2.56	−1.53	5.71	2.75	−1.70	−2.32	−5.26	2.72	−1.51	4.08	2.23	1.41
2007	−1.08	−4.00	−2.32	6.50	4.96	3.66	−2.54	−3.73	5.20	4.32	1.16	6.47
2008	6.44	6.57	−0.21	0.34	−0.94	2.04	−4.19	0.08	5.55	4.73	2.02	3.72[E]

E=estimated

Campbell & Company, Inc. — Financial Metals & Energy — Large Program

Annual Performance Breakdown

	Yearly Statistics	
Year	Return	Drawdown
2008	0.69%	
2007	−13.35%	−17.76%
2006	5.48%	−8.89%
2005	11.05%	−5.39%
2004	6.96%	−12.98%

(continues)

Yearly Statistics		
Year	**Return**	**Drawdown**
2003	20.41%	−5.29%
2002	16.39%	−8.09%
2001	6.21%	−9.62%
2000	14.32%	−4.12%
1999	6.81%	−4.83%
1998	20.07%	−5.88%
1997	18.75%	−7.57%
1996	35.96%	−5.63%
1995	19.46%	−4.91%
1994	−16.76%	−16.76%
1993	4.68%	−14.59%
1992	13.47%	−10.52%
1991	31.12%	−9.35%
1990	35.24%	−11.50%
1989	42.23%	−11.58%
1988	7.96%	−6.90%
1987	64.38%	−13.91%
1986	−30.45%	−41.92%
1985	33.05%	−14.51%
1984	26.96%	−5.50%
1983	−10.34%	−10.34%

Month by Month Returns

					Month by Month Returns							
Year	Jan	Feb	Mar	Apr	May	Jun	Jul	Aug	Sep	Oct	Nov	Dec
1983	—	—	—	-0.40	0.18	-3.71	3.27	-1.47	0.83	-4.18	-1.93	-3.21
1984	1.27	2.12	2.44	0.09	9.78	-5.50	6.86	-1.34	8.32	2.79	-3.12	1.49
1985	3.63	11.59	0.74	5.97	2.92	-2.18	5.48	-3.63	-11.29	3.95	10.45	3.40
1986	-6.28	17.84	6.48	-7.87	5.01	-17.68	5.21	7.61	-17.22	-11.74	-11.84	1.84
1987	33.71	3.23	13.51	15.39	-4.17	-3.21	9.80	-1.12	2.71	-13.45	-0.53	2.11
1988	-0.08	2.39	-1.88	-5.12	1.63	8.29	-0.68	-0.22	4.80	-0.06	-0.35	-0.42
1989	7.90	-1.99	10.74	1.94	13.72	1.88	0.55	-0.81	-4.27	-6.88	2.46	12.88
1990	3.00	0.59	3.37	4.62	-11.50	8.29	10.04	12.30	2.59	1.25	-1.35	-0.54
1991	-7.89	-1.59	20.41	-1.87	2.81	1.49	-7.96	3.79	6.07	0.63	-2.03	17.45
1992	-5.45	-3.58	1.04	-2.79	1.14	10.66	10.41	5.00	-2.17	-4.67	6.26	-1.34
1993	-0.71	13.74	-5.79	2.99	2.81	2.55	5.55	-4.33	-4.83	-6.19	0.59	-0.08
1994	-4.67	-6.81	7.00	-1.77	-2.78	5.25	-4.36	-3.79	6.92	0.36	-7.02	-5.07
1995	-4.53	5.85	9.58	2.08	0.88	-0.90	-4.05	5.83	-3.47	1.20	-0.24	6.82
1996	5.46	-5.63	5.62	3.49	-1.71	1.29	0.01	1.78	2.47	12.06	12.22	-4.30
1997	5.26	2.26	-2.08	-3.84	-1.84	2.23	9.27	-5.14	4.23	2.39	0.57	4.50
1998	3.25	-2.38	4.95	-5.90	4.34	2.04	-3.68	9.23	2.97	4.42	-0.50	0.67
1999	-4.83	1.45	0.87	5.60	-3.25	4.63	-0.15	1.22	1.76	-4.25	0.53	3.64
2000	3.70	-0.34	-1.96	-1.86	2.74	1.96	-1.72	3.08	-3.23	3.19	5.98	2.38
2001	-1.09	0.71	6.96	-8.08	1.23	-1.71	1.45	2.10	6.94	4.97	-9.62	3.71
2002	-0.71	-1.98	-1.60	-4.03	4.12	7.73	7.64	3.61	3.90	-4.75	-1.31	3.65
2003	7.75	7.71	-4.38	2.77	2.09	-0.77	-4.55	2.42	-1.37	2.85	0.79	4.29
2004	2.36	10.79	0.94	-6.67	-0.54	-3.14	-0.61	-1.10	-1.54	2.41	4.04	0.78
2005	-2.16	-1.10	0.12	0.50	5.00	6.24	1.01	-5.39	3.75	3.85	2.12	-2.76
2006	2.01	-1.58	4.27	-2.76	-2.78	-0.41	-0.10	-0.36	-2.78	1.76	0.80	7.81
2007	2.49	-5.58	-3.22	2.18	5.72	4.15	-10.81	-6.70	1.92	5.61	-6.14	-2.18
2008	-0.43	1.50	-0.15	-2.81	2.22	5.57	-1.28	-1.57	-1.59	-1.09	-1.35	0.60[E]

E=estimated

Chesapeake Capital Corporation — Diversified Program

Annual Performance Breakdown

Yearly Statistics		
Year	Return	Drawdown
2008	15.43%	
2007	2.33%	–23.36%
2006	10.88%	–10.17%
2005	–1.14%	–5.80%
2004	4.84%	–16.12%
2003	23.08%	–11.11%
2002	11.07%	–4.75%
2001	–7.98%	–15.15%
2000	5.23%	–11.66%
1999	3.30%	–12.59%
1998	16.31%	–5.40%
1997	9.94%	–7.88%
1996	15.05%	–7.64%
1995	14.09%	–7.48%
1994	15.87%	–8.52%
1993	61.82%	–2.69%
1992	1.81%	–16.62%
1991	12.51%	–8.58%
1990	43.12%	–4.61%
1989	28.30%	–20.58%
1988	48.91%	–19.05%

Month by Month Returns

					Month by Month Returns							
Year	Jan	Feb	Mar	Apr	May	Jun	Jul	Aug	Sep	Oct	Nov	Dec
1988	—	−2.63	−6.89	−10.71	6.93	32.42	−9.41	6.85	2.03	10.65	11.06	7.04
1989	4.93	−5.42	6.64	−8.82	22.38	−8.28	11.66	−11.75	−2.82	−7.40	3.90	28.56
1990	0.49	3.37	8.62	4.37	−4.61	1.77	6.25	15.15	0.60	1.86	−0.25	0.11
1991	−1.29	4.84	2.32	−2.80	0.27	−1.25	−1.75	−3.32	4.39	4.21	−4.68	12.08
1992	−10.98	−2.86	0.53	−0.44	−3.66	6.52	12.96	3.16	−6.78	5.21	2.27	−1.93
1993	0.42	15.99	5.86	7.38	0.40	0.98	9.49	5.88	−2.63	−0.06	1.03	5.77
1994	−3.33	−4.88	0.09	−0.60	9.06	7.02	−1.70	−2.98	3.49	1.97	4.83	2.86
1995	−3.23	−4.39	8.60	1.45	6.84	0.88	−3.09	−2.66	0.20	−1.11	1.76	9.18
1996	1.69	−4.26	0.28	10.16	−3.04	3.27	−7.64	0.57	6.47	5.92	6.57	−4.30
1997	1.86	5.48	−1.24	−2.41	−2.28	1.44	6.24	−7.88	5.06	−2.34	1.70	4.88
1998	−1.29	6.06	3.65	−2.16	3.62	−0.67	3.03	7.27	−0.59	−3.21	−1.68	1.80
1999	−2.76	1.90	−2.65	8.42	−8.71	3.57	−4.80	3.37	1.98	−7.88	4.16	8.49
2000	−0.87	0.92	1.88	−3.80	0.63	−0.99	−3.71	3.90	−7.30	−0.62	7.42	8.80
2001	−0.43	3.75	4.98	−7.50	−1.43	0.16	−3.06	−3.40	7.15	5.01	−10.09	−1.92
2002	−2.11	−1.79	2.43	−3.27	2.26	4.19	2.84	2.55	3.81	−2.63	−1.58	4.31
2003	6.52	3.61	−8.76	0.29	5.35	−5.65	−1.85	2.42	−2.78	15.48	1.91	6.61
2004	1.63	5.05	−2.70	−6.05	−0.50	−2.90	−1.86	−3.23	3.50	2.32	8.89	1.53
2005	−3.82	0.46	0.92	−3.62	−1.25	3.40	0.45	4.70	−1.10	−4.75	4.33	1.97
2006	5.54	−0.70	5.37	3.19	−1.50	−0.74	−2.13	−4.66	−1.53	1.38	3.38	3.35
2007	2.63	−2.33	−1.27	4.53	5.48	0.80	−8.30	−16.42	11.42	10.64	−6.73	5.57
2008	2.35	17.15	−7.49	0.63	2.07	9.48	−9.39	−7.50	−7.20	7.29	6.44	4.19

Clarke Capital Management, Inc. — Millennium Program

Annual Performance Breakdown

Yearly Statistics		
Year	Return	Drawdown
2008	94.66%	
2007	14.86%	-16.57%
2006	9.61%	-15.76%
2005	-13.48%	-16.98%
2004	10.49%	-10.06%
2003	40.66%	-18.26%
2002	34.62%	-14.58%
2001	-0.56%	-11.90%
2000	42.52%	-4.18%
1999	5.18%	-7.82%
1998	36.98%	-21.31%

Month by Month Returns

Month by Month Returns											
Year	Jan	Feb	Mar	Apr	May	Jun	Jul	Aug	Sep	Oct	Nov	Dec
1998	0.29	-6.94	-3.17	-12.67	16.89	-7.02	4.13	29.81	16.26	-6.90	5.45	3.51
1999	-1.68	1.12	-0.42	3.43	-6.49	5.09	4.74	-0.08	0.92	-7.82	7.39	-0.03
2000	3.09	0.77	-2.66	1.16	5.35	3.01	-3.26	5.96	-2.17	-2.05	12.57	16.11
2001	2.38	0.71	8.60	-9.15	2.88	-5.37	2.26	-0.26	-0.23	7.54	-7.28	-0.65
2002	-3.42	-5.54	-1.58	-8.12	2.06	16.44	11.26	8.14	2.35	-7.54	-5.51	27.63
2003	10.11	16.15	-18.26	4.31	25.01	-10.09	-4.13	2.5	3.36	8.23	-3.43	8.11
2004	-4.74	6.96	1.96	-7.36	8.06	-7.55	6.80	-8.91	11.60	1.97	9.39	-5.11

					Month by Month Returns							
Year	Jan	Feb	Mar	Apr	May	Jun	Jul	Aug	Sep	Oct	Nov	Dec
2005	−6.53	−4.64	3.24	−1.83	10.75	0.32	−10.71	12.22	−13.50	−4.02	5.76	−2.02
2006	−3.71	−3.54	0.64	20.25	2.15	−3.62	−10.47	−2.38	8.92	−1.37	4.41	1.04
2007	2.45	−8.61	−3.14	−0.76	−2.95	3.92	1.40	−7.13	19.36	7.95	2.97	1.28
2008	5.94	27.36	12.76	6.76	11.93	−0.81	−16.44	3.90	5.01	10.80	4.96	1.81

Drury Capital, Inc. — Diversified Trend Following Program

Annual Performance Breakdown

Yearly Statistics		
Year	Return	Drawdown
2008	76.17%	
2007	5.05%	−10.61%
2006	−15.40%	−19.40%
2005	−10.47%	−15.91%
2004	7.27%	−19.08%
2003	25.77%	−12.77%
2002	5.55%	−14.83%
2001	20.62%	−9.34%
2000	15.80%	−6.76%
1999	10.46%	−10.07%
1998	47.21%	−7.82%
1997	30.42%	−13.12%

Month by Month Returns

Month by Month Returns												
Year	**Jan**	**Feb**	**Mar**	**Apr**	**May**	**Jun**	**Jul**	**Aug**	**Sep**	**Oct**	**Nov**	**Dec**
1997	—	—	—	—	−4.57	14.98	12.49	−2.12	−2.08	−9.35	17.34	3.64
1998	7.84	6.11	6.60	−5.46	7.78	2.20	−1.38	19.34	−5.22	−2.74	4.25	2.46
1999	0.06	6.05	−2.82	4.46	−5.56	−0.36	−4.43	8.54	−3.59	−1.24	5.20	4.88
2000	−5.58	0.35	−1.59	11.91	1.14	−4.41	1.49	4.92	−1.70	3.26	6.33	−0.12
2001	−6.20	4.95	15.48	−4.19	2.41	4.97	−3.66	2.03	6.23	3.82	−9.34	4.82
2002	0.52	−1.32	−2.05	−3.68	−5.13	11.62	4.82	3.75	4.35	−9.42	−5.97	10.19
2003	7.76	6.94	−6.32	−4.10	9.42	−6.35	−4.41	−0.87	4.17	13.80	−1.03	6.64
2004	2.45	11.09	2.33	−6.97	−6.06	−1.21	−0.45	−5.85	7.78	−1.13	7.20	−0.36
2005	−2.34	−4.57	0.27	−5.56	−4.02	−2.42	−0.65	1.83	1.15	0.95	7.85	−2.78
2006	−0.51	−0.69	0.37	2.38	−2.15	−1.28	−6.44	−1.22	0.91	−4.47	−6.34	3.38
2007	3.33	−3.51	0.08	3.21	3.39	7.79	−5.60	−5.31	2.93	−0.67	3.56	−3.29
2008	6.78	11.17	−8.45	−5.44	7.44	6.63	−9.45	1.92	16.95	23.37	6.57	5.45

DUNN Capital Management, Inc. — World Monetary Assets

Annual Performance Breakdown

Yearly Statistics		
Year	**Return**	**Drawdown**
2008	51.47%	
2007	7.58%	−36.36%
2006	3.62%	−26.06%
2005	−16.39%	−23.92%
2004	−11.71%	−34.97%
2003	−13.40%	−28.86%
2002	54.05%	−23.41%

Yearly Statistics		
Year	**Return**	**Drawdown**
2001	1.12%	−23.52%
2000	13.22%	−41.41%
1999	13.14%	−10.97%
1998	13.67%	−18.05%
1997	44.42%	−12.02%
1996	58.38%	−17.46%
1995	98.63%	−6.50%
1994	−19.32%	−35. 13%
1993	60.04%	−5.00%
1992	−21.77%	−23.62%
1991	16.92%	−14.90%
1990	51.69%	−11.20%
1989	30.49%	−28.69%
1988	−18.77%	−22.66%
1987	72.15%	−7.18%
1986	3.42%	−26.89%
1985	−21.85%	−49.83%
1984	5.02%	−0.00%

Month by Month Returns

						Month by Month Returns						
Year	Jan	Feb	Mar	Apr	May	Jun	Jul	Aug	Sep	Oct	Nov	Dec
1984	—	—	—	—	—	—	—	—	—	—	11.00	18.00
1985	6.20	10.00	−7.30	−13.10	21.70	−6.80	−8.40	−13.50	−30.70	6.70	13.60	10.00
1986	−1.50	24.50	11.90	−5.60	−6.00	−14.00	−4.20	12.50	0.60	−2.80	−6.20	−0.10
1987	8.80	−1.80	7.20	31.60	−2.70	−4.60	6.00	−3.00	5.50	−5.60	17.80	2.00
1988	0.70	4.30	−6.50	−2.50	3.90	−0.60	−1.80	−2.70	2.00	1.90	−0.70	−16.70
1989	21.10	−4.20	9.30	6.10	20.00	3.20	8.20	−13.00	−1.60	−16.70	7.30	−5.40
1990	23.50	5.30	6.10	6.80	−11.20	4.00	1.40	2.10	3.80	−0.40	5.40	−1.20
1991	−7.00	−4.50	10.30	−4.50	−5.00	−0.50	−2.50	9.90	9.20	−14.90	1.20	31.20
1992	−14.50	−0.90	4.00	−15.10	−0.40	13.00	11.40	9.20	−8.20	−5.40	−4.30	−8.10
1993	3.00	14.00	−3.30	12.40	3.40	0.90	7.30	8.40	−5.00	1.60	1.00	6.00
1994	−1.70	−5.30	14.90	7.00	5.20	3.30	−13.40	−17.70	−4.70	−1.00	0.70	−4.20
1995	0.50	13.70	24.40	3.80	−2.60	−3.60	0.60	18.50	−6.50	10.80	11.20	4.40
1996	15.80	−13.30	9.60	9.20	−1.20	0.60	−12.40	−5.20	12.60	20.30	26.90	−7.10
1997	17.80	−0.20	2.20	−6.50	−5.90	10.40	16.80	−10.20	6.50	−0.60	9.80	1.50
1998	4.20	−5.30	4.00	−11.00	−4.80	−0.40	−1.40	27.50	16.20	3.80	−13.70	0.30
1999	−13.20	3.90	4.20	4.10	7.60	9.60	0.50	5.80	3.60	−7.00	1.30	−5.50
2000	6.90	−2.90	−17.30	−12.40	−7.60	−3.90	0.56	3.29	−9.70	9.12	28.04	29.39
2001	7.72	0.55	6.26	−8.96	−0.91	−8.31	0.09	6.47	1.13	20.74	−23.52	6.73
2002	3.03	−8.07	2.39	−5.71	5.41	24.24	14.82	10.50	9.10	−12.27	−12.70	21.34
2003	6.94	13.83	−22.44	1.57	9.45	−8.07	−4.75	16.70	−7.63	−4.23	−4.45	−4.47
2004	−2.86	8.38	−2.90	−18.35	−6.84	−9.86	−5.16	9.29	1.58	7.93	5.32	−0.69
2005	−4.09	−6.72	−4.04	−15.01	13.03	12.23	−1.89	−5.46	−3.51	−0.94	6.00	−3.88
2006	−3.63	−1.37	12.42	9.38	−7.78	−1.63	−5.69	−8.76	−5.22	5.93	4.35	8.41
2007	6.21	−8.30	−3.36	8.22	11.77	7.39	−17.75	−22.63	16.90	3.00	7.78	6.55
2008	19.94	29.55	−10.13	−6.55	1.67	3.56	−10.18	−9.26	1.02	21.09	7.77	2.60

Eckhardt Trading Company — Standard Program

Annual Performance Breakdown

Yearly Statistics		
Year	**Return**	**Drawdown**
2008	13.07%	
2007	35.62%	−4.06%
2006	2.56%	−6.40%
2005	8.57%	−1.86%
2004	4.49%	−10.98%
2003	15.01%	−2.45%
2002	11.07%	−5.49%
2001	5.34%	−4.65%
2000	17.94%	−5.07%
1999	−4.54%	−10.83%
1998	26.57%	−8.61%
1997	45.63%	−6.19%
1996	48.22%	−17.26%
1995	46.02%	−21.43%
1994	−11.69%	−12.93%
1993	57.63%	−8.28%
1992	−7.54%	−14.07%
1991	16.89%	−20.83%

Month by Month Returns

						Month by Month Returns						
Year	Jan	Feb	Mar	Apr	May	Jun	Jul	Aug	Sep	Oct	Nov	Dec
1991	−12.10	2.90	7.10	−9.10	−12.90	12.40	−1.50	−1.00	6.64	0.25	2.09	27.50
1992	−15.27	−7.56	−5.70	2.22	−3.45	9.35	11.43	7.51	−1.18	−4.35	7.70	−4.60
1993	−1.38	9.63	−8.28	9.41	3.81	12.13	9.41	4.85	−6.67	1.74	4.90	9.45
1994	−18.30	−0.70	10.58	2.17	5.05	1.66	−0.10	−8.59	13.36	−10.50	8.74	−10.45
1995	−1.39	8.85	14.13	3.21	20.13	−1.32	−10.31	−3.27	−2.80	−5.58	9.24	12.20
1996	8.72	−5.40	2.60	17.48	−9.28	−3.32	−4.28	−1.20	17.55	16.24	11.43	−5.51
1997	12.66	6.91	6.60	1.24	1.89	5.39	9.18	−4.11	6.51	−0.41	−3.54	−2.35
1998	4.77	2.48	−3.60	−5.17	1.89	1.57	−1.59	25.28	0.18	0.39	−0.10	0.65
1999	1.49	5.12	−6.18	−2.59	−2.43	1.43	5.18	−5.62	3.31	−2.86	0.04	−0.73
2000	−2.14	−0.61	−1.94	−0.29	1.88	−1.45	−2.71	0.43	1.48	0.83	12.30	10.02
2001	1.63	−1.07	0.40	−0.48	3.40	−3.28	−1.42	5.87	−3.28	5.58	−2.36	0.76
2002	2.69	−4.55	−0.99	3.92	−0.68	2.59	2.24	−0.34	−1.01	−1.90	−1.40	10.79
2003	1.56	7.26	−0.58	0.31	4.78	−0.80	−1.55	0.44	0.15	−0.70	0.86	2.69
2004	−2.22	4.28	−0.75	−4.37	0.04	−3.65	−2.69	4.40	0.86	5.96	4.38	−1.16
2005	−3.38	0.23	1.33	−1.79	6.16	3.25	−0.20	3.72	−1.86	0.31	0.59	0.27
2006	0.67	−2.13	−4.36	4.92	1.34	1.83	−3.54	1.83	−1.79	0.66	6.05	−2.33
2007	0.38	0.68	−4.06	3.21	1.71	5.47	1.26	−1.76	12.07	5.54	3.22	4.02
2008	1.85	10.01	0.21	0.14	1.70	3.10	−5.34	−2.71	2.65	0.17	1.20	0.04

John W. Henry & Company, Inc.— Financials and Metals Program

Annual Performance Breakdown

	Yearly Statistics	
Year	Return	Drawdown
2008	39.30%	
2007	–9.25%	–21.64%
2006	–8.52%	–19.56%
2005	–17.34%	–18.22%
2004	6.01%	–33.33%
2003	19.41%	–11.35%
2002	45.05%	–14.27%
2001	7.15%	–17.83%
2000	13.04%	–25.88%
1999	–18.69%	–23.90%
1998	7.21%	–18.30%
1997	15.26%	–13.53%
1996	29.67%	–5.53%
1995	38.52%	–4.04%
1994	–5.32%	–14.31%
1993	46.85%	–1.98%
1992	–10.89%	–39.53%
1991	61.88%	–15.45%
1990	83.60%	–22.73%
1989	34.62%	–37.17%
1988	4.02%	–19.93%
1987	252.42%	–27.59%
1986	61.55%	–19.88%
1985	20.66%	–34.68%
1984	9.93%	–3.16%

Month by Month Returns

| | | | | | Month by Month Returns | | | | | | | |
Year	Jan	Feb	Mar	Apr	May	Jun	Jul	Aug	Sep	Oct	Nov	Dec
1984	—	—	—	—	—	—	—	—	—	1.61	−3.16	11.72
1985	6.62	17.71	−9.28	−7.77	−7.69	−1.75	41.26	−10.12	−27.32	6.37	26.63	1.93
1986	4.79	21.87	−6.30	3.67	−17.52	17.57	24.95	9.42	−0.23	2.56	−3.56	−0.46
1987	33.01	12.10	34.24	18.23	−7.16	−10.69	12.25	−14.61	−8.89	28.02	32.54	21.21
1988	−12.56	9.77	−2.30	−15.02	0.28	44.19	5.47	6.89	−8.09	2.50	5.18	−19.19
1989	31.69	−8.66	8.51	3.17	37.03	−6.63	4.43	−8.17	−14.92	−17.53	21.63	−4.53
1990	27.98	19.50	11.40	2.41	−22.73	6.91	12.16	11.16	8.32	−5.01	3.09	−3.68
1991	−2.28	3.80	4.46	−0.79	−0.32	−1.29	−13.39	4.78	25.80	−7.74	6.62	39.37
1992	−18.03	−13.53	2.98	−12.17	−5.68	21.90	25.46	10.18	−5.23	−4.50	−0.80	−2.59
1993	3.34	13.89	−0.30	9.34	3.35	0.12	9.69	−0.78	0.22	−1.10	−0.33	2.88
1994	−2.93	−0.55	7.21	0.89	1.29	4.47	−6.11	−4.12	1.49	1.65	−4.38	−3.51
1995	−3.76	15.67	15.35	6.10	1.24	−1.66	−2.33	2.08	−2.13	0.31	2.64	1.65
1996	5.99	−5.53	0.66	2.28	−1.74	2.25	−1.13	−0.76	3.22	14.33	10.95	−2.55
1997	4.41	−2.23	−0.69	−2.85	−8.33	4.15	15.75	−3.65	2.20	2.02	2.48	2.86
1998	−3.50	−3.98	−1.56	−7.93	3.18	−4.84	−0.92	17.50	15.26	−3.78	−7.50	8.87
1999	−4.84	0.90	−2.56	1.63	5.89	6.12	−2.30	−3.15	−7.01	−8.12	−3.18	−2.78
2000	−3.59	−6.20	−2.28	2.51	−2.06	−8.97	−1.74	−0.43	−6.20	9.39	13.33	23.02
2001	3.34	2.53	12.84	−8.30	1.01	−4.14	−4.44	8.47	5.41	4.64	−17.83	7.44
2002	−0.81	−6.00	−5.45	−1.04	11.01	28.33	11.25	3.59	7.39	−8.53	−6.28	10.01
2003	11.38	4.51	−3.48	1.85	9.11	−4.96	−3.36	2.52	−3.86	0.65	−2.71	7.89
2004	1.66	6.53	−6.50	−10.73	−5.52	−5.45	−10.59	5.08	0.51	14.07	18.72	2.66
2005	−9.48	−6.74	−5.90	−1.70	8.67	9.37	−3.78	−12.82	−2.51	4.45	9.36	−4.63
2006	−2.47	−8.51	11.20	13.04	1.39	−12.10	−2.97	11.15	−3.78	−9.38	6.06	−8.24
2007	2.20	−10.45	−12.50	7.89	6.10	9.67	−11.58	3.14	2.27	−1.58	1.67	−3.28
2008	14.11	4.53	8.91	−15.47	1.14	−1.63	−10.73	3.87	0.45	27.25	7.30	7.30

Millburn Ridgefield Corporation — Diversified Program

Annual Performance Breakdown

	Yearly Statistics	
Year	Return	Drawdown
2008	20.70%	
2007	12.85%	–14.84%
2006	6.13%	–13.50%
2005	–3.89%	–7.85%
2004	–3.83%	–23.57%
2003	1.56%	–12.81%
2002	24.55%	–11.87%
2001	–5.80%	–14.44%
2000	12.70%	–13.14%
1999	–1.99%	–13.56%
1998	7.11%	–8.86%
1997	12.68%	–9.76%
1996	17.33%	–11.58%
1995	32.76%	–3.09%
1994	11.78%	–8.92%
1993	10.88%	–8.06%
1992	17.30%	–11.06%
1991	4.44%	–10.87%
1990	53.01%	–5.66%
1989	–0.94%	–28.13%
1988	2.70%	–12.52%
1987	35.80%	–14.86%
1986	–19.36%	–33.47%
1985	22.50%	–16.98%

(continues)

Yearly Statistics		
Year	Return	Drawdown
1984	21.72%	−14.10%
1983	−9.44%	−14.79%
1982	29.35%	−11.00%
1981	38.50%	−10.72%
1980	64.38%	−4.09%
1979	58.38%	−2.45%
1978	18.64%	−18.82%
1977	3.72%	−13.60%

Month by Month Returns

Month by Month Returns											
Year	Jan	Feb	Mar	Apr	May	Jun	Jul	Aug	Sep	Oct	Nov	Dec
1977	—	−1.07	2.27	6.23	−7.51	1.21	6.84	−4.37	−9.65	4.80	−3.62	10.57
1978	6.33	3.91	13.76	−17.86	12.78	−2.57	8.54	0.59	5.34	12.01	−14.17	−5.42
1979	−2.45	5.52	0.66	6.82	4.45	7.41	−1.76	1.82	14.84	−0.74	5.42	6.11
1980	20.82	3.81	8.62	−2.97	5.25	3.44	1.18	−2.32	−1.81	7.59	3.75	5.44
1981	11.39	10.40	−8.62	9.48	7.43	9.74	6.96	−0.15	−3.60	−4.79	8.24	−10.00
1982	4.77	8.68	9.14	−1.38	−0.82	8.99	−11.00	3.32	7.66	−4.04	−2.57	5.49
1983	6.28	−1.29	−2.12	−0.42	1.13	−6.95	−1.11	5.57	−2.05	2.25	−7.08	−3.13
1984	5.03	0.05	1.08	2.45	4.76	−6.11	19.22	−9.05	4.14	−2.80	−6.69	11.04
1985	5.69	7.69	−4.65	−2.12	−4.52	−2.12	14.68	−2.75	−14.63	9.15	12.43	5.61
1986	3.84	14.91	1.59	−7.05	−2.74	−9.34	5.98	7.22	−18.35	−6.21	−5.36	−1.44
1987	14.52	0.16	3.34	10.29	−3.59	−3.63	1.12	−3.72	−5.88	1.66	9.67	9.44
1988	−8.23	1.30	−4.11	−1.87	6.09	17.89	−9.26	−0.47	0.67	1.64	6.11	−4.27

Month by Month Returns

Year	Jan	Feb	Mar	Apr	May	Jun	Jul	Aug	Sep	Oct	Nov	Dec
1989	3.18	−4.67	7.53	−1.51	17.04	−8.11	−3.62	−8.53	−2.74	−8.78	4.74	7.93
1990	4.13	4.21	2.99	2.40	−5.66	3.51	16.05	3.39	2.67	7.65	3.00	0.24
1991	−5.32	1.40	2.60	−0.09	−1.13	1.63	−4.02	−6.09	0.91	−0.30	0.10	16.35
1992	−8.53	−1.34	−0.72	−0.73	0.90	14.25	8.87	7.56	−0.19	−3.95	2.66	−0.73
1993	−2.69	5.78	−0.70	5.76	−1.79	−2.54	5.11	−8.06	1.09	−0.70	1.33	9.02
1994	−7.56	−1.47	7.67	−2.27	4.63	5.80	−3.00	−5.26	3.68	3.02	4.76	2.46
1995	−3.09	6.81	16.85	4.64	−1.10	0.99	−2.48	1.43	−1.84	0.06	0.19	7.90
1996	7.43	−11.05	0.80	5.72	−6.72	3.91	1.37	−1.88	2.79	10.64	3.96	1.08
1997	8.14	5.72	−2.83	−3.01	1.50	0.52	8.15	−8.52	1.20	−2.22	−0.31	5.02
1998	2.87	−2.71	1.14	−7.38	4.04	2.32	−4.96	6.94	5.53	−1.84	−0.75	2.71
1999	−4.01	3.08	1.21	5.51	−3.34	5.80	−3.82	1.17	0.73	−11.81	2.19	2.68
2000	1.99	−1.73	−4.55	0.67	−1.94	−4.43	−1.85	3.23	−2.77	4.50	6.02	14.41
2001	0.62	−1.54	9.12	−5.39	1.89	−2.24	−5.38	3.26	−2.85	4.20	−8.21	1.85
2002	1.88	−4.31	1.05	−3.26	6.01	13.44	6.06	1.55	6.62	−8.06	−4.14	7.38
2003	4.28	6.91	−9.34	−0.07	10.74	−4.10	1.95	2.05	−0.96	−8.93	−3.11	4.14
2004	1.27	4.01	−1.59	−10.53	−2.38	−4.31	−4.89	−2.33	1.01	6.73	9.74	0.80
2005	−3.72	−0.05	−3.40	−4.61	219	4.36	−0.16	1.18	5.33	−3.44	7.05	−0.22
2006	6.00	−1.01	2.41	4.10	−6.37	−2.11	−3.71	−1.67	−0.32	3.40	0.04	6.03
2007	1.71	−3.24	2.79	6.45	6.83	3.37	−4.92	−10.43	6.59	6.55	−3.39	1.56
2008	1.53	6.71	−2.51	−1.14	1.37	6.54	−3.33	−4.28	3.00	8.33	1.85[E]	1.09

E = estimated

Rabar Market Research, Inc. — Diversified

Annual Performance Breakdown

	Yearly Statistics	
Year	Return	Drawdown
2008	18.32%	
2007	15.12%	−6.79%
2006	9.23%	−8.23%
2005	−5.78%	−8.90%
2004	−2.81%	−24.33%
2003	23.93%	−10.40%
2002	24.57%	−7.68%
2001	0.77%	−9.36%
2000	1.79%	−11.88%
1999	−9.27%	−16.25%
1998	24.29%	−7.65%
1997	11.39%	−9.06%
1996	0.66%	−12.89%
1995	12.57%	−29.82%
1994	33.91%	−9.46%
1993	49.74%	−13.39%
1992	−4.36%	−10.02%
1991	−5.74%	−18.91%
1990	122.71%	−13.61%
1989	10.00%	−27.77%

Month by Month Returns

					Month by Month Returns							
Year	Jan	Feb	Mar	Apr	May	Jun	Jul	Aug	Sep	Oct	Nov	Dec
1989	−0.77	−3.57	13.82	−0.18	13.76	−2.61	−2.84	−13.76	2.69	−13.81	5.24	17.01
1990	1.89	7.76	12.16	16.71	−13.61	9.50	16.06	21.80	10.40	4.87	2.51	−2.45
1991	−7.43	−7.75	2.26	−5.58	−1.17	3.32	−8.12	−2.93	2.43	0.66	−0.27	22.14
1992	−12.26	−3.31	0.57	−2.13	−0.77	5.47	12.93	7.70	−7.12	−0.69	1.45	−3.93
1993	−0.12	14.17	0.22	10.89	3.45	−1.28	14.75	−3.89	−4.10	−6.03	5.63	10.07
1994	−10.51	−6.02	19.43	2.47	11.40	18.00	−4.31	−4.42	3.35	−4.17	10.65	−1.25
1995	−9.45	14.00	15.25	5.84	8.91	−2.45	−9.28	−8.66	−9.11	−4.48	2.42	14.20
1996	−0.13	−9.52	−1.49	3.33	−3.45	1.54	−2.13	−1.30	3.75	10.75	5.95	−5.08
1997	5.37	5.07	−0.64	−6.41	−2.10	−0.11	14.84	−7.75	3.11	−3.33	0.51	4.24
1998	2.28	1.55	0.00	−6.43	4.17	2.12	1.16	19.37	6.10	−4.05	−3.75	1.60
1999	−1.90	3.70	−4.30	3.30	−6.90	0.00	−2.90	−0.40	0.10	−6.00	2.10	4.30
2000	−0.70	0.20	−2.10	−5.30	−0.10	−3.70	−1.20	4.70	−1.80	0.40	5.60	6.50
2001	1.50	0.30	4.80	−4.60	−2.00	−1.80	0.60	−1.60	2.00	6.40	−8.10	4.20
2002	−0.70	−4.00	2.30	−6.00	6.80	11.40	7.90	3.20	3.50	−3.50	−2.10	4.90
2003	3.40	5.20	−10.40	4.20	10.80	−2.60	−0.40	0.00	1.30	4.00	−1.50	9.40
2004	2.70	8.30	−1.20	−13.10	−3.80	−4.60	−2.10	−1.90	0.90	3.10	11.90	−0.80
2005	−6.40	5.20	−3.80	−5.30	4.40	3.00	−0.30	−1.80	1.70	−3.70	3.10	−1.20
2006	5.40	−3.40	3.80	8.90	−0.80	−3.90	−3.60	2.10	−0.60	−1.60	5.20	−1.70
2007	−1.30	−4.20	−2.70	5.90	5.90	3.40	−3.10	−2.30	9.80	6.00	−3.80	1.80
2008	1.77	12.91	−1.42	1.87	4.42	3.01	−4.10	−2.43	−2.02	1.19	0.76	2.02

Sunrise Capital Partners LLC—Expanded Diversified

Annual Performance Breakdown

Yearly Statistics		
Year	Return	Drawdown
2008	29.80%	NA
2007	3.90%	NA
2006	9.00%	NA
2005	−2.40%	NA
2004	6.00%	NA
2003	17.40%	NA
2002	14.50%	NA
2001	13.60%	NA
2000	8.20%	NA
1999	4.40%	NA
1998	25.80%	NA
1997	20.70%	NA
1996	19.30%	NA
1995	11.50%	NA
1994	1.60%	NA
1993	1.50%	NA
1992	−0.90%	NA
1991	33.50%	NA
1990	54.10%	NA
1989	27.00%	NA

Month by Month Returns

					Month by Month Returns							
Year	Jan	Feb	Mar	Apr	May	Jun	Jul	Aug	Sep	Oct	Nov	Dec
1989	13.51	−20.34	13.12	0.04	24.91	0.02	−8.78	−6.07	−8.42	−3.68	10.41	19.05
1990	7.75	−0.74	6.16	8.92	−9.94	4.92	12.61	14.16	9.84	0.20	0.21	−6.98
1991	−11.27	−1.60	24.29	3.18	−1.34	9.61	−15.51	−11.24	4.72	−2.31	8.45	32.54
1992	−13.33	−8.97	−3.60	−3.34	2.01	10.83	14.92	15.72	−5.24	−3.42	1.69	−3.68
1993	−8.31	17.39	−1.66	3.24	3.97	2.47	10.22	−10.23	−4.64	−11.83	−5.98	11.51
1994	−1.30	−3.48	0.19	−7.09	5.19	11.77	−4.24	−10.99	2.48	10.82	3.92	−3.16
1995	−8.46	4.71	19.10	2.45	−3.77	−0.74	−1.94	−0.44	−2.67	0.75	−0.84	5.17
1996	0.54	−5.80	4.53	9.28	0.11	−0.56	−0.77	−0.49	0.93	6.85	1.29	2.73
1997	4.56	8.59	1.48	−0.46	4.39	−2.86	5.95	−3.32	−1.53	−1.18	1.82	2.25
1998	1.37	3.28	2.66	1.59	2.65	3.34	−0.61	9.54	3.21	−1.02	−4.71	2.51
1999	−0.88	5.14	−1.44	4.18	−1.20	2.18	−1.53	−0.13	0.42	−4.08	4.36	−2.20
2000	3.78	−3.31	−1.51	−4.65	−1.43	−0.46	0.43	3.91	−1.28	0.07	6.16	6.95
2001	1.67	3.74	7.27	−6.25	3.27	−1.27	−1.63	2.49	7.36	6.25	−10.33	1.88
2002	−2.52	−2.83	0.30	0.94	4.26	8.59	1.59	0.66	6.06	−3.74	−5.06	6.39
2003	9.16	4.62	−6.15	0.09	5.24	−3.66	−1.71	0.18	−3.40	5.98	−1.08	8.28
2004	0.98	7.67	2.35	−4.77	−1.28	−2.81	−1.60	−4.21	0.71	3.45	4.87	1.19
2005	−6.09	−0.12	−0.56	−1.39	−0.42	−0.27	−2.42	0.11	1.14	1.06	5.52	1.38
2006	0.47	−0.04	3.20	3.45	0.85	−0.91	−4.05	−1.26	−0.10	3.44	1.53	2.39
2007	3.38	−2.93	−4.80	6.26	3.46	1.60	−6.28	−13.91	6.52	9.10	1.52	2.32
2008	6.14	8.87	−1.36	−2.57	2.95	2.29	−4.40	−2.72	2.07	12.63	3.02	0.80

Superfund

Annual Performance Breakdown

	Yearly Statistics	
Year	**Return**	**Drawdown**
2008	47.71%	
2007	−9.91%	−25.14%
2006	13.17%	−26.07%
2005	−9.12%	−22.92%
2004	11.19%	−28.22%
2003	26.33%	−27.04%
2002	69.21%	−22.15%
2001	42.59%	−18.76%
2000	40.15%	−10.42%

Month by Month Returns

						Month by Month Returns						
Year	Jan	Feb	Mar	Apr	May	Jun	Jul	Aug	Sep	Oct	Nov	Dec
2000	12.32	−5.63	−2.45	−0.75	6.45	0.71	−8.55	12.32	−6.91	−3.09	8.94	26.19
2001	3.56	4.57	9.95	−8.60	1.89	5.02	1.11	10.27	28.42	5.27	−14.62	−4.85
2002	1.06	−2.69	−5.46	−0.64	3.56	23.54	17.67	15.23	9.01	−17.23	−5.94	24.42
2003	19.99	15.52	−23.21	1.06	9.89	−8.56	−3.14	2.62	−5.87	10.23	−2.54	16.28
2004	1.96	14.05	−0.54	−19.92	4.70	−10.20	1.70	−5.75	8.19	5.88	15.42	0.75
2005	−12.48	2.54	4.26	−15.46	1.65	5.98	−0.05	0.59	3.41	−13.00	14.20	3.24
2006	8.26	−4.37	4.33	4.66	−9.42	−3.70	−13.75	−1.73	8.73	7.98	−0.88	16.36
2007	0.19	−10.67	−5.69	10.93	5.99	3.76	−13.16	−13.80	7.49	12.77	−8.54	5.42
2008	−3.77	22.39	1.49	−2.65	9.51	13.98	−14.87	−11.55	4.87	24.83	3.17	—

Transtrend B.V.—Diversified Trend Program—Enhanced Risk (USD)

Annual Performance Breakdown

| Year | Yearly Statistics | |
	Return	Drawdown
2008	29.38%	
2007	22.38%	−7.18%
2006	12.04%	−8.50%
2005	5.99%	−3.48%
2004	12.82%	−9.41%
2003	8.48%	−6.78%
2002	26.26%	−4.38%
2001	26.36%	−3.12%
2000	12.40%	−4.82%
1999	−2.21%	−8.59%
1998	21.95%	−5.46%
1997	37.93%	−8.58%
1996	31.68%	−7.10%
1995	29.09%	−6.29%

Month by Month Returns

						Month by Month Returns						
Year	Jan	Feb	Mar	Apr	May	Jun	Jul	Aug	Sep	Oct	Nov	Dec
1995	–6.16	9.57	10.15	2.16	6.49	3.63	–3.70	–0.58	1.75	–3.81	2.07	5.70
1996	5.38	–6.65	–0.48	8.59	–4.40	–0.30	3.88	7.26	7.51	10.37	1.46	–3.12
1997	9.64	5.12	–2.17	–4.07	–0.62	0.20	19.27	1.02	1.87	–8.58	5.72	7.95
1998	0.25	0.21	2.79	–5.43	3.55	1.36	–4.75	19.57	1.93	0.86	–1.06	2.70
1999	–3.86	1.22	–2.77	3.11	–3.10	4.51	1.95	–2.51	0.63	–6.82	1.84	4.29
2000	1.55	–1.99	–2.29	0.14	2.52	–2.44	–0.77	1.81	0.62	2.54	5.97	4.47
2001	0.72	0.60	6.75	–1.48	1.29	–1.36	4.72	2.37	7.82	1.07	–3.12	4.86
2002	–1.17	–0.69	2.00	–0.99	2.34	8.41	5.97	2.78	3.44	–2.72	–1.71	6.58
2003	5.18	4.03	–5.04	3.77	5.81	–2.45	–2.36	–0.10	–2.04	2.48	–0.69	0.22
2004	2.08	4.95	–2.18	–3.17	–0.31	–2.35	–1.34	–0.42	1.63	3.20	8.97	1.71
2005	–4.35	2.74	2.03	–3.48	1.03	4.02	3.26	–0.49	1.80	–0.67	3.40	–3.00
2006	1.78	–2.26	0.89	1.94	–3.78	–1.26	–3.69	4.72	0.12	4.56	3.68	5.29
2007	1.64	–4.07	–3.24	5.69	6.84	3.65	–2.50	–2.44	7.81	9.02	–2.16	1.32
2008	–0.48	5.55	1.33	0.59	3.28	3.03	–2.38	–1.38	4.95	7.12	2.57	2.29

Winton Capital Management Ltd —
Diversified Winton Futures Fund

Annual Performance Breakdown

	Yearly Statistics	
Year	Return	Drawdown
2008	21.08%	
2007	17.97%	–9.65%
2006	17.84%	–4.53%
2005	9.73%	–8.94%
2004	22.62%	–11.79%

Yearly Statistics		
Year	Return	Drawdown
2003	27.76%	−10.80%
2002	18.33%	−8.60%
2001	7.12%	−11.88%
2000	10.43%	−11.68%
1999	15.08%	−14.56%
1998	52.17%	−5.70%
1997	3.49%	−0.00%

Month by Month Returns

Month by Month Returns											
Year	Jan	Feb	Mar	Apr	May	Jun	Jul	Aug	Sep	Oct	Nov	Dec
1997	—	—	—	—	—	—	—	—	—	−12.97	9.96	8.14
1998	1.50	3.27	7.38	−1.63	8.53	2.97	1.51	10.99	4.51	−5.70	1.15	9.50
1999	−1.38	3.61	−3.98	10.51	−8.39	5.29	−2.01	−3.47	−0.16	−6.20	13.93	9.04
2000	−3.96	1.72	−3.28	2.06	−0.26	−1.28	−4.58	3.23	−7.76	2.09	7.33	16.81
2001	4.38	0.57	7.09	−5.31	−2.61	−2.66	0.66	0.56	4.64	13.75	−7.10	−5.15
2002	−10.13	−6.04	12.62	−3.76	−3.96	7.95	4.71	6.04	7.63	−7.96	−0.69	14.16
2003	5.95	11.95	−10.80	2.45	10.19	−5.20	−0.68	0.62	0.26	4.72	−2.48	10.27
2004	2.72	11.56	−0.80	−8.62	−0.28	−2.96	1.33	3.09	5.14	4.03	6.37	−0.19
2005	−5.38	6.58	4.64	−4.21	6.62	3.13	−1.85	7.63	−6.17	−2.95	7.32	−4.37
2006	4.20	−2.58	4.01	5.66	−2.94	−1.17	−0.47	4.54	−1.10	1.48	3.24	2.14
2007	3.83	−5.93	−3.95	6.46	5.05	1.91	−1.18	−0.88	6.99	2.52	2.42	0.24
2008	3.85	7.95	−0.66	−0.99	1.99	5.06	−4.63	−3.00	−0.41	3.73	4.97	2.17

Risk Disclaimer

Short-Term Trading

C

Ed Seykota was asked at Seykota.com:

"I am new to trend following and wish to ask you what your favorite chart is for determining a given market's trend? Daily, weekly, yearly, hourly?"

Seykota responded:

"Hmmm...your list seems to lack scaling options for minute, second, and millisecond. If you want to go for the really high-frequency stuff, you might try trading visible light, in the range of one cycle per 10–15 seconds. Trading gamma rays, at around one cycle per 10–20 seconds, requires a lot of expensive instrumentation, whereas you can trade visible light 'by eye.' I don't know of even one short-term trader, however, who claims to show a profit at these frequencies. In general, higher-frequency trading succumbs to declining profit potential against nondeclining transaction costs. You might consider trading a chart with a long enough time scale that transaction costs are a minor factor—something like a daily price chart, going back a year or two."

He's barely rated a mention in the nation's most important newspapers, but pay close attention to what Institutional Investor wrote about him... "Jim Simons [president of Renaissance Technologies and operator of the Medallion Fund] may very well be the best money manager on earth."

Long Island Business News

Toby Crabel has made a 180-degree turn from discretionary to systematic trading. In the early days, he used discretion to devise the system-generated signals and to decide whether or not to take the trade signals. "However, I have now come to the conclusion that systematic trading is more suited to me... It's only one in 500 or so cases that we do not trade a signal because of execution problems or some other technical reason... Now I am less emotionally involved in the markets and I believe being more objective helps."

Managed Account Reports

I agree with Seykota's wisdom, but he is not saying short-term is impossible. There are shorter-term systematic traders who have done quite well (Toby Crabel and Jim Simons, for example). They would agree with Seykota that their style is hard. The shorter you go, the more the need for great execution, fantastic data, and multiple systems. To be a great shorter-term mechanical trader is a different animal than trend following, but it is a style that a select few have mastered.

Personality Traits of Successful Traders D

I am grateful for the following contribution from Brett Steenbarger.

In my book *The Psychology of Trading*, I referred to personality traits that tend to distinguish successful traders from less successful ones. Several of these traits are also likely to influence the degree of success traders are likely to have in adopting a trend following approach to trading. Following are several self-assessment questions that might be useful in determining whether you'll face particularly great challenges in riding market trends. Please write down "yes" or "no" answers to each of the 12 questions before reading further:

1. When something goes against you in the market, do you often find yourself venting your frustration?

2. Do you enjoy (or as a child did you enjoy) roller coasters or other thrill rides?

3. Do you often find yourself procrastinating over work?

4. Do you consider yourself moody—sometimes rather up, sometimes rather down?

5. Would you generally prefer going out and partying with friends rather than staying at home with a good book or movie?

> *Luck is a dividend of sweat. The more you sweat, the luckier you get.*
>
> Ray Kroc, founder of McDonalds

SAT tests are designed by huge panels of experts in education and psychology who work for years to design tests in which not one single question measures any bit of knowledge that anyone might actually need in the real world. We should applaud kids for getting lower scores.

Dave Barry

6. Do you often find yourself apologizing to others because you forgot to do something you were supposed to do?

7. Are you generally high-strung, tense, or stressed?

8. If given the choice at a buffet, would you prefer to try exotic foods you've never heard of rather than familiar dishes?

9. When you have a task that needs to be done around the house, do you tend to take a quick and dirty approach, rather than a meticulous, painstaking approach?

10. After a losing trade, do you often feel guilty or get down on yourself?

11. Have you experimented with or regularly used two or more recreational drugs (other than alcohol) in your life?

12. Are you often late for appointments or for social plans you've made?

If you indicated "yes" to most or all of questions 1, 4, 7, and 10, you most likely score high on a trait called "neuroticism." Neuroticism is the tendency toward negative emotional experience, and it shows up as anger, anxiety, or depression.

If you responded "yes" to most or all of questions 2, 5, 8 and 11, you probably score high on a trait called "openness to experience." Openness reflects a tendency toward sensation seeking and risk-taking.

If you answered "yes" to most or all of questions 3, 6, 9, and 12, you potentially score low on a trait called "conscientiousness." Conscientiousness measures the degree to which an individual is oriented toward duty, responsibility, and dependability.

Other things being equal, the ideal personality pattern for trend following is one of high conscientiousness, low neuroticism, and low openness. A good trend follower sticks with rules and systems (conscientious), won't impulsively enter or exit trades on the whim of emotion (neuroticism), and will trade for profits, not stimulation (low openness). In my experience, some of the best systems traders are among the least flashy people. They are meticulous and conscientious about their research and execution, and they don't let their emotions or needs pull them from their discipline.

Conversely, individuals who are high risk-takers and who crave novelty, stimulation, and action often take impulsive and imprudent risks. Frequently, the neurotic emotions kick in after a series of losing high-risk trades. Such individuals are trading for excitement and self-validation, not just profits. Even if they are given a tested, profitable trading system, they will not be able to follow it faithfully.

System traders often focus their research and energy on defining the optimal parameters for a system's profitability. Equally important is finding a trading strategy that meshes with one's personality. Traders who are relatively risk-averse may trade shorter time frames or smaller positions than those who are risk-tolerant. Traders with a higher need for novelty and stimulation may benefit from trading a greater number of stocks or markets rather than focusing on a relative few. Are some personalities simply unsuited for trading? I would say yes, just as some personalities are not cut out to be fighter pilots or surgeons. It is difficult to imagine a trader enjoying ongoing success without the capacity for disciplined risk-taking.

Personality testing options can be found at www.knowyourtype.com. Myers-Briggs testing can be useful for all traders from beginner to advanced.

It is not at all unusual to find that a trader is losing with a trend following approach because he acts out unmet personality needs in the market. One of the best trading strategies one can employ is to find adequate outlets for attention and affection, achievement, self-esteem, emotional well being, and excitement outside of trading. Sometimes traders I talk with try to impress me by explaining that trading is their entire life. They do not realize that their very "passion" and "obsession" with the markets are likely to sabotage them, imposing undue pressures and interference. If you have a trading system and you faithfully execute that system, trading should be reasonably boring and routine. Better to enjoy roller coasters outside of market hours than ride them with your equity curve!

Brett N. Steenbarger, Ph.D. is Associate Professor of Psychiatry and Behavioral Sciences at SUNY Upstate Medical University in Syracuse, NY. He is also an active trader and writes occasional feature articles on market psychology for MSN's Money site (www.moneycentral.com). Many of Dr. Steenbarger's articles and trading strategies are archived on his website, www.brettsteenbarger.com.

Personality testing options can be found at www.knowyourtype.com.

Trend Following Models

E

Paul Mulvaney of Mulvaney Capital provided the following visual models of trend following.

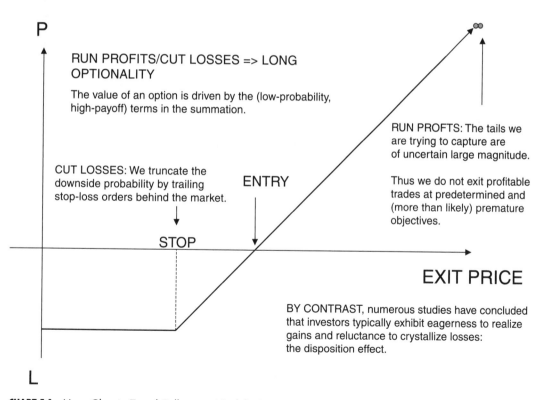

RUN PROFITS/CUT LOSSES => LONG OPTIONALITY

The value of an option is driven by the (low-probability, high-payoff) terms in the summation.

CUT LOSSES: We truncate the downside probability by trailing stop-loss orders behind the market.

ENTRY

STOP

RUN PROFTS: The tails we are trying to capture are of uncertain large magnitude.

Thus we do not exit profitable trades at predetermined and (more than likely) premature objectives.

EXIT PRICE

BY CONTRAST, numerous studies have concluded that investors typically exhibit eagerness to realize gains and reluctance to crystallize losses: the disposition effect.

CHART E.1: How Classic Trend Following Models Generate Payout Source: Mulvaney Capital Management Ltd.

*Man can learn nothing
unless he proceeds from
the known to the
unknown.*

Claude Bernard

According to Mulvaney, the "hockey stick" diagram (Chart E.1) depicts how classic trend following models generate payouts analogous to long options positions. We know from options theory that the value of an option is dominated by the low probability/large magnitude events. The diagonal line slopes upward to infinity. Trend followers do not predict the extent of price changes but seek to capture large outsize moves over significant periods of time. The horizontal line represents the truncation of risk by stop placement and can be likened to paying a finite premium for an option.

Mulvaney notes that trend following does not rely on a unidirectional, single-market position as buy-and-hold stock investing does. A single trend following model has multiple sources of return, morphing itself into whatever and wherever the market is. As you can see from the Mulvaney Capital P&L chart (Chart E.2), the typical trend follower's portfolio is well diversified, allowing it to profit from the tendency of markets to trend at different times.

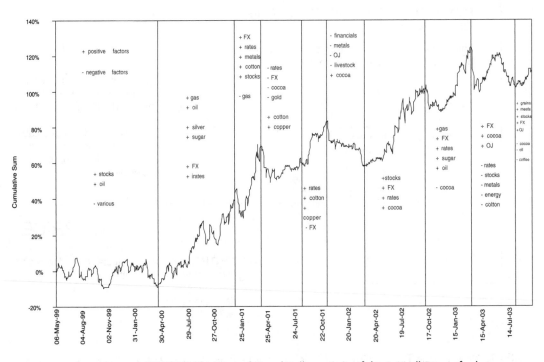

CHART E.2: The Typical Trend Follower's Portfolio Is Well Diversified Source: Mulvaney Capital Management Ltd.

Mulvaney concludes:

"Two lessons derive from the empirical data. Price changes in financial and commodity markets are approximately uncorrelated over time and thus are not predictable. This is the Martingale property: The best estimate of tomorrow's price is today's price. This is absolutely not saying that profitable systems cannot be designed, just that mean returns cannot be estimated, in a strict econometric sense. This observation underpins a 'run profits' strategy. By contrast, systematic profit-taking at calculated objectives is a form of mean estimation and is untenable. On the other hand, the volatility of financial and commodity markets changes over time and exhibits autocorrelation. Returns of like magnitude tend to be clustered over time. Volatility tends to come in waves, so that financial markets are characterized by tranquil and volatile periods. Large price changes tend to be followed by large changes and small changes by small changes, but of either sign. As a result, predictive models for volatility can be derived. In modeling terms, this means we do estimate the volatility of returns, detecting nascent trends when price changes exceed previous volatility estimates and a tail starts to form."

The vertical thinker says, "I know what I am looking for." The lateral thinker says, "I am looking but I won't know what I am looking for until I have found it."

Edward de Bono

Trading System Example from Mechanica

F

"Part of back-testing is to determine position sizing and risk management strategies that fit within your drawdown tolerance envelope."
—Ed Seykota[1]

In this appendix, Bob Spear shows how a trader might construct a simple, mechanical trend following system on Trading Recipes Portfolio Engineering Software. His newest software, surpassing Trading Recipes, is called Mechanica (www.mechanicasoftware.com).

Grow your own dope— plant an economist.

Graffiti seen at London School of Economics

For this example we start with a broad look at the system's trading ideas, which echo many of the ideas discussed in this book. We construct a hypothetical portfolio and run a backtest up to a certain point in time. Then, we examine in detail how the software enters, sizes, and manages a trade. Afterwards, we run our backtest to the end of our data and examine the results without and with money management.

Please note that we provide this information to illustrate a concept; I do not necessarily recommend that anyone "trade" this system, nor do we offer it as trading advice.

System Background Information

Our sample trend following system enters on an 89-day price breakout and exits on a 13-day price breakdown, bets 2 percent of equity on every trade, and implements a mechanism to ensure that

385

we don't risk too much. This system is run over a small portfolio of futures markets. Portfolio selection is a critical element of trading performance, but we did not put the portfolio used here under a microscope.

Chart F.1 shows the markets included in the sample portfolio.

CHART F.1: Markets Included in Sample Portfolio

Sector	Market	Symbol	Exchange
Currencies	British Pound	BP	CME (day)
	Canadian Dollar	CD	CME (day)
	Japanese Yen	JY	CME (day)
	Swiss Franc	SF	CME (day)
	U.S. Dollar Index	DX	NYBT
Energies	Crude Oil	CL	NYMEX
	Heating Oil	HO	NYMEX
	Natural Gas	NG	NYMEX
	Unleaded Gas	HU	NYMEX
Grains	Corn	C_	CBT (day)
	Soybean Oil	BO	CBT (day)
	Wheat—KC	KW	KCBT
Softs	Coffee	KC	NYBT
	Cotton	CT	NYBT
	Sugar #11	SB	NYBT

Our test comprises in-sample data only; we do not verify our in-sample results with out-of-sample data. Before risking real money in the market, you'd be prudent to test several samples.

System Details

Before we review portfolio-level performance, we examine the code used in Trading Recipes to generate entry and exit signals and to size positions (money management). Please note that words in

ALL CAPS represent elements from Trading Recipes' programming language, whereas words following an apostrophe are explanatory comments.

```
SYSTEM = 1                              'unique ID # for this system
COL1 = ATR[15]                   '15-day avg true range of current market
MANAGER[1] = COL1[1] * POINTVALUE    'dollar value of that volatility
COL2 = MAX[H,89,1] + TICK[1]          '89-day breakout for long entry
COL3 = MIN[L,13,1] — TICK[1]          '13-day breakdown for long exit
COL4 = MIN[L,89,1] — TICK[1]          '89-day breakout for short entry
COL5 = MAX[H,13,1] + TICK[1]          '13-day breakdown for short exit
```

Each day, we calculate the following values.

As it processes each day of each market, our system will search for a breakout to enter a trade (long or short):

```
BUYSTOP = COL2                              'long entry stop
SELLSTOP = COL4                             'short entry stop
```

If an entry signal is generated, the system executes position-sizing rules to determine how many contracts (futures) or shares (equities) to trade.

In the rules that follow, you can see that we risk 2 percent of our equity on each trade. However, we trade conservatively in that we trade *the lesser quantity of contracts* as calculated by 2 percent divided by new risk (defined as the dollar value of the absolute value of [entry – stop]) or 2 percent divided by twice the dollar value of 15-day average volatility.

```
STARTUPCASH = 1000000                       'start with $1 million
STARTDATE = 19910101                     '10-year in-sample dataset
ENDATE = 20001231
MEMORY[1] = (TOTALEQUITY * .02) / NEWRISK
                               'risk 2% of equity / dollar risk on trade
MEMORY[2] = (TOTALEQUITY * .02) / (MANAGER[1] * 2)
                             'risk 2% of equity / dollar value of volatility
IF MEMORY[1] < MEMORY[2] THEN MEMORY[2] = MEMORY[1]
                               'put lesser of two values into MEM2
IF MEMORY[2] > 100 THEN MEMORY[2] = 100   'don't trade too large
            NEWCONTRACTS = MEMORY[2]       'use value of MEM2 to size position
```

Once in a trade, our trend following system will search for a breakdown to exit a trade (long or short):

```
SELLSTOP = COL3                        'long exit stop
BUYSTOP = COL5                         'short exit stop
```

A Canadian Dollar Trade

Let's follow a Canadian Dollar trade to see exactly how our trend following system enters, sizes, and exits a trade.

On December 14, 1994, the Canadian Dollar hit an 89-day low (as represented by the line in the midst of the price bars) intraday. Because our trend following system had a sell stop "on the floor," the order was filled and the system went short. (See Chart F.2.)

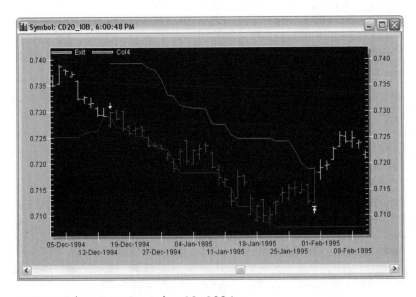

CHART F.2: Short Entry December 12, 1994

It indicates the trailing stop (a 13-day high) via the line above the price bars. While in a trade, Trading Recipes compares daily data to that line. If a day's price range touches that line, as it does on January 31, 1995, then the exit stop is hit and a buy order is generated to cover the short.

How was the position sized? Let's review our sizing rules in the context of the equity level when the entry signal was generated.

After our portfolio was marked-to-market at the close on December 13, 1994, we had $2,205,963 in equity. As it sizes the Canadian Dollar entry, our system calculates the following values (please note that a 1.0 move in the Canadian Dollar is worth $100,000 per our data setup):

```
MEMORY[1] = (TOTALEQUITY * .02) / NEWRISK
Where TOTALEQUITY = $2,205,963
      TOTALEQUITY * .02 = $44,119.26
      NEWRISK = ABS(.7273 − .7392) * $100,000 = $1190
Thus  MEMORY[1] = $44,119.26 / $1190 = 37.0750084

MEMORY[2] = (TOTALEQUITY * .02) / (MANAGER[1] * 2)
Where TOTALEQUITY = $2,205,963
      TOTALEQUITY * .02 = $44,119.26
      MANAGER[1] = .0023 * $100,000 = $230
      MANAGER[1] * 2 = $460
Thus  MEMORY[2] = $44,119.26 / $460 = 95.91143478

IF MEMORY[1] < MEMORY[2] THEN MEMORY[2] = MEMORY[1]
Where MEMORY[1] is indeed < MEMORY[2], so MEMORY[2] = 37.0750084

IF MEMORY[2] > 100 THEN MEMORY[2] = 100
Where the condition evaluates to false

NEWCONTRACTS = MEMORY[2]
Where Trading Recipes rounds down and sizes the position at 37 contracts
```

By taking the smaller of two possible position sizes, this example illustrates clearly one of the maxims of trend following: Bet conservatively so that you might live to see another day.

System Performance

We can use some of Trading Recipes' analysis tools to see how our trend following system performed over the entire portfolio. The portfolio summary provides a wealth of useful information. Chart F.3 shows the statistics for our 10-year in-sample test over 15 markets. Note that, for the sake of simplicity, commission and slippage costs (which can be significant) were not factored into the backtest.

CHART F.3: 10-Year In-Sample Test

Initial Balance	1,000,000	$ Won	13,774,599
Net Win Loss	5,732,456	$ Lost	8,770,406
Ending Equity	6,732,456	Incentive + Fees	0
ROI	573.25%	Other Credits	3,143
Compound Annual ROI	21.02%	Other Debits	0
Max Drawdown %	23.05%		
Max Drawdown % Date	19931101		
		Long Wins	113
Longest Drawdown in Years	0.28	Long Losses	150
Longest Drawdown Start Date	19920901	Short Wins	132
Longest Drawdown End Date	19940506	Short Losses	181
MAR Ratio	0.91	Long $ Won	8,030,086
Sharpe Ratio	1.02	Long $ Lost	4,104,701
Return Retracement Ratio	2.88	Short $ Won	5,744,513
Sterling Ratio	0.68	Short $ Lost	4,665,705
Std. Dev. Daily % Returns	1.23%	Largest Winning Trade	480,563
Average Expectation Value	20.33	Largest Losing Trade	141,900
Expectation	32.79%	Average Winning Trade	56,223
DU Area / DD Area	1.21	Average Losing Trade	26,497
Percent New Highs	6.61%	Max Consecutive Wins	8
		Max Consecutive Losses	15
Trades	576	Days Winning	1,350
Trades Rejected	85	Days Losing	1,176
Wins	245		
Losses	331	Number of Margin Calls	0
Percent Wins	42.53%	$ Largest Margin Call	0
Avg $Win to Avg $Loss	2.12		

Average Days in Winning Trade	37	Size Adjustments	0
Average Days in Losing Trade	15	Size Adjusted Items	0
Start Date	19910102		
End Date	20001231	Total Slippage + Commission	0
Max Items Held	588	PSR run time (H:M:S)	0:00:03
Total Items Traded	18,879		

To see how our equity curve looked in relationship to our drawdown, we can chart the logarithmic equity curve (see Chart F.4). Note that through 1992 and 1993, the curve failed to gain traction, as it was hampered by large drawdowns—drawdowns that proved to be historic. But in mid-1994, the system hit its stride, and the equity curve began a nice trajectory upward.

The search for truth is more precious than its possession.

Albert Einstein[2]

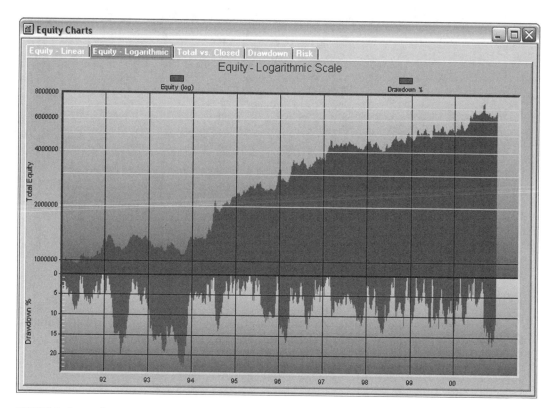

CHART F.4: Logarithmic Equity Curve

To see how our system performs in rolling, annual blocks of time, we can chart the 12-month rolling returns (see Chart F.5). Note how frequently these rolling returns result in positive gains— an excellent sign of robustness.

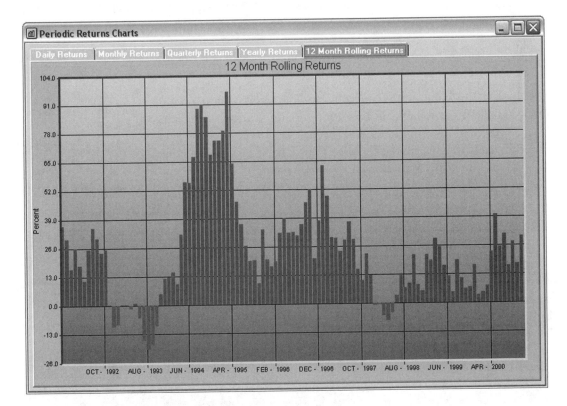

CHART F.5: Twelve-Month Rolling Returns

Summary

In this appendix, I presented a simple trend following system in the context of a portfolio, discussed the rules and calculations in detail, and examined the results via tables and charts. This is the type of process all trend followers go through in their trading.

Notes:

Bob Spear is the creator of Trading Recipes software. For more information about Trading Recipes, see www.tradingrecipes.com and his newest software Mechanica (www.mechanicasoftware. com). You may also find software from Trading Blox and Tim Arnold (www.tradingblox.com) is a very useful systems testing tool. Additionally, Volker Knapp and Dion Kurczek at Wealth Lab have created a loyal following with their systems testing software (www.wealth-lab.com).

Critical Questions for Trading Systems

G

There are many questions you should ask when building and testing a trend following trading system. Here are a few:

1. What are the largest actual and simulated drawdowns experienced? What was the maximal loss in equity—simulated and actual—in a single day?

2. What is the maximum number of consecutive losing months the system has sustained?

3. How often do drawdowns occur?

4. Are drawdowns typically short-lived, or do they develop gradually?

5. On the average, how long does it take to recover all losses incurred during a drawdown? What is the longest it has taken to complete a recovery from the trough of a drawdown?

6. Is the risk of each trade quantified? If so, what variables are included when making the calculation? Is the procedure accomplished by the computer or "by hand?"

7. How is the overall risk controlled?

8. Are there circumstances under which all trading could be halted to avoid further losses? If so, what are they? If not, why not?

9. Are there markets in which the trading system consistently performed poorly? If so, why does it not work well in those markets?

On the Cuban Revolution:

Michael: "I saw an interesting thing happen today. A rebel was being arrested by the military police, and rather than be taken alive, he exploded a grenade he had hidden in his jacket. He killed himself, and he took a captain of the command with him."

Random observer: "Those rebels, you know they're crazy."

Michael: "Maybe so but it occurred to me—the soldiers are paid to fight. The rebels aren't."

Hyman Roth: "What does that tell you?"

Michael: "They could win."[3]

10. Does the system adapt quickly or slowly to changes in market volatility?

11. Does the system have a way to minimize losses caused by whipsaws in the market?

12. Does the system permit discontinuation of trading when equity falls to a prespecified point and call for resumption of trading when market conditions warrant?

13. What principles establish stop placement?

14. How much does portfolio diversification reduce risk in the trading system?[2]

For more information on these types of questions, including additional study materials and personal instruction, please see: www.turtletrader.com/order.html.

Resources

Educational web sites from Michael Covel for trend followers include:

- www.turtletrader.com
- www.michaelcovel.com
- www.trendfollowing.com
- www.brokemovie.com

There are many who find a good alibi far more attractive than an achievement. For an achievement does not settle anything permanently. We still have to prove our worth anew each day: we have to prove that we are as good today as we were yesterday. But when we have a valid alibi for not achieving anything, we are fixed, so to speak, for life.

Eric Hoffer

Endnotes

Preface

1. Recruitment ad for Shackleton's Antarctic Expedition. *The Times*, London, 1913. Believed to have been posted in the personals section.

2. Van K. Tharp, *Trade Your Way to Financial Freedom*. New York: McGraw-Hill, 1999.

About the Author

1. Denise G. Shekerjian, *Uncommon Genius*. New York: Penguin Books, 1990.

Chapter 1

1. See *www.mises.org*.

2. Robert Koppel, *The Intuitive Trader*, Hoboken, NJ: John Wiley & Sons, Inc., 1996, 88.

3. Ludwig von Mises, *Human Action: A Treatise on Economics*. 4th revised ed. Irvington-on-Hudson, NY: The Foundation for Economic Education, Inc., 1996, printed 1998. First published in 1949.

4. Jack Schwager, *Market Wizards: Interviews with Top Traders*. New York, NY: Harper Collins, 1993.

5. Ludwig von Mises, *Human Action: A Treatise on Economics*. 4th revised ed. Irvington-on-Hudson, NY: The Foundation for Economic Education, Inc., 1996, printed 1998. First published in 1949.

6. Barclay Trading Group, Ltd. *Barclay Managed Futures Report*. Vol. 3, No. 3 (Third quarter 1992), 3.

7. Allison Colter. Dow Jones. July 13, 2001.

8. *Trading System Review*, Futures Industry Association Conference, November 2, 1994.

9. Jack Schwager, *Getting Started in Technical Analysis*. Hoboken, NJ: John Wiley & Sons, Inc., 1999.

10. The History of the Motley Fool. Fool.com, November 4, 2003. See *www.fool.com*.

11. The State of the Industry. *Managed Account Reports, Inc*. June 2000.

12. John Allen Paulos. *A Mathematician Plays the Stock Market*. New York, NY: Basic Books, 2003, 47.

13. Quantitative Strategy: Does Technical Analysis Work? Equity Research, Credit Suisse First Boston. September 25, 2002.

14. Daniel P. Collins in *Futures*, October 2003.

15. Disclosure Document. John W. Henry & Company, Inc. August 22, 2003.

16. Disclosure Document. John W. Henry & Company, Inc. August 22, 2003.

17. Carla Cavaletti, Top Traders Ride 1996 Trends. *Futures*. (March 1997), 68.

18. Jack Schwager, *Getting Started in Technical Analysis*. Hoboken, NJ: John Wiley & Sons, Inc., 1999.

19. Ginger Szala, Abraham Trading: Trend Following Earns Texas Sized Profits. *Futures* (March 1995), 61.

20. Desmond MacRae, Valuing Trend-Followers' Returns. *Managed Account Reports*, Inc. No. 242 (April 1999), 12.

21. Speech given to financial consultants on November 17, 2000. See *www.jwh.com*.

22. Presentation in Geneva, Switzerland on September 15, 1998.

23. *Futures*. Vol.22, No.12 (November 1993), 98.

24. *AIMA Newsletter*, June 2001. Alternative Investment Management Association.

25. Morton S. Baratz, *The Investor's Guide to Futures Money Management*. Columbia, MD: Futures Publishing Group, 1984.

26. Guest Article, 249. *Managed Account Reports* (November 1999), 9.

27. Speech given to financial consultants on November 17, 2000. See *www.jwh.com*.

28. From Upstairs/Downstairs Seminar with Tom Baldwin. Futures Industry Association, 1994.

29. Performance Review, February 1999. John W. Henry & Company, Inc.

30. Tass Twenty Traders Talk. Held June 29, 1996 at the Montreal Ritz Carlton Hotel in Montreal, Canada.

31. Jack Schwager, *Market Wizards: Interviews with Top Traders*. New York: Harper Business, 1989.

32. Riva Atlas, Macro, Macro Man. *Institutional Investor Magazine*. 1996.

33. Trend Following: Performance, Risk and Correlation Characteristics. White Paper. Graham Capital Management.

34. Trend Following: Performance, Risk and Correlation Characteristics. White Paper. Graham Capital Management.

35. Trends in Currency Markets: Which Way the $? *AIMA Newsletter*, June 2002. Alternative Investment Management Association.

36. The Trading Tribe at Seykota.com. See *www.seykota.com/tribe/*.

37. Mary Greenebaum, Funds: The New Way to Play Commodities. *Fortune*, November 19, 1979.

38. Brett N. Steenbarger, *The Psychology of Trading*. Hoboken, NJ: John Wiley & Sons, Inc., 2002, 316–317.

39. Brenda Ueland, *How to Write*. 10th ed. New York, NY: Graywolf Press, 1997. First published 1938.

40. Bruce Cleland, Campbell and Co. *Futures* (March 2004), 72.

41. David Whitford, *Why Owning the Boston Red Sox Is Like Running a Successful* Hedge Fund. *Fortune Small Business* (October 25, 2003).

42. The Whizkid of Futures Trading. *Business Week* (December 6, 1982), 102.

43. Anonymous, "Super Trader" in Van Tharp, Two Contrasting Super Traders.

Chapter 2

1. Jim Rogers, *Investment Biker*. New York: Random House, 1994.

2. Thomas Friedman, *The Lexus and the Olive Tree*. New York: Farrar, Straus, and Giroux, 1999.

3. Leah McGrath Goodman, *Trader Monthly*; www.traderdaily.com/magazine/article/17115.html.

4. Leah McGrath Goodman, *Trader Monthly*; www.traderdaily.com/magazine/article/17115.html.

5. Leah McGrath Goodman, *Trader Monthly*; www.traderdaily.com/magazine/article/17115.html.

6. The Winton Papers. www.wintoncapital.com.

7. Daniel P. Collins, Seeding Tomorrow's Top Traders; Managed Money; Dunn Capital Management Provides Help to Commodity Trading Advisor Start-ups. *Futures*, No. 6, Vol. 32, 67, (May 1, 2003) ISSN: 0746-2468.

8. In J. R. Newman (ed.) *The World of Mathematics*. New York: Simon and Schuster, 1956.

9. Jim Collins, *Good to Great*, New York: Harper Business, 2001.

10. Robert Koppel, *The Intuitive Trader*. Hoboken, NJ: John Wiley & Sons, Inc., 1996, 74.

11. The Reason Foundation. See *www.reason.org*.

12. Daniel P. Collins, Seeding Tomorrow's Top Traders; Managed Money; Dunn Capital Management Provides Help to Commodity Trading Advisor Start-ups. *Futures*, No. 6, Vol. 32, 67, (May 1, 2003) ISSN: 0746-2468.

13. Tricycle Asset Management, part of the *Market Wizards* Tour. Held on May 15, 2003 in Saskatoon, Saskatchewan.

14. Tricycle Asset Management, part of the *Market Wizards* Tour. Held on May 15, 2003 in Saskatoon, Saskatchewan.

15. Tricycle Asset Management, part of the *Market Wizards* Tour. Held on May 15, 2003 in Saskatoon, Saskatchewan.

16. Amy Rosenbaum, 1990s Highs and Lows: Invasions, Persuasions and Volatility. *Futures*, Vol. 19, No. 14 (December 1990), 54.

17. Andrew Osterland, For Commodity Funds, It Was as Good as It Gets. *Business Week* (September 14, 1998).

18. Jack Reerink, Dunn: Slow Reversal Pays Off. *Futures*, Vol. 25, No. 3 (March 1996).

19. Mike Mosser, Learning from Legends. *Futures*, Vol. 29, No. 2 (February 2000).

20. How Managed Money Became a Major Area of the Industry; Futures Market. *Futures*, Vol. 21, No. 9 (July 1992), 52.

21. Daniel P. Collins, Bob Pardo: Perfecting a Model. *Futures*, Vol. 31, No.13 (October 2002), 90.

22. Denise G. Shekerjian, *Uncommon Genius*. New York: Penguin Books, 1990.

23. Mary Ann Burns, Industry Icons Assess the Managed Futures Business. *Futures Industry Association* (May/June 2003).

24. Jack Reerink, Dunn: Slow Reversal Pays Off. *Futures*, Vol. 25, No. 3 (March 1996).

25. Carla Cavaletti, Comeback Kids: Managing Drawdowns According to Commodity Trading Advisors. *Futures* Vol. 27, No. 1 (January 1998), 68.

26. Excerpt from Dunn Capital Management Monthly Commentary for February 2003.

27. Barclay Trading Group, Ltd. *Barclay Managed Futures Report*. Vol. 3, No. 3 (Third quarter 1992), 2.

28. Monster.com ad.

29. Ginger Szala, John W. Henry: Long-Term Perspective. *Futures* (1987).

30. Presentation in Geneva, Switzerland on September 15, 1998.

31. Lois Peltz, *The New Investment Superstars*. New York: John Wiley & Sons, Inc., 2001.

32. Mary Ann Burns, Industry Icons Assess the Managed Futures Business. *Futures Industry Association* (May/June 2003).

33. Mark S. Rzepczynski, John W. Henry & Co. Year in Review, December 2000.

34. Oliver Conway, Cover story about John W. Henry & Company, Inc. *Managed Derivatives* (May 1996).

35. W.H. Auden and L. Kronenberger (eds.). *The Viking Book of Aphorisms*. New York: Viking Press, 1966.

36. Michael Peltz, John W. Henry's Bid to Manage the Future. *Institutional Investor* (August 1996).

37. Ginger Szala, John W. Henry: Long-term Perspective. *Futures* (1987).

38. Lois Peltz, *The New Investment Superstars*. New York: John Wiley & Sons, Inc., 2001.

39. Speech given to financial consultants on November 17, 2000. See *www.jwh.com*.

40. Lois Peltz, *The New Investment Superstars*. New York: John Wiley & Sons, Inc., 2001.

41. 2002 Year in Review. John W. Henry & Company, Inc.

42. Futures Industry Association Conference Seminar. *Trading System Review*, November 2, 1994.

43. John W. Henry, Morgan Stanley Dean Witter Achieve Conference. Naples, Florida, November 17, 2000.

44. Presentation in Geneva, Switzerland on September 15, 1998.

45. Presentation in Geneva, Switzerland on September 15, 1998.

46. Presentation in Geneva, Switzerland on September 15, 1998.

47. FIA Research Division dinner held in New York City on April 20, 1995.

48. Jack Schwager, *The Market Wizards*. New York: Harper Business, 1989, 172.

49. The Trading Tribe at Seykota.com. See *www.seyokota.com/tribe/*.

50. Email to *TurtleTrader.com*.

51. Daniel P. Collins, Long-Term Technical Trend-Following Method for Managed Futures Programs. *Futures*, Vol 30, No. 14 (November 2001); 22.

52. The Trading Tribe at Seykota.com. See *www.seyokota.com/tribe/*.

53. Thom Hartle, ed., Ed Seykota of Technical Tools. *Technical Analysis of Stocks & Commodities*, Vol. 10, No. 8 (August 1992), 328–331. (Used with permission; www.traders.com.)

54. Thom Hartle, ed., Ed Seykota of Technical Tools. *Technical Analysis of Stocks & Commodities*, Vol. 10, No. 8 (August 1992), 328–331. (Used with permission; www.traders.com.)

55. Thom Hartle, ed., Ed Seykota of Technical Tools. *Technical Analysis of Stocks & Commodities*, Vol. 10, No. 8 (August 1992), 328–331. (Used with permission; www.traders.com.)

56. Thom Hartle, ed., Ed Seykota of Technical Tools. *Technical Analysis of Stocks & Commodities*, Vol. 10, No. 8 (August 1992), 328–331. (Used with permission; www.traders.com.)

57. Shawn Tully, Princeton's Rich Commodity Scholars. *Fortune* (February 9, 1981), 94.

58. The Trading Tribe at Seykota.com. See *www.seyokota.com/tribe/*.

59. *http://sysdyn.clexchange.org/sd-intro/home.html.*

60. Kelly, J. L., Jr., A New Interpretation of Information Rate. *Bell System Technical Journal* (July 1956), 917–926.

61. The Trading Tribe at Seykota.com. See *www.seyokota.com/tribe/*.

62. Jack Reerink, The Power of Leverage. *Futures*, Vol. 24, No. 4 (April 1995), 59.

63. Gibbons Burke, How to Tell a Market by Its Covers: Financial Market Predictions Based on Magazine Covers. *Futures*, Vol. 22, No. 4 (April 1993), 30.

64. Your Trading Edge. See *http://www.yte.com.au*.

65. Joe Niedzielski, Wild Market Swings Take Toll on Commodity Trading Advisers. *Dow Jones Newswires*, April 25, 2000.

66. H. Weyl, Mathematics and the Laws of Nature. In I. Gordon and S. Sorkin (eds.) *The Armchair Science Reader*. New York: Simon and Schuster, 1959.

67. Darrell R. Jobman, How Managed Money Became a Major Area of the Industry. *Futures* Vol. 21, No. 9 (July 1992), 52.

68. Futures Industry Association Conference Excerpt. Campbell and Company.

69. Mary Ann Burns, Industry Icons Assess the Managed Futures Business. *Futures Industry Association* (May/June 2003).

70. Value of Adding Managed Futures. Marketing Documents. Campbell and Company.

71. 2003 Disclosure Document. Campbell and Company.

72. Desmond McRae, 31-Year Track Record of 18.1%. *Managed Account Reports: Extracting Inherent Value from Managed Futures* (March 2003).

73. Barclay Trading Group, Ltd. *Barclay Managed Futures Report*. Vol. 2, No. 3 (Third quarter 1991), 2.

74. The Futures and Industry Association's Future and Options Expo '98. Held at the Sheraton Chicago Towers & Hotel in Chicago, Ill., on October 14–16, 1998.

75. The Futures and Industry Association's Future and Options Expo '98. Held at the Sheraton Chicago Towers & Hotel in Chicago, Ill., on October 14–16, 1998.

76. The Futures and Industry Association's Future and Options Expo '98. Held at the Sheraton Chicago Towers & Hotel in Chicago, Ill., on October 14–16, 1998.

77. The Futures and Industry Association's Future and Options Expo '98. Held at the Sheraton Chicago Towers & Hotel in Chicago, Ill., on October 14–16, 1998.

78. The Futures and Industry Association's Future and Options Expo '98. Held at the Sheraton Chicago Towers & Hotel in Chicago, Ill., on October 14–16, 1998.

79. Chuck Epstein, The World According to J. Parker. *Managed Account Reports* (November 1998).

80. Barclay Trading Group, Ltd. *Barclay Managed Futures Report*. Vol. 2, No. 3 (Third quarter 1991), 7.

81. Barclay Trading Group, Ltd. *Barclay Managed Futures Report*. Vol. 2, No. 3 (Third quarter 1991), 2.

82. Simon Romero, A Homespun Hedge Fund, Tucked Away in Texas. *New York Times*, December 28, 2003, Business, 1.

83. *Futures* (March 1995).

84. Simon Romero, A Homespun Hedge Fund, Tucked Away in Texas. *New York Times*, December 28, 2003, Business, 1.

85. See *www.abrahamtrading.com*.

86. Ayn Rand, *The Fountainhead*. New York: Bobbs-Merrill Company, 1943.

87. Simon Romero, A Homespun Hedge Fund, Tucked Away in Texas. *New York Times*, December 28, 2003, Business, 1.

88. Jack Schwager, *Market Wizards: Interviews with Top Traders*. New York: New York Institute of Finance, 1989.

89. Stanley W. Angrist, Commodities: Winning Commodity Traders May Be Made, Not Born. *The Wall Street Journal*, September 5, 1989.

90. Greg Burns, Rich Dennis: A Gunslinger No More. *Business Week* (April 7, 1997).

91. Susan Abbott, Richard Dennis: Turning a Summer Job into a Legend. *Futures* (September 1983), 58.

92. Susan Abbott, Richard Dennis: Turning a Summer Job into a Legend. *Futures* (September 1983), 59.

93. Susan Abbott, Richard Dennis: Turning a Summer Job into a Legend. *Futures* (September 1983), 57.

94. Susan Abbott, Richard Dennis: Turning a Summer Job into a Legend. *Futures* (September 1983), 58.

95. Paul Rabar, Managed Money: Capitalizing on the Trends of 1990. *Futures* Vol. 20, No. 3 (March 1991).

96. Jack Schwager, *Market Wizards: Interviews with Top Traders*. New York: New York Institute of Finance, 1989.

97. Barbara Dixon, Richard Donchian: Managed Futures Innovator and Mentor. *Futures Industry Association*.

98. William Baldwin, Rugs to Riches (Section: The Money Men), *Forbes* (March 1, 1982).

99. Barbara Dixon, Richard Donchian: Managed Futures Innovator and Mentor. *Futures Industry Association*.

100. Barbara Dixon, Richard Donchian: Managed Futures Innovator and Mentor. *Futures Industry Association*.

101. Barbara Dixon, Richard Donchian: Managed Futures Innovator and Mentor. *Futures Industry Association*.

102. William Baldwin, Rugs to Riches (Section: The Money Men), *Forbes* (March 1, 1982).

103. Barbara Dixon, Richard Donchian: Managed Futures Innovator and Mentor. *Futures Industry Association*.

104. William Baldwin, Rugs to Riches (Section: The Money Men), *Forbes* (March 1, 1982).

105. Futures Industry Association Review: Interview: Money Managers. See *www.fiafii.org*.

106. Barbara S. Dixon, Discretionary Accounts. *Managed Account Reports*. Report No. 20, No. 14, 5.

107. Barbara S. Dixon, Discretionary Accounts. *Managed Account Reports*. Report No. 20, No. 14, 5.

108. Edwin Lefevre. *Reminiscences of a Stock Operator*. New York: George H. Doran Company, 1923.

109. Andrew Leckey, Dabble, Don't Dive, in Futures. *Chicago Tribune,* October 2, 1986, C1.

110. Dickson G. Watts, *Speculation as a Fine Art*. Reprint. Flint Hill, Virgina: Fraser Publishing Co., 1997.

Chapter 3

1. Sir Arthur Conan Doyle, "A Scandal in Bohemia" in *The Adventures of Sherlock Holmes*. New York: A. L. Burt, 1892.

2. Alexander M. Ineichen, *Absolute Returns*. New York, John Wiley & Sons, Inc., 2003, 19.

3. Disclosure Document. John W. Henry & Company, Inc., August 22, 2003.

4. BMFR. Barclay Trading Group (First Quarter 2003).

5. International Traders Research Star Ranking System Explanation. See *http://managedfutures.com*.

6. Ludwig von Mises, *Human Action: A Treatise on Economics*. 4th revised ed. Irvington-on-Hudson, NY: The Foundation for Economic Education, Inc., 1996, printed 1998. First published 1949.

7. Larry Harris, *Trading and Exchanges: Market Microstructure for Practitioners*. New York: Oxford University Press, 2003.

8. David Greising, How Managed Funds Managed to Do So Poorly. *Business Week*, No. 3294 (November 23, 1992), 112.

9. Daniel P. Collins, The Return of Long-Term Trend Following. *Futures*, Vol. 32, No. 4 (March 2003), 68–73.

10. Desmond McRae, Top Traders. *Managed Derivatives* (May 1996).

11. Trend Following: Performance, Risk and Correlation Characteristics. White Paper, Graham Capital Management.

12. Larry Harris, *Trading and Exchanges: Market Microstructure for Practitioners*. New York: Oxford University Press, 2003.

13. Ben Warwick, The Holy Grail of Managed Futures (cover story). *Managed Account Reports* (MAR), No. 267 (May 2001), 1.

14. The Trading Tribe at Seykota.com. See *www.seyokota.com/tribe/*.

15. Definition from the Institutional Advisory Services Group (IASG). See *www.iasg.com*.

16. Laurie Kaplan, Turning Turtles into Traders. *Managed Derivatives* (May 1996).

17. Marketing Materials. Dunn Capital Management, Inc.

18. Carla Cavaletti, Comeback Kids: Managing Drawdowns According to Commodity Trading Advisors. *Futures*, Vol. 27, No. 1 (January 1998), 68.

19. Michael Peltz, John W. Henry's Bid to Manage the Future. *Institutional Investor* (August 1996).

20. D. Harding, G. Nakou and A. Nejjar, "The Pros and Cons of Drawdown as a Statistical Measure of Risk for Investments." *AIMA Journal*, April 2003, 16–17.

21. Carla Cavaletti, Comeback Kids: Managing Drawdowns According to Commodity Trading Advisors. *Futures*, Vol. 27, No. 1 (January 1998), 68.

22. *The Value of a Long-Term Perspective*. Marketing Document. John W. Henry and Company, Inc. October 1999.

23. Carla Cavaletti, Comeback Kids: Managing Drawdowns According to Commodity Trading Advisors. *Futures*, Vol. 27, No. 1 (January 1998), 68.

24. Thomas F. Basso, When to Allocate to a CTA?—Buy Them on Sale.

25. New Fans for Managed Futures. *Euromoney Institutional Investor PLC* (February 1, 2003), 45.

26. InvestorWords.com. See *http://investorwords.com*.

27. Julius A. Staniewicz, Learning to Love Non-Correlation. *Investor Support*. John W. Henry & Company, Inc.

28. Ginger Szala, Tom Shanks: Former "Turtle" Winning Race the Hard Way. *Futures*, Vol. 20, No. 2 (January 15, 1991), 78.

29. Carla Cavaletti, Turtles on the Move. *Futures*, Vol. 27 (June 1998), 79.

30. Laurie Kaplan, Turning Turtles into Traders. *Managed Derivatives* (May 1996).

31. Larry Harris, *Trading and Exchanges: Market Microstructure for Practioners*. New York: Oxford University Press, 2003.

32. Larry Harris, The Winners and Losers of the Zero-Sum Game: The Origins of Trading Profits, Price Efficiency and Market Liquidity. Draft 0.911, May 7, 1993.

33. Larry Harris, The Winners and Losers of the Zero-Sum Game: The Origins of Trading Profits, Price Efficiency and Market Liquidity. Draft 0.911, May 7, 1993.

34. Larry Harris, The Winners and Losers of the Zero-Sum Game: The Origins of Trading Profits, Price Efficiency and Market Liquidity. Draft 0.911, May 7, 1993.

35. Danny Hakim, Huge Losses Move Soros to Revamp Empire. *The New York Times*. May 1, 2000.

36. Enoch Cheng. "Of Markets and Morality ..." *Café Bagola* weblog, August 27, 2002. See *http://bagola.blogspot.com/2002_08_25_bagola_archive.html*.

37. Ayn Rand, "Philosophical Detection," *Philosophy: Who Needs It?* Edited by Leonard Peiikoff. Indianapolis: Bobbs-Merrill, 1998.

38. Written testimony submitted for the Record of Lawrence Parks, Executive Director, The Foundation for the Advancement of Monetary Education. Before the Subcommittee on Capital Markets, Securities, and GSE's; House Committee on Banking and Financial Services, United States House of Representatives. Hearing on Hedge Funds, March 3, 1999.

39. Danny Hakim, Huge Losses Move Soros to Revamp Empire. *The New York Times*. May 1, 2000.

40. Danny Hakim, Huge Losses Move Soros to Revamp Empire. *The New York Times*. May 1, 2000.

41. In re Merrill Lynch & Co. Inc. Research Reports Securities Litigation, 02 MDL 1484. Ruling by Federal Judge Milton Pollack dismissing class-action claims brought against Merrill Lynch & Co. and its former analyst Henry Blodgett.

42. Gregory J. Millman, *The Chief Executive* (January–February 2003).

43. Bill Dries, *Futures* (August 1995), 78.

Chapter 4

1. Nassim Taleb, *Fooled by Randomness*. New York: Texere, 2001.

2. Herb Greeenberg, Answering the Question—Who Wins From Derivatives Losers. *The San Francisco Chronicle*, March 20, 1995, D1.

3. Herb Greeenberg, Answering the Question—Who Wins From Derivatives Losers. *The San Francisco Chronicle*, March 20, 1995, D1.

4. Alexander M. Ineichen, *Absolute Returns*. New York: John Wiley & Sons, Inc., 2003, 416.

5. Michael J. Mauboussin and Kristen Bartholdson, Integrating the Outliers: Two Lessons from the St. Petersburg Paradox. *The Consilient Observer*. Vol. 2, No. 2 (Credit Suisse First Boston, January 28, 2003).

6. Jason Russell. See *www.jrussellcapital.com*.

7. Trend Following: Performance, Risk, and Correlation Characteristics. White Paper, Graham Capital Management.

8. Thomas S. Y. Ho and Sang Bin Lee, *The Oxford Guide to Financial Modeling*. Oxford University Press, 2004, 559.

9. Ginger Szala, Barings Abyss. *Futures*, Vol. 24, No. 5 (May 1995), 68.

10. Carolyn Cui and Ann Davis, "Some Trend-Following Funds Are Winners in Rough Market." *Wall Street Journal*, November 5, 2008.

11. John W. Henry & Company, Inc., 1998 Corporate Brochure. See *www.jwh.com*.

12. Mark S. Rzepczynski, President, John W. Henry and Co., Presentation. See *www.jwh.com*.

13. Erin E. Arvedlund, Swinging for the Fences: John W. Henry's Managed Futures Funds Are Striking Out. *Barrons* (December 4, 2000).

14. Speech given to financial consultants on November 17, 2000. See *www.jwh.com*.

15. Erin E. Arvedlund, Whiplash! Commodity-Trading Advisers Post Sharp Gains. *Barrons* (January 15, 2001).

16. Fast Finish Makes 2000 a Winner. *Managed Account Reports*, No. 263 (January 2001).

17. Speech given to financial consultants on November 17, 2000. See *www.jwh.com*.

18. Pallavi Gogoi, Placing Bets in a Volatile World. *Businessweek* (September 30, 2002).

19. Email to *TurtleTrader.com*.

20. Barclay Managed Futures Report. Barclay Trading Group (Fourth Quarter 2002).

21. Larry Swedroe, Buckingham Asset Management. See: *http://www.bamstl.com/*.

22. The Trading Tribe at Seykota.com. See *www.seyokota.com/tribe/*.

23. Paul Barr, Trending Markets Lead to Profit: September 11 example will go in case studies. *Money Management World* (September 25, 2001).

24. Trillion Dollar Bet. *Nova*, No. 2075. Airdate: February 8, 2000.

25. Broadcast Transcript, Trillion Dollar Bet. *Nova*, No. 2075. Airdate: February 8, 2000.

26. Kevin Dowd, Too Big to Fail? Long-Term Capital Management and the Federal Reserve. Cato Institute Briefing Paper, No. 52 (September 23, 1999).

27. Roger Lowenstein, *When Genius Failed*. New York: Random House, 2000, 34.

28. Roger Lowenstein, *When Genius Failed*. New York: Random House, 2000, 69.

29. Roger Lowenstein, *When Genius Failed*. New York: Random House, 2000, 69.

30. Clay Harris and Wiliam Hall, Top-Tier Departures Expected at UBS. *Financial Times*: London Edition, October 2, 1998, 26.

31. Organization for Economic Cooperation and Development, The LTCM crisis and its Consequences for Banks and Banking Supervision, June 1999.

32. The Futures and Industry Association's Future and Options Expo '98. Held at the Sheraton Chicago Towers & Hotel in Chicago, Ill. on October 14–16 1998.

33. Presentation in Geneva, Switzerland on September 15, 1998.

34. Broadcast Transcript, Trillion Dollar Bet. *Nova*, No. 2075. Airdate: February 8, 2000.

35. See *www.pbs.org*.

36. Roger Lowenstein, *When Genius Failed*. New York: Random House, 2000, 71.

37. Andrew Osterland, For Commodity Funds, It Was as Good as It Gets. *Businessweek* (September 14, 1998).

38. John W. Meriwether, Letter to Investors, September 1998.

39. Broadcast Transcript, Trillion Dollar Bet. *Nova*, No. 2075. Airdate: February 8, 2000.

40. Bruce Cleland, Campbell and Co., The State of the Industry. *Managed Account Reports*, Inc. (June 2000).

41. Robert Lenzner, Archimedes on Wall Street. *Forbes* (October 19, 1998).

42. Kevin Dowd, Too Big to Fail? Long-Term Capital Management and the Federal Reserve. Cato Institute Briefing Paper, No. 52 (September 23, 1999).

43. Malcolm Gladwell, *The New Yorker*, April 22 and 29, 2002.

44. G. K. Chesterton, "The Point of a Pin" in *The Scandal of Father Brown*. London, Cassell and Company, 1935.

45. Philip W. Anderson, "Some Thoughts About Distribution in Economics, " in W. B. Arthur, S. N. Durlaf, and D.A. Lane, eds. *The Economy as an Evolving Complex System II*. Reading, MA: Addison-Wesley, 1997, 566.

46. Dan Colarusso, Gray Monday's First Casualty: Famed Soros Confidant Victor Niederhoffer. *TheStreet.com* (October 29, 1997).

47. Mark Etzkorn. Bill Dunn and Pierre Tullier: The Long Run (Trader Profile). *Futures*, Vol. 26, No. 2 (February 1997).

48. David Henry, *USA Today*, October 30, 1997.

49. *http://www.thestreet.com/funds/fwfeatures/626822.html.*

50. Source: *Barclay Managed Futures Report.*

51. Mark Etzkorn, Bill Dunn and Pierre Tullier: The Long Run (Trader Profile). *Futures*, Vol. 26, No. 2 (February 1997).

52. Source: *The Stark Report* (Second Quarter 1997).

53. Greg Burns, Whatever Voodoo He Uses, It Works: Trader Victor Niederhoffer Is as Eccentric as He is Contrarian. *Businessweek* (February 10, 1997).

54. Greg Burns, Whatever Voodoo He Uses, It Works: Trader Victor Niederhoffer Is as Eccentric as He is Contrarian. *Businessweek* (February 10, 1997).

55. George Soros. *Soros on Soros*. New York: John Wiley & Sons, Inc., 1995.

56. Victor Niederhoffer and Laurel Kenner, Why the Trend Is Not Your Friend. *The Speculator: MSN Money* (May 2, 2002). See *moneycentral.msn.com.*

57. Victor Niederhoffer and Laurel Kenner, *Practical Speculation*. Hoboken, NJ: John Wiley & Sons, Inc., 2003, 74.

58. Victor Niederhoffer and Laurel Kenner, *Practical Speculation*. Hoboken, NJ: John Wiley & Sons, Inc., 2003, 2.

59. Victor Niederhoffer, *The Education of a Speculator*. New York: John Wiley & Sons, Inc., 1997.

60. Greg Burns, Whatever Voodoo He Uses, It Works: Trader Victor Niederhoffer Is as Eccentric as He Is Contrarian. *Businessweek* (February 10, 1997).

61. Malcolm Gladwell, *The New Yorker*, April 22 and 29, 2002.

62. Source: IFCI International Financial Risk Institute.

63. Mark Hawley, Dean Witter Managed Futures, Futures Industry Association Dinner, New York City, April 20, 1995.

64. Presentation in Geneva, Switzerland on September 15, 1998.

65. Sharon Reier, Easy to Beat Up, Hard to Kill. *The International Herald Tribune* (March 23, 2002). See www.iht.com.

66. Ed Krapels, Re-examining the Metallgesellschaft Affair and its Implication for Oil Traders. *Special Report Oil & Gas Journal* (March 26, 2001).

67. Ed Krapels, Re-examining the Metallgesellschaft Affair and its Implication for Oil Traders. *Special Report Oil & Gas Journal* (March 26, 2001).

68. John Digenan, Dan Felson, Robert Kelly, and Ann Wiemert, Metallgesellschaft AG: A Case Study. *The Journal of Research and Ideas on Financial Markets and Trading, Stuart School of Business*, Illinois Institute of Technology.

69. Lewis Carroll, *Through the Looking Glass*, 1872.

70. The Value of a JWH Investment as a Portfolio Diversifier. Marketing Materials. John W. Henry and Company, September 1998.

71. Marketing Materials. John W. Henry and Company, September 1998.

72. Barclay Trading Group, Ltd., Technical vs. Fundamental: How Do Traders Differ? *Barclay Managed Futures Report*, Vol. 2, No. 3 (2000).

73. Sir Arthur Conan Doyle, *The Sign of Four*. London and New York: Pitman and Sons, 1890.

74. Christopher L. Culp, *Media Nomics* (April 1995), 4.

75. The Coming Storm, *The Economist* (February 17, 2004), see *www.economist.com/buttonwood*.

76. Emanuel Derman, *The Journal of Derivatives* (Winter, 2000), 64.

77. Frederic Townsend, *Futures* (December 2000), 75.

78. Another Two Bites the Dust. *Derivative Strategies* (May 16, 1994), 7.

Chapter 5

1. Michael J. Mauboussin and Kristen Bartholdson, The Babe Ruth Effect: Frequency versus Magnitude *The Consilient Observer*. Vol. 1, No. 2 (Credit Suisse First Boston, January 29, 2002).

2. Michael Lewis, *Moneyball: The Art of Winning an Unfair Game*. New York: W.W. Norton and Company, 2003.

3. Michael Lewis, *Moneyball: The Art of Winning an Unfair Game*. New York: W.W. Norton and Company, 2003.

4. Michael Lewis, *Moneyball: The Art of Winning an Unfair Game*. New York: W.W. Norton and Company, 2003.

5. The Trading Tribe at Seykota.com. See *www.seyokota.com/tribe/*.

6. Earnshaw Cook, *Percentage Baseball*. Baltimore: Waverly Press, 1964.

7. Rob Neyer, A New Kind of Baseball Owner. *ESPN.com*, August 15, 2002.

8. Richard Driehaus, Unconventional Wisdom in the Investment Process. Speech given in 1994.

9. John Dorschner, Boca Raton, Fla.-Based Firm Is a Standout in Futures. *The Miami Herald*, January 27, 2001.

10. Greg Burns, Former 'Turtle' Turns Caution into an Asset. *Chicago Sun-Times*, May 29, 1989, 33.

11. Rob Neyer, Examining the Art of Evaluating: Q&A with Michael Lewis. *ESPN.com*, May 13, 2003.

12. Michael Lewis, *Moneyball: The Art of Winning an Unfair Game*. New York: W.W. Norton and Company, 2003.

13. James Surowiecki, The Buffett of Baseball. *The New Yorker* (September 23, 2002).

14. Rob Neyer, Red Sox Hire James in Advisory Capacity. *ESPN.com*, November 7, 2002.

15. Bill James, Red Sox Hire. Baseball Abstract. *USA Today*, November 15, 2002.

16. James Surowiecki, The Buffett of Baseball. *The New Yorker* (September 23, 2002).

17. Ben McGrath, The Professor of Baseball. *The New Yorker* (July 14, 2003), 38.

18. John W. Henry, quoted in *The New York Times*, September 26, 2002.

19. Rob Neyer, Red Sox Hire James in Advisory Capacity. *ESPN.com*, November 7, 2002.

20. Jon Birger, Baseball by the Numbers. *Money* (April 2003), 110.

21. Jon Birger, Baseball by the Numbers. *Money* (April 2003), 110.

22. Jon Birger, Baseball by the Numbers. *Money* (April 2003), 110.

23. Thomas Boswell, Evaluation by Numbers Is Beginning to Add Up. *Washington Post*, May 29, 2003, D01.

24. Jon Birger, Baseball by the Numbers. *Money* (April 2003), 110.

25. Rob Neyer, Red Sox Hire James in Advisory Capacity. *ESPN.com*, November 7, 2002.

26. Eric Perlmutter, Little Not Big Enough for Sox. *The Brown Daily Herald*, October 29, 2003.

27. Michael Lewis, Out of Their Tree. *Sports Illustrated*, Vol. 100 No. 9 (March 1, 2004), 7.

28. Stephen Jay Gould, *Triumph and Tragedy in Mudville: A Lifelong Passion for Baseball*. New York: W.W. Norton and Company, 2003, 176–177.

29. Stephen Jay Gould, *Triumph and Tragedy in Mudville: A Lifelong Passion for Baseball*. New York: W.W. Norton and Company, 2003, 176–177.

30. Jeff Merron, The Worst Sports Moves of 2003. *Espn.com*.

31. In H. Eves, *Mathematical Circles Squared*. Boston: Prindle, Weber and Schmidt, 1972.

Chapter 6

1. *Financial Trader*, Vol. 1, No. 7 (September/October 1994), 26.2.

2. Jason Russell, Hedgehogcapital.com. See *www.hedgehogcapital.com*.

3. Gerard Jackson, *Brookesnews.com*, April 21, 2003.

4. Jason Zweig, Do You Sabotage Yourself? *Business 2.0* (May 2001).

5. David Dreman, *Contrarian Investment Strategies*. New York: Simon & Schuster, 1998.

6. Lao Tsu, Verse XXXIII, *Tao Te Ching*.

7. Steven Pearlstein, The New Thinking about Money Is That Your Irrationality Is Predictable. *The Washington Post*, January 27, 2002, H01.

8. Daniel Goleman, What Makes a Leader? *Harvard Business Review*, 1998.

9. Harris Collingwood, The Sink or Swim Economy. *The New York Times*, June 8, 2003.

10. Jack D. Schwager, *The New Market Wizards*. New York: Harper Business, 1992.

11. Ayn Rand, *Atlas Shrugged*. New York: Random House, 1957.

12. *Animal House*. Universal Pictures, 1978. Written by Harold Ramis, Douglas Kenney, and Chris Miller.

13. Daneen Skube, Self Knowledge Keys. *The Seattle Times*, 2002.

14. *Futures*, Vol. 22, No. 12. (November 1993), 98.

15. Alexis de Tocqueville, *Democracy in America*. New York: G. Dearborn and Co., 1838.

16. Daniel Goleman, *Emotional Intelligence*. New York: Bantam, 1995.

17. Daniel Goleman, "What Makes a Leader?" *Harvard Business Review*, 1998.

18. Daniel Goleman, "What Makes a Leader?" *Harvard Business Review*, 1998.

19. Ayn Rand, *Atlas Shrugged*. New York: Random House, 1957.

20. Denise G. Shekerjian, *Uncommon Genius*. New York: Penguin Books, 1990.

21. Daniel Goleman, "What Makes a Leader?" *Harvard Business Review*, 1998.

22. Tom Girard, The Wizards Cast a Spell. *Financial Trader*, No. 4 (July 1995).

23. Gustave Le Bon, *The Crowd: A Study of the Popular Mind*. London: T.F. Unwin, 1925.

24. Ayn Rand, *Atlas Shrugged*. New York: Random House, 1957.

25. Tom Girard, The Wizards Cast a Spell. *Financial Trader*, No. 4 (July 1995).

26. Tom Girard, The Wizards Cast a Spell. *Financial Trader*, No. 4 (July 1995).

27. Jack D. Schwager, *The New Market Wizards*. New York: Harper Business, 1992, 416.

28. The Trading Tribe at Seykota.com. See *www.seykota.com/tribe/*.

29. Ludwig von Mises, *Human Action*. New Haven, CT: Yale University Press, 1963.

30. Jack Schwager, *Getting Started in Technical Analysis*. New York: John Wiley & Sons, Inc., 1999.

31. Robert Koppel, *The Intuitive Trader*. New York: John Wiley & Sons, Inc., 1996, 74.

32. David Nusbaum, Mind Games; Trading Behavior. *Futures*, Vol. 23, No. 6 (June 1994), 60.

33. Michelle Conlin, *Businessweek* (June 30, 2003).

34. Michael J. Mauboussin and Kristen Bartholdson, All Systems Go: Emotion and Intuition in Decision-Making. *The Consilient Observer*, Vol. 3, No. 2 (January 27, 2004).

35. Jack D. Schwager, *The New Market Wizards*. New York: Harper Business, 1992.

36. Michael Crichton, *The Lost World*. New York: Knopf, 1995.

37. Educated in England, Lee Kuan Yew led Singapore to independence and served as its first prime minister. He was regularly re-elected from 1959 until he stepped down in 1990. Under his guidance, Singapore became a financial and industrial powerhouse, despite a lack of abundant natural resources.

38. Alan Greenberg, *Memos from the Chairman*. New York: Workman Publishing, 1996.

39. Anna Muoio, All The Right Moves—If You See a Good Idea, Look for a Better One. *Fast Company*, No. 24 (May 1999), 192.

40. Jason Russell. See *www.jrussellcapital.com*.

41. Robert B. Zajonc, Feeling and Thinking: Preferences Need No Inferences, *American Psychologist*, 35, 1980, 151–175.

42. Antonio R. Damasio, *Descartes' Error: Emotion, Reason, and the Human Brain*. New York: Avon Books, 1994, xii.

Chapter 7

1. Lewis Carroll, *Alice's Adventures in Wonderland*. 1865.

2. Gerd Gigerenzer and Peter M. Todd, *Simple Heuristics That Make Us Smart*. New York: Oxford University Press, 1999, 28.

3. Robert Rubin, Harvard Commencement Address before the graduating class of 2001. See *www.commencement.harvard.edu/2001/rubin.html*.

4. Carla Fried, The Problem with Your Investment Approach. *Business 2.0* (November 2003), 146.

5. *Seykota.com*.

6. Thomas A. Stewart, How to Think With Your Gut, *Business 2.0* (November 2002). See http://www.business20.com/articles/mag/print/ 0,1643,44584,FF.html.

7. See *www.2think.org*.

8. Gerd Gigerenzer and Peter M. Todd, *Simple Heuristics That Make Us Smart*. New York: Oxford University Press, 1999, 14.

9. Stephen Hawking, *A Brief History of Time*. New York: Bantam Books, 1988.

10. Gerd Gigerenzer and Peter M. Todd, *Simple Heuristics That Make Us Smart*. New York: Oxford University Press, 1999, 358.

11. *Futures*, Vol. 22, No.12 (November 1993), 98.

12. Gerd Gigerenzer and Peter M. Todd, *Simple Heuristics That Make Us Smart*. New York: Oxford University Press, 1999, 361.

13. Gerd Gigerenzer, Smart Heuristics. Edge Foundation, Inc., March 31, 2003. See *www.edge.org*.

14. Bruce Bower, For Sweet Decisions, Mix a Dash of Knowledge with a Cup of Ignorance. *Science News*, Vol. 155, No. 22 (May 29, 1999). See www.sciencenews.org.

15. Presentation before the New York Mercantile Exchange.

16. Anna Muoio, All The Right Moves—If You See a Good Idea, Look for a Better One. *Fast Company*, No. 24 (May 1999), 192.

17. Market Commentary. John W. Henry and Company.

18. Daniel P. Collins, Building a Stronger Fort (Trader Profile: Yves Balcer and Sanjiv Kumar). *Futures*, Vol. 21, No. 6 (May 1, 2003), 82.

19. Gerd Gigerenzer, Smart Heuristics. Edge Foundation, Inc., March 31, 2003. See *www.edge.org*.

20. David Leonhardt, Caution Is Costly, Scholars Say. *The New York Times*, July 30, 2003.

21. Clayton M. Christensen, *The Innovator's Dilemma*. Boston: Harvard Business School Press, 1997.

22. Tom Girard, The Wizards Cast a Spell, *Financial Trader*, No. 4 (July 1995).

23. Michael J. Mauboussin and Kristen Bartholdson, Be the House: Process and Outcome in Investing. *The Consilient Observer*, Vol. 2, No. 19 (Credit Suisse First Boston, October 7, 2003).

24. J. Edward Russo and Paul J. H. Schoemaker, *Winning Decisions*. New York: Doubleday, 2002.

Chapter 8

1. Thomas Harris, *The Silence of the Lamb*s. New York: St. Martin's Press, 1988.

2. Definition of physics taken from *Webster's Revised Unabridged Dictionary*. Springfield, MA: G.C. Merriam, 1913.

3. The Trading Tribe at Seykota.com. See *www.seyokota.com/tribe/*.

4. Jessica James and Neil Johnson, Physics and Finance. *Visions: Briefing Papers for Policy Makers*. Institute of Physics and IOP Publishing Ltd., 1999–2000.

5. Pierre Simon, Marquis de LaPlace, *Theorie Analytique des Probabilites*, 1812.

6. See *www.criticalthinking.org*.

7. See *www.criticalthinking.org*.

8. Darrell Huff, *How to Take a Chance*. New York: W.W. Norton and Company, 1959.

9. Manus J. Donahue III, An Introduction to Chaos Theory and Fractal Geometry, 1997. See *www.duke.edu/~mjd/chaos/chaosh.html*.

10. Donald Rumsfeld, Secretary of Defense. *Washington Post* editorial, 2003.

11. Gerd Gigerenzer, Smart Heuristics. Edge Foundation, Inc., March 31, 2003. See *www.edge.org*.

12. Elementary Concepts in Statistics. See *http://statsoftinc.com/textbook/stathome.html*.

13. National Institute of Standards and Technology. See *www.itl.nist.gov*.

14. Michael J. Mauboussin and Kristen Bartholdson, A Tail of Two Worlds, Fat Tails and Investing. *The Consilient Observer*, Vol. 1, No. 7 (Credit Suisse First Boston, April 9, 2002).

15. Lux, Ha, The Secret World of Jim Simons. *Institutional Investor*, Vol. 34, No. 11 (November 1, 2000), 38.

16. Lux, Ha, The Secret World of Jim Simons. *Institutional Investor*, Vol. 34, No. 11 (November 1, 2000), 38.

17. Jerry Parker, The State of the Industry. *Managed Account Reports, Inc.* (June 2000).

18. Daniel P. Collins, Chenier: Systematizing What Works (Trader Profile). *Futures*, Vol. 32, No. 9 (July 1, 2003), 86.

19. Roger Lowenstein, *Wall Street Journal*, June 13, 2003.

20. Benoit B. Mandelbrot, A Multifractal Walk Down Wall Street. *Scientific American*, Vol. 280, No. 2 (February 1999), 70–73.

21. Larry Swedroe, Buckingham Asset Management. See *http://www.bamstl.com/*.

22. Larry Swedroe, Buckingham Asset Management. See *http://www.bamstl.com/*.

23. Mark Rzepczynski, Ph.D., Return Distribution Properties of JWH Investment Programs, Stock and Bond Indices, and Hedge Funds. *John W. Henry and Co.*, No. V, June 2000.

24. National Institute of Standards and Technology. See *www.itl.nist.gov*.

25. National Institute of Standards and Technology. See *www.itl.nist.gov*.

26. Jim Rogers, *Investment Biker*. New York: Random House, 1994.

27. Larry S. Liebovitch, Two Lessons from Fractals and Chaos. *Complexity*, Vol. 5, No. 4 (2000), 34–43.

28. The Paula Gordon Show. See *http://www.paulagordon.com/shows/bak/*.

Chapter 9

1. Of Pimps, Punters and Equities. *The Economist* (March 24, 2001).

2. *Crossfire*. CNN (December 21, 1999).

3. Richard Rudy, Buy and Hold: A Different Perspective. *Barclay Managed Futures Research* (Fourth quarter 2001).

4. Buy it now! For a fine keepsake of the Internet boom! Review of *Dow 36000* by James Glassman, Amazon.com, November 7, 2001.

5. Jerry Parker, The State of the Industry. *Managed Account Reports, Inc.* (June 2000).

6. Richard Rudy, Buy and Hold: A Different Perspective. *Barclay Managed Futures Research* (Fourth quarter 2001).

7. William R. Gallacher, *Winner Take All*. New York: McGraw-Hill, 1994.

8. David Dukcevich. *Forbes* (May 6, 2002).

9. James Cramer, Host, CNBC, Kudlow and Cramer. Yahoo! Chat, September 7, 2000.

10. News Release. Berkshire Hathaway, Inc. May 22, 2002.

11. *Washington Post*, March 6, 2003, E01.

12. James K. Glassman, *Washington Post*, December 9, 2001.

13. *Moneyline*. CNN (December 23, 1999).

14. James K. Glassman, *Washington Post*, February, 17, 2002.

15. *Street Sweep*. CNN (April 4, 2000).

16. Jennifer Karchmer, Tiger Management Closes: Julian Robertson Plans to Return Money to Shareholders after Losses in Value Stocks. *CNNfn*, March 30, 2000: 6:59 p.m. EST.

17. Aaron L. Task, Requiem for a Heavyweight. *TheStreet.com*.

18. *Larry King Live. CNN* (March 2001).

19. Edward Clendaniel, After the Sizzle Comes the Fizzle. *Forbes.com*, March 25, 2002.

20. Allan Sloan, *Washington Post*, March 26, 2002, E01.

21. Alan Abelson, Up and Down Wall Street. *Barrons*, Monday, December 15, 2003.

22. See *http://www.charlotte.com/mld/observer/business/3560508.htm*.

23. David Rode and Satu Parikh, An Evolutionary Approach to Technical Trading and Capital Market Efficiency. The Wharton School, University of Pennsylvania, May 1, 1995.

24. The Trading Tribe at Seykota.com. See *www.seykota.com*.

25. See *http://www.turtletrader.com/images/merrill.gif* to view this direct mail marketing flyer.

26. Jerry Garcia and Robert Hunter, "Casey Jones." Originally appears on The Grateful Dead, *Workingman's Dead,* 1970.

27. David Whitford, Why Owning the Boston Red Sox Is Like Running a Successful Hedge Fund. *Fortune Small Business* (October 25, 2003).

28. Dave Barry. February 3, 2002.

Chapter 10

1. The Trading Tribe at Seykota.com. See *www.seykota.com*.

2. Marketing materials. Dunn Capital Management, Inc.

3. Leon G. Cooperman, CNBC Interview with Ron Insana. Leon G. Cooperman founded Omega Advisors, Inc., a $3.5 billion hedge fund based in New York City. Prior to starting Omega, Mr. Cooperman spent 25 years at Goldman, Sachs & Co., where he was a general partner and chairman and Chief Executive Officer (CEO) of Goldman's Asset Management division. Mr. Cooperman received his MBA from Columbia University and his undergraduate degree from Hunter College.

4. Commencement address given before the graduating class of 1989, University of Georgia, June 17, 1989.

5. Gibbons Burke, Managing Your Money. *Active Trader* (July 2000).

6. Mark Rzepczynski, Portfolio Diversification: Investors Just Don't Seem to Have Enough. *JWH Journal*.

7. Jack Reerink, The Power of Leverage. *Futures*, Vol. 24, No. 4 (April 1995).

8. Edward O. Thorp, *The Mathematics of Gambling*. Hollywood, CA, 1984.

9. Larry Harris, *Trading and Exchanges: Market Microstructure for Practitioners*. New York: Oxford University Press, 2003.

10. Going Once, Going Twice. *Discover* (August 2002), 23.

11. Jim Little, Sol Waksman, A Perspective on Risk. *Barclay Managed Futures Report*.

12. Craig Pauley, How to Become a CTA. Based on Chicago Mercantile Exchange Seminars, 1992–1994. June 1994.

13. Thomas L. Friedman, *The Lexus and The Olive Tree*. New York: Farrar, Straus, Giroux, 1999.

14. Gibbons Burke, Managing Your Money. *Active Trader* (July 2000).

15. Craig Pauley, How to Become a CTA. Based on Chicago Mercantile Exchange Seminars, 1992–1994. June 1994.

16. Ed Seykota and Dave Druz, Determining Optimal Risk. *Technical Analysis of Stocks and Commodities Magazine*, Vol. 11, No. 3, March 1993. 122–124. See *www.traders.com*. Used with permission.

17. Gibbons Burke, Gain Without Pain: Money Management in Action. *Futures*, Vol. 21, No. 14 (December 1992), 36.

18. Tom Basso, How to Become a CTA. Based on Chicago Mercantile Exchange Seminars, 1992–1994. June 1994.

19. Carla Cavaletti, Comeback Kids: Managing Drawdowns According to Commodity Trading Advisors. *Futures*, Vol. 27, No. 1 (January 1998), 68.

20. Michael Peltz, John W. Henry's Bid to Manage the Future. *Institutional Investor* (August 1996).

21. InterMarket, *The Worldwide Futures and Options Report*. Chicago: InterMarket Publishing Group, July 1984.

22. The Trading Tribe at Seykota.com. See *www.seykota.com*.

23. Oliver Conway, Cover story about John W. Henry & Company, Inc. *Managed Derivatives* (May 1996).

24. Ted Williams, *The Science of Hitting*. New York: Simon & Schuster, 1986, 7.

25. Desmond McRae, 31-Year Track Record of 18.1%. *Managed Account Reports: Extracting Inherent Value from Managed Futures* (March 2003).

26. Daniel Colton, Trading the Pain Threshold (Trader Profile: Mark van Stolk). *Futures* (November 2003), 98.

27. Ludwig von Mises, *Human Action: A Treatise on Economics*. 4th revised ed. Irvington-on-Hudson, NY: The Foundation for Economic Education, Inc., 1996, printed 1998. First published 1949.

28. Ellyn E. Spragins, Gary Weiss, and Stuart Weiss, Contrarians. *Business Week*, The Best of 1986 (December 29, 1986), 74.

29. *Washington Post*, December 9, 2001.

30. Jack D. Schwager, *The New Market Wizards*. New York: HarperBusiness, 1992.

31. Jerry Parker, The State of the Industry. *Managed Account Reports, Inc.* (June 2000).

32. Bruce Terry, *Managed Account Reports* (September 2001).

33. Morton Baratz, Do Trend Followers Distort Futures Prices? *Managed Account Reports*, No. 43, 9.

34. Sharon Schwartzman, Computers Keep Funds in Mint Condition: A Major Money Manager Combines the Scientific Approach with Human Ingenuity, *Wall Street Computer Review*, Vol. 8, No. 6 (March 1991), 13.

35. Sharon Schwartzman, Computers Keep Funds in Mint Condition: A Major Money Manager Combines the Scientific Approach with Human Ingenuity. *Wall Street Computer Review*, Vol. 8, No. 6 (March 1991), 13.

36. Thomas L Friedman, *The Lexus and the Olive Tree*. New York: Farrar, Straus, Giroux, 1999.

37. Barclay Trading Group, Ltd., *Barclay Managed Futures Report*, Vol. 4, No. 1 (First quarter 1993), 3.

38. Barclay Trading Group, Ltd., *Barclay Managed Futures Report*, Vol. 4, No. 1 (First quarter 1993), 10.

39. Presentation in Geneva, Switzerland on September 15, 1998.

40. Trading System Review. Futures Industry Association Conference Seminar on November 2, 1994.

41. Tom Basso, How to Become a CTA. Based on Chicago Mercantile Exchange Seminars, 1992–1994. June 1994.

42. Leo Melamed, *Escape to the Futures*. New York: John Wiley & Sons, Inc., 1996.

Chapter 11

1. The Trading Tribe at Seykota.com. See *www.seykota.com*.

2. Alexander M. Ineichen, *Absolute Returns*. New York: John Wiley & Sons, Inc., 2003, 64.

3. Keith Campbell, Campbell & Co., *Managed Account Reports*.

4. Carla Cavaletti, Turtles on the Move, *Futures*, Vol. 27, No. 6 (June 1998), 77.

5. Jerry Parker, The State of the Industry. *Managed Account Reports, Inc.* (June 2000).

6. Thomas Scheeweis, Dealing with Myths of Hedge Fund Investment. *The Journal of Alternative Investments* (Winter 1998).

7. Who's to Blame Next? *Asterias Info-Invest*, Editoral. London, Asterias, Ltd.

8. Jerry Parker, The State of the Industry. *Managed Account Reports, Inc.* (June 2000).

9. Carla Cavaletti, Comeback Kids: Managing Drawdowns According to Commodity Trading Advisors. *Futures,* Vol. 27, No. 1 (January 1998), 68.

10. Richard Dennis, The State of the Industry. *Managed Account Reports, Inc.* (June 2000).

11. Bill Dunn, MAR's Mid Year Conference on Alternative Investment Strategies held June 22–24, 1999.

12. Van Tharp's Interview with Two Super Traders.

13. Max Gunther, *The Zurich Axioms*. New York: New American Library, 1985.

14. W.H. Auden and L. Kronenberger (eds.), *The Viking Book of Aphorisms*. New York: Viking Press, 1966.

Appendix A

1. **Systematic:** Having clearly defined rules that can be defined mathematically and tested empirically.

2. **Long volatility:** An investing strategy that tends to benefit from increasing volatility and/or persistent directional trends. Often associated with strategies employed by commodity trading advisors from the managed futures industry.

3. **Penny stock:** Loosely defined as stock with a low nominal share price that typically trades in the over-the-counter market, often an OTC Bulletin Board or Pink Sheets quoted stock.

4. **Recorded percent return:** ((exit price / entry price) –1)

5. **Recorded initial risk:** (absolute_value((stop loss price / entry price) –1))

6. **Short selling:** The selling of a security that the seller does not own with the goal of buying the security back at a lower price, thus profiting from a decline.

7. **Buy-in:** When a short seller is forced to repurchase the shorted share in order to deliver them to the rightful owner.

8. **Portfolio stimulation:** This historical simulation was generated using the www.PowerST.com strategy testing software.

9. **Ex-dividend date:** The first day of the ex-dividend period. The day upon which the stock will typically fall by an amount equal to the anticipated dividend. Owners of record prior to the ex-dividend date are entitled to the dividend proceeds.

Appendix F

1. The Trading Tribe at Seykota.com. See *www.seykota.com/tribe/*.

2. *The American Mathematical Monthly*, Vol. 100, No. 3.

Appendix G

1. In J. R. Newman (ed.), *The World of Mathematics*. New York: Simon and Schuster, 1956.

2. Morton S. Baratz, *The Investor's Guide to Futures Money Management*. Columbia, MD: Futures Publishing Group, 1984, 78–79.

3. Mario Puzo, *The Godfather*. New York: Putnam, 1969 (also screenplay with Francis Ford Coppola, 1972, Paramount Pictures).

Bibliography

Abbott, Susan. Turning a Summer Job into a Legend. *Futures*, Vol. 12, No. 9 (September 1983): 57–59.

Amin, Gaurav. S., and Kat, Harry M. Who Should Buy Hedge Funds? The Effects of Including Hedge Funds in Portfolios of Stocks and Bonds. ISMA Centre for Education and Research in Securities Markets. Working Paper Series (2002).

Angrist, Stanley W. *Sensible Speculation in Commodities or How to Profit in the Bellies, Bushels and Bales Markets*. New York: Simon and Schuster, 1972.

Aronson, Mark. Learning from a Legend. *Trading Advisor Review* (June 1997).

Baratz, Morton S. *The Investor's Guide to Futures Money Management*. Columbia, MD: Futures Publishing Group, 1984.

Barber, Brad and Terrance Odean. Trading Is Hazardous to Your Wealth: The Common Stock Investment Performance of Individual Investors. *Journal of Finance*, Vol. LV, No. 2 (April 2000): 773–806.

Basso, Thomas F. When to Allocate to a CTA? Buy Them on Sale (1997).

Basso, Thomas F. The Driving Force Behind Profits in the Managed Futures Industry. Trendstat Capital Management, Inc. (1998).

Basso, Thomas F. Some Leverage Is Good, Too Much Is Dangerous. Trendstat Capital Management, Inc. (March 1999).

Basso, Thomas F. Study of Time Spent in Trending and Sideways Markets. Trendstat Capital Management, Inc. (1999).

Bernstein, Peter L. *Against the Gods: The Remarkable Story of Risk*. Canada: John Wiley & Sons, Inc., 1996.

Bogle, John. C. *Common Sense on Mutual Funds*. New York: John Wiley & Sons, Inc., 1999

Borish, Peter. Managed Money. *Futures,* Vol. 27, No. 3 (March 1998).

Brealey, Richard and Stewart C. Myers. *Principles of Corporate Finance*, Fifth Edition. New York: Irwin McGraw Hill, 1996.

Brooks, Chris, and Harry M. Kat. The Statistical Properties of Hedge Fund Index Returns and Their Implications for Investors. *Journal of Alternative Investment*, 5 (2002): 26–44.

Brorsen, B.W. and S.H. Irwin. Futures Funds and Price Volatility. *Review of Futures Markets* 6 (1987): 119–135.

Burke, Gibbons. Your Money. *Active Trader* (July 2002): 68–73.

Burns, Greg. A Gunslinger No More. *Businessweek* (April 7, 1997): 64–72.

Canoles, W. Bruce, Sarahelen R. Thompson, Scott H. Irwin, and Virginia G. France. An Analysis of the Profiles and Motivations of Habitual Commodity Speculators. Working Paper 97-01, Office for Futures and Options Research, University of Illinois, Champagne-Urbana (1997).

Cavaletti, Carla. 1997's Home Run Hitters. *Futures*, Vol. 27, No. 3 (March 1998).

Chandler, Beverly. *Managed Futures*. England: John Wiley & Sons Inc., 1994.

Chang, E.C. and B. Schachter. Interday Variations in Volume, Variance and Participation of Large Speculators. Working Paper, Commodity Futures Trading Commission, 1993.

Christensen, Clayton M. *The Innovator's Dilemma: When New Technologies Cause Great Firms to Fail*. Boston: Harvard Business School Press, 1997.

Christensen, Clayton M. and Matt Verlinden. Disruption, Disintegration, and the Dissipation of Differentiability. Harvard Business School Working Paper, 2000.

Clendaniel, Edward. Bubble Troubles. *Forbes* (March 25, 2002).

Collins, James C. and Jerry I. Porras. *Built to Last: Successful Habits of Visionary Companies*. New York: Harper Business, 1994.

Collins, Jim. *Good to Great*. New York: Harper Business, 2001.

Commodity Futures Trading Commission, Division of Economic Analysis. Survey of Pool Operators in Futures Markets with an Analysis of Interday Position Changes. Washington, D.C., 1991.

de Tocqueville, Alexis. *Democracy in America*. New York: Vintage Books, 1959.

Diz, Fernando. How do CTAs' Return Distribution Characteristics Affect Their Likelihood of Survival? *Journal of Alternative Investments*, Vol. 2, No. 2 (Fall 1999): 37–41.

Douglas, Mark. *The Disciplined Trader: Developing Winning Attitudes*. New York: New York Institute of Finance, 1990.

Eales, J.S., B.K. Engel, R.J. Hauser, and S.R. Thompson. Grain Price Expectations of Illinois Farmers and Grain Merchandisers. *American Journal of Agricultural Economics*, 72 (1990): 701–708.

Ecke, Robert. Allocation to Discretionary CTAs Grow as Market Stalls. *Barclay Trading Group Roundtable*, Vol. 9, No. 3 (Third quarter, 1998).

Eckhardt, William. The c-Test. *Stocks and Commodities*. Vol. 12, No. 5 (1994): 218–221.

Edwards, Franklin R., and Mustafa Onur Caglayan. Hedge Fund and Commodity Fund Investment Styles in Bull and Bear Markets. *Journal of Portfolio Management*, 27 (2001): 97–108

Ellis, Charles D. *Winning the Loser's Game*, Third ed. New York: McGraw Hill, 1998.

Energy Traders on the Verge of Extinction. *Barclay Trading Group Roundtable*, Vol. 8, No. 3 (Third quarter, 1997).

Epstein, Richard A. *The Theory of Gambling and Statistical Logic*. San Diego, CA: Academic Press, Inc., 1995.

Fabozzi, Frank J., Francis Gupta, and Harry M. Markowitz. The Legacy of Modern Portfolio Theory. Institutional Investor, Inc., 2002.

Feynman, Richard P., as told to Ralph Leighton. *"What Do You Care What Other People Think?" Further Adventures of a Curious Character*. New York: W.W. Norton & Company, 1988.

Fleckenstein, Bill. The Long and Short of Short-Selling (September 2002). See *http://moneycentral.msn.com*.

Forrester, Jay W. *Principles of Systems*. Cambridge, MA: Wright-Allen Press, Inc., 1968.

Forrester, Jay W. System Dynamics and the Lessons of 35 Years, in *The Systemic Basis of Policy Making in the 1990s*, Kenyon B. De Greene, ed., 1991.

Friedman, Thomas L. *The Lexus and the Olive Tree*. New York: Farrar, Straus, Giroux, 1999.

Fung, William and David A. Hsieh. Asset-Based Hedge-Fund Styles and Portfolio Diversification, *Financial Analyst Journal* (September 2001).

Fung, William, and David A. Hsieh. Hedge-Fund Benchmarks: Information Content and Biases, *Financial Analyst Journal* (2002).

Fung, William and David A. Hsieh. Pricing Trend Following Trading Strategies: Theory and Empirical Evidence (1998).

Fung, William, and David A. Hsieh. The Risk in Hedge Fund Strategies: Theory and Evidence from Fixed Income Funds. *Journal of Fixed Income*, 14 (2002).

Gadsden, Stephen. Managed the Future. *The MoneyLetter*, Vol. 25, No. 20 (October 2001).

Gallacher, William R. *Winner Take All*. New York: McGraw-Hill, 1994.

Gann, W.D. *How to Make Profits Trading in Commodities*. Pomeroy: Library of Gann Publishing Co. Inc., 1951.

Garber, Peter M. *Famous First Bubbles: The Fundamentals of Early Manias*. Cambridge, MA: MIT Press, 2000.

Gardner, B.L. Futures Prices in Supply Analysis. *American Journal of Agricultural Economics*, 58 (1976): 81–84.

Gary, Loren. The Right Kind of Failure. *Harvard Management Update*.

Gigerenzer, Gerd and Peter M. Todd. *Simple Heuristics That Make Us Smart*. Oxford: Oxford University Press, 1999.

Gilovich, Thomas, Robert Valone, and Amos Tversky. The Hot Hand in Basketball: On the Misperception of Random Sequences. *Cognitive Psychology*, 17 (1985): 295–314.

Ginyard, Johan. Position-Sizing Effects on Trader Performance: An Experimental Analysis. Uppsala University, Department of Psychology, 2001.

Goldbaum, David. Technical Analysis, Price Trends, and Bubbles.

Gould, Stephen Jay. *Full House*. New York: Three Rivers Press, 1996.

Gould, Stephen Jay. The Streak of Streaks. *The New York Times Review of Books* (Aug. 18, 1988). See *www.nybooks.com/articles/4337*.

Grof, Stanisslav. *The Adventure of Self-Discovery: Dimensions of Consciousness and New Perspectives in Psychotherapy and Inner Exploration*. Albany: State University of New York, Press, 1988.

Hakim, Danny. Hedging Learned at the Family Farm. *The New York Times*, July 26, 2002.

Harlow, Charles V. D.B.A. and Michael D. Kinsman, Ph.D, CPA. The Electronic Day Trader & Ruin. *The Graziadio Business Report* (Fall 1999).

Harris, Larry. *Trading and Exchanges*. New York: Oxford University Press, 2003.

Harris, Lawrence. The Winners and Losers of the Zero-Sum Game: The Origins of Trading Profits, Price Efficiency and Market Liquidity. University of Southern California (1993)

Haun, Bruce. Rebalancing Portfolios Lowers Volatility and Stabilizes Returns. B. Edward Haun & Company (June 1994).

Irwin, Scott H. and Satoko Yoshimaru. Managed Futures Trading and Futures Price Volatility (1996).

Jaeger, Lars. *Managing Risk in Alternative Investment Strategies*. Upper Saddle River, NJ: Financial Times Prentice Hall, 2002

Jakiubzak, Ken. KmJ: Ready for Anything. *Futures*, Vol. 29, No. 3 (March 2000).

Kahneman, Daniel and Amos Tverksy. Prospect Theory: An Analysis of Decision Under Risk. *Econometrica*, 47 (1979): 263–291.

Kaplan, Laurie. Turning Turtles into Traders. *Managed Derivatives* (May 1996).

Karas, Robert. Looking Behind the Non-Correlation Argument. See *www.aima.org/aimasite/research/lgtoct99.htm*.

Kat, Harry M. Managed Futures and Hedge Funds: A Match Made in Heaven. Working Paper (November 2002).

Kaufman, Perry. *Trading Systems and Methods*, Third Edition. New York: John Wiley and Sons, Inc., 1998.

Klein, Gary. *Sources of Power: How People Make Decisions*. Cambridge, MA: MIT Press, 1998.

Krauland, and P.C. Mabon. Going Once, Going Twice. *Discover* (August 2002).

Le Bon, Gustave. *The Crowd: A Study of the Popular Mind*. Atlanta: Cherokee Publishing Company, 1982.

Lefevre, Edwin. *Reminiscences of a Stock Operator*. Canada: John Wiley & Sons, Inc., 1994.

Lerner, Robert L. The Mechanics of the Commodity Futures Markets, What They Are and How They Function. Mount Lucas Management Corp., 2000.

Liebovitch, L. S. *Fractals and Chaos Simplified for the Life Sciences*. New York: Oxford University Press, 1998.

Liebovitch, L. S., A. T. Todorov, M. Zochowski, D. Scheurle, L. Colgin, M. A. Wood, K. A. Ellenbogen, J.M. Herre, and R.C. Bernstein. Nonlinear Properties of Cardiac Rhythm Abnormalities. *Physical Review*, 59 (1999): 3312–3319.

Livermore, Jesse L. *How to Trade in Stocks: The Livermore Formula for Combining Time Element and Price*. New York: Duel, Sloan & Pearce, 1940.

Lukac, L. P., B. W. Brorsen, and S. H. Irwin. The Similarity of Computer Guided Technical Trading Systems. *Journal of Futures Markets*, 8 (1988): 1–13.

Lungarella, Gildo. Managed Futures: A Real Alternative. White Paper.

Mackay, Charles LL.D. *Extraordinary Popular Delusions and the Madness of Crowds*. New York, 1841.

MacRae, Desmond. Dealing with Complexities. *Trading Focus* (July 1998).

Martin, George. Making Sense of Hedge Fund Returns: What Matters and What Doesn't. *Derivatives Strategies* (2002).

Mauboussin, Michael J., Alexander Schay and Stephen Kawaja. Counting What Counts. Credit Suisse First Boston Equity Research (February 4, 2000).

Mauboussin, Michael J. and Kristen Bartholdson. Stress and Short-Termism. *The Consilient Observer*, Vol. 1, No. 9 (Credit Suisse First Boston, May 2002).

Maubossin, Michael and Kristen Bartholdson. Whither Enron? Or Why Enron Withered. *The Consilient Observer*, Vol. 1, No. 1 (Credit Suisse First Boston, January 2002).

Mosser, Mike. Learning from Legends. *Futures*, Vol. 29, No. 2 (Feb. 2000).

Nacubo Endowment Study. Washington, D.C.: National Association of College and University Business Officers, 1999.

Niederhoffer, Victor and Laurel Kenner. *Practical Speculation*. Hoboken, NJ: John Wiley & Sons Inc., 2003.

Odean, Terrance. Are Investors Reluctant to Realize Their Losses? *Journal of Finance*, 53 (October 1998): 1775–1798.

O'Donoghue, Ted and Matthew Rabin. Choice and Procrastination. University of California at Berkeley, Department of Economics. Working Paper E00-281 (June 3, 2001).

Oldest CTAs in the Industry Have Survived and Thrived. *Barclay Trading Group Roundtable*, Vol. 6, No. 3 (Third quarter, 1995).

Peltz, Lois. The Big Global Macro Debate. *Market Barometer* (April 1998): 9–13.

Peltz, Lois. *The New Investment Superstars*. Canada: John Wiley & Sons, Inc., 2001.

Peters, E.E. *Fractal Market Analysis*. New York: John Wiley & Sons, Inc., 1994.

Rand, Ayn. *Atlas Shrugged*. New York: Random House, 1957.

Rand, Ayn. *The Fountainhead*. New York: Bobbs-Merrill Company, 1943.

Rappaport, Alfred. *Creating Shareholder Value: A Guide for Managers and Investors*. New York: The Free Press, 1998.

Rappaport, Alfred and Michael J. Mauboussin. *Expectations Investing*. Boston: Harvard Business School Publishing, 2001.

Reerink, Jack. Seidler's Returns Fuel Comeback. *Futures*, Vol. 24, No. 3 (March 1995).

Rogers, Jim. *Investment Biker*. New York: Villard Books, 1994.

Russo, J. Edward and Paul J. H. Schoemaker. Managing Overconfidence. *Sloan Management Review* (Winter 1992).

Rzepczynski, Mark. The End of the Benign Economy and the New Era for Managed Funds. *MFA Reporter* (John W. Henry & Company, Inc, 2001).

Rzepczynski, Mark S. Market Vision and Investment Styles: Convergent versus Divergent Trading. *The Journal of Alternative Investments*, Vol. 2, No. 1 (Winter 1999): 77–82.

Schneeweis, Thomas, and Georgi Georgiev. The Benefits of Managed Futures. CISDM and School of Management at University of Massachusetts (2002).

Schneeweis, Thomas, and Spurgin, Richard. *Quantitative Analysis of Hedge Fund and Managed Futures Return and Risk Characteristics, in Evaluating and Implementing Hedge Fund Strategies*, Second Edition, R. Lake ed., 2002.

Schwager, Jack D. *Getting Started in Technical Analysis*. New York: John Wiley & Sons, Inc., 1999.

Schwager, Jack D. *Market Wizards: Interviews with Top Traders*. New York: HarperBusiness, 1989.

Schwager, Jack D. *The New Market Wizards: Conversations with America's Top Traders*. New York: HarperBusiness, 1992.

Schwed Jr., Fred. *Where Are the Customers' Yachts?* Canada: John Wiley & Sons, Inc., 1995.

Seykota, Ed and Dave Druz. Determining Optimal Risk. *Stocks and Commodities*, Vol. 11, No. 3: 122–124.

Shapiro, Carl and Hal R. Varian. *Information Rules: A Strategic Guide to the Network Economy*. Boston: Harvard Business School Press, 1999.

Shefrin, Hersh and Meir Statman. The Disposition to Sell Winners Too Early and Ride Losers Too Long: Theory and Evidence. *Journal of Finance*, 40 (1985): 777–790.

Shekerjian, Denise. *Uncommon Genius*. New York: Penguin Books, 1990.

Shiller, Robert J. *Irrational Exuberance*. Princeton, NJ: Princeton University Press, 2000.

Shiller, Robert J. Do Stock Prices Move Too Much to Be Justified by Subsequent Changes in Dividends? *American Economic Review*, 71 (1981).

Sloan, Allen. Even With No Bull Market, Baby Boomers Can Thrive. March 2002. See *www.washingtonpost.com*.

Slywotzky, Adrian J. *Value Migration: How to Think Several Moves Ahead of the Competition*. Boston: Harvard Business School Press, 1996.

Smant, Dr. D.J.C. Famous First Bubbles, South Sea Bubble? *The Fundamentals of Early Manias*. October 2001.

Soros, George. *The Alchemy of Finance: Reading the Mind of the Market*. New York: John Wiley & Sons, Inc., 1994.

Spurgin, Richard. Some Thoughts on the Source of Return to Managed Futures. CISDM and School of Management at University of Massachusetts.

Steinhardt, Michael. *No Bull: My Life In and Out of Markets*. Canada: John Wiley & Sons, Inc., 2001.

Stendahl, David, Staying Afloat. *Omega Research* (1999).

Szala, Ginger. William Eckhardt: Doing by Learning. *Futures,* Vol. 21, No. 1 (January 1992).

Taleb, Nassim Nicholas. *Fooled By Randomness*. New York: Texere, 2001.

Teweles, Richard J. and Frank J. Jones. *The Futures Game. Who Wins? Who Loses? Why?* New York: McGraw-Hill, 1987.

Thaler, Richard H. Mental Accounting Matters. *Journal of Behavioral Decision Making*, 12 (1999): 183–206.

Thaler, Richard H. Saving, Fungibility, and Mental Accounts. *Journal of Economic Perspectives*, Vol. 4, No. 1 (Winter 1990): 193–205.

Tharp, Van K. *Trade Your Way to Financial Freedom*. New York: McGraw-Hill, 1999.

Thorp, Edward O. *Beat the Dealer*. New York: Vintage Books, 1966.

Toffler, Alvin. *Future Shock*. New York: Bantam Books, 1971.

Tully, Shawn. Princeton's Rich Commodity Scholars. *Fortune,* 9 (February 1981): 94.

Tversky, Amos and Daniel Kahneman. Belief in the Law of Small Numbers. *Psychological Bulletin*, 76 (1971): 105–110.

Tzu, Sun. *The Art of War*. Boston and London: Shambhala, 1988.

Ueland, Brenda. *If You Want to Write: A Book About Art, Independence and Spirit*. Saint Paul, MN: Graywolf Press, 1937.

Vince, Ralph. *Portfolio Management Formulas*. Canada: John Wiley & Sons, Inc., 1990.

Vince, Ralph. *The New Money Management*. New York: John Wiley & Sons, Inc., 1995.

von Mises, Ludwig. *Human Action: A Treatise on Economics*. New York: The Foundation for Economic Education, Inc., 1996. First published 1949.

Watts, Dickson G. *Speculation as a Fine Art and Thoughts on Life*. New York: Traders Press, 1965.

Where, Oh Where Are the .400 Hitters of Yesteryear. *Financial Analysts Journal* (November/December 1998): 6–14.

Williamson, Porter B. *General Patton's Principles for Life and Leadership*. Tuscon, AZ: MSC, Inc., 1988.

Wolfram, Stephen. *A New Kind of Science*. Champaign, IL: Wolfram Media, Inc., 2002.

Wolman, William and Anne Colamosca. *The Great 401(k) Hoax*. Cambridge, MA: Perseus Publishing, 2002.

Yeung, Albert, Mika Toikka, Pankaj N. Patel, and Steve S. Kim. Quantitative Strategy. Does Technical Analysis Work? Credit Suisse First Boston. September 25, 2002.

Index

Abbey National Bank, 149
Abelson, Alan, 240
Abraham Trading Company, 75, 77, 148, 347-348
Abraham, Malouf, 75
Abraham, Mark, 9, 11, 264
Abraham, Salem, 12, 74, 76-77, 90, 124, 136-138, 182, 256, 289-290
absolute returns, 98-99
Absolute Returns (Ineichen), 277
acceptance of trend following, 278-279, 285-288
Adam, Harding, and Lueck (AHL), 29, 254
Adam, Michael, 29
AIG, 294, 296
Altegris, 296
Altucher, James, 292
analysts' advice, trusting, 241-243
Anderson, Philip, 164
Anderson, Sparky, 186
Animal House (film), 197
Aristotle, 212, 242
Arnold, Tim, 393
Asian Contagion, 164-168
Asymmetrical Leverage (ASL), 287
Atlas Shrugged (Rand), 198
averaging losers, 235, 237-238

Bacon, Louis, 20, 62, 289
Bagehot, Walter, 49
Baha, Christian, 12, 29, 124, 137, 257, 281, 289, 297
Baldwin, William, 85
Bank of Italy, 156
Bankers Trust, 153
Baratz, Morton S., 16
Barings Bank, xix, 45, 124-125, 168-172
Barrons, 143
Barry, Dave, 145, 244, 378
Bartholdson, Kristen, 124, 181, 218, 226
Bartiromo, Maria, 237
Baruch, Bernard, 262

baseball analogy, 181-182
   and Beane, 185-186
   Boston Red Sox, 188-190
   decision making, 212-217
   and Henry, 186-188
   home runs, 182-185
Basso, Tom, 6, 110, 231, 258, 264, 270
Beane, Billy, 185-186, 190
Bear Stearns, 153
A Beautiful Mind (film), 251
behavioral finance
   commitment to success, 206-208
   and curiosity, 204-206
   and emotional intelligence, 200-201
   and Faulkner, 201-202
   overview, 193-194
   prospect theory, 194-199
   and Seykota, 202-204
benchmarks, 226
   absolute returns versus, 98-99
   and Campbell, 69-70
Bergin, Martin, 39
Berkshire Hathaway, 234
Bernard, Claude, 382
bet sizing, 256-259
Bhardwaj, Geetesh, 294-296
Bird, Larry, 56, 189, 261
Black, Fischer, 152
Black-Scholes Option Pricing Formula, 152, 154
Blackstar Funds, LLC, 307
blind risk, 250
Bogle, John C., 218
Bok, Derek, 5
Borish, Peter, 18
Borne, Ludwig, 89
Boston Red Sox, 188-190
Boswell, Thomas, 187
Boyd, Jack, xiv
Brady, David, 149

Bragg, William, xix
British Petroleum, 149
British pound trading, 36-38, 131
Brody, Harvey, 47
The Brown Daily Herald, 188
bubbles. *See* events
Buddha, 223
"The Buffett of Baseball" (newsletter), 185
Buffett, Warren, 111, 234-235, 286
Burke, Gibbons, 248, 256, 291
Bush, George W., 7
Business Week, 102
Buy and Hold: A Different Perspective (Rudy), 232
buy-and-hold strategy, 232-234
    compounding versus, 240
buy-in, defined, 422

calculated risk, 250
California energy crisis, 145-146
Campbell & Co., 12-13, 16, 67, 69, 148, 157, 349-351
Campbell, Keith, 6, 67-71, 90, 157, 278, 281-282
    background, 68-69
    drawdowns and, 69-70
    performance data, 70-71
Canadian dollar trade (trading system example),
    388-389
Capitalism Distribution (trend following on stocks),
    331-337
Caray, Harry, 47
Carroll, Lewis, 175, 211
change, inevitability of, 14
chaos theory, 224-229
charts (trend following on stocks), 338-346
Chase Manhattan, 153
Chenier, Jean-Jacques, 227
Chesapeake Capital, 72, 148, 157, 267, 352-353
Chesterton, G. K., 162
Cheval, Liz, 289
Chicago Mercantile Exchange, 3
Christensen, Clayton M., 216
Citigroup, 292
City of Fort Worth retirement fund, 149
Clarke Capital Management, 127, 354-355
Clarke, Michael, 29, 124, 127, 263, 281, 286, 289
Cleland, Bruce, 24, 67, 69, 149, 156
clients
    alignment with traders, 281-282
    of Dunn Capital Management, 43-44
    expectations of, 84
    explaining trend following to, 280-281
coffee trading, 135
Coggan, Philip, 289
Cognitrend GMBH, 28
coin toss example (risk and reward), 251
Collins, Jim, xviii, 33
commitment
    to success, 206-208
    to trend following, 282-284
Commodities Corporation, 61-62, 263
compounding, 229-230, 240
computer technology, 268-272
Conrad, Chet, 68
Cook, Earnshaw, 182, 185
Cool Hand Luke (film), 97
Cooperman, Leon, 247
correlation
    lack of, 70-71
    of performance data, 111, 113-114
correlation coefficient, 112
Covel, Michael, 144
Cowles, Alfred, 134
Crabel, Toby, 176, 286, 376
Cramer, James, 8, 234

Crapple, George, 121, 289
crashes. *See* events
Credit Suisse, 156
Crichton, Michael, 204
Cripps, Richard, 285
critical thinking, 222-224
criticism of trend following, 290-296
Crittenden, Eric, 268, 307
crude oil trading, 130, 173
Cruden, Christopher, 21
Cuban, Mark, 219, 292
Culp, Christopher, 124, 177
Curie, Marie, 19
curiosity and behavioral finance, 204-206
curve fitting, 268-272

Darwin, Charles, 10
data integrity issues (trend following on stocks), 308
Davis, Miles, 65
DAX (2002), trend-followers and, 142
day trading, limitations of, 272
de Boer, Harold M., 278
de Bono, Edward, 383
Dean Witter, 153, 170
decision making, 211-219
    baseball analogy, 212, 214-215, 217
    innovation and, 216-217
    Occam's razor, 212-213
    with price, 18-20
    process versus outcome, 218-219
    simplicity in, 213-216
    speed in, 213-216
decreasing leverage/returns, 281-282
delisted stocks (trend following on stocks), 326
Dellutri, Dale, 79
Dennis, Richard, 19, 25, 58, 72, 78-84, 113, 260,
    281-282
    students of, 78-79
    Turtle selection process, 79-83
Deoteris, Peter, 291
depression, as reaction to stress, 197
derivatives, 234-235
Derman, Emanuel, 179
Desai, Dinesh, 91, 104, 289
DiLaura, Chauncey, 203, 258
discipline and behavioral finance, 196
discretionary trading systems, 11-12
diversification, 254-256
dividend adjustments (trend following on stocks),
    327-330
Dixon, Barbara, 86, 88-90, 268-269
Dockray, Geoff, 75
dollar (U.S.) trading, 128, 136, 139, 162
dollar-cost averaging, 235, 237-238
Donahue, Manus J., III, 224
Donchian, Richard, 29, 60-61, 85-90, 201, 238, 270
    background, 85-86
    students of, 88-90
    trading guidelines of, 87-88
Douglas, Mark, 256
Dow 36,000 (Glassman), 231-232
Doyle, Arthur Conan, 97, 177
drawdowns, 106-111. *See also* losses
    and Campbell, 69-70
    and Dunn, 42
    and recoveries, 138-144
Dresdner, 156
Driehaus, Richard, 183
Dries, Bill, 120
Drury Capital, performance data, 355-356
Drury, Bernard, 29, 124, 127, 262, 281, 286, 289
Druyan, Ann, 221
Druz, David, 60, 63, 65-66, 110, 120, 138, 250, 269

Dunn Capital Management, 13, 32, 100, 106, 123, 144, 146-147, 155, 157, 163, 165, 259, 282
  atmosphere of, 39-40
  clients and, 43-44
  drawdowns and, 106-107
  job posting, 44-45
  monthly newsletter, 42-43
  performance data, 356-358
Dunn, Bill, xix, 32-45, 54, 72, 78-79, 84, 90, 102, 106, 109-110, 124, 136, 138, 155, 157, 163, 166, 178, 182, 247, 281-282, 289, 294
  background, 38-39
  clients and, 43-44
  drawdowns, 42
  performance data, 34-38
  profit targets, lack of, 40-41
  risk management systems, 33, 41-42
Dunn, Daniel, 32, 146, 163
Dunn, Dennis D., 85

Eastwood, Clint, 237
Eckhardt Trading Company, 359-360
Eckhardt, William, 19, 78, 124, 138, 202, 204, 206, 266, 289
The Economist, 178, 231
ED & F Man, 287
Efficient Market Hypothesis, 152, 288
Ehrlich, Marty, 151
Einstein, Albert, 154, 190, 217, 225, 391
Elam, Brett, 86
Emotional Intelligence (Goleman), 200-201
energy crisis in California, 145-146
Enron, 144-150, 236
entry (trend following on stocks), 309
equity curve trading, 110
Euribor trading, 132
Euro chart (2002), trend-followers and, 140
Euro-Bund chart (2002), trend-followers and, 142
Eurodollar chart (1998), trend-followers and, 161
EuroSwiss trading, 133
events
  Asian Contagion, 164-168
  Barings Bank collapse, 168-172
  first Gulf War, 176-178
  future issues, 178-179
  Long-Term Capital Management (LTCM) collapse, 151-164
  Metallgesellschaft (MG), 172-175
  overview, 123-125
  stock market bubble of 2000-2002, 138-151
  stock market crash of 1987, 176
  stock market crash of 2008, 126-138
Everest Capital, 156
ex-dividend date, defined, 422
example of trading system. *See* trading system example
exchanges, defined, 3
exiting
  losing positions, 262-263
  in trend following on stocks, 311-312
  winning positions, 263-265
expectancy studies (trend following on stocks), 313-317
explaining trend following to clients, 280-281

Faith, Curtis, 79
false parallels, avoiding, and behavioral finance, 197
Fama, Eugene, 152, 155
FAQs
  Can you offer insight on computers and curve fitting?, 268-272
  How much money do I need?, 266-267
  Is trend following for stocks?, 267-268

What are the limitations of day trading?, 272
What is a good example of the wrong way to view a trade?, 273-274
fashion metaphor, 50
fat tails, 228
Faulkner, Charles, 3, 15, 21, 28, 33, 66, 193-194, 197-198, 201-203, 206-208, 214, 223, 253, 282, 299-302
Fawcett, George, 273
Federal Reserve announcements, reaction to, 56-57
Feinstein, Diane, 146
Feynman, Richard, 16
"fight-or-flight" mode, 197
First Gulf War, 176-178
five-year notes trading, 130
Florida Marlins, 187
Forrester, Jay, 62-63
Fouts, Roger, 209
Franiak, Frank J., 167
Freud, Sigmund, 206, 221
Friedman, Thomas, 28, 143, 256, 267
FTSE chart (2002), trend-followers and, 141
fundamental analysis, 7-9, 177, 212
Futures and Options Expo, 72
futures exchanges, 3
Futures Magazine, xvi

Galilei, Galileo, 68
Galton, Francis, 32
game theory, 251
game, trading as, 277-278
Garcia, Jerry, 243
Gardner, David, 9
Gardner, Tom, 9
Gartman, Dennis, 116
"The Gartman Letter," 116
Gawande, Atul, 209
generalists, trend followers as, 28
German Bund chart (1998), trend-followers and, 159
Gigerenzer, Gerd, 211, 213-214, 216, 224
Gladwell, Malcolm, 158, 169
Glassman, James, 231-232, 235
gold trading, 129
Goldman Sachs, 153
Goleman, Daniel, 196, 200-201
Good to Great (Collins), xviii, 33
Goodman, Marc, 105
Gould, Stephen Jay, 189
government, market system and, 4
Graham Capital Management, 21, 147
greed and behavioral finance, 196
Greenberg, Alan "Ace", 205
Griffin, Ken, 111
Griffith, Bill, 18
Gulf War (first), 176-178
Gunther, Max, 283

Hamer, Jim, 66
Harding, David, xv, xx, 29-32, 105, 109, 124, 182, 199, 215, 230, 281, 289, 295
Harris, Larry, 114-115, 278
Harrison, Alfred, 235
"Has Trend Following Changed?" (panel discussion), 15
Hawking, Stephen, 213
"heat" of portfolio, 258
Heebner, Ken, 111, 286
Henry, John W., xiv, xix, 7, 11, 14, 18, 25, 45-57, 69, 78, 84, 90, 98, 104, 124, 127, 138, 143-144, 146, 154, 157, 170-171, 176, 182-186, 190, 215, 269, 282, 289, 293
  background, 47-49
  baseball analogy, 186-188

Federal Reserve announcements, reaction to, 56-57
investment philosophy of, 49-51
prediction and, 46-47
Q&A with, 53-55
research and, 52-53
system, lack of change in, 55-56
Heraclitus, 54
High Risk Opportunity Fund, 156
Hite, Larry, xvi, 24, 123, 218, 265, 268, 277, 281, 283, 286, 288-289
Ho, Thomas, 125
Hochenberger, Fred, 125
Hoenig, Jonathan, 10, 202, 234, 238, 255, 266
Hoffer, Eric, xx, 397
hog trading, 134
Holy Grails
  and Buffett, 234-235
  buy-and-hold strategy, 232-234
  dollar-cost averaging, 235, 237-238
  overview, 231-232
  retirement plans, 238-241
  stock tips, 241-243
home runs (in baseball analogy), 182-185
Hormats, Robert, 267
Horne, Timothy P., 167
Hostetter, Amos, 60-62, 207-208
"hot hands" phenomenon, 189
Houthakker, Hendrik, 289
Hovey, Gail, 240
How to Trade in Stocks: The Livermore Formula for Combining Time, Element, and Price (Livermore), 92
human behavior. *See* behavioral finance

Icahn, Carl, 111
"illusion of control," 194
impulsiveness and behavioral finance, 196
inefficiency of markets, 288-290
Ineichen, Alexander, 98, 124, 277
innovation, decision making and, 216-217
The Innovator's Dilemma (Christensen), 216
An Introduction to Chaos Theory and Fractal Geometry (Donahue), 224
Investment Biker (Rogers), 229
investment philosophies
  described, 4-6
  and Henry, 49-51
investors, traders versus, 6-7

J.P. Morgan, 153
Jaffe, Charles A., 268
Jagr, Jaromir, 266
James, Bill, 185-187, 190
Japanese banks, losses in Enron scandal, 149
Japanese yen, 34-36, 57
job posting at Dunn Capital Management, 44-45
John Hancock Financial Services, 149
John W. Henry & Company, 13, 16, 47, 70, 109, 127, 138, 147, 157, 228, 361-362
Johnson, Magic, 261
Jones, Paul Tudor, 18, 21, 62, 235
Jong, Erica, 247

Kahneman, Daniel, 194-195
Kandel, Myron, 236
Kansas Public Employees Retirement System, 149
Katir, Easan, 64
Kelly, J. L., Jr, 62
Kerkorian, Kirk, 111
Killian, Mike, 125
Kingman, Dave, 143, 183-184
Klingler, James, 107
Klopenstein, Ralph, 39
Knapp, Volker, 393

Knoepffler, Alejandro, 273
Koppel, Ted, 117
Kovner, Bruce, 62, 282, 285, 289
Kozloff, Burt, 16
Kroc, Ray, 377
Kurczek, Dion, 393
kurtosis (statistics), 228

Lange, Harry, 111
Lao Tsu, 195
"law of small numbers," 195
Le Bon, Gustave, 201
leadership traits, 201
"Learning to Love Non-Correlation" (research paper), 112
Lector, Hannibal, 221
Lee Kuan Yew, 205
Lee, Sang, 125
Leeson, Nick, 124-125, 168-172
Lefevre, Edwin, 91
Legg Mason, 285-286
Leggett, Robert, 241
Lehman Brothers, 153
Leonardo da Vinci, 242
leverage, decreasing returns and, 281-282
Levine, Karen, 203
Lewis, Michael, 184, 188
Liechtenstein Global Trust, 156
limitations of day trading, 272
linear versus nonlinear world, 224-229
Litner, John, 86
Little, Grady, 188-189
Little, Jim, 69, 71, 151, 253, 261
Litvinenko, Alexander, 199
Livermore, Jesse, 22, 90-93, 131, 236
Lo, Andrew, 271
Lombardi, Vince, 65, 176
Long Island Business News, 375
Long Term Capital Management (LTCM), xix, 118, 151-164, 272, 280, 293
long volatility, defined, 422
losers
  averaging, 235, 237-238
  winners versus, 123-125
losing investment philosophies, 4-6
losing positions, when to exit, 262-263
losses. *See also* drawdowns
  handling, 22-23, 195-196
  Long-Term Capital Management (LTCM) collapse, 156
  zero-sum trading, 114-120
lottery example (risk and reward), 250-251
Lowenstein, Roger, 259
Lueck, Martin, 29
lumber trading, 134
Lynch, Peter, 110

Madoff, Bernard, 22, 223
The Man Group, 15, 29, 148, 157-158, 287
Managed Account Reports, 376
Mandelbrot, Benoit B., 228
manias, prospect theory, 194-199
Marcus, Michael, 19, 60, 62, 285
Marino, Dan, 261
market
  defined, 3-4
  inefficiency of, 288-290
  role of speculation in, 6
market price. *See* price
market theories
  fundamental analysis, 7-9
  technical analysis, 9-11
Market Wizards (Schwager), xvi, 58
Markowitz, Harry, xx, 86
Martin, Michael, 64

Martinez, Pedro, 186, 188
Mauboussin, Michael, 124, 181, 218, 226, 286
McCann, Timothy, 285
McCarver, Tim, 214
Meaden, Nicola, 102
Mechanica software, 385-393
mechanical trading systems, 11-12
Melamed, Leo, 123, 273-274
Memos from the Chairman (Greenberg), 205
Mencken, H. L., 50
mentors to Seykota, 61-63
Meriwether, John W., 152, 155
Merrill Lynch, 153, 243
Merton, Robert, 152
Metallgesellschaft (MG), 172-175
Millburn Ridgefield Corporation, 54, 111, 363-365
Miller, Bill, 111, 286
Miller, Merton, 152, 154
Millman, Gregory J., 119
minimum stock price (trend following on stocks), 331
Mint Investments, xvi
misconception of trend following, 279-280
models of trend following, 381-383
money, role of, 198-199
money management, 256-259. *See also* risk management
Moneyball (Lewis), 181-182
Montana, Joe, 261
monthly newsletter of Dunn Capital Management, 42-43
Montier, James, 215
Morgan Stanley, 153
Motley Fool, 9
Mulvaney Capital Management, 136, 138
Mulvaney, Paul, 17, 124, 127, 172, 255, 259, 381-383
Munger, Charlie, 234
mutual fund industry, 296

NASDAQ, 3, 111, 233
Nash Equilibrium, 252
Nash, John, 251
National Institute of Standards and Technology, 225, 228-229
natural gas trading, 144-150
negative skew (statistics), 228
Neuro-Linguistic Programming (NLP), 201
The New Market Wizards (Schwager), 202, 300
New York Stock Exchange, 3
New York Yankees, 186, 188
Newton, Isaac, 238
Neyer, Robert, 188
Niederhoffer, Victor, 100, 164-168, 272, 289
Nightline (television program), 116
Nikkei 225 stock index, 131, 168-172, 238
Nin, Anais, 150, 273
NLP (Neuro-Linguistic Programming), 201
nonlinear versus linear world, 224-229
normal distributions, 226-227
numbers, trusting, 18

Oakland A's, 185-186
objectivity and behavioral finance, 196
Occam's razor, 212-213
Odean, Terrence, 212
Ostgaard, Stig, 126, 129
outcome versus process, 218-219
Oxford Dictionary, 213
The Oxford Guide to Financial Modeling (Ho and Lee), 125

panics. *See* events
parallels, avoiding, and behavioral finance, 197
Pardo, Robert, 38
Parker, Jerry, 9, 71-74, 76, 78-79, 90, 98, 102, 114, 124, 138, 154, 157, 162, 177, 193, 227, 232, 267, 279-281, 289, 305

Parks, Lawrence, 117-118
passion in trend following, 23-24
patience and behavioral finance, 196
Patton, George S., Jr., xiii, 280, 297
Pauley, Craig, 253
penny stock, defined, 422
Percentage Baseball (Cook), 185
performance data
    Abraham Trading Company, 136-137, 290, 347-348
    absolute returns, 98-99
    Barings Bank, 169-171
    Campbell & Company, 70-71, 349-351
    Chesapeake Capital Corporation, 352-353
    Clarke Capital Management, 354-355
    correlation, 111, 113-114
    drawdowns and, 106-111
    Drury Capital, 355-356
    Dunn Capital Management, 34-38, 356-358
    Eckhardt Trading Company, 359-360
    Enron scandal/natural gas trading, 144-150
    John W. Henry & Company, 361-362
    Long-Term Capital Management (LTCM), 157-162
    Metallgesellschaft (MG), 174
    Millburn Ridgefield Corporation, 363-365
    Niederhoffer, 166
    Nikkei 225 stock index, 238
    overview, 97
    Rabar Market Research, 366-367
    stock market bubble of 2000-2002, 138
    Seykota, 59
    Sunrise Capital, 368
    Superfund, 126-131, 370
    trading system example, 389-392
    Transtrend, 371-372
    Vandergrift, 132-134
    volatility and, 99-105
    Winton Capital Management, 372-373
    zero-sum trading, 114-120
personality traits of successful traders, 377-379
personalizing trading systems, 265
physics, defined, 221
Pickens, T. Boone, xx, 111
Platinum Grove, 164
Plato, 36
Pollack, Milton, 119
portfolio diversification, 254-256
portfolio management system example (trend following on stocks), 321
portfolio risk example (trend following on stocks), 323-326
portfolio stimulation, defined, 422
position sizing, 256-259
positive skew (statistics), 228
pound trading, 36-38, 131
predictions
    and Henry, 46-47
    in trend following, 20-22
predictive technical analysis, 9-10
present, avoiding, and behavioral finance, 197
price
    decision making with, 18-20
    determining, 3-4
    as objective data, 17-18
price analysis. *See* technical analysis
process versus outcome, 218-219
profit targets, 40-41, 263-265
profits, allowing to run, 20-22
prospect theory, 194-199
The Psychology of Trading (Steenbarger), 377
Purcell, Ed, 189

Quantum Fund (Soros), 156
quarterly performance constraints, 177-178

questions. *See also* FAQs
  critical thinking and, 222-224
  seminal to trading systems, 253-265

Rabar Market Research, 366-367
Rabar, Paul, 83, 289
Rand, Ayn, 75, 117, 198, 200-201
rand trading, 56
ranking systems, 99-100
reactive technical analysis, 10-11, 292
Reason Magazine, 33
recorded initial risk, defined, 422
recorded percent return, defined, 422
recoveries and drawdowns, 108, 138-144
Redstone, Sumner, 272
Reminiscences of a Stock Operator (Lefevre), 91
Rensink, Ronald A., xiii
research and Henry, 52-53
responsibility and trend following, 282-284
retirement plans, 149, 238-241
returns, decreasing leverage and, 281-282
revenge, buy-and-hold strategy and, 233
reward, risk and, 248-252
Ridgefield, Millburn, 282
risk
  reward and, 248-252
  in star ranking systems, 100
  types of, 250
  volatility versus, 104
risk assessment, 199
risk management, 256-259
  and Dunn, 33, 41-42
  elements of, 252
risk measurement, standard deviation as, 226-227
risk premiums, 15
Robertson, Julian, 20, 156, 177-178, 237
Robusta Coffee trading, 135
robustness of trading systems, 269, 271
Rogers, Jim, 27, 229
Romaine, Rob, 274
Rothbard, Murray N., 219
Rother, John, 240
Rubin, Robert, 211
Rudy, Richard, 232
Rulle, Michael, 20-21, 103, 124
Rumsfeld, Donald, 224
Russell 3000 Index, 332-336
Russell, Bertrand, 23, 242, 283
Russell, Jason, 65, 104, 124, 193, 282
Russo, Edward, 218
Ruth, Babe, 181, 183-184, 243
Rzepczynski, Mark S., 51, 102, 143, 249, 287

S&P chart (1998), trend-followers and, 160
S&P chart (2002), trend-followers and, 139
sabermetrics, 185
SABR (Society for American Baseball Research), 185
Sabre Fund Management, 29
Sagan, Carl, 194, 221
Salomon Brothers, 71
Samuelson, Robert, 116
Sanford, Charles, 248
Sapolsky, Robert, 197
Schoemaker, Paul, 218
Scholes, Myron, 152, 155, 164
Schwager, Jack, xvi, 58, 300
science of trading
  chaos theory, 224-229
  compounding, 229-230
  critical thinking, 222-224
  overview, 221-222
self-awareness, 200

self-regulation, 200
sell strategy, 262-263
September 11, 2001 terrorist attacks, 150-151
serial correlation, 255
Seykota, Ed, 4, 8, 12, 19, 23, 25, 39, 58-66, 78, 84-85, 90, 104, 120, 151, 179, 182, 201, 209, 212, 219, 221, 234, 241, 247, 252-253, 258, 261, 263, 266, 274, 277, 282, 295, 301, 375-376, 385
  background, 60-61
  behavioral finance, 202-204
  lessons from, 63-64
  mentors to, 61-63
  performance data, 59
  students of, 64-66
Shanks, Tom, 289
Sharpe ratio, 103, 281, 295-296
Sharpe, William, 86
Shearson American Express, 86
Shekerjian, Denise, 40, 201
short selling, 318-, 422
short-term trading, 375-376
Simms, Jim, 149
Simon, Pierre, 222
Simons, Jim, 171, 226-227, 269, 272, 376
Simple Heuristics That Make Us Smart (Gigerenzer and Todd), 213
simplicity in decision making, 213-216
skew (statistics), 227-228
Sloan, Alan, 18, 239
Smith, Grant, 286
Smith, Greg, 75
Smith, Vernon, 194
Society for American Baseball Research (SABR), 185
Soros, George, 116-119, 156, 167, 177
South African rand, 56
Spear, Bob, 385-393
speculation
  defined, 3, 92
  role in market, 6
speed in decision making, 213-216
standard deviation, as risk measurement, 226-227
star ranking systems, 99-100, 166
The Stark Report, 166
starting capital, 266-267
statistical thinking, 225-226
Steenbarger, Brett, 23, 285, 377-379
Steidlmayer, J. Peter, 299
stock bubbles and crashes, 238-241
  bubble of 2000-2002, 138-151
  crash of 1987, 176
  crash of 2008, 126-138
stock tips, 241-243
stocks, trend following and, 267-268, 307-346
  Capitalism Distribution, 331-337
  data integrity issues, 308
  delisted stocks, 326
  dividend adjustments, 327-330
  entry, 309
  example charts, 338-346
  exit, 311-312
  expectancy studies, 313-317
  minimum stock price, 331
  portfolio management system example, 321
  portfolio risk example, 323-326
  short selling, 318
  taxes and, 318-320
stops. *See* exiting
stress, reaction to, 197
students
  of Dennis, 78-79
  of Donchian, 88-90
  of Seykota, 64-66

success
    commitment to, 206-208
    of trend following, 15-17
Sundt, Jon C., 55, 118, 235, 290, 297
sunk cost, defined, 195
Sunrise Capital, 124, 281, 289, 368
Superfund, 126-132, 370
Swedroe, Larry, 150, 227
Swiss Franc chart (1998), trend-followers and, 160
"Swiss skiing" example, 202
system dynamics, 62-63
systematic, defined, 422

T-bond chart (2002), trend-followers and, 141
Taleb, Nassim, 123, 347
taxes, trend following on stocks and, 318-320
Taylor, Hunt, 180
Teacher Retirement System of Texas, 149
technical analysis, 9-11
    predictive, 9-10
    reactive, 10-11, 292
technical indicators, 261-262
Templeton, John, 15
10 Year T-Note chart (1998), trend-followers and, 158
Terence (Publius Terentius Afer), 180
terrorist attacks of September 11, 2001, 150-151
Terry, Bruce, 267
Tharp, Van, xvii
Thompson, Hunter S., 115, 179
Tiger Fund, 156, 237
Tocqueville, Alexis de, 199
Todd, Peter, 211, 213-214
Toffler, Alvin, 14, 43, 204, 260, 279
Townsend, Frederic, 179
traders
    alignment with clients, 281-282
    investors versus, 6-7
trades, example of wrong way to view, 273-274
trading, as game, 277-278
Trading Recipes Portfolio Engineering Software, 385
trading system example, 385-393
    background information, 385-386
    Canadian dollar trade, 388-389
    system details, 386-388
    system performance, 389-392
trading systems
    critical questions for, 395-396
    discretionary versus mechanical, 11-12
    overview, 247
    personalizing, 265
    questions seminal to, 253-265
    risk and reward, 248-252
    robustness of, 269-271
    trend following philosophy, 12-15
Trading Tribe, 202
Trading Tribe Process (TTP), 203
transparency, 154, 162
TransTrend, 29, 124, 127, 281, 289, 371-372
trend following
    acceptance of, 278-279, 285-288
    criticism of, 290-296
    misconception of, 279-280
    passion in, 23-24
    philosophy of, 12-15
    predictions in, 20-22
    responsibility and commitment to, 282-284
    on stocks. See stocks, trend following and
    success of, 15-17
    understand and explaining to clients, 280-281
Tropin, Ken, 271, 274, 289
trusting numbers, 18
truth, refusal of, and behavioral finance, 196

TTP (Trading Tribe Process), 203
Turtles, 78-79, 281
    correlation, 113-114
    selection process, 79-83
Tversky, Amos, 189

U.S. dollar trading, 128, 136, 139, 162
U.S. National Agricultural Library, 53
U.S. T-Bond chart (1998), trend-followers and, 159
UBS, 156
Ueland, Brenda, 24
uncertainty, reaction to, 197
understanding trend following, 280-281
upside volatility, 102-105

value-at-risk (VAR) models, 180
van Stolk, Mark, 262
Vandergrift, Justin, 110, 132-134, 255
Vanguard, 295
VAR (value-at-risk) models, 180
Varanedoe, J. Kirk T., 214
Vician, Thomas, Jr., 40, 66, 243, 272
volatility, 99-105
    measuring, 180
    risk versus, 104
    upside volatility, 102-105
Voltaire, xvii
von Metternich, Klemens, 270
von Mises, Ludwig, xviii, 3, 97, 99, 202, 264

Wachtel, Larry, 235
Waksman, Sol, 253
Watts, Dickson, 92
Weaver, Earl, 182
web sites, 397
Weill, Sandy, 156
Weintraub, Neal T., 233
Wells, Herbert George (H.G.), 225
Welton, Patrick, 15
what to trade, 254-256
when to buy/sell, 259-262
whipsaws, 263
Wigdor, Paul, 126
Wilcox, Cole, 268, 307
William of Occam, 213
Williams, Ted, 261
winners
    Long-Term Capital Management (LTCM) collapse,
        156-164
    losers versus, 123-125
"The Winners and Losers of the Zero-Sum Game: The
    Origins of Trading Profits, Price Efficiency and
    Market Liquidity" (white paper) (Harris), 115
winning investment philosophies, 4-6
winning positions, when to exit, 263-265
Winton Capital Management, 29, 372-373
Winton Futures Fund, 230
"The Winton Papers" (Harding), 31
Wittgenstein, Ludwig, 395
Womack, Kent, 241
The World is Flat (Friedman), 143
WorldCom, 241
Wright, Charlie, 244

Yahoo!, 217
Yahoo! Finance, 8
yen trading, 34-36, 57, 140, 161

zero-sum trading, 114-120
Zimmer, Don, 186

TRENDFOLLOWING

FREE TREND FOLLOWING DVD

Contact Information: *Please fill out all fields to receive free DVD*

Name:

Company Name:

Address 1:

Address 2:

City:

State:

Postal Code:

Country:

Phone:

Fax:

E-mail:

How did you hear about the book *Trend Following*:

To receive FREE Trend Following DVD please send completed form to:

Trend Following
c/o Michael Covel
11654 Plaza America Drive, # 224
Reston, VA 20190
USA

You can also claim the FREE DVD by filling in form at:
www.trendfollowing.com/2009.html